THE
LEARNING
CURVE

Recent Titles from QUORUM BOOKS

THE LEARNING CURVE

A Management Accounting Tool

Ahmed Belkaoui

Foreword by H. Peter Holzer

Q

Quorum Books
Westport, Connecticut · London, England

Library of Congress Cataloging-in-Publication Data

Belkaoui, Ahmed, 1943–
    The learning curve.

    Bibliography: p.
    Includes index.
    1. Learning curve (Industrial engineering)   2. Labor
productivity.   3. Costs, Industrial.   4. Managerial
accounting.   I. Title.
T60.35.B46   1986   658.3′124   85–9438
ISBN 0–89930–132–0 (lib. bdg.: alk. paper)

Library of Congress Catalog Card Number: 85–9438
ISBN: 0–89930–132–0

First published in 1986 by Quorum Books

Greenwood Press
A division of Congressional Information Service, Inc.
88 Post Road West, Westport, Connecticut 06881

Printed in the United States of America

The paper used in this book complies with the
Permanent Paper Standard issued by the National
Information Standards Organization (Z39.48–1984).

10 9 8 7 6 5 4 3 2 1

Copyright Acknowledgments

Grateful acknowledgment is given for permission to reprint the article appearing in *Cost and Management* by Woody M. Liao, November/December 1983, by permission of the Society of Management Accountants of Canada.

To Hédi J. and Janice M. Belkaoui

CONTENTS

EXHIBITS

FOREWORD

Professor Belkaoui has undertaken to write this comprehensive volume on the theoretical and practical aspects of using the learning curve for management planning and control. Learning curve models are based on functions distinct from the traditional cost functions of management accounting because they assume non-linearity. Such models may prove particularly valuable where the underlying of non-linear cost behavior corresponds to reality. Uses of linear models in such situations could lead to significant planning errors and non-optimal decisions.

Outdated cost accounting and control systems have recently been criticized for distorting the realities of production performance. Today's world of multinational companies requires finer analytical tools to meet management needs. The learning curve models of this book should certainly be given careful consideration when we modernize our accounting and control systems.

To the student and teacher of management accounting, the book offers a systematic and comprehensive discussion of learning curve models. For management and accounting practitioners the book should serve as a useful reference to planning models that are applicable in many practical situations. The principal merit of the book lies in the systematic presentation of planning and control models that would otherwise be available only by consulting numerous different sources. Dr. Belkaoui is to be commended for another valuable contribution to the literature of management accounting.

H. Peter Holzer

PREFACE

People learn by repeating tasks. As they learn, their time performance improves according to a predictable pattern often called the learning curve. The curve describes a decreasing relationship between output quantities and quantities of certain inputs (mainly direct-labor hours) when learning inducement improvement is present. When this learning phenomenon exists in a given task and is detected and used for decision making, there are potential cost savings and useful managerial applications. In short, the learning curve is a very important managerial accounting tool. Given the predictable improvement in time as production increases, the curve may provide valuable information for decision making. Applications are possible in the areas of cost estimation, warrant maintenance and maintenance force, make or buy decisions, work-accident experience, standard costs and efficiency variance analysis, external reporting, cost reduction, price estimation, capital budgeting, break-even analysis, and other decision contents.

Accordingly, this book explains and elaborates on (1) the history and various geometries of the curve, (2) the techniques of using the log-linear model, (3) the various practical applications of the phenomenon, and (4) the possible limitations as well as the ways of implementing the learning curve.

The book will be of definite interest to all management accountants and decision makers involved in resource allocation decisions and facing various structural tasks conducive to the learning effect. With productivity emerging as the important target of business and governmental agencies, learning and its quantification and internalization in day-to-day measurement and decisions will be a central concern. This book fills a gap by providing an exhaustive view of the phenomenon as presented in the academic and professional literatures. It will serve academicians as well as practitioners interested in incorporating the phenomenon in their classes or their practices.

THE
LEARNING
CURVE

1

THE LEARNING CURVE: HISTORY AND GEOMETRY

> The industrial learning curve thus embraces more than the increasing skill of an individual by repetition of a simple operation. Instead, it describes a more complex organism—the collective efforts of many people, some in line and others in staff positions, but all aiming to accomplish a common task progressively more efficiently.[1]

1.1. Definition

The improvement in labor time is generally referred to as resulting from productivity. If the improvement is, however, repetitive and predictable, it is considered as resulting from learning. In effect, progress depends on people learning, and a conventional hypothesis in industry is that they learn according to a predictable pattern often called the learning curve. The learning curve describes the empirical relationships between output quantities and quantities of certain inputs (mainly direct-labor hours) where learning inducement improvement is present. It portrays the concept that the cumulative average unit cost decreases systematically by a common percentage each time the volume of production increases geometrically (that is, increases by doubling). The phenomenon is helpful in the investigation of the cost behavioral patterns, cost estimation, and decision making in general.[2] In effect the forecasting of labor input and its impact on various economic decisions has been a laborious and time-consuming job. The learning curve is intended to make such forecasting easier, quicker, and much more accurate.

In brief, learning curves are applicable to all the aspects of production planning and control where there are tasks subject to improvement.

1

Exhibit 1.1 shows a schematic representation of how learning curves can influence the use of production resources. Synonyms for the learning curve include the manufacturing progress function, cost-quantity relationship, cost curve, product acceleration curve, improvement curve, performance curve, experience curve, and efficiency curve. In this book the term *learning curve* will be used throughout.

1.2. History and Theory

The learning curve was first recognized in the aircraft industry,[3] where any reduction in the considerable number of direct-labor hours needed for assembly work is quickly recognized and formalized. However, the learning curve was not translated into an empirical theory curve until 1925, when it was observed in a military manufacturing operation. Some eleven years later, T. P. Wright disclosed the results of empirical tests of the learning curve. He observed that on the average, when output doubled in the aircraft industry, the labor requirements decreased by about 20 percent; in other words, there was an 80 percent learning factor.[4]

Interest in such a discovery applied to a wartime situation; the U.S. Defense Department commissioned the Stanford Research Institute to study the direct-labor input required for aircraft production in a number of firms. The resulting learning curves had a common characteristic: an 80 percent improvement rate. From 1909, when the first Model T Ford was produced, until 1926, productivity improved along an 86 percent learning curve.[5] Evidence of improvement over sixteen years and on sixteen million items was found in a human-paced operation that involved assembling candy boxes. The learning continued for the production of tens of millions of units in a machine-paced operation.[6]

The learning curve theory is based on a simple principle of human nature: People learn from experience. As workers repeat a task, they become more efficient at it. The net result is a reduced use of direct-labor hours per unit. This improvement can be regular enough to follow a predictable pattern that should apply to any task or job in any industry. The early literature considered the learning improvement possible only in labor-intensive, discontinuous forms of manufacture, such as airframe assembly.[7] It was later proved, however, that the improvement could take place in continuous and capital-intensive forms of manufacture. Industries where the learning phenomenon is applicable include the petroleum, refining, and basic chemical industries. Finally, learning was found to exist in process-oriented contexts as well as in job-order production,[8] and in mature phases of production as well as in start-up phases.[9]

Exhibit 1.1
Integration of Learning Curves and Production Resources

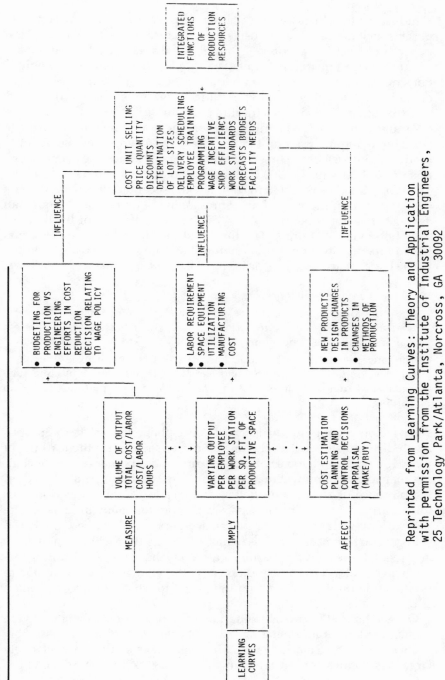

Reprinted from _Learning Curves: Theory and Application_ with permission from the Institute of Industrial Engineers, 25 Technology Park/Atlanta, Norcross, GA 30092

3

Industries in which the learning curve phenomenon was found applicable include machine-intensive manufacturing (steel mills and glass, paper, and electrical products),[10] automotive assembly,[11] apparel manufacture, large musical instruments and electromechanical assembly,[12] housing construction,[13] machine tools,[14] petroleum refining,[15] clerical operations,[16] printing and typesetting,[17] machine shop processes,[18] electronic (radar),[19] and electrical manufacture.[20]

As an example of the learning phenomenon, assume that the average labor hours required per unit are reduced by 30 percent as the quantity produced doubles. If the first unit takes 100 hours, then the average for 2 units is 70 hours (0.7 × 100 hours), or a total of 140 hours for 2 units. Therefore, the time required to complete the second unit equals 40 hours (140 − 100). Continuing this line of reasoning, 4 units would require an average of 49 hours per unit (0.7 × 70 hours), and a total of 196 hours (4 × 49 hours) for all 4 units. The third and fourth units require 56 hours (196 hours required for 4 units minus 140 hours required for 2 units).

The basic doctrine of the learning curve can be summarized as follows:

1. Where there is life, there can be learning.
2. The more complex the life, the greater the rate of learning. Man-paced operations are more susceptible to learning or can give greater rates of progress than machine-paced operations.
3. The rate of learning can be sufficiently regular to be predictive. Operations can develop trends which are characteristic of themselves. Projecting such established trends is more valid than assuming a level performance or no learning.[21]

What factors account for the learning curve phenomenon? It is appropriate to distinguish between the impact of two factors: (1) the learning in the literal sense on the part of the workers, and (2) other factors, including management innovation. Although these factors operate together, the presence of a consistent behavior indicates that of the various factors, learning in the literal sense is the predominant influence. The nonlearning factors, such as new machinery, time studies, or design changes, do bring some labor savings; however, they will probably have an irregular effect on the learning curve. Furthermore, the learning factors will be subject to two conditions: (1) the predisposition of an operation to an improvement, and (2) the extent to which the predisposition is used.

On one hand, the predisposition to an improvement is related to the human content of an operation. It is reflected in the ratio of assembly (human content) to machine work. In assembly work there are relatively large possibilities for learning; in machine work the improvement is constrained by the fact that the machines cannot "learn" to run any faster. The following rates are often employed as possible benchmarks:

75% assembly labor, 25% machine labor: 80% curve
50% assembly labor, 50% machine labor: 85% curve
25% assembly labor, 75% machine labor: 90% curve[22]

On the other hand, the extent to which the predisposition is used may depend on the following two factors:

1. The effect of faith. A positive attitude toward the possibility of learning can reinforce progress. Winfred B. Hirschmann states: "If progress is believed possible, it will likely be sought; and if it is looked for, there is some possibility of finding it. Conversely, if improvements are considered unlikely, there will be little urge to seek them. A defeatist philosophy can be engendered which so debilitates an effort that it helps to produce the very condition it assumes."[23]

2. The presence of open-ended expectations. The absence of "ceiling psychology" may create a predisposition to learning and permit improvement to continue. Some companies obtain more rapid progress when the workers are not informed of the target rate.

1.3. Learning Curve Geometry

Since the discovery of the learning curve and the publication in 1936 of the first article formulating the theory of learning curves, various geometric versions have been proposed. The more well known are these:

1. The log-linear model
2. Pegels's exponential function
3. Levy's adaptation function
4. The Stanford-B model
5. DeJong's learning formula with an incompressibility factor
6. The S-curve
7. Glover's learning formula with a work commencement factor

Common to all these models, however, is the need to estimate these two basic parameters:

1. Input resources associated with the production of the first unit
2. The learning curve characteristic or some measure of the rate reduction

These various models are described next. It is, however, appropriate to note that the log-linear model has been and still is, by far, the most useful model. The other models are described because they have been found and may be found in the future to be applicable to some manufacturing experiences.

1.4. The Log-Linear Model

The log-linear model or constant percentage model basically states that the improvement in productivity is fairly constant as output increases. It follows the mathematical power function

$$\gamma = KX^n$$

where

γ = the number of direct-labor hours required to produce the xth unit,
K = the number of direct-labor hours required to produce the first unit,
X = the cumulative unit number,
n = $\log \phi / \log 2$ = learning index,
ϕ = the learning rate,
$1 - \phi$ = the progress ratio.

Assume that a company's rate of learning, like the aircraft industry's, is 80 percent. On an arithmetic chart with linear coordinates, the relationship between the cumulative average direct-labor hours and the cumulative units of production is portrayed by a curve showing a rapid decline that trails off (see Exhibit 1.2). The same curve on a logarithmic chart will follow a straight declining rate (see Exhibit 1.3). The portrayal of the learning phenomenon as a straight line is generally preferred for practical reasons.

1.5. Pegels's Exponential Function

As an alternative to the power function formulation of the log-linear model, various authors proposed models based on exponential functions. As an example, Pegels proposed an alternative algebraic function, an exponential-type function, to complement or replace the power function approach.[24] The functions are expressed as follows:

1. The marginal cost per unit index for the xth unit, $M{\cdot}C(x)$ is as follows:

$$MC(x) = \alpha a^{x-1} + \beta$$

Exhibit 1.2
Cumulative Average Labor Time at 80 Percent Learning Rate

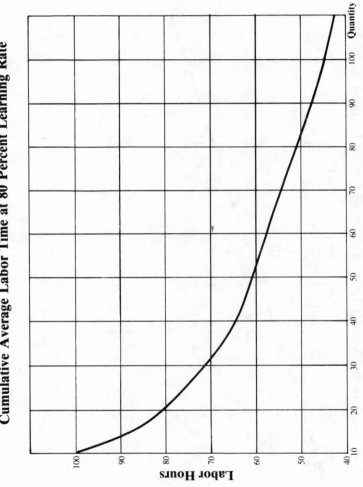

Note: Plotted on arithmetic paper, it forms an abrupt, sloping path that is difficult to project.

Exhibit 1.3
Cumulative Average Labor Time at 80 Percent Learning Rate

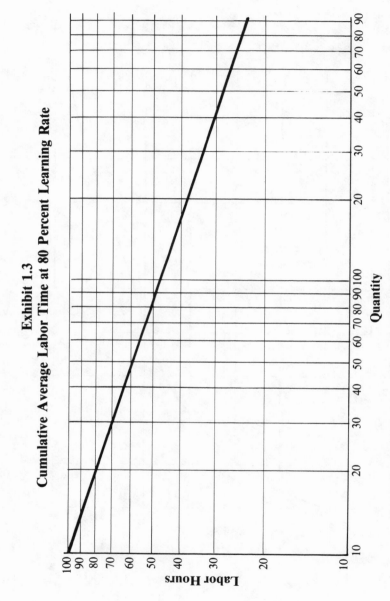

Note: Plotted on a log-log scale, it is a descending straight line, easy to extend and easy to read off.

where α, β, and a are empirically based parameters.

2. By integrating across x yields $TC(x)$ which is the total cost index up to the xth unit in terms of the marginal cost per unit index, in other words:

$$TC(x) = \int(\alpha a^{x-1} + \beta)dx + C = \frac{\alpha a^{x-1}}{lna} + \beta x + C$$

where α, β, and a are empirically based parameters, and C is a constant to be derived after the parameters have been derived. In fact, the constant C can be derived by letting $MC(1) = TC(1) = AC(1)$, which yields

$$C = \alpha - \frac{\alpha}{lna}.$$

3. The average cost $AC(x)$ of the first x units produced in marginal cost index terms or cumulative average cost can be derived as follows:

$$AC(x) = \frac{TC(x)}{x} = \frac{\alpha a^{x-1}}{xlna} + \beta + \frac{c}{x}.$$

The main assumption in the exponential function formulation is that the marginal cost of the first unit, $MC(1) = y_0$, is assumed to be known and will be set equal to the index value of one. In other words, $y_0 = \alpha + \beta = 1.00$.

In comparing the merits of his model to the other power function models, Pegels concluded as follows:

The proposed exponential model is only slightly more difficult to apply than the common power function model. Although there are three parameters to be estimated, one of these, β, is based on subjective estimates or historically based subjective estimates. The other two parameters, a and b, can be as readily determined as the two power function parameters. Since the exponential function is based on a zero-to-one marginal cost index, applying the exponential function requires slightly more training and care.[25]

In addition, the basic power function has the disadvantage of showing both marginal and average costs decreasing with increasing output, while in the exponential function the marginal cost becomes constant after a certain number of units produced.

1.6. Levy's Adaptation Function

Levy[26] cites two shortcomings of the log-linear model—namely, it does not recognize the leveling off of production rate, and it does not give insight into factors that may influence learning. The new type of learning function which he proposes is particularly useful in showing how a firm can adapt itself to the learning process and isolate the variables which influence learning. Levy's function has the following form:

$$MC = [1/\beta - (1/\beta - x^b/a)C^{-cx}]^{-1}$$

where MC = marginal cost, a and b are the parameters that are analogous to the power function parameters, C is a third parameter to be estimated, and β is the production index for the first unit. The function of the parameter C is to flatten the curve for large values of x. In other words, Levy's learning function reaches a plateau and does not continue to decrease or increase as does the power function.

1.7. The Stanford-B Model

The search for something other than the log-linear model stems from the fact that the linear model does not always provide the best fit in all situations. A Stanford study found that the linear formulations of the learning curve may be inappropriate for some World War II data. Instead the following equation, usually referred to as the Stanford-B formula or the learning formula with a B-factor,[27] was found to be more representative:

$$y = a(X + B)^n$$

where

y = direct-man hours required for cumulative unit number x,
a = constant, equivalent to the cost of the first unit when B = 0,
n = exponent describes slope of the asymptote (-0.5 is a typical value),
B = constant which may be expressed as the number of units theoretically produced prior to the first unit acceptance, or the equivalent units of experience available at the start of a manufacturing process ($1 < B < 10$ and 4 is a typical value).

The Stanford study found that n for 29 cases ranged between -0.397 and -0.599 (66.1% and 75.9% slopes) with a mean value of -0.499. In fact, the Boeing Company found that the Stanford-B model was the best for the manufacturing of the Boeing 707 if it is modified to incorporate design differences for special customers' requirements.[28] The modified progress curve developed suffers, however, from the following limitations:

1. It assumes that the learning experienced on any component is fully retained, no matter how much time elapses before the same work is repeated. Modifying the assumption will lead to a more cumbersome formulation and has not been attempted.

2. When the number of versions in a family of airplanes gets large, the computations become extensive. The difficulty is relieved if attention is restricted to a smaller number of versions in a combination with the version to be estimated. These will be ones which share the most work with this version and contribute the most experience.[29]

The Stanford-B model includes as a main feature the B factor which measures design differences or complexities beyond the control of management know-how or the amount of engineering or retooling. Another explanation is that the Stanford-B model accounts for previous learning retained by using a scale of displacement B.

Note that setting $n = 0.5$, the Stanford-B model yields a unit learning curve equation as follows:

$$y = a/\sqrt{x + B}.$$

With B = 0, the same equation becomes

$$y = ax^{-0.5}$$

which is equivalent to a 70.7 percent linear unit time reduction curve.

A typical learning curve of the Stanford-B type is asymptotic to a straight line with slope n and approaches such a line over its entire length as B approaches zero. The main result of the B factor is that the curve tends to follow a convex shape in the early part of a program.

There is at least one known attempt at evaluating the superiority of the Stanford curve over the conventional log-linear curve. Hoffman used the same data used by the Stanford Research Institute and concludes that there is little basis for choice between the two curves in spite of the fact that in several cases the inclusion of parameter B did result in smaller sums of squared deviations.[30]

1.8. DeJong's Learning Formula with an Incompressibility Factor

DeJong proposed a version of the power function which suggests parameters to be assigned for the proportion of manual activity in a given task.[31] When the activities are mainly controlled by manual operations, the time is compressible as successive units are completed. If machine time was dominant in the cycle of activities, the time will be less compressible as the number of units increases. Accordingly, DeJong introduced an incompressibility factor M in the log-linear model to take into account the man-machine ratio and the asymptotic behavior of the curve when it approaches a limit of unit time as the number of units increases. This model generates, then, two components: a fixed component which is set equal to the irreducible portion of the task and a variable component which is subject to learning. It has the following form:

$$MC = a[M + (1 - M)/X^n]$$

where

> MC = marginal time for the xth unit,
> a and n are parameters analogous to the power function,
> M is the factor of incompressibility.

The incompressibility factor suggested by DeJong is often 0.25 for manually dominated activities and 0.50 for machine-dominated activities. When M is zero, the DeJong formulation becomes the log-linear model, which would happen in a situation of a completely manual situation. In a machine-dominated situation, M approaches 1, and the expected unit time is a constant, thus $MC = a$. Exhibit 1.4 shows a set of curves for various values of M, for all of which the learning exponent is $n = 0.32$. The incompressibility factor indicates the inability to reduce production time as the number of cycles is repeated. A completely machine-dominated operation would be unlikely to improve and thus possess high incompressibility. In addition, the model demonstrates a practical limit to the amount of learning or improvement. The curve ultimately approaches a plateau as the number of units increases.

1.9. The S-Curve

Another curve useful when the data "miss" the straight learning curve is the somewhat S-shaped curve. For example, Carr proposed an S-type function which was based on the assumption of a gradual start-up.[32] An S-type function has the shape of the cumulative normal distribution function for the start-up curve and the shape of an operating characteristics function for the learning curve. Several factors appear to contribute to this pattern:

1. The early stages of production are a time of partial experimentation by all personnel. Various approaches are tried in learning to use prescribed tooling and methods, which preclude rapid improvement. Further, last minute changes in design and materials sometimes hit during this period, and these prevent the solidification of techniques necessary for rapid learning or initial low cost.

Exhibit 1.4
Learning Curve with an Incompressibility Factor for Various Values of *M*

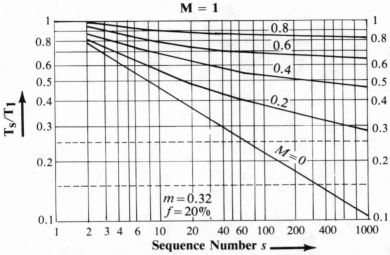

Note: The fall in $T_S T_1$ according to formula (3) for various values of *M* and for *m* = 0.32.

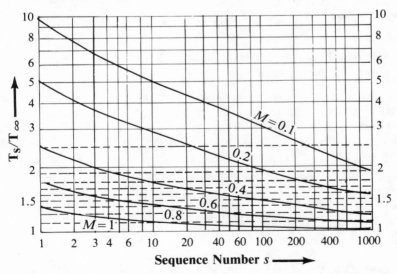

Note: The fall in $T_S T_\infty$ according to formula (4) for a number of values of *M* and for *m* = 0.32.

13

2. As corrections are made to toolings and methods, a rapid reduction in cost is possible for some time. For our assembly operation, the learning slope often reaches 50 percent during the period, compared with a norm of 75 percent.

3. Finally, however, the "water" has been taken out of the costs and we settle down to a more routine activity—the slope activity. The slope of learning now proceeds somewhat more slowly than average, say at 80 percent for assembly.[33]

Because the Stanford-B may better fit the early part of the curve and the DeJong model the latter part, one approach may be to combine these two models to obtain an S-curve such as:

$$MC = a[M + (1 - M)(x + B)^n].$$

To solve this equation, however, assumptions have to be made to preselect the incompressibility M and equivalent experience units B and a to solve for a value of n. In other words, values for any of the unknown can be determined given a logical preselection of the other three independent variables.

Another procedure for the determination of the coefficients of the S-curve is to look at it as a smooth "cubic curve." In such a case the model $\log MC = A + B(\log x) + C(\log x^2) + D(\log X^3)$ represents the cubic curve on a log-log plot. The fitting of a cubic curve to actual time can then be accomplished by the use of any polynomial fit program from the available computer library statistical routines.

1.10. Glover's Learning Formula with a Work Commencement Factor

In contrast to other theories which were based on an analysis of the output of complete factories, Glover examined studies of the gain in speed skill of individuals before extending the model to complete departments of companies.[34] A model derived for the learning of individuals in experimental psychology was found applicable to learning of all kinds in industry. It is expressed as follows:

$$\sum_{i=1}^{n} y_i + C = a \left(\sum_{i=1}^{n} x_i \right)^m$$

where y_i and x_i are interchangeable in the sense that either may represent time or quantity, C is a commencement factor, a is the time of the first cycle, and n is the index of the curve $= 1 + b$. If Σy is used to represent the total elapsed time, then x_i will normally be unity, that is,

$$\sum_{i=1}^{n} x_i = n$$

and

$$\sum_{i=1}^{n} y_i + C = an^m.$$

The model differs from the conventional power function of the introduction of the work commencement factor C. The rationale for such adjustment is stated as follows:

The nature of logarithmic scales tends to exaggerate any early deviation from the straight line, and it is not surprising that, if only a few cycles of practice can upset a laboratory experiment, lack of understanding of the importance of recording exact times in industry can cause a curve to be obtained instead of a straight line. The "work commencement" factor C in the model is, in effect, a factor of ignorance concerning the commencement of a job. As has been stated, there is reason to think that when C is not zero, the data relating to the time of commencement may be inaccurate. The reader may synthesize such inaccuracies by taking data which is known to yield a straight line relationship and introduce a fictitious constant error into either the time or practice scales.[35]

1.11. Conclusions

The learning curve is a very important management accounting tool. Given the predictable improvement in time as production increases, the curve provides valuable information for decision making. This chapter defines the concept of the learning phenomenon and elaborates on its history and theory. Many geometric versions of the learning curve proposed in the literature and in practice were presented:

1. The log-linear model
2. Pegels's exponential function
3. Levy's adaptation function
4. The Stanford-B model
5. DeJong's learning formula with an incompressibility factor
6. The S-curve
7. Glover's learning formula with a work commencement factor

The reason for the proliferation of new models other than the log-linear model stems from the fact that the linear model does not always provide the best fit in all situations. The log-linear model is, however, the most widely discussed, taught, and used model. Given that relative superiority is attributed to each of these models and specific industrial applications of these models are presented, it is recommended that new users of learning curves should make some test runs in their choice of the learning curve models most appropriate to their case.

Notes

1. Winfred B. Hirschmann, "Profit from the Learning Curve," *Harvard Business Review* (January–February 1964), p. 128.

2. Ahmed Belkaoui, "Costing Through Learning," *Cost and Management* (May–June 1976), pp. 36–40.

3. Miguel Reguero, *An Economic Study of the Military Plane Industry* (Wright-Patterson Air Force Base, Ohio: Department of the Air Force, 1957), p. 213.

4. T. P. Wright, "Factors Affecting the Cost of Airplanes," *Journal of Aeronautical Science* (February 1936), pp. 122–128.

5. Hirschmann, "Learning Curve," p. 136.

6. Ibid.

7. Frank J. Andress, "The Learning Curve as a Production Tool," *Harvard Business Review* (January–February 1954), p. 87.

8. Nicholas Baloff, "The Learning Curve: Some Controversial Issues," *Journal of Industrial Economics* (January 1966), p. 278.

9. Hirschmann, "Learning Curve," p. 136.

10. N. Baloff, "Startups in Machine Intensive Production Systems," *Journal of Industrial Engineering* (July 1966), p. 26.

11. N. Baloff, "Extension of the Learning Curve—Some Empirical Results," *Operational Research Quarterly* (Vol. 22, No. 4, 1971), pp. 329–40.

12. R. W. Conway and Andrew Schultz, Jr., "The Manufacturing Progress Function," *Journal of Industrial Engineering* (January–February 1959).

13. J. R. DeJong, "The Effects of Increasing Skill on Cycle Time and Its Consequences for Time Standards," *Ergonomics* (November 1957).

14. W. Z. Hirsch, "Manufacturing Progress Functions," *Review of Economics and Statistics* (Vol. 34, May 1952), pp. 143–155.

15. Winfred B. Hirschmann, "Profit–From the Learning Curve," *Harvard Business Review* (January–February, 1964).

16. M. D. Kilbridge, "A Model for Industrial Learning Costs," *Management Science* (Vol. 8, No. 4, July 1962).

17. F. K. Levy, "Adaptation in the Production Process," *Management Science* (April 1965).

18. G. Nadler and W. D. Smith, "Manufacturing Progress Functions for Types of Processes," *International Journal of Production Research* (June 1963).

19. L. E. Preston and E. C. Keachie, "Cost Functions and Progress Functions: An Integration," *American Economic Review* (March 1964).

20. E. Turban, "Incentives During Learning—An Application of the Learning Curve Theory and a Survey of Other Methods," *Journal of Industrial Engineering* (December 1968).

21. Hirschmann, "Learning Curve," p. 136.

22. Thomas G. Vayda, "How to Use the Learning Curve for Planning and Control," *Cost and Management* (July–August 1972), p. 28.

23. Hirschmann, "Learning Curve," p. 134.

24. C. C. Pegels, "On Startup or Learning Curves: An Expanded View," *AIIE Transactions* (Vol. 1, No. 3, September 1969), pp. 216–222.

25. Ibid., p. 220.

26. Levy, "Adaptation in the Production Process," pp. B136–B154.

27. Harold Asher, "Cost-Quantity Relationships in the Airplane Industry," Report No. R-291, The Rand Corporation, Santa Monica, Calif., July 1, 1956.

28. A. Garg and P. Milliman, "The Aircraft Progress Curve—Modified for Design Changes," *Journal of Industrial Engineering* (Vol. 12, No. 23, January–February 1961), pp. 23–28.

29. Ibid., p. 113.

30. F. S. Hoffman, "Comments on the Modified Form of the Aircraft Progress Functions," Report No. RN-464, The Rand Corporation, Santa Monica, Calif., 1950.

31. DeJong, "The Effects of Increasing Skill on Cycle Time," pp. 51–60.

32. G. W. Carr, "Peacetime Cost Estimating Requires New Learning Curves," *Aviation* (Vol. 45, April 1946).

33. E. B. Cochran, "New Concepts of the Learning Curve," *Journal of Industrial Engineering* (July–August, 1960), p. 324.

34. J. H. Glover, "Manufacturing Progress Functions. I. An Alternative Model and Its Comparison with Existing Functions," *International Journal of Production Research* (Vol. 4, No. 4, 1966), pp. 279–300.

35. Ibid., p. 283.

2

THE LOG-LINEAR MODEL

The learning curve is a well-accepted model in the production and managerial accounting literature. Although various mathematical models have been suggested as descriptive of the phenomenon, only one—the constant-percentage or log-linear model—is widely used and discussed in the managerial accounting literature. The log-linear model basically states that the improvement in productivity is fairly constant as output increases. Accordingly, this chapter elaborates on the models, formulae, and mechanics of the log-linear model. A basic knowledge of the working of these models is important for an efficient implementation in actual managerial situations.

2.1. The General Model: The Constant Percentage Model

The learning phenomenon based on the constant-percentage model is generally expressed by the mathematical function

$$(Y, I_* \text{ or } M) = ax^b$$

where the right side of the function is defined as

a = the number of direct-labor hours required to produce the first unit of output,

b = the learning exponent derived from $\dfrac{\log r}{\log f}$

where

r = the rate of learning or improvement represented by the constant percentage decrease in hours,

f = the factor increase in output (usually discussed in terms of 2).

As can be seen from the formulae, the dependent variable is represented by either Y, I_* or M. This is due to the existence of three types of learning curve models which differ in their definition of the dependent variable. They are the average time model, the marginal time model, and the individual unit-time model. They may be defined as follows:

1. The average time model specifies that the new cumulative average time per unit (Y) will decrease by a constant percentage (r) as the cumulative production doubles.
2. The marginal time model specifies that the new marginal time per unit (M) will decrease by a constant percentage (r) as cumulative production doubles.
3. The individual unit-time model specifies that the new individual time per unit (I_*) will decrease by a constant percentage (r) as cumulative production doubles.

In what follows I will explain each of these models, present a synthesis of the three models, provide guidance for the choice of one of these models, and elaborate on the relationships between the percentage of learning and the b parameter (the learning exponent).

2.2. The Average Time Model

As stated earlier the average time model specifies the relationship between the cumulative average time per unit (Y) and the cumulative production (X). More precisely, the basic formulae for the average time or average curve specifies that the new cumulative time per unit (Y) will decrease by a constant percentage (r) as the cumulative production doubles. Besides the average time, the model provides formulae for the total time or total curve, the individual time or individual curve, and the marginal time or marginal curve.

Formula 1 computes the average curve Y (that is, the average cumulative labor hours, labor dollars, or material cost for all units produced up to any particular point):

$$Y = aX^b \qquad (1)$$

where

Y = average cumulative labor hours, labor dollars, or material costs for X number of units,
a = theoretical value or actual value (if known) of the first unit,
X = cumulative number of units produced,
b = slope coefficient, exponent, or learning index. It is always negative, since the cost or number of hours is decreasing.

A much more used logarithmic version of formula 1 is

$$\log Y = (\log a) + (b \log X).$$

Formula 2 computes the total curve T (that is, the total labor hours required to produce a predetermined number of units):

$$T = YX = XaX^b = aX^{b-1} \tag{2}$$

where T = total labor hours required to produce a predetermined number of units.

Formula 3 computes the individual unit time I (that is, the change in successive times):

$$I = aX^{b+1} - a(X - 1)^{b+1} \tag{3}$$

Formula 4 computes the marginal curve M (that is, the relative change in total time to produce the xth unit, or slope of total time):

$$M = dt/dn = (b + 1)aX^b \tag{4}$$

where M = marginal time to produce the xth unit.

To apply any of the four formulae, the value of the exponent b is first computed as follows:

$$b = \log r/\log 2$$

or

$$\log r = b \log 2.$$

To illustrate the average time model, let us assume that (1) it takes 800 hours to produce the first unit of a product, and (2) an 80 percent learning rate is found to exist in the average assembly time when cumulative production doubles. Determine the value of b and the cumulative average labor hours for 4 units of output by first determining the value of b:

$$b = \log (0.80)/\log 2$$

Then inserting the appropriate values obtained from Exhibit 2.1:

$$b = \frac{9.9031 - 10}{0.301} = -0.322$$

Exhibit 2.1
Common Logarithms of Numbers

Number	0	1	2	3	4	5	6	7	8	9	Avg. diff.
1.0	0.0000	0043	0086	0128	0170	0212	0253	0294	0334	0374	
1.1	0414	0453	0492	0531	0569	0607	0645	0632	0719	0755	
1.2	0792	0828	0864	0899	0934	0969	1004	1038	1072	1106	
1.3	1139	1173	1206	1239	1271	1303	1335	1367	1399	1430	
1.4	1461	1492	1523	1553	1584	1614	1644	1673	1703	1732	
1.5	1761	1790	1818	1847	1875	1903	1931	1959	1987	2014	
1.6	2041	2068	2095	2122	2148	2175	2201	2227	2253	2279	
1.7	2304	2330	2355	2380	2405	2430	2455	2480	2504	2529	
1.8	2553	2577	2601	2625	2648	2672	2695	2718	2742	2765	
1.9	2788	2810	2833	2856	2878	2900	2923	2945	2967	2989	
2.0	0.3010	3032	3054	3075	3096	3118	3139	3160	3181	3201	21
2.1	3222	3243	3263	3284	3304	3324	3345	3365	3385	3404	20
2.2	3424	3444	3464	3483	3502	3522	3541	3560	3579	3598	19
2.3	3617	3636	3655	3674	3692	3711	3729	3747	3766	3784	18
2.4	3802	3820	3838	3856	3874	3892	3909	3927	3945	3962	17
2.5	3979	3997	4014	4031	4048	4065	4082	4099	4116	4133	17
2.6	4150	4166	4183	4200	4216	4232	4249	4265	4281	4298	16
2.7	4314	4330	4346	4362	4378	4393	4409	4425	4440	4456	16
2.8	4472	4487	4502	4518	4533	4548	4564	4579	4594	4609	15
2.9	4624	4639	4654	4669	4683	4698	4713	4728	4742	4757	15

	0	1	2	3	4	5	6	7	8	9	
3.0	0.4771	4786	4800	4814	4829	4843	4857	4871	4886	4900	14
3.1	4914	4928	4942	4955	4969	4983	4997	5011	5024	5038	14
3.2	5051	5065	5079	5092	5105	5119	5132	5145	5159	5172	13
3.3	5185	5198	5211	5224	5237	5250	5263	5276	5289	5302	13
3.4	5315	5328	5340	5353	5366	5378	5391	5403	5416	5428	13
3.5	5441	5453	5465	5478	5490	5502	5514	5527	5539	5551	12
3.6	5563	5575	5587	5599	5611	5623	5635	5647	5658	5670	12
3.7	5682	5694	5705	5717	5729	5740	5752	5763	5775	5786	12
3.8	5798	5809	5821	5832	5843	5855	5866	5877	5888	5899	11
3.9	5911	5922	5933	5944	5955	5966	5977	5988	5999	6010	11
4.0	0.6021	6031	6042	6053	6064	6075	6085	6096	6107	6117	11
4.1	6128	6138	6149	6160	6170	6180	6191	6201	6212	6222	10
4.2	6232	6243	6253	6263	6274	6284	6294	6304	6314	6325	10
4.3	6335	6343	6355	6365	6375	6385	6395	6405	6415	6425	10
4.4	6435	6444	6454	6464	6474	6484	6493	6503	6513	6522	10
4.5	6532	6542	6551	6561	6571	6580	6590	6599	6609	6618	10
4.6	6628	6637	6646	6656	6665	6675	6684	6693	6702	6712	10
4.7	6721	6730	6739	6749	6758	6767	6776	6785	6794	6803	9
4.8	6812	6821	6830	6839	6848	6857	6866	6875	6884	6893	9
4.9	6902	6911	6920	6928	6937	6946	6955	6964	6972	6981	9

Exhibit 2.1 (continued)

Number	0	1	2	3	4	5	6	7	8	9	Avg. diff.
5.0	0.6990	6998	7007	7016	7024	7033	7042	7050	7059	7067	9
5.1	7076	7084	7093	7101	7110	7118	7126	7135	7143	7152	8
5.2	7160	7168	7177	7185	7193	7202	7210	7218	7226	7235	8
5.3	7243	7251	7259	7267	7275	7284	7292	7300	7308	7316	8
5.4	7324	7332	7340	7348	7356	7364	7372	7380	7388	7396	8
5.5	7404	7412	7419	7427	7435	7443	7451	7459	7466	7474	8
5.6	7482	7490	7497	7505	7513	7520	7528	7536	7543	7551	8
5.7	7559	7566	7574	7582	7589	7597	7604	7612	7619	7627	8
5.8	7634	7642	7649	7657	7664	7672	7679	7686	7694	7701	7
5.9	7709	7716	7723	7731	7738	7745	7752	7760	7767	7774	7
6.0	0.7782	7789	7796	7803	7810	7818	7825	7832	7839	7846	7
6.1	7853	7860	7868	7875	7882	7889	7896	7903	7910	7917	7
6.2	7924	7931	7938	7945	7952	7959	7966	7973	7980	7987	7
6.3	7993	8000	8007	8014	8021	8028	8035	8041	8048	8055	7
6.4	8062	8069	8075	8082	8089	8096	8102	8109	8116	8122	7
6.5	8129	8136	8142	8149	8156	8162	8169	8176	8182	8189	7
6.6	8195	8202	8209	8215	8222	8228	8235	8241	8248	8254	7
6.7	8261	8267	8274	8280	8287	8293	8299	8305	8312	8319	6
6.8	8325	8331	8338	8344	8351	8357	8363	8370	8376	8382	6
6.9	8388	8395	8401	8407	8414	8420	8426	8432	8439	8445	6

x	0	1	2	3	4	5	6	7	8	9	
7.0	0.8451	8457	8463	8470	8476	8482	8488	8494	8500	8506	6
7.1	8513	8519	8525	8531	8537	8543	8549	8555	8561	8567	6
7.2	8575	8579	8585	8591	8597	8603	8609	8615	8621	8627	6
7.3	8633	8639	8645	8651	8657	8663	8669	8675	8681	8686	6
7.4	8692	8698	8704	8710	8716	8722	8727	8733	8739	8745	6
7.5	8751	8756	8762	8768	8774	8779	8785	8791	8797	8802	6
7.6	8808	8814	8820	8825	8831	8837	8842	8848	8854	8859	6
7.7	8865	8871	8876	8882	8887	8893	8899	8904	8910	8915	6
7.8	8921	8927	8932	8938	8943	8949	8954	8960	8965	8971	6
7.9	8976	8982	8987	8993	8998	9004	9009	9015	9020	9025	5
8.0	0.9031	9036	9042	9047	9053	9058	9063	9069	9074	9079	5
8.1	9085	9090	9096	9101	9106	9112	9117	9122	9128	9133	5
8.2	9138	9143	9149	9154	9159	9165	9170	9175	9180	9186	5
8.3	9191	9196	9201	9206	9212	9217	9222	9227	9232	9238	5
8.4	9243	9248	9253	9258	9263	9269	9274	9279	9284	9289	5
8.5	9294	9299	9304	9309	9315	9320	9325	9330	9335	9340	5
8.6	9345	9350	9355	9360	9365	9370	9375	9380	9385	9390	5
8.7	9395	9400	9405	9410	9415	9420	9425	9430	9435	9440	5
8.8	9445	9450	9455	9460	9465	9469	9474	9479	9484	9489	5
8.9	9494	9499	9504	9509	9513	9518	9523	9528	9533	9538	5

Exhibit 2.1 (continued)

Number	0	1	2	3	4	5	6	7	8	9	Avg. diff.
9.0	0.9543	9547	9552	9557	9562	9566	9571	9576	9581	9586	5
9.1	9590	9595	9600	9605	9609	9614	9619	9624	9628	9633	5
9.2	9638	9643	9647	9652	9657	9661	9666	9671	9675	9680	5
9.3	9685	9689	9694	9699	9703	9708	9713	9717	9722	9727	5
9.4	9731	9736	9741	9745	9750	9754	9759	9763	9768	9773	5
9.5	9777	9782	9786	9791	9795	9800	9805	9809	9814	9818	5
9.6	9823	9827	9832	9836	9841	9845	9850	9854	9859	9863	4
9.7	9868	9872	9877	9881	9886	9390	9894	9899	9903	9908	4
9.8	9912	9917	9921	9926	9930	9934	9939	9943	9948	9952	4
9.9	9956	9961	9965	9969	9974	9978	9983	9987	9991	9996	4

$\log \pi = 0.4071$ $\qquad \log \pi/2 = 0.1961$ $\qquad \log \pi^2 = 0.9943$

$\log \theta = 0.4343$ $\qquad \log (0.4343) = 0.6378 - 1$ $\qquad \log \sqrt{\pi} = 0.2486$

These pages give the common logarithms of numbers between 1 and 10, correct to four places. Moving the decimal point n places to the right [or left] in the number is equivalent to adding n [or $-n$] to the logarithm. Thus, $\log 0.017453 = 0.2419 - 2$, which may also be written 2.2419 or $8.2419 - 10$.

$\log (ab) = \log a + \log b$ $\qquad \log (a^N) = \log a$

$\log \left(\dfrac{a}{b}\right) = \log a - \log b$ $\qquad \log (N\sqrt{a}) = \dfrac{1}{N} \log a$

Next, the four formulae—the average time, the total time, the individual unit-time, and the marginal time—may be used to determine the average labor hours, the total labor hours, the individual unit labor hours, and the marginal labor hours required for different numbers of units as shown in Exhibit 2.2 and graphed in Exhibits 2.3 and 2.4.

2.3. The Marginal Time Model

As stated earlier, the marginal time model specifies the relationship between the marginal time per unit (M) and the cumulative production (X). More precisely the basic formulae for the marginal time or marginal curve specifies that the new marginal time per unit (M) will decrease by a constant percentage (r) as cumulative production doubles. Besides the marginal time, the model provides formulae for the total time or total curve, the individual time or individual curve, and the average time or average curve.

Formula 1 computes the marginal curve M (that is, the marginal labor hours, labor dollars, or material cost for all units produced up to any particular point):

$$M = aX^b_{**} \tag{1}$$

where

M = marginal time per unit for X_{**} numbers of units produced,
a = number of hours to build the first unit,
X = number of units completed,
b = learning factor.

Formula 2 computes the total time T_*:

$$T_{**} = \int_o^x Y \tag{2}$$

$$T = \frac{a}{b+1}(X^{b+1})$$

where T = total labor hours needed to produce a predetermined number of units.

Formula 3 computes the average time Y_*:

$$Y_{**} = \frac{T}{x} = \frac{a}{b+1}(X^b_{**}) \tag{3}$$

Exhibit 2.2
Average, Total, Marginal, and Individual Unit Hours (Average Time Model)

Units	Cumulative Units	Average Time	Total Time	Marginal Time	Individual Unit Time*
1	1	$800\ (1)^{-0.322} = 800$	$800\ (1)^{-0.678} = 800$	$800 \times 0.678\ (1)^{-0.322} = 542$	800
1	2	$800\ (2)^{-0.322} = 640$	$800\ (2)^{-0.678} = 1280$	$800 \times 0.678\ (2)^{-0.322} = 434$	480
1	3	$800\ (3)^{-0.322} = 562$	$800\ (3)^{-0.678} = 1680$	$800 \times 0.678\ (3)^{-0.322} = 381$	400
1	4	$800\ (4)^{-0.322} = 512$	$800\ (4)^{-0.678} = 2048$	$800 \times 0.678\ (4)^{-0.322} = 574$	368
1	5	$800\ (5)^{-0.322} = 476$	$800\ (5)^{-0.678} = 2380$	$800 \times 0.678\ (5)^{-0.322} = 322$	332
1	6	$800\ (6)^{-0.322} = 449$	$800\ (6)^{-0.678} = 2694$	$800 \times 0.678\ (6)^{-0.322} = 304$	314
1	7	$800\ (7)^{-0.322} = 427$	$800\ (7)^{-0.678} = 2993$	$800 \times 0.678\ (7)^{-0.322} = 289$	299
1	8	$800\ (8)^{-0.322} = 409$	$800\ (8)^{-0.678} = 3272$	$800 \times 0.678\ (8)^{-0.322} = 277$	279
1	9	$800\ (9)^{-0.322} = 394$	$800\ (9)^{-0.678} = 3548$	$800 \times 0.678\ (9)^{-0.322} = 267$	276
1	10	$800\ (10)^{-0.322} = 381$	$800\ (10)^{-0.678} = 3811$	$800 \times 0.678\ (10)^{-0.322} = 258$	263

Exhibit 2.3

80 Percent Average Time Curve, Arithmetic Graph

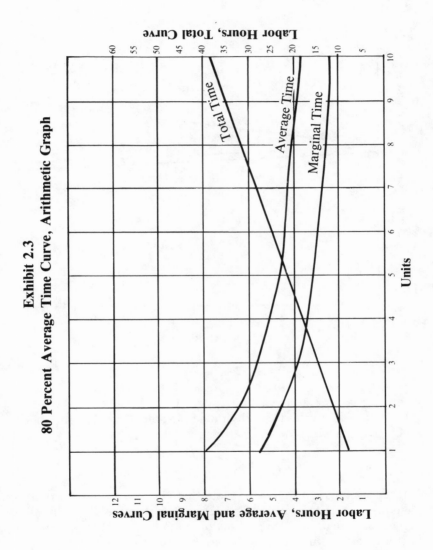

Exhibit 2.4
80 Percent Average Time Curve, Logarithmic Graph

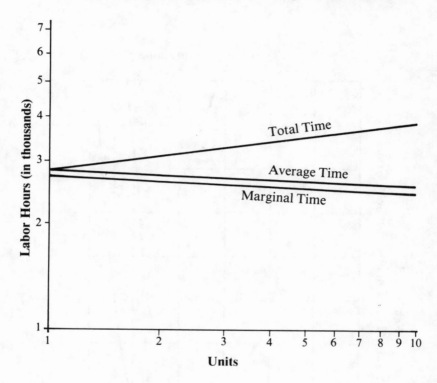

where Y_{**} = average labor hours required to build a number of units.

Formula 4 computes the individual unit-time, I_* (that is, the change in successive times):

$$I_{**} = aX_*^{b+1} - a(X_{**}-1)^{b+1} \tag{4}$$

To apply these formulae, assume that (1) it takes 700 hours to complete the first unit of output, and (2) an 80 percent learning curve exists in the marginal time when production doubles. As in the earlier example (in the average time model), b may be found to be equal to -0.3200. Inserting the proper values in the form formulae will yield the marginal time, total time, and average time for different levels of production as shown in Exhibit 2.5 and graphed in Exhibits 2.6 and 2.7.

Exhibit 2.5
Marginal, Total, and Average Hours (Marginal Time Model)

Units	Cumulative Units	Marginal Time	Total Time	Average Time
1	1	$700(1)^{-0.322} = 700$	$\dfrac{700}{0.678} \times (1)^{0.678} = 1{,}032$	$700(1)^{-0.322} = 1{,}032$
1	2	$700(2)^{-0.322} = 559$	$\dfrac{700}{0.678} \times (2)^{0.678} = 1{,}651$	$700(1)^{-0.322} = 825$
1	3	$700(3)^{-0.322} = 491$	$\dfrac{700}{0.678} \times (3)^{0.678} = 2{,}173$	$700(1)^{-0.322} = 724$
1	4	$700(4)^{-0.322} = 448$	$\dfrac{700}{0.678} \times (4)^{0.678} = 2{,}641$	$700(1)^{-0.322} = 660$
1	5	$700(5)^{-0.322} = 416$	$\dfrac{700}{0.678} \times (5)^{0.678} = 3{,}073$	$700(1)^{-0.322} = 614$
1	6	$700(6)^{-0.322} = 393$	$\dfrac{700}{0.678} \times (6)^{0.678} = 3{,}478$	$700(1)^{-0.322} = 579$
1	7	$700(7)^{-0.322} = 374$	$\dfrac{700}{0.678} \times (7)^{0.678} = 3{,}860$	$700(1)^{-0.322} = 551$
1	8	$700(8)^{-0.322} = 358$	$\dfrac{700}{0.678} \times (8)^{0.678} = 4{,}226$	$700(1)^{-0.322} = 528$
1	9	$700(9)^{-0.322} = 345$	$\dfrac{700}{0.678} \times (9)^{0.678} = 4{,}577$	$700(1)^{-0.322} = 508$
1	10	$700(10)^{-0.322} = 333$	$\dfrac{700}{0.678} \times (10)^{0.678} = 4{,}917$	$700(1)^{-0.322} = 491$

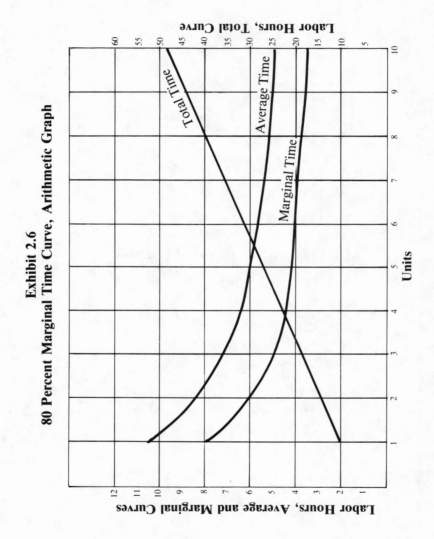

Exhibit 2.6
80 Percent Marginal Time Curve, Arithmetic Graph

32

Exhibit 2.7
80 Percent Marginal Time Curve, Logarithmic Graph

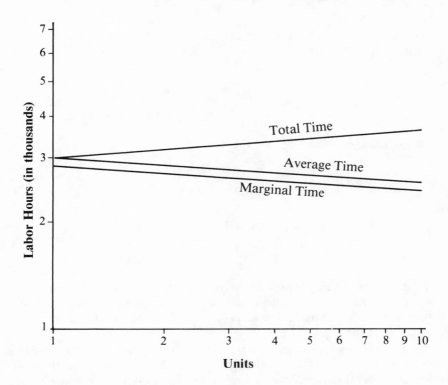

2.4. The Individual Unit-Time Model

As stated earlier, the individual unit model specifies that the new individual time per unit (I_*) will decrease by a constant percentage (r) as cumulative production doubles. More precisely, the basic formulae for the individual unit-time or unit-time curve specifies that the new individual time per unit (I_*) will decrease by a constant percentage (r) as cumulative production doubles. Besides the individual time, the models provide formulae for the total time or total curve, the average time or average curve, and the marginal time or marginal curve.

Formula 1 computes the individual time curve, I_{**} (that is, the time required to build a predetermined number of units X_{**}):

$$I_* = aX_*^b \tag{1}$$

where

a = time required to build the first unit,
X_* = cumulative number of units produced,
b = learning index.

Formula 2 computes the total time T_{**} (that is, the total time required to build a predetermined number of units X_{**}):

$$^*T_* = \sum_{n=1}^{X^*} an^b \tag{2}$$

Formula 3 computes the average time, Y_{**}:

$$Y_* = \frac{T^*}{X^*} = \sum_{n=1}^{X^*} an^b/X_* \tag{3}$$

Formula 4 computes the marginal time M_*:

$$M_* = dT_*/dX_* \tag{4}$$

To illustrate the individual time curve, let us assume that (1) it takes 100 hours to build the first unit, and (2) an 80 percent learning curve is found to exist in the assembly time of an individual unit when production doubles.

As in the earlier examples, b may be found to be equal to -0.328. Inserting the proper values in the four formulae will yield the individual time, the total time, and the average time, as shown in Exhibit 2.8.

2.5. Distinguishing among the Three Forms of the Constant Percentage Learning Curve Model

The three models differ in their definition of the dependent variable (the left side of the equation) which is subject to the learning phenomena.

1. In the average time model, the dependent variable is the new cumulative average time per unit Y.
2. In the unit time model, the dependent variable is the individual time per unit, I_*.
3. In the marginal time model, the dependent variable is the marginal time per unit, M_{**}.

It is important to determine which is the correct dependent variable which is subject to the learning phenomena because it dictates the types

Exhibit 2.8
Individual Unit-Time Computations

* Units	Individual Unit Time	Total Time	Average Time
1	100	100	100
2	80	180	90
3	70.21	250.21	83.40
4	64	314.21	78.75
5	59.56	373.77	74.75
6	56.17	429.94	71.65
7	53.45	483.39	69.06
8	51.20	534.59	66.83
9	49.25	583.84	64.87
10	47.62	631.46	63.14

of formulae to be used. The formulae for the three types of models are summarized in Exhibit 2.9.

2.6. Which Model to Use

The process being studied determines whether the average time, the marginal time, or the individual unit time should be used. The procedure consists of the following steps:

1. Collecting average time, marginal time, and individual unit-time information and cumulative output information.
2. Plotting the information on a log-log graph and the line providing the best visual fit between, on one hand, the average time, the managerial time, or the individual time information and, on the other hand, the cumulative output defines the model to be used.

Exhibit 2.9
Three of the Forms of the Constant Percentage Learning Curve Model

	Cumulative Average Model, $X \in (0,+\infty)$	Individual Unit Model, $X_* \in (0,1,2,\ldots\infty)$	Marginal Unit Model $X_{**} \in (0,+\infty)$
Total Time of Cumulative Output	$T = KX = aX^{b+1}$	$T_* = \sum_{n=1}^{X_*} an^b$	$T_{**} = \int_0^{X_{**}} M$ $= \frac{a}{b+1}(X^{b+1})$
Average Time of Cumulative Output	Fitted $Y = aX^b$	$Y_* = T_*/X_*$ $= \sum_{n=1}^{X_*} an^b / X_*$	$Y_{**} = \frac{T_{**}}{X_{**}}$ $= \frac{a}{b+1}(X^b_{**})$
Individual Unit Time	$I = aX^{b+1} - a(X-1)^{b+1}$	Fitted $I_* = aX_*^b$	$I_{**} = \frac{a}{b+1}(X_{**}^{b+1}) - \frac{a}{b+1}(X_{**}-1)^{b+1}$
Marginal Time	$M = dT/dX = (b+1)aX^b$	not defined	$M = aX_{**}^b$

Exhibit 2.10
Relationship between Percentage of Learning (*r*) and Exponent (*b*)

r	b	1+b
51	-0.97143	0.028570
52	-0.94342	0.056580
53	-0.91594	0.084060
54	-0.88997	0.110030
55	-0.86250	0.137500
56	-0.83650	0.163500
57	-0.81097	0.189030
58	-0.78588	0.214120
59	-0.76121	0.238790
60	-0.736966	0.263034
61	-0.713119	0.286881
62	-0.689660	0.310340
63	-0.666576	0.333424
64	-0.643856	0.356144
65	-0.621488	0.378512
66	-0.599462	0.400538
67	-0.577767	0.422233
68	-0.556393	0.443607
69	-0.535332	0.464668
70	-0.514573	0.485427
71	-0.494109	0.505891
72	-0.473931	0.526069
73	-0.454032	0.545968
74	-0.434403	0.565597
75	-0.415037	0.584963
76	-0.395929	0.604071
77	-0.377070	0.622930
78	-0.358454	0.641546
79	-0.340075	0.659925
80	-0.321928	0.678072
81	-0.304006	0.695994
82	-0.286304	0.713696
83	-0.268817	0.731183
84	-0.251539	0.748461
85	-0.234465	0.765535
86	-0.217591	0.782409
87	-0.200913	0.799087
88	-0.184425	0.815575
89	-0.168123	0.831877
90	-0.152003	0.847997
91	-0.136062	0.863938
92	-0.120294	0.879706
93	-0.104697	0.895303
94	-0.089267	0.910733
95	-0.074006	0.925994
96	-0.058894	0.941106
97	-0.043943	0.956057

Exhibit 2.11

Computed Values of X^b for 80 Percent and 90 Percent Curves: 50 Units

X (unit number)	80% curve (b = -.3219)	90% curve (b = -.1520)	X (unit number)	80% curve (b = -.3219)	90% curve (b = 0.1520)
1	1.0000	1.0000	26	.3504	.6094
2	.7999	.9000	27	.3461	.6059
3	.7021	.8462	28	.3421	.6026
4	.6400	.8100	29	.3379	.5994
5	.5957	.7830	30	.3346	.5963
6	.5617	.7616	31	.3311	.5934
7	.5345	.7440	32	.3277	.5905
8	.5120	.7290	33	.3245	.5878

n			n		
9	.4930	.7161	34	.3214	.5851
10	.4766	.7047	35	.3184	.5825
11	.4621	.6946	36	.3155	.5800
12	.4494	.6854	37	.3128	.5776
13	.4380	.6771	38	.3101	.5753
14	.4276	.6696	39	.3075	.5730
15	.4182	.6626	40	.3050	.5708
16	.4096	.6561	41	.3026	.5687
17	.4017	.6501	42	.3002	.5666
18	.3944	.6445	43	.2980	.5646
19	.3876	.6392	44	.2958	.5626
20	.3819	.6342	45	.2937	.5607
21	.3753	.6295	46	.2916	.5588
22	.3697	.6251	47	.2896	.5570
23	.3645	.6209	48	.2876	.5552
24	.3595	.6169	49	.2857	.5535
25	.3548	.6131	50	.2839	.5518

3. To be more exact in determining whether the average time, marginal time, or individual unit time applies, perform a logarithmic linear regression of either one of the possible dependent variables with the output, that is, log (time, average, total, or individual unit) = log a + b log (cumulative units).

The model which provides the best statistical fit in terms of the highest coefficient of determination, R^2, should be used as the right model for the observed learning phenomenon.

2.7. Relationships between Percentage of Learning and Parameter b

To simplify the computations necessary in the applications of the learning curve, the relationships between the percentage of learning (r) and the exponent (b) can be established for all possible values of r. In general, the relationship is computed as b = log 2/log 2.

For example, for 2 = 70 percent, b = -0.51457. Exhibit 2.10 establishes this relationship for all values of r ranging from 51 through 97, and it can be used as an expedient way to find the appropriate value of b.

Another way to simplify the computations is to use Exhibit 2.11 which shows the computed values of x^b for curves of 80 and 90 percent. A more complete exhibit is shown in Appendix 4-A.

2.8. Conclusions

This chapter presented the formulae and fundamentals behind the constant percentage models. Because these models differ in their definition of the dependent variables, true models were explained by the average time model, the marginal time model, and the individual unit-time model. The chapter explained each of these models, presented a synthesis of each, provided guidance for the choice of one of these models, and elaborated on the relationships between the percentage of learning and the learning exponent.

3

LEARNING CURVE
APPLICATIONS

Any operation can always be performed better each succeeding time. That pattern of improvement, time, and cost reduction can be sufficiently regular to be predictive. That is the essential principle of the learning phenomenon. Chapters 1 and 2 presented various learning curve models. This chapter focuses on the possible learning curve applications in production and management accounting. Cases examined include basic application, cost estimation, warranty maintenance and maintenance force, make or buy decisions, work-accident experience, standard costs and efficiency variance analysis, external reporting, cost reduction, price estimation, capital budgeting, and break-even analysis.

3.1. Formulae for Determining the Slope

The average time model of the log-linear model is represented by the formula

$$Y = ax^{-b}.$$

If production doubles, then the formula becomes

$$Y^1 = a(2x)^{-b}.$$

Given that learning ($r\%$) takes place when production doubles, then

$$r\% = \frac{Y^1}{Y} = \frac{a(2x)^{-b}}{ax^{-b}} \qquad \text{or} \qquad r\% = 1^{-b} = \frac{1}{2^b}.$$

If we take the logarithm of both sides and solve for b, then we obtain

$$b = \frac{\log r\%}{\log 2}.$$

For example, the slope b for a 50 percent curve is

$$b = \frac{\log \text{ of } .90}{\log \text{ of } 2} = \frac{9.95424 - 10}{0.30103} = \frac{-.04576}{.30108} = -.15201.$$

3.2. Cost Estimation

The learning curve can be used in cost estimation. Cost estimation when cumulative costs are known and when the learning phenomenon is in effect consists of estimating the coefficients of the learning curve from past data using the logarithmic linear equation

$$\log Y = \log a - b \log x.$$

In one method, the regression analysis of the logarithmic data on y and x using the least-squares method will provide a regression line. Its slope coefficient, exponent, or learning constant can be determined using the least-squares method as follows:

$$b = \frac{N\Sigma(XY) - (\Sigma X)(\Sigma Y)}{N\Sigma(X^2 - (\Sigma X)^2}$$

where

N = number of observations for which cost and hours are available,
XY = product of log y and log x,
X = log of the cumulative production,
Y = log of the cumulative labor hours.

For a first example, suppose you were provided the data in Exhibit 3.1 disclosing only the first three columns: column (a) for the weeks, column (b) for total production, column (c) for direct-labor hours. On the basis of these data two new columns are added: column (d) for cumulative units completed and column (e) for cumulative direct-labor hours. The data for columns (d) and (e) are then plotted on a log-log graph. If the scatter diagram indicates the presence of a learning phenomenon, then we need to determine the following information to insert in the formula for the slope coefficient:

Exhibit 3.1
Practical Example for Computing the Learning Factor

Week (a)	Total Production (b)	Direct Labor Hours (c)	Cumulative Units Completed (d)	Cumulative Direct Labor Hours (e)
1	10	174.0	10	174.0
2	10	110.0	20	290.0
3	20	491.6	40	481.6
4	40	318.4	80	800.0
5	80	528.0	100	1328.0
6				

Week	X	Y	log X	log Y	log X log Y	log X
1	10	17.40	1.00000	1.24054920	1.2405	1.0000
2	20	14.50	1.30103	1.16136800	1.5110	1.6929
3	40	12.04	1.60206	1.08062650	1.7312	2.5667
4	80	10.00	1.90309	1.00000000	1.9031	3.6218
5	100	8.30	2.20412	0.91907809	2.0258	4.8581
			8.01030	5.40162170	8.4116	13.7392

Inserting the correct values in the formula yields

$$b = \frac{5(8.4116) - 8.010(5.4016)}{5(13.7392) - (8.0103)^2} = -0.267.$$

Next the learning rate (2) can be determined as follows:

$$b = \log 2/\log 2 \text{ or}$$
$$\log r = b \log 2$$
$$= -0.267(0.3010) = -0.080367$$
$$r = 83.3\%$$

The other method of finding the learning rate is the doubling approach. Basically, it reads the gain time over any doubled quantity. The learning factor can be expressed as the ratio between the time taken to produce Z units and the cumulative time to produce $2Z$ units.

If double quantities are not available, use instead the following formula:

$$r = \frac{\log (\text{cost 2/cost 1})}{\log (\text{quality 2/quality 1})}$$

Using the data from Exhibit 3.1, the learning rate may be computed as follows. If the time to produce 10 units is 174 hours and the cumulative time for 20 units is 290 hours, the learning factor is equal to

$$(290/20 \div (174/10) \times 100\% = 83.3\%.$$

After determining the learning rate using either the regression approach or the doubling approach, any of the computational formulae described in Chapter 2 can be used to compute the average cumulative labor hours, unit labor hours, total labor hours, or marginal hours required to produce a specific number of units. Exhibit 3.2 shows the

Exhibit 3.2
Results of the Cost Estimation

Weeks	Cumulative Average Direct Labor Hours per Unit (CADLH)	Computation of CADLH	Total Direct Labor Hours	Individual Direct Hours Hours
1	17.40	17.4 x 0.83	17.40	17.40
2	14.50	14.5 x 0.83	29	11.60
3	12.04	12.04x 0.83	36.12	7.12
4	10.00	10 x 0.83	40	3.88
5	8.30	8.3 x 0.83	41.50	1.5

results of these computations. Finally, assuming the rate of learning will continue beyond total estimated production of 80 units, the learning curve can be used to make cost estimates.

3.3. Warranty Maintenance and Maintenance Force

The learning phenomenon has been used in both the areas of warranty maintenance and estimating the size of a maintenance force.

In the area of warranty maintenance, Kneip[1] suggested that a progress function exists in the relationship of a product's maintenance requirement to cumulative production. Whereas in the conventional application of the learning phenomenon, the dependent variable (cost r labor time) is a production efficiency variable, in the maintenance progress function, the dependent variable is a quality, reliability, and serviceability characteristic. The results of regression analysis on two products showed that the maintenance progress function exists, that it relates warranty period maintenance to cumulative production, and that the relationship is logarithmic. Kneip also made the following interesting note:

Progress in a product's maintenance requirement is thus a characteristic of the organization, dependent upon both its structure and personnel, as well as the nature of the product. It cannot be overemphasized that progress is neither automatic nor self-perpetuating, but is the result of continual effort toward improvement. Furthermore, its use as a management control device involves the possibility of actually impeding progress that might otherwise have been attained through the selection of a progress rate too slow to provide challenging objectives. The selection of the progress rate is a critical decision in the application of the function.[2]

In the area of maintenance force, Clarke[3] used the learning phenomenon to predict the required size of a plant's maintenance force.

3.4. Make or Buy Decisions

Learning curves are very helpful in make or buy decisions, which involve a choice between the cost of producing an item and the cost of purchasing it. The learning curve can provide the data for determining the necessary labor hours and the cost of producing the item. There are other costs involved, of course, but the labor costs are usually considered more illustrative. Once they have been determined, the make or buy decision is reduced to simpler terms.

Andress gives the following illustration of the usefulness of the learning curve in make or buy decisions.[4] An aircraft company is faced with an economic slowdown and the necessity of reconsidering some existing subcontracts. It produces a landing flap assembly in its own plant as well as subcontracting it to another company. An existing subcontract to be considered for cancelling was for 372 landing flap assemblies. In examining its learning curve, the aircraft company noticed that it produced 165 assemblies with a unit time of 445 hours for the 165th unit and that it would take a total labor cost of 111,000 hours if it decides to make the 372 additional units. On the other side, the subcontractor relying also on the learning curve has produced the 165th unit with a unit time of 402 hours—43 hours less than the aircraft company. However, he found that the additional 372 units would require 164,000 hours, or 53,000 more than the aircraft company. Obviously the short-run analysis using the learning curve argued in this case for making rather than subcontracting.

Using the same example as the one used by Andress, Katz cautions that the decision may very well hinge on the nature of the future demand. He states:

In the short run (for the first 372 units) it would be more economical to cancel the subcontract. In the long run, however, it would be less expensive to leave the work with the subcontractor, as he could produce the product for 10% less labor once it fabricated as many units as the company. Therefore, this decision would hinge largely on the profitability of future demand for these products. Since, in the particular case under consideration, the future demand was considered very difficult to measure, the decision was to make the units in the house and cancel the subcontract.[5]

To use another illustration of the use of the learning curve in make or buy decisions, let's assume that the XYZ Company purchases 800 pumps from the ABC Company. The price was set last year at $70 per unit. Given the higher price, the XYZ Company decided to make some cost estimates to consider the feasibility of making rather than buying the pumps. The following estimates were made for an assembly run of 100 units:

Purchased components	$ 1,300	
Assembly labor	4,000	
Variable factory overhead	4,000	(100% of assembly labor)
Fixed factory overhead	5,000	
General and administrative overhead	3,200	
	$17,500	

A conventional make or buy analysis would compare the incremental costs with the supplier's price. In this case the incremental price will include only the relevant costs, that is, purchased components, assembly labor, and variable factory overhead. The incremental price is computed as follows:

	Cost of 100 pumps assembly run	Per unit
Purchased component	$1,300	$13
Assembly labor	4,000	40
Variable factory overhead	4,000	40
	$9,300	$93

In this case the XYZ Company must elect to buy the pumps rather than make them given that the supplier's price of $70 per unit is lower than the company's cost of $93.

If, however, the XYZ Company was experiencing an 80 percent learning factor, the analysis used would be different. With an 80 percent learning phenomenon the XYZ's assembly labor and variable overhead costs should decrease by 20 percent every time there is a doubling of cumulative production. The following labor cost and variable overhead cost behavior by lots would occur:

Quantity		Cumulative average labor cost per unit
Per lot	Cumulative	
100	100	$40
100	200	32 (40 × .8)
200	400	25.6 (32 × .8)
400	800	20.48 (25.6 × .8)

This means that the average cumulative cost of the assembly labor for the first 800 pumps is $20.48 per pump. A revised analysis which considers an 80 percent learning cost per unit factor is shown below:

Incremental Costs to Manufacture 800 Pumps

Purchased components	$13
Assembly labor	20.48
Variable factory overhead	20.48

Total incremental cost	$53.96
Cost to purchase	$70.00
Savings if pumps are manufactured	$16.04

Therefore, if XYZ Company is experiencing an 80 percent learning curve, it should manufacture the pumps rather than purchase them.

3.5. Work-Accident Experience

Work-accident is an unfortunate but recurring event in all types of human endeavors. Public data on the subject are available in most industries. Among those industries which collect, tabulate, and publish the work-accident experience of its member firms is the American Petroleum Industry. In that industry "disabling injury" and the computation of injury experience are accomplished on the basis of USASI Standard Z16.1.[6] One of the statistics defined by that standard is this:

$$\text{Disabling injury frequency rate} = \frac{\text{No. of disabling injuries} \times 1,000,000}{\text{No. of man hours worked}}$$

The assumption taken in the foundation of the standard is that in every unit of time some constant number of exposures occurs and is some multiple of the duration. Greenberg[7] argued that the method was misleading and that the denomination of the standard should be in units of production rather than in units of time, especially in light of evidence that the incidence of accidents was highly negatively correlated with productivity. He also found that accident experience follows a learning curve pattern, showing a decreasing trend in accident sequence as productivity increases. In fact, using mining industry data, Greenberg[8] showed again in another study that mining accidents also conformed to a learning model. Such accident-experience learning curves may be used to evaluate the effectiveness of a safety program and to open new possibilities in the analysis and prevention of accident occurrence.

3.6. Standard Costs and Efficiency Variance Analysis

A standard cost is a forecast of what costs should be used as a basis of cost control and as a measure of productive efficiency when ultimately compared with actual costs. In a traditional labor variance analysis, where standard costs are compared to actual costs, the standard cost is assumed to be a constant amount per unit of output. The analysis proceeds generally by dichotomizing the difference between the actual cost and the flexible budget into wage rate and efficiency variances as follows:

$$WRV = H_a (r_a - r_s)$$

$$EV = r_s (H_a - H_s)$$

where

WRV = wage rate variance,
EV = efficiency variance,
H_a = actual labor hours,
r_a = actual wage rate per hour,
r_s = standard wage rate per hour,
H_s = standard labor hours.

This traditional labor variance analysis rests in the assumption that no learning phenomenon is affecting labor usage and that it is realistic to assume that standard labor is constant over the total production of the period.

If learning was present, then the assumption of constant standard cost is unrealistic and the traditional labor variance analysis inapplicable. In such a case, it would be preferable to consider one of two possible approaches:

1. One approach would be to use "moving standard costs" rather than "constant standard costs." The moving standard costs would be computed on the basis of the relevant learning curve formulae.
2. A second approach would be to dichotomize the traditional labor efficiency variance into (a) labor efficiency variance due to learning, and (b) a labor efficiency variance due to factors other than the learning factors.[9]

To illustrate the three possible approaches, the traditional and the two approaches incorporating the learning effect, let's use this example: The XYZ Company makes personal computers. Its engineering department has determined that 800 direct-labor hours are necessary to assemble the first unit of a new model and that an 80 percent learning phenomenon is present in the assembling process. The standard direct-labor rate per hour is $20. During the month of January, 10 personal computers were assembled in 800 hours. The actual direct-labor rate per hour is $75. Discussion of the three approaches to labor variance analysis follows:

FIRST APPROACH: NO LEARNING EFFECT INCLUDED IN THE ANALYSIS

Under this approach the traditional labor variance analysis consists of computing a labor rate variance and a labor efficiency variance based on a standard labor hours per unit of 100. It will be computed as follows:

Actual Rate × Actual Hours	Standard Rate × Actual Hours	Standard Rate × Standard Hours
$25 × 7,800 = $195,000	$20 × 7,800 = $156,000	$20 × 8,000 = $160,000

$39,000 (Unfavorable) $4,000 (Favorable)
Labor Rate Variance   Labor Efficiency Variance

SECOND APPROACH: LEARNING EFFECT CONSIDERED WITH MOVING STANDARD COSTS

The standard labor hours per unit is adjusted to take into account the learning effect resulting in the use of a moving standard cost. In such case, the standard direct-labor hours allowed for actual production of 20 personal computers is derived using the learning curve formulae as follows:

$$\$10(ax^b) = 10 \times 800 \times 10^{\log .2 \cdot \frac{\log .8}{}} = 3810$$

Therefore, the analysis can now proceed as follows:

Actual Rate × Actual Hours	Standard Rate × Actual Hours	Standard Rate × Standard Hours
$25 × 7,800 = $195,000	$20 × 7,800 = $156,000	$20 × 3,810 = $76,200

$39,000 (Unfavorable) $79,800 (Unfavorable)
Labor Rate Variance   Labor Efficiency Variance

As can be seen by the analysis, the labor efficiency variance is $79,800 unfavorable taking the learning effect into account rather than $4,000 favorable effect in the traditional approach.

THIRD APPROACH: TOTAL CONSIDERATION OF THE LEARNING EFFECT

In this case the traditional labor efficiency variance is dichotomized into both a labor efficiency variance due to the learning effect and a labor efficiency variance due to factors other than the learning factors.

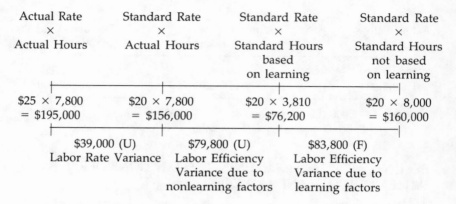

Actual Rate × Actual Hours	Standard Rate × Actual Hours	Standard Rate × Standard Hours based on learning	Standard Rate × Standard Hours not based on learning
$25 × 7,800 = $195,000	$20 × 7,800 = $156,000	$20 × 3,810 = $76,200	$20 × 8,000 = $160,000
	$39,000 (U) Labor Rate Variance	$79,800 (U) Labor Efficiency Variance due to nonlearning factors	$83,800 (F) Labor Efficiency Variance due to learning factors

This approach shows the whole picture by disclosing the pure efficiency variance due to the nonlearning factors and the learning efficiency variance due to the learning effect. This approach should allow for a better analysis and effective control of labor cost.

3.7. External Reporting

External reporting may be affected by the learning phenomenon. It may be suggested that the cost savings due to the learning effect should be abstracted from the profit so actual increased productivity can be examined rather than productivity due to a repetition of tasks.

A more important problem is the distortion of profit that can occur when production costs follow the learning curve phenomenon if two conditions exist: (1) the contract(s) cover two or more periods, and (2) the unit price is based on a cumulative average cost permit.

To correct for the possible misstatement of profit, Wayne J. Morse has shown that a cost allocation model based on the learning phenomenon will disclose the relationships between efforts and accomplishments better than the conventional method.[10]

To illustrate the problem of profit misstatement and how to correct it with the learning curve allocation model, let us use the data shown in

Exhibit 3.3. Let us also assume that 40 units are sold in 19 × 1, and 120 units are sold in 19 × 2; the unit selling price is $50 per unit in both years; the factory overhead and the direct-labor cost are each incurred at the rate of $5 per direct-labor hour; and the material cost is $1 per unit.

Exhibit 3.3 shows the income statements for both years under the conventional method of matching actual costs with revenues and the learning curve allocation model. Under the conventional method the company shows a loss of $608 the first year followed by a profit (net income) of $1,168 in the second year; the learning curve cost allocation model shows a profit of $140 in the first year and a profit of $420 the second year. Notice that the total profit for the two years is $560 under both methods.

To avoid such reporting differences which may adversely affect the market image of the firm, Morse proposed the following reporting system:

As production takes place, any excess of the projected cost of each unit over the expected average cost of all anticipated production is charged to a deferred production expense account, and inventory is charged with an amount equal to the expected average unit cost of all anticipated production. When the projected unit cost is less than the expected average unit cost of all anticipated production, this difference is deducted from the deferred production expense account, and inventory is charged with an amount equal to the expected average unit cost of all anticipated production. As production takes place, any differences between actual and projected costs are written off as a period variance unless a change in a parameter of the model occurs.[11]

Applying this reporting system to the previous problem yields the following journal entries:

Year 1
| Deferred Production Expenses | $748 | |
| Work in Process | | 748 |

To defer the differences between the actual costs of $2,408 and average cumulative costs of $1,660

Year 2
| Finished Goods | $748 | |
| Deferred Production Expenses | | 748 |

To change the differences between the actual costs of $4,232 and average cumulative costs of $4,980

Exhibit 3.3
Income Statements Comparing Conventional Method with Learning Curve Model

Income Statements

Prepared Matching Actual Costs with Revenues

	19x1 (40 Units Sold)	19x2 (120 Units Sold)
Sales at $50 per Unit	$2,000	$6,000
Costs of Goods Sold		
Overhead and Labor		
$(\$5 \times \dfrac{481.6 \text{ hours}}{40} \times 40)$	2,408	
$(\$5 \times \dfrac{318.4 + 528}{120} \times 120)$		4,232
Material at $5 per Unit	200	600
Costs of Goods Sold	$2,608	$4,832
Net Income	$ (608)	$1,168

54

Prepared Using Learning Curve Cost Allocation Model

	19x1 (40 Units Sold)	19x2 (120 Units Sold)
Sales at $50 per Unit	$2,000	$6,000
Costs of Goods Sold		
Overhead and Labor		
($5 x 8.3 x 40)	1,660	
($5 x 8.3 x 120)		4,980
Material at $5 per Unit	200	600
Costs of Goods Sold	$1,860	$5,580
Net Income	$ 140	$ 420

3.8. Cost Reduction

Finding ways to reduce costs sometimes may be crucial to firms and is a necessity most of the time. The learning phenomenon and the learning curve offer opportunities for cost reduction programs in general and in the preproduction planning and the product redesign areas in particular.

In the preproduction planning stage, the type of learning curve to be used subsequently may be affected by the level and content of organizational planning. More precisely, the more preplanning that is done in all aspects associated with the launching of a new product, the lower the cost of the initial unit. With the cost of the initial unit being the starting point of the learning phenomenon, the lower it is through effective preproduction planning, the greater the savings generated by the resulting learning curve. Various studies, including an empirical one,[12] have pinpointed the impact of preproduction planning on the time taken to produce the first unit and the dynamic rate resulting during the course of production.[13]

Other authors have emphasized the importance of proper preproduction planning undertaken at the initial stages to lessen the scope of improvement during the course of production, which results in a flatter function, lying considerably below one which depicts a smaller amount of preproduction planning. Bhada identifies the following factors which influence initial cost and production time, indirectly affecting the dynamic rate:

Anticipated duration of the production run

Estimated rate of output

The type of tooling utilized

The degree of detail presented by engineering specifications

Effort expanded on settling problems regarding manufacturing design and inspection procedures

The degree of coordination achieved between different functions within the organization

The importance given to proper working methods, planning and shop organization

The influence of experience gained on similar product and processes[14]

The impact of preproduction planning was even demonstrated in an experiment investigating the impact of types of organization structures on complex problem solving. Note: "Groups with higher initial performance (*a* values) demonstrated relatively smaller indices of performance improvement than groups that began with relatively lower initial performance."[15]

In the same vein, Abernathy and Baloff examined the supply-demand imbalances during the preproduction stage and suggested that effective and proper planning at the production marketing phase would help prevent costly imbalances because the rate of increase in productivity was different from the rate of increase in sales.[16]

In the redesigning state of a product, the learning curve may also be used to reduce the cost and help estimate the engineering effort required to do the job. More explicitly, it can be applied to the engineering effort in repeated design passes directed toward the reduction of total cost of the first unit. Bruns[17] presented a two-dimensional model relating the curve of the manufacturing learning improvement to the engineering learning improvement curve. Bruns shows that the unit cost depends on the engineering design as well as a manufacturing cost factor and uses the model to determine how many engineering design passes are needed to drive the product cost down to some predetermined target. The model allows reconciliation of the various approaches to new-product development where, on one side, researchers and scientists are attempting to build the first unit of some useful object at any cost, and, on the other side, engineers are trying to reduce cost while meeting given requirements. Bruns concludes:

In any event, whether engineering learning improvement is applied objectively or intuitively, this procedure warns the manager that the engineering effort to achieve a goal can vary widely, and may be beyond the range of interest or capability. New materials, processes, or designs and new personnel suggest possible reduction of costs through redesign. Conversely, experienced people and a steady technology suggest that great cost progress at small expense should not be expected.[18]

3.9. Price Estimation

The learning curve is a study tool that can help managers understand and predict trends in cost. As such it can also be used to develop price strategies aimed at controlling market share and profitability.

In general there are four price strategies as shown in Exhibits 3.4, 3.5, 3.6, and 3.7.

During phase A of the pattern shown in Exhibit 3.4, the dominant producer creates a price umbrella by keeping the price constant (or showing little decline), which may attract more producers. During phase B the price declines as a result of a price war where aggressive competitors strive for dominance. Finally, during phase C the price war

Exhibit 3.4
Pattern of Costs and Prices in Three Phases

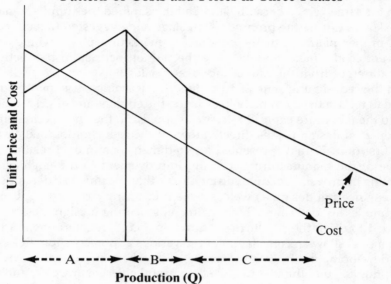

Exhibit 3.5
Pattern of Costs and Prices in a Parallel Pattern

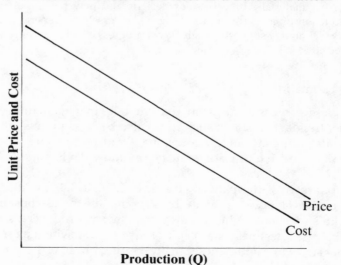

is over, and a more stable and competitive situation is established among the price war survivors. The weak producers may have been eliminated or have differentiated their product.

The pattern in Exhibit 3.5 is simpler. Given that the cost function (Y) follows the pattern $Y = KX^b$, the dominant producer may adopt a parallel stable pattern for the price function: $Y^1 = K^1X^b$, where Y^1 is the average price and K^1 the price of the first unit. This may discourage the entry of competitors. Although initial margins are small, final margins are usually greater.

The pattern in Exhibit 3.6 is known as preemptive pricing. Basically prices are set using the learning curve as an anchor. They are set at low levels with slim margins but which will generate higher sales volume and profits. The preemptive pricing strategy was successfully used by the so-called trusts of the late nineteenth century. The strategy consists of deferring the rewards and using the low prices generated on the basis of the learning curve to create a shakeout in the industry. Preemptive

Exhibit 3.6
A Preemptive Pricing Strategy

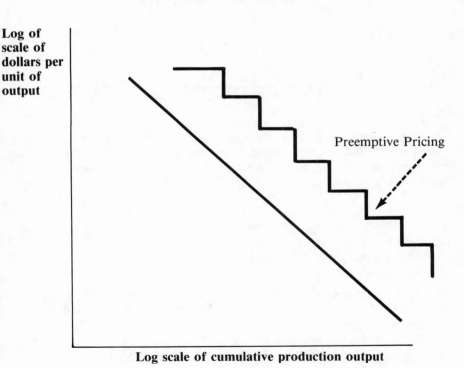

Log scale of cumulative production output

Exhibit 3.7
Pricing Strategy Using a Price Umbrella

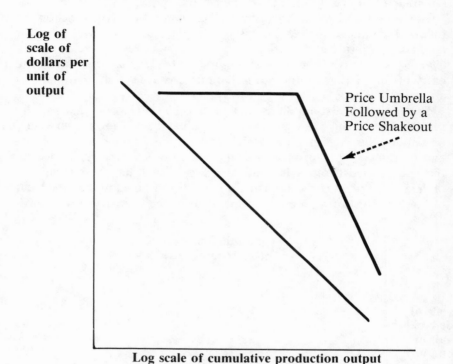

Log scale of cumulative production output

pricing is not successful in those situations where there is a constant need for product model changes or new-product introductions. The following features were found to be important for an effective use of preemptive pricing:

1. The expected product life is long.
2. The product is standardized, like a commodity, with little risk that consumer tastes will suddenly turn against it.
3. The expected growth of the market is rapid.
4. The apparent slope of the learning curve is steeper, since the learning curve in that instance can constitute a substantial barrier to the entry of other firms into the industry.
5. The product is not patent protected.
6. The company is not particularly strapped for cash.[19]

The pattern shown in Exhibit 3.7 consists of a price umbrella at a high price followed by a sudden price shakeout. It is an aggressive strategy aimed at eventual industry shakeout and "brutal" elimination of competitors.

Although other price patterns may exist, the predictive ability of the learning curve can be generally used as a determinant in estimating the number of labor hours required for production. This facilitates the seller's pricing of the output, of course. Thus, given a knowledge of prime costs, the labor hours determined from the learning curve can be used as an allocation base for other indirect costs. Furthermore, the buyer, aware of the learning characteristics of the seller's costs, may be willing initially to pay a higher price that is to be reduced as the supplier's production increases and its costs begin declining.

3.10. Capital Budgeting

For most companies capital budgeting is a very serious and precarious proposition, and any reduction in the uncertainty of the potential cash flow is desirable. First, in a capital budgeting situation the company is likely to be at the top of its learning curve; hence, it can derive significant labor and time savings estimates from the curve. Second, the greater the proposition of labor assembly time, the more likely the curve will explain cost behavior. Third, the more planning the company does, the more useful will be the predictive aspects of learning curves.

As an example of the application of the learning curve, let's assume the following fictional example of the XYZ Company which is considering the investment of $50,000 in equipment having a five-year expected life and no salvage value. The investment is expected to generate a cumulative expected demand of 200 units composed of 25, 40, 60, 40, and 35 units per year for the respective five years. The required minimum rate of return is 20 percent. The engineering estimation led to the following costs for 200 units of production: direct material, $500; direct labor ($5 per hour for an average per unit of 100 hours), $500; variable factory overhead (50% of direct labor), $250; variable selling and administration (10% of the sales price of $2,500 per unit), $250. The total fixed costs are estimated to be $5,000 per year. Based on these data the capital budgeting analysis will proceed as illustrated in Exhibit 3.8. It shows that a net present value in favor of production equals $6,739.

The XYZ Company has, however, determined that an 80 percent learning rate is applicable to both labor and variable overhead. It concluded that the capital budgeting analysis should instead include the correct time required as determined by the learning curve. Using the

Exhibit 3.8
Capital Budgeting Analysis with Constant Average Costs and 20 Percent Rate of Return

Year	(1) Demand	(2) Total Contribution Margin*	(3) Fixed Costs	(4) Net Cash Flow (2)-(3)	(5) Discount Factor 20%	(6) Discounted Net Cash Flow (4) x (5)
0				(95,000)	1.000	(95,000)
1	25	$25,000	$5,000	20,000	.8333	16,666
2	40	40,000	5,000	35,000	.6944	24,304
3	60	60,000	5,000	55,000	.5787	31,828.5
4	40	40,000	5,000	35,000	.4823	16,880.5
5	35	35,000	5,000	30,000	.402	12,060

Net present value $6,739.

*2,500 Revenue - 1,500 variable costs.

62

information that the first four prototypes required 1761.2 hours, it pro-
ceeded to compute the parameters of the learning curve b and a from the
average model

$$y = ax^b$$

where

> y = cumulative average time,
> a = time required for the first unit,
> b = learning exponent,
> x = cumulative production.

For an 80 percent learning curve, b was rapidly determined to be equal to
$-.3219$. Given that it took 1761.2 hours for the first four prototypes, the
cumulative average hours per unit is

$$y = 1761.2 \text{ hours}/4 = 440.3 \text{ hours}.$$

Using the logarithmic form of the equation $y = ax^b$, we can solve for a as
follows:

$$\log y = \log a + b \log X$$
$$\log 440.3 = \log a + (-.3219) \log 2$$
$$a = 55.04$$

Using the information obtained $a = 55.04$, $b = -.3219$, the marginal
formula

$$y = (b + 1)ax^b$$

and the demand distribution (25, 40, 60, 40, and 35), we can obtain the
respective marginal time required (4,882 hours, 4,452 hours, 5,204
hours, 3,108 hours, and 2,444 hours). All this information may then be
used in the capital budgeting analysis with learning-based costs as
shown in Exhibit 3.9. It shows a negative present value of $161.14. Using
the improved cost projections of the learning curve, the capital budgeting analysis argues against the proposed investment.

3.11. Break-Even Analysis

Break-even analysis or cost-volume-profit (*CVP*) analysis is an established managerial tool that attempts to formulate a firm's cost and reve-

Exhibit 3.9
Capital Budgeting Analysis with Learning-Based Costs and 20 Percent Rate of Return

Year	(1) Demand	(2) Marginal Labor Hours Required	(3) Revenues (1) x $2,500	(4) Labor and Variable Factory Overhead Cost (2) x $7.50	(5) Other Costs 5,000 + (7.50) (1)	(6) Net Cash Flow (3)−(4)+(5)	(7) Discount Factor	(8) Discounted Cash Flow (7) x (6)
0						$ (95,000)	1.0000	$ (95,000)
1	25	4,882	$ 62,500	$36,615	$23,750	2,315	.8333	1,929.08
2	40	4,452	100,000	33,390	35,000	31,610	.6944	21,949.98
3	60	5,204	150,000	39,030	50,000	60,970	.5787	35,283.33
4	40	3,018	100,000	22,635	35,000	42,365	.4823	20,432.63
5	35	2,444	87,500	18,330	31,250	37,920	.402	15,243.84

Net present value   (161.14)

nue functions and the relationships between the two. Basically, it involves an examination of cost and revenue behavioral patterns and their relationships with profit. The analysis separates costs into fixed and variable components and determines the level of activity where costs and revenues are in equilibrium. The cost-volume-profit analysis is a normative model for understanding the relationships between the cost, revenue, and profit structures of a firm. It is a key factor in all decisions based on selling prices, variable costs, and fixed costs.

The conventional approach to break-even analysis is used to compute the break-even volume or level of activity for which the profit generated is zero and beyond which any increase in production will lead to positive results on profit. The break-even point corresponds to the volume of activity at which total revenues equal total costs. In other words:

$$r = P_q - (F + V_q)$$

where

$$
\begin{aligned}
r &= \text{profit before income taxes,} \\
P &= \text{unit selling price,} \\
q &= \text{sales volume in units,} \\
F &= \text{total fixed costs,} \\
V &= \text{unit variable cost.}
\end{aligned}
$$

The break-even point at which sales equal total costs and profits equal zero may be found as follows:

$$P_q^* - (F + V_q^*) = 0$$

where q^* = break-even volume. Consequently, we may write

$$q^* = \frac{F}{P - V}$$

where $P - V$ = contribution margin permit. Therefore, the break-even point equals the ratio of total fixed costs (F) divided by the contribution margin per unit $(P - V)$.

To illustrate consider the following example. Susan Pineda plans to open a frozen yogurt business. She determined the following revenue and expense relationships:

	Dollars	Percent
Sales price per cup of yogurt	.50	100
Variable expense per cup	.30	60

Monthly fixed expenses
Rent	$1,000
Wages	1,500
Payroll fringe costs	550
Other fixed costs	6,450
Electricity	500
	$10,000

The break-even analysis proceeds as follows:

1. The unit contribution margin or excess of unit sales price over unit variable cost is

$$P - V = \$.50 - \$.30 = \$.20.$$

2. The break-even point in terms of units sold is

$$q^* = \frac{\$10,000}{\$.20} = 50,000 \text{ cups per month.}$$

The above "conventional" break-even analysis assumes linearity for both the costs and the reverse functions. With regard to costs, the linearity assumption means that the unit variable cost is a constant. In other words, no learning is taking place to reduce the unit variable cost. Needless to say, this is a very limiting assumption. The unit variable cost, in general, and the unit labor cost in particular may be subject to the learning phenomenon. A declining labor cost due to the learning phenomenon would substantially change break-even analysis and improve its use as a tool for planning and control of operations. In fact, various authors have attempted to present models for cost-volume-profit analysis which incorporate a nonlinear cost function to express the effects of employee learning. Their contributions are examined next.

Brenneck[20] was one of the first to integrate conventional break-even analysis with the learning curve theory. He argued that as the cycle time per unit decreases because of learning, both the unit direct-labor cost and variable cost will drop. He concludes that such a decrease in cost should be incorporated in the conventional break-even analysis to improve its reliability.

McIntyre[21] examined also the effects of the break-even equation and solution. This analysis follows.

The profit equation without learning is

$$r = px - cyx - f$$

where

$$r = \text{profit}$$

that is, x units would be produced by n labor teams of one or more employees each, with each team producing x/n units. To determine the break-even point, the last equation must be set equal to zero and solved for x. Due to the exponential form of the equation and the presence of fixed cost, it is not possible to present a general solution for this break-even quantity. The cumulative break-even volume may be determined for specific values of the parameters, however, by using the method of successive approximation to solve the equation for $M = 0$.[22]

Pegels[23] used start-up curves to determine the break-even point. Using the marginal time model, he suppresses total costs as

$$TC(x) = \frac{a}{1 - b}x^{1 - b} + cx$$

where cx is a variable cost that is not affected by learning. He also sequences the revenue function as

$$R(x) = px.$$

The break-even point is where $TC(x) = R(x)$ which after solving for n gives the following break-even point x_B:

$$x_B = \left[\frac{a}{(p - c)(1 - b)} \right]^{1/b}$$

If the cost of the first unit is $AC(1)$, then the break-even formula becomes

$$x_B = \left[\frac{aAC(1)}{(1 - b)(p - c)} \right]^{1/b}$$

p = selling price per unit less all variable costs other than labor costs,
c = labor costs per unit of time,
f = fixed costs per period,
y = cumulative average production time per unit after x units have been produced.

The average time model, which states that cumulative average time per unit will be reduced by $1 - R$ every time production doubles is

$$Y = ax^b$$

where

Y = the cumulative average production time per unit after x units have been produced,
a = the time required to produce the first unit,
x = cumulative production,
b = index of learning = log R/log 2,
R = learning rate.

The profit equation which incorporates the learning phenomenon will be as follows:

$$r = px - cax^{b+1} - f.$$

If there were n production processes operating simultaneously, the profit equation will be

$$r = px - nca\ (x/n)^{b+1} - f$$

As an example, suppose that $AC(1) = \$400$, $p = \$300$, and $c = \$200$. For $\alpha = 80$, $b = 0.32193$, and $a = 0.67807$, one finds that

$$x_B = \left[\frac{AC(1)}{p-c}\right]^{1/b} = \left[\frac{400}{100}\right]^{3.10627} = 74.2.$$

In other words, the break-even volume is approximately 75 units.

3.12. Conclusions

The learning curve is a practical managerial accounting tool. Its derivation is straightforward as illustrated in Chapters 1 and 2. If a process is found to be conducive to the learning phenomenon, practical applications and savings are possible to obtain. This chapter illustrated some of the savings and potential applications of the learning phenomenon. Examples of applications examined included basic applications, cost estimation, warranty maintenance and maintenance force, make or buy decisions, work-accident experience, standard costs and efficiency variance analysis, external reporting, cost reduction, price estimation, capital budgeting, and break-even analysis.

Notes

1. J. G. Kneip, "The Maintenance Progress Function," *Journal of Industrial Engineering* (November–December 1965), pp. 398–400.

2. Ibid., p. 399.

3. Stuart Clark, "Applying Learning Curves to the Maintenance Force," *Plant Engineering* (August 1967), pp. 126–127.

4. Frank Andress, "The Learning Curve as a Production Tool," *Harvard Business Review* (Vol. 32, No. 1, 1954), pp. 87–97.

5. Richard Katz, "Understanding and Applying Learning Curves," *Automation* (November 1969), p. 53.

6. United States of America Standards Institute, U.S.A., *Standard Method of Recording and Measuring Work Injury Experience* (Z16.1) (New York, 1967).

7. Leo Greenberg, "The Measurement of Work-Accident Experience in the American Petroleum Industry," *American Society of Safety Engineers* (Vol. 15, No. 2, 1970), pp. 11–13.

8. Leo Greenberg, "Why the Mine Injury Picture Is Out of Focus," *Mining Engineering* (March 1971), pp. 51–53.

9. Woody M. Liao, "Consideration of Learning Effects in Efficiency Variance Analysis," *Cost and Management* (January–February 1982), pp. 30–32.

10. Wayne J. Morse, "Reporting Production Costs That Follow the Learning Curve Phenomenon," *Accounting Review* (October 1972), pp. 761–773.

11. Ibid., p. 764.

12. Harold Asher, "Cost-Quantity Relationships in the Airframe Industry," Report No. R-291, The Rand Corporation, Santa Monica, Calif., July 1, 1956.

13. R. W. Conway, and A. Schultz, "The Manufacturing Progress Function," *Journal of Industrial Engineering* (January–February 1959), pp. 39–54.

14. Yezdi K. Bhada, "Dynamic Cost Analysis," *Management Accounting* (July 1970), p. 12.

15. Selwyn W. Becker and Nicholas Baloff, "Organization Structure and Complex Problem Solving," *Administrative Science Quarterly* (Vol. 14, No. 2, 1969), p. 266.

16. W. J. Abernathy and Nicholas Baloff, "A Methodology for Planning New Product Start-Ups," *Decision Sciences* (Vol. 4, No. 1, 1973), pp. 1–6.

17. J. H. Bruns, "Forecasting the Cost of Redesign," *Machine Design* (March 5, 1970), pp. 113–115.

18. Ibid., p. 115.

19. Roger W. Schmenner, *Production/Operations Management: Concepts and Situations* (Chicago, Ill.: SRA, 1984), p. 490.

20. R. Brenneck, "Breakeven Charts Reflecting Learning," *NAA Bulletin* (Vol. 40, No. 10, 1959), p. 34.

21. E. V. McIntyre, "Cost-Volume-Profit Analysis Adjusted for Learning," *Management Science* (Vol. 24, No. 2, 1977), pp. 149–160.

22. Ibid., p. 152.

23. C. Carl Pegels, "Start Up or Learning Curves—Some New Approaches," *Decision Sciences* (Vol. 7, No. 4, 1976), pp. 705–713.

APPENDIX: THE EFFECTS OF LEARNING ON COST-VOLUME-PROFIT ANALYSIS

by Woody M. Liao, University of Houston

Cost-volume-profit (CVP) analysis is widely used in profit planning and decision making. In recent years, the CVP model has been extended to consider such factors as uncertainty [13], [11], [14], non-linear cost and revenue functions [8], [7], income tax effect [15] and inflationary costs and prices [5]. However, little attention has been given to the effect of learning on CVP analysis [3], [6], [17], [10].

The learning phenomenon, which tends to decrease the marginal cost as the cumulative output increases, occurs in many manufacturing situations. For example, learning has been found to operate in labor-intensive industries [1], capital-intensive industries [12], and process-oriented as well as job-order production [2]. As Summers and Welsch [18] state, practically all manufacturing operations are subject to learning effects in some way.

The purpose of this paper is to incorporate learning effects into CVP analysis for managerial profit planning. First, the effect of learning on CVP analysis is explored. Then, an incorporation of learning effects into CVP analysis is proposed. Finally, examples are developed to illustrate the proposed approach and demonstrate its feasibility.

The effect of learning on CVP analysis

A mathematical expression of the traditional CVP analysis is:

$$Z = P.Q - V.Q - FC \qquad (1)$$

where
Z = Total profits
P = Unit selling price
V = Unit variable cost
Q = Quantity produced and sold
FC = Total fixed costs

Woody M. Liao, PhD, CPA, CMA, is an associate professor of accounting in the College of Business Administration, University of Houston. His publications have appeared in *The Accounting Review, Journal of Accountancy, Management Accounting, Decision Sciences, Managerial Planning*, and other leading journals. He is a member of AAA, NAA, AIDS, and IMA.

This traditional cost-volume-profit analysis is a static model. The analysis implicitly assumes that the learning effect does not exist. In many manufacturing processes, however, the assumption of no learning effect is not true. In such cases, learning would result in a lower unit variable cost as efficiency increases. The decrease of unit variable cost due to learning will in turn affect the contribution margin and thus the results of CVP analysis over the learning period. Therefore, if a firm is confronted with a situation where learning effects may be realized, the use of CVP analysis without consideration of learning effects most likely will result in misleading information. In such a case, the incorporation of learning effects into CVP analysis will provide more meaningful information.

CVP analysis with consideration of learning effects

Mathematically, the learning effect is expressed by an exponential function as:[1]

$$Y = a \cdot Q^b \qquad (2)$$

where
Y = Average number of labor hours per unit required to produce Q units
a = Number of labor hours required to produce the first unit
Q = Cumulative number of units produced
b = Index of learning which is the log of the learning rate divided by log 2, i.e., $b = \dfrac{\log (\text{learning rate})}{\log 2}$

Accordingly, the total labor hours required, T, to produce Q units of the product can be determined as:

$$T = Q \cdot Y = a \cdot Q^{b+1} \qquad (3)$$

On the other hand, if T is given, the total number of units of the produce that can be produced is determined by:

$$Q = (T/a)^{1/(b+1)} \text{ — — - - - -} \qquad (4)$$

Therefore, if total cumulative direct labor hours available up to the end of period n is T_n (i.e. $T_n = \sum_{i=1}^{n} t_i$, where t_i is total direct labor hours available in period i), the total quantity of the product that can be produced in period n is:

$$Q_n = \left(\frac{T_n}{a}\right)^{1/(b+1)} - \left(\frac{T_{n-1}}{a}\right)^{1/(b+1)} \quad (5)$$

In other words, the total number of units that can be produced in period n is equal to total cumulative production up to the end of period n minus total cumulative production up to the end of period (n-1). Therefore, given a learning index and the total budgeted direct labor hours in each period, total budgeted production in each period can be estimated by Equation (5). Furthermore, budgeted profit in period n can be determined as (assume direct costing[2] or no change in inventory levels):

$$Z_n = (P-VSE) \cdot Q_n - (DM \cdot Q_n) + t_n \cdot (DL+VOH) - FC \quad (6)$$

where

VSE = Variable selling expense per unit
DM = Direct material cost per unit
DL = Direct labor rate per hour
VOH = Variable overhead rate per direct labor hour
All other notations are defined as before.

The consideration of learning effects can also be extended to the determination of the breakeven point. At the breakeven point, total revenues equal total costs, i.e.,

$$P \cdot Q_{be} = (VSE \cdot Q_{be}) + (DM \cdot Q_{be}) + t_{be(n)} \cdot (DL+VOH) + FC \quad (7)$$

where

Q_{be} = the breakeven point in units
$t_{be(n)}$ = the number of direct labor hours required to produce Q_{be} in period n.

In order to determine the breakeven point (Q_{be}) in Equation (7), $t_{be(n)}$ must be transformed into a function of Q_{be}. The transformation can be made by examining the relationship between Q_{be} and $t_{be(n)}$ in a given period n as follows:

From Equation (5), the breakeven point in quantity in period n can be defined as:

$$Q_{be} = \left[\frac{T_{n-1} + t_{be(n)}}{a}\right]^{\frac{1}{(b+1)}} - \left[\frac{T_{n-1}}{a}\right]^{\frac{1}{(b+1)}} \quad (8)$$

By rearranging Equation (8), we obtain

$$t_{be(n)} = a \cdot \left[Q_{be} + \left(\frac{T_{n-1}}{a}\right)^{\frac{1}{(b+1)}}\right]^{(b+1)} - T_{n-1} \quad (9)$$

Substituting $t_{be(n)}$ from Equation (9) in Equation (7), we have

$$(P-VSE-DM) \cdot (Q_{be}) - a \cdot \left[Q_{be} + \left(\frac{T_{n-1}}{a}\right)^{\frac{1}{(b+1)}}\right]^{(b+1)}$$
$$\cdot (DL+VOH) + T_{n-1} \cdot (DL + VOH) - FC = 0 \quad (10)$$

Therefore, the breakeven point for period n can be determined by solving Equation (10) for Q_{be}.

An example

A firm is initiating a new product which can be sold for $2,010 per unit with a variable selling expense of $10 per unit. According to the firm's engineering studies, one unit of the new product requires $100 of direct material and the number of direct labor hours required to produce the first unit is $200. The variable overhead rate is $2 per direct labor hour and the direct labor rate is $6 per hour. From past experience, the firm expects a direct labor learning rate of 90% in manufacturing the product. The budgeted direct labor hours available and fixed cost related to the production of the new product for the first six months are 3,000 hours and $20,000 per month, respectively.

In this example, the firm's budgeted production and budgeted profit for each of the six months can be determined by use of Equations (5) and (6). The results are shown in Table 1:

Table 1

Budgeted Production and Budgeted Profit

Month	Budgeted Production (Q_n)	Budgeted Profit (Z_n)
1	24.37 units	$ 2,303
2	30.82	14,556
3	33.84	20,396
4	35.96	24,324
5	37.62	27,378
6	39.01	30,119

Due to the labor learning effects, unit direct labor cost and variable overhead cost decrease as more units are produced. As shown in Table 1, with the same number of direct labor hours available in each month, the learning experience increases (at a diminishing rate) the production and profit in each successive month as cumulative output increases.

Using Equation (10), the breakeven point for each period can be determined by solving each of the following equations for Q_{be}:

Period 1: $1900(Q_{be}) - 1600(Q_{be})^{.848} - 20,000 = 0$
Period 2: $1900(Q_{be}) - 1600(Q_{be} + 24.36)^{.848} + 4000 = 0$
Period 3: $1900(Q_{be}) - 1600(Q_{be} + 55.15)^{.848} + 28,000 = 0$
Period 4: $1900(Q_{be}) - 1600(Q_{be} + 88.95)^{.848} + 52,000 = 0$
Period 5: $1900(Q_{be}) - 1600(Q_{be} + 124.86)^{.848} + 76,000 = 0$
Period 6: $1900(Q_{be}) - 1600(Q_{be} + 162.44)^{.848} + 100,000 = 0$

Table 2

Breakeven Point for Each Month

Month	Breakeven Point in Units
1	22.19
2	18.13
3	16.95
4	16.31
5	15.87
6	15.56

To solve the above equations with non-integer exponentials, Newton's method of approximation[3] provides a convenient and efficient method. A computer program has been written using Newton's method of approximation to solve the above equations for the breakeven point in each month. They can also be solved on some calculators. The resultant breakeven point for each month is given in Table 2.

Again, the reduction in variable cost because of learning will influence the point at which the firm will break even in each month. As shown in Table 2, the point at which the firm will break even in each successive month as more units are produced and more learning is gained. It should be noted that the results in Table 2 assume that all 3,000 direct labor hours are utilized in each month and each month's budgeted production in Table 1 is achieved. If fewer than 3,000 direct labor hours are utilized in a period, the proposed approach is still useful. In such a case, T_{n-1} in Equation (10) is the total cumulative labor hours utilized up to the end of period n-1.

The above analysis is useful for considering learning effects in CVP analysis for a case where the learning rate is known with certainty or managers have a reliable estimate of the learning rate. But estimates of learning rates may be subject to a certain degree of uncertainty. In such a situation, the analysis can be improved by considering uncertainty in the estimation of learning rates. Such a consideration may significantly affect the determination of budgeted profit and breakeven point. Practical techniques have been developed for business applications of probability concepts in profit planning under conditions of uncertainty. For example, three techniques suggested in the literature are: the PERT - like approach, the probability - tree approach, and the simulation approach [6]. These three approaches can be used to solve the problem with uncertainty in estimation of learning for CVP analysis.

Conclusion

The traditional CVP analysis has been extended to consider the effects of several important factors such as uncertainty, non-linear cost and revenue functions, income tax effect, and inflationary costs and prices. But

little attention has been given to the effect of learning on CVP analysis.

Learning has significant effects on CVP analysis. Learning will not only affect the distribution of profits, but also change the traditional breakeven analysis. This paper has demonstrated the effect of learning on CVP analysis and developed a model for determining the breakeven point and budgeted profits with consideration given to learning effects.

---

[1] Direct labor hours are assumed to be the scarce resource subject to learning in this article. Other scarce resources such as materials and machine hours may also be subject to learning.

[2] If the absorption costing system is used, fixed manufacturing costs must be adjusted by the change in inventory levels.

[3] See any standard quantitative methods or operations research textbook. For example, Samuel B. Richmond, *Operations Research for Management Decisions*, The Roland Press Company, 1968), pp. 92-96.

REFERENCES

[1] Andress, Frank J., "The Learning Curve as a Production Tool," *Harvard Business Review* (January-February 1954), pp. 87-97.

[2] Baloff, Nicholas, "The Learning Curve—Some Controversial Issues," *Journal of Industrial Economics* (July 1966), pp 275-282.

[3] Brenneck, R., "Breakeven Charts Reflecting Learning," *NAA Bulletin* (January 1959), p. 34.

[4] Conway, R.W., "Some Tactical Problems in Digital Simulation," *Management Science* (October 1963), p. 49.

[5] Dhavale, D., "Cost-Volume-Profit Analysis With Inflationary Costs and Prices," *Proceedings of the National Meeting of the American Institute for Decision Sciences* (1976), pp. 108-111.

[6] Ferrara, W.L. and Hayya, J.C., "Toward Probabilistic Budgeting," *Management Accounting* (October 1970), pp. 23-28.

[7] Givens, H.R., "An Application of Curvilinear Breakeven Analysis," *The Accounting Review* (January 1966), pp. 141-143.

[8] Goggans, T.P., "Breakeven Analysis With Curvilinear Functions," *The Accounting Review* (October 1965), pp. 867-871.

[9] Harris, L.B.C. and Stephens, W.L., "Learning Curve Applications," *Proceedings of the Southeastern Regional Meeting of the American Accounting Association* (April 1977), pp. 301-305.

[10] Harvey, David W., "Financial Planning Information for Production Start-ups," *The Accounting Review* (October 1976), pp. 838-845.

[11] Hilliard, J.E. and Leitch, R.A., "Cost-Volume-Profit Analysis Under Uncertainty: A Log Normal Approach," *The Accounting Review* (January 1975), pp 69-80.

[12] Hirschmann, Winfred B., "Profit from the Learning Curve," *Harvard Business Review (January-February 1964), pp. 125-139.*

[13] Jaedick, R.K. and Robichek, A.A., "Cost-Volume-Profit Analysis Under Conditions of Uncertainty," *The Accounting Review* (October 1964), pp. 917-926.

[14] Liao, M., "Model Sampling: A Stochastic Cost-Volume-Profit Analysis," *The Accounting Review* (October 1964), pp. 780-790.

[15] Morse, W.J., "The Effect of Taxes on Cost-Volume-Profit Analysis," *Proceedings of the National Meeting of the American Institute for Decision Sciences* (1976), pp. 411-414.

[16] Pegels, C. Carl, "Start Up or Learning Curves—Some New Approaches," *Decision Sciences* (October 1976), pp. 705-713.

[17] Richmond, Samuel B., *Operations Research for Management Decisions* (The Roland Press Company, 1968).

[18] Summers, Edward L. and Glenn A. Welsch, "How Learning Curve Models Can Be Applied to Profit Planning," *Management Services* (March-April 1970), pp. 45-50.

4

THE LEARNING CURVE: POSSIBLE LIMITATIONS

The learning curve is a very important management tool. Given the predictable improvement in time as production increases, the curve provides valuable information for decision making. Chapter 1 defined the concept of the learning phenomenon, elaborated on its history and theory, and presented many geometric versions of the learning curve model. Chapter 2 focused on the models, formulae, and mechanics of the log-linear models. Finally, Chapter 3 presented a detailed list of the possible applications of the learning curve phenomenon. The three chapters presented the positive aspects of this managerial accounting tool. However, like any normative model, the learning curve phenomenon suffers from some limitations which must be corrected or taken into account before any efficient implementation can take place. Therefore, this chapter elaborates on the possible limitations inherent in the implementation of the learning curve phenomenon.

4.1. Influence of Causal Factors

Common to all the learning curve models is the need to estimate these two basic parameters: (1) input resources associated with the production of the first unit, and (2) the learning curve characteristic or some measure of the rate reduction.

The exact determination of these two parameters is essential to the validity of the use of the learning curve. There are, however, factors which may affect the exact determination of these parameters. Hammer, for example, alluded to the fact that the incurring of more effort in the preproduction stage would lower the initial cost while the incurring of more resources during the production stage would increase the learning rate and cost reduction as production accumulates.[1] Conway and Schultz attempted to categorize the factors which influence cost initially and during production.[2] The preproduction factors which will have a bearing on initial cost and influence the number of opportunities for cost reduction subsequently include the following:

1. Tooling—type of tooling used and degree of completion or development prior to production.
2. Equipment and Tool Selection—volume for which production was planned.
3. Product Design—extent to which manufacturability was considered and the degree of change required subsequently. Degree to which product design and manufacturing engineering were coordinated prior to initiation of production.
4. Methods—the degree to which work methods in detail are predesigned and the effort devoted to associated jig fixture design, flow analysis, etc.
5. State of the Art—relationship between the difficulty of the task and the ability of the organization to perform it.
6. Magnitude of the Design Effort—time and effort devoted to the problem of preproduction manufacturing design, specification, test, inspection, etc.
7. Shop Organization—including branding methods, preproduction training, skill, planning organization, etc.[3]

All these factors suggest that to be useful the determination of the first piece cost of any item should be made far in advance of production.

The production factors which will influence learning subsequently include the following:

1. Tooling—changes during production, method of increasing capacity for increasing demand (replication or redesign of production method).
2. Methods—changes during production, work simplification and similar programs, operator originated changes, method of capacity increase.
3. Design Changes—degree to which manufacturing and product designs are changed to allow minor economies, specification and inspection changes as experience is gained.
4. Management—improved planning, scheduling and supervision to encourage progress, increase effectiveness, diminish delays and idle time.
5. Volume Changes—changes in rate or anticipated duration of production which affect other factors and decisions.
6. Quality Improvements—the gradual reduction of re-work and repair operations, the reduction of scrap losses.

7. Incentive Pay Plans—manner in which administered, when installed.
8. Operator Learning—degree to which operations decrease time utilized in execution of a specific task.[4]

All these factors affect the determination of the basic parameters of the learning curve and may cause the learning relationship computed to differ under various circumstances. The last factor, operator learning, has been considered by some writers to be the most important causal factor in those cases where the operator can contribute improvements in task method.[5,6] Others maintain that in most cases the tooling, flow, and methods changes are the most significant causal factors of the learning phenomenon. They result more from management effort than operator learning.[7] A more reasoned position is that the learning curve depends equally on both factors. More precisely, this position is supported by McCampbell and McQueen,[8] who maintain that the function is based on the following:

1. The human element (man's ability to learn and improve and the elimination of direct thought-process activities through repetition).
2. The natural process of methods improvements and his foreman.
3. More efficient material handling, transportation, pallet moving, and so forth.
4. Less percentage owed to scrap, rejection, and re-works.

4.2. Measurement and Aggregation Problems

In trying to determine the parameters of the learning curves in industrial situations, the cost analyst should beware of various measurement problems reported in the literature and in practice. Some of these problems follow:

1. The accuracy of the industrial data may be in doubt in most firms which use individual incentives such as piece rates for wage payment and control purposes. In effect such situations may create an environment in which output is restricted, actual times are seldom accurately recorded, and considerable doubt exists as to the validity of operator times charged to direct versus indirect labor accounts.[9]
2. The determination of the production count may be difficult because such factors as varying lot sizes, varying lead times, and varying schedules distort the association between costs and production quantities.
3. The learning curve is generally determined for an aggregation rather than individual operations. What items to aggregate to determine the learning curve is a difficult and serious question. The aggregation may be determined

following the organization of the facility and the method of production or following the inherent characteristics of operations performed and the components of the product or operation. The problems of what to aggregate may be exacerbated by the mechanics of aggregation when product is produced at different times in different lots.

Some writers have preferred to work from disaggregated data before determining the learning curve for a product or assembly. For example McCampbell and McQueen[10] maintained that the learning curve model for a product would depend on each type of operation and its corresponding percentage of total unit labor:

$$C = (X_1)\,(Y_1) + (X_2)(Y_2) + \ldots + (X_n)(Y_n)$$

where

C = the learning curve for an assembly,
X_i = % of the labor for each operation,
Y_i = % curve of each operation,
n = operation number.

For example, suppose:

Machining: 30% of the labor with a curve of 100%

Punch Press: 20% with 80% curve

Burring, Sanding, Hand Forming: 10% with 90% curve

Assembly: 40% with 70% curve

then, the curve for this product is 83%.

A fourth problem can be added:

4. Whatever learning rate is found, it is important *not* to think of it as universal. Overwhelming evidence shows that the rate of learning differs between products, manufacturing facilities, and industries. To think otherwise is illogical and hard to verify empirically. Progress does exist for some operations but not necessarily at the same rate. No give slope is universal. Even if a given slope seems to be recurring, the learning functions are generally determined with tolerable amounts of error. "There is no such thing as a fundamental law of progress such as the '80% learning curve' used in the aircraft industry."[11]

One interesting finding reported is that it is common to find different learning curve ratios for similiar products within a given production facility, and identical products produced in different production facilities.[12] Another extensive study of data gathered in machine shops found, however, that while each basic manufacturing operation has an individual learning function for a product, it is based on a time-proportion weighted combination of individual progress functions.[13]

4.3. Narrow Understanding of the Causes and Existence of the Learning Curve

One of the deficiencies in the learning curve literature is the narrow understanding of the causes and existence of the learning curve. The causes and existence of the learning phenomenon have been typically associated with clearing, or adaptation on the part of direct-labor workers, especially those involved in assembly. In general the contribution of engineers and indirect labor to the learning curve phenomenon has been ignored. In short, the learning phenomenon has been limited to direct-labor, manual adaptation to repetitive tasks and has eliminated the machine-paced or machine-intensive manufacture.

Some authors have considered the generality of the learning phenomenon and criticized the narrow understanding of the causes and existence of the learning curve. For example Baloff states: "However, the emphasis on direct-labor learning as the primary cause of the learning phenomenon and the implications for machine-intensive manufacture that have been drawn from it appear to have very limited applicability."[14]

What Baloff was alluding to is the generally accepted thesis in a variety of machine-intensive industries that a distinct learning phenomenon occurs during the start-up or debugging of new products and new production processes. An example of the learning phenomenon in the debugging of automated processes was provided by Bright.[15] This learning or debugging is not necessarily the result of an improvement in direct labor but more likely in direct labor, indirect labor, and technical personnel. In these cases, it is more the effort of engineers and other indirect-labor employees that generated the learning in the start-up or debugging. According to Baloff, this learning includes "such cognitive activities as redesigning the product or process, altering raw-material and end-product quality specifications, evolving more effective maintenance procedures and finding the proper operating (balance) of a manufacturing process."[16]

4.4. Uncertainty as to the Nature of the Learning Curve Model

Another deficiency in the learning curve literature is the uncertainty as to the actual form or statement of the learning curve model. There is not one single model of the learning curve. As seen in Chapter 1, the following seven models are possible:

1. The log-linear model
2. Pegels's exponential function
3. Levy's adaptation function
4. The Stanford-B model
5. DeJong's learning formula with an incompressibility factor
6. The S-curve
7. Glover's learning formula with a work commencement factor

Some of these models have also been described by Carlson. [17,18] Given that relative superiority is attributed to each of these models and specific industrial applications have been presented, it is recommended that new users of learning curves should make some test runs in their choice of the learning curve model most appropriate to their case.

4.5. Dubious Practices in the Estimation of Parameters

One of the major deficiencies in the learning curve literature is the dubious practice in the estimation of the b parameter in the learning curve model. As one may see by a cursory review of major cost account textbooks,[19] it is the practice to simplify the parameter estimation problem by assuming that the b parameter retain the same constant value from start-up to start-up, i.e., "empirical parameter value." Baloff calling for more empirical investigation to shake the tenacity of this unfortunate assumption states:

This is not meant to eschew the role of empirical investigation, however, for it is clear that the generalization of the learning curve techniques will ultimately depend on empirical demonstration of the phenomenon in a variety of contents. Empiricism can make a further contribution in scrutinizing such dubious practices as the constant b parameter value and "interminable progress" assumptions that have plagued past applications of the learning curve.[20]

In fact, evidence of the instability of the b parameter has been reported by Alchian[21] in different airframe start-ups during World War II, Asher[22] for a number of other postwar airframe start-ups, Conway and Schultz[23] in the electronics industry, and Hirsh[24] in the start-ups of machine tools.

4.6. Separating the Wheat from the Chaff

The learning curve may be used by management as an artificial device to secure contracts and justify their cost estimates. In other words management may estimate their labor requirements with a false learning curve presumably based on empirical performance. If the contract is accepted, the learning curve-based estimates are used to prove its own existence. In other words the reduced labor became cursed by budgetary action more than by improved productivity through learning. This artificial technique may be produced by (1) increasing the labor content of the first unit or setting it at a very high point, (2) fluctuating labor classifications by frequently shifting the designation of workers between "direct" or "support/indirect" and hence reducing the labor content on a specific unit, (3) using manufacturing methods and tooling changes to create a reduction in the labor content, and (4) using at the start of the process small manufacturing lot sizes resulting in a high labor content for the first unit. These are some of the factors which obscure the true significance of the learning curve by causing it to reflect budgetary- and management-directed influence more than the increased productivity resulting from skill acquired in reflective operations. These factors which obscure the true significance of the learning phenomenon have been mostly noted to last in the aerospace industry. That industry is conducive to the use of the learning curve as an artificial device because of specific conditions in that industry that are outlined as follows:

1. Profit is a negotiated element, dependent on cost.
2. There is little direct incentive to reduce cost, and there is incentive to maintain a high cost level.
3. The basic product starts the production cycle with relatively little definition, thus requiring much rework, modification and delays and an abundance of manpower to cope with those problems.
4. The customer may direct changes to be made that are outside of the contractor's original contract scope, and the contractor anticipates this by carrying additional personnel.
5. Objective manufacturing criteria generally are not used to achieve the most efficient production.
6. Variable-type time allowances that are often the basis for staffing tend to create the appearance of a "cost reduction curve."
7. There is customer emphasis on reduction curves which stimulates contractors to "sell" and emphasize reduction curves.[25]

Given these conditions which may also exist in other industries, the challenge to management and to other parties is to separate the wheat from the chaff and to identify the real learning curve if there is one.

4.7. Illusory Savings and Verification

Illusory savings may be the result of errors in the selection of labor hour data to be used in plotting the curve.[26] First, automation may lead to a reduction in labor input per unit. Second, a direct-labor savings may disguise a greater use of indirect labor. Third, a change in the "labor mix" through hiring more qualified workers may lead to savings in direct-labor hours and an increase in direct-labor cost. Finally, the savings in labor may be due to a change in volume rather than to learning. All this creates a problem of verification. The problem of verification pertains mainly to the possibility of obtaining inaccurate data for direct labor, and to the potential inability to isolate accurately the learning factor that led to the reduction in direct labor. As a result, the learning curve in its present state has been criticized as failing to be a "scientific tool."[27]

4.8. Negative or Defeatist Attitudes of Employees

The negative or defeatist attitudes of employees may act as a barrier to the implementation or acceptance of the learning curve. Attitudes which ignore, belittle, or negate the presence of learning threaten the applicability of the learning phenomenon. For the learning phenomenon to be used effectively, positive attitudes have to be generated from the employee. Faith in the phenomenon is important. If progress is believed possible, then the learning phenomenon has a chance to occur. Open-ended expectations and the absence of "ceiling psychology" are two factors most conducive to a learning effect. Some companies have been reported to have obtained more progress when the workers are not informed of the target rate. This is possible because the target set does not become a self-fulfilling prophecy. Finally, credibility in the phenomenon and its possibilities act as a major drive for its use. As Hirschmann states:

If the premise is valid that learning performance can be an underlying natural characteristic, then such performance should be found not only for more types of activities already recognized as responsive, but also for operations not previously reported or believed possible. Petroleum refining is considered to have such operations. It is characterized by large investments in heavy equipment, and is so highly automated that learning is thought to be nonexistent or too small to be of value.[28]

What Hirschmann is alluding to is progress by serendipity whereby the assumption that continual progress can occur may also create an atmosphere conducive to a learning phenomenon. He states again:

Nevertheless, discovering such performance for operations previously considered unresponsive does provide additional tangible evidence that learning can be an underlying natural characteristic of organized activity. It does not merely extend the catalog of learning curves. Instead, it can help to breed the correction that such performance should be found elsewhere, and thereby lead not only to scrutinizing all operations to see which additional ones are susceptible, but to assuming that all operations have learning curve potential and to devising ways of making this potential a reality. Thus, it is prudent to reflect learning potential in plans and forecasts.[29]

White[30] goes further by suggesting the use of learning curve theory to predict expected improvement in advance and sets these goals as an incentive to accomplishment.

4.9. Anomalies in the Learning Curve Shape

It is common practice to assume that improvement in direct-labor activity associated with a start-up will continue throughout the production history of the product. These assumptions are at best tenuous. For example, Asher found evidence of plateaus developing in the start-up histories of several postwar airframes produced in the United States.[31] Similarly, Conway and Schultz found distinct steady-state conditions occurring at the end of several new product start-ups.[32] It is generally more accepted that there are several variations to the smooth learning curve forms, mainly with respect to the start-up point. The steepness of some curves may be due to an assumed high labor requirement. For example, if the proportion of assembly work was supposed to be lower, the downward slope of the curve would not be as steep. In addition to the steepness, there may be anomalies to the learning curve shape. Hirschmann listed the following possible anomalies to the learning curve shape.[33]

1. A leveling off or a toe up may occur due to such factors as the closing of operations at the end of a contract. The costs may increase, which is a condition known in the industry as reverse learning.
2. An aberration may also occur in the middle of the curve.

Hence, if the production process is interrupted for a significant length of time, resumption of the work will reflect a sharp increase in the learning curve. The aberration may be due to inefficiencies resulting from the employees' loss of skill and from the reorganization costs. Such a situation is called a scallop. It may also result from the change in the design of a product followed by two costs: (1) the cost of added design less the quoted cost of the design removed, and (2) a loss of learning resulting in not being able to produce an assembly at the full quantity contracted.

Hirschmann listed a third anomaly:

3. A leveling down or a toe down may result from major innovations or sudden improvements in the learning process.

Exhibit 4.1 portrays the possible anomalies in the learning curve.

The leveling-off phenomenon has been observed by others and labeled as the phenomenon of plateauing. The results of the empirical analysis of different start-ups showed that the learning phenomenon occurs regularly, is generally pronounced, but is ultimately followed by plateauing or steady-state conditions. Baloff states the findings as follows:

1. There is clear indication that a definite learning phenomenon occurs regularly in the several forms of manufacture investigated, and that this phenomenon is common to both new process and new product start-ups.

Exhibit 4.1
Anomalies in the Learning Curve

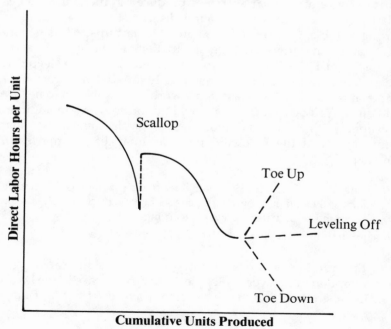

Cumulative Units Produced

2. The productivity consequences of the phenomenon are generally pronounced; all of the start-ups were marked by large regular increases in productivity for some months following the inception of manufacture.

3. These productivity increases do not continue interminably; they are typically
   interrupted by the eventual development of a distinct steady-state operating
   condition.[34]

In fact, Baloff observed plateauing in both machine-intensive manufacturing[35] as well as labor-intensive manufacturing,[36] with more like-
lihood of it happening in the machine-intensive cases where management is not willing to invest in capital to sustain learning. The two
phases of plateauing in the learning curve are shown in Exhibit 4.2.
Another interruption in the learning phenomenon can be caused by

Exhibit 4.2
The Two Phases of Plateauing in the Learning Curve

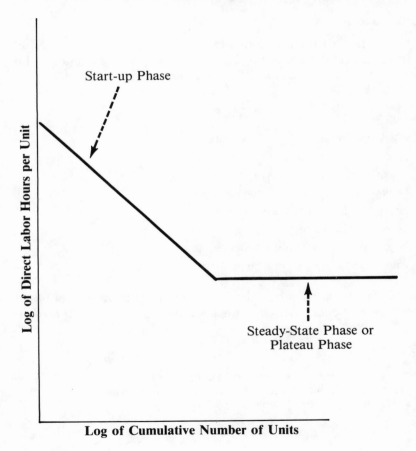

production breaks. The production break is the time lapse between the completion of a contract for the manufacture of certain units of equipment and the commencement of a follow-on order for identical units.

Anderlohr[37] focused on production breaks between manufacturer lots and the resulting loss of learning which takes place.[38] The following five factors associated with loss of learning are identified: production personnel learning, supervisory learning, continuity of production, improvement of special tooling, and improvement of methods. In fact, all the interruptions identified in this section lead to some form of learning loss. For example, Hall[39] suggested that design changes lead to two costs:

1. The cost of added design less the quoted cost of the design removed.
2. Loss of learning resulting in not being able to produce an assembly at the full quantity contracted.

4.10. Conclusions

While the first three chapters focused on the positive aspects of the learning curve, this chapter elaborated on the possible limitations inherent in the implementation of the learning curve phenomenon. They include the following:

1. Influence of causal factors
2. Measurement and aggregation problems
3. Narrow understanding of the causes and existence of the learning curve
4. Uncertainty as to the nature of the learning curve model
5. Dubious practices in the estimation of parameters
6. Separating the wheat from the chaff
7. Illusory savings and verification
8. Negative or defeatist attitudes of employees
9. Anomalies in the learning curve shape

These limitations must be either corrected or taken into account before an efficient implementation of the learning curve model can take place.

Notes

1. K. F. Hammer, "An Analytical Study of 'Learning Curves' as a Means of Relating Labor Requirements to Production Quantities" (unpublished Master's essay, Cornell University, September 1954).

2. R. W. Conway and Andrew Schultz, Jr., "The Manufacturing Progress Function," *Journal of Industrial Engineering* (January–February 1959), pp. 39–54.

3. Ibid., p. 42.

4. Ibid.

5. F. Andress, "The Learning Curve as a Production Tool," *Harvard Business Review* (Vol. 32, No. 1, 1954), pp. 87–97.

6. W. Z. Hirsch, "Manufacturing Progress Functions," *Review of Economics and Statistics* (Vol. 34, May 1952), pp. 143–155.

7. Conway and Schultz, "The Manufacturing Progress Function," p. 42.

8. G. W. McCampbell and C. W. McQueen, "Cost Estimating from the Learning Curve," *Aero Digest* (73, 1956), pp. 36.

9. Conway and Schultz, "The Manufacturing Progress Function," pp. 43–44.

10. McCampbell and McQueen, "Cost Estimating from the Learning Curve."

11. Ibid., p. 53.

12. Conway and Schultz, "The Manufacturing Progress Function."

13. G. Nadler and W. D. Smith, "Manufacturing Progress Functions for Types of Processes," *International Journal of Production Research* (June 1963).

14. Nicholas Baloff, "The Learning Curve—Some Controversial Issues," *Journal of Industrial Economics* (No. 3, July 1966), p. 276.

15. J. R. Bright, *Automation and Management* (Boston: Harvard University, 1958), especially Chapters 9 and 11.

16. Baloff, "The Learning Curve," p. 277.

17. J. G. Carlson, "How Management Can Use the Improvement Phenomenon," *California Management Review* (Vol. 3, No. 2, 1961), pp. 83–94.

18. J. G. Carlson, "Cubic Learning Curves: Decision Tool for Labor Estimating," *Manufacturing Engineering and Management* (Vol. 71, No. 5, 1973), pp. 22–25.

19. A. Belkaoui, *Cost Accounting, A Multidimensional Emphasis* (Hinsdale, Ill.: Dryden Press, 1983).

20. Baloff, "The Learning Curve," p. 283.

21. A. Alchian, "Reliability of Progress Curves in Airframe Production," Report No. RM-260-1, The Rand Corporation, Santa Monica, Calif., February 1958.

22. H. Asher, "Cost-Quality Relationship in the Airframe Industry," Report No. R-291, The Rand Corporation, Santa Monica, Calif., July 1, 1956.

23. Conway and Schultz, "The Manufacturing Progress Function."

24. Hirsch, "Manufacturing Progress Functions," pp. 134–155.

25. Samuel L. Young, "Misapplications of the Learning Curve Concept," *Journal of Industrial Engineering* (August 1966), p. 414.

26. Andress, "The Learning Curve as a Production Tool," p. 90.

27. E. L. Summers and G. A. Welsch, "How Learning Curve Models Can Be Applied to Profit Planning," *Management Sciences* (March–April 1970), pp. 45–50.

28. Winfred B. Hirschmann, "Learning Curve," *Chemical Engineering* (March 30, 1964), p. 97.

29. Winfred B. Hirschmann, "Profit from the Learning Curve," *Harvard Business Review* (Vol. 42, No. 1, 1964), p. 139.

30. James M. White, "The Use of the Learning Curve Theory in Setting Man-

agement Goals," *Journal of Industrial Engineering* (November–December 1961), pp. 409–411.

31. Asher, "Cost-Quantity Relationship in the Airframe Industry."

32. Conway and Schultz, "The Manufacturing Progress Function," pp. 39–54.

33. Hirschmann, "Profit from the Learning Curve," pp. 126–127.

34. Nicholas Baloff, "Startups in Machine Intensive Production Systems," *Journal of Industrial Engineering* (January 1966), pp. 25–32.

35. Ibid.

36. Nicholas Baloff, "Extension of the Learning Curve—Some Empirical Results," *Operational Research Quarterly* (Vol. 22, No. 4, 1971), pp. 329–340.

37. George Anderlohr, "Determining the Cost of Production Breaks," *Management Review* (December 1969), pp. 16–19.

38. Ibid., p. 16.

39. L. H. Hall, "Experience with Experience Curves for Aircraft Design Changes," *NAA Bulletin* (Vol. 39, No. 4, 1957), pp. 59–66.

APPENDIX: COMPUTED VALUES OF X^b FOR LEARNING RATES 60 PERCENT TO 96 PERCENT AND FOR UNITS 1 TO 8,000

Unit	60	65	70	75	80	81	82
1	1.000000	1.000000	1.000000	1.000000	1.000000	1.000000	1.000000
2	0.600000	0.650000	0.700000	0.750000	0.800000	0.810000	0.820000
3	0.445019	0.505213	0.568180	0.633836	0.702104	0.716065	0.730127
4	0.360000	0.422500	0.490000	0.562500	0.640000	0.656100	0.672400
5	0.305410	0.367789	0.436846	0.512745	0.595637	0.613068	0.630786
6	0.267011	0.328389	0.397726	0.475377	0.561683	0.580012	0.598704
7	0.238337	0.298388	0.367397	0.445916	0.534490	0.553458	0.572855
8	0.216000	0.274625	0.343000	0.421875	0.512000	0.531441	0.551368
9	0.198041	0.255240	0.322829	0.401748	0.492950	0.512748	0.533085
10	0.183246	0.239063	0.305793	0.384559	0.476510	0.496585	0.517244
11	0.170816	0.225313	0.291157	0.369643	0.462111	0.482403	0.503321
12	0.160207	0.213453	0.278408	0.356533	0.449346	0.469810	0.490937
13	0.151030	0.203094	0.267174	0.344883	0.437916	0.458516	0.479815
14	0.143002	0.193952	0.257178	0.334437	0.427592	0.448301	0.469741
15	0.135913	0.185812	0.248208	0.324996	0.418199	0.438996	0.460554
16	0.129600	0.178506	0.240100	0.316406	0.409600	0.430467	0.452122
17	0.123937	0.171906	0.232726	0.308544	0.401683	0.422606	0.444342
18	0.118825	0.165906	0.225980	0.301311	0.394360	0.415326	0.437130
19	0.114183	0.160424	0.219780	0.294625	0.387555	0.408555	0.430415
20	0.109948	0.155391	0.214055	0.288419	0.381208	0.402234	0.424141
21	0.106064	0.150750	0.208748	0.282637	0.375267	0.396312	0.418257
22	0.102490	0.146454	0.203810	0.277233	0.369689	0.390747	0.412723
23	0.099187	0.142463	0.199201	0.272165	0.364436	0.385502	0.407504
24	0.096124	0.138744	0.194886	0.267400	0.359477	0.380546	0.402568
25	0.093275	0.135268	0.190835	0.262970	0.354784	0.375853	0.397891
26	0.090618	0.132011	0.187022	0.258662	0.350332	0.371398	0.393448
27	0.088132	0.128951	0.183425	0.254642	0.346102	0.367161	0.389220
28	0.085801	0.126069	0.180024	0.250828	0.342073	0.363124	0.385188
29	0.083611	0.123349	0.176803	0.247201	0.338231	0.359271	0.381337
30	0.081548	0.120778	0.173745	0.243747	0.334559	0.355587	0.377654

Unit	60	65	70	75	80	81	82
31	0.079601	0.118341	0.170838	0.240452	0.331046	0.352060	0.374125
32	0.077760	0.116029	0.168070	0.237305	0.327680	0.348678	0.370740
33	0.076016	0.113831	0.165430	0.234293	0.324450	0.345432	0.367488
34	0.074362	0.111739	0.162908	0.231408	0.321347	0.342311	0.364360
35	0.072791	0.109744	0.160496	0.228641	0.318362	0.339308	0.361349
36	0.071295	0.107839	0.158186	0.225983	0.315488	0.336414	0.358446
37	0.069870	0.106018	0.155972	0.223428	0.312717	0.333624	0.355645
38	0.068510	0.104276	0.153846	0.220969	0.310044	0.330930	0.352940
39	0.067211	0.102606	0.151803	0.218599	0.307462	0.328327	0.350325
40	0.065969	0.101004	0.149838	0.216314	0.304966	0.325810	0.347795
41	0.064779	0.099466	0.147947	0.214109	0.302552	0.323373	0.345345
42	0.063639	0.097987	0.146123	0.211978	0.300214	0.321013	0.342971
43	0.062545	0.096565	0.144365	0.209918	0.297948	0.318725	0.340668
44	0.061494	0.095195	0.142667	0.207924	0.295751	0.316505	0.338433
45	0.060484	0.093874	0.141027	0.205994	0.293619	0.314350	0.336262
46	0.059512	0.092601	0.139441	0.204124	0.291549	0.312256	0.334153
47	0.058576	0.091371	0.137906	0.202310	0.289537	0.310222	0.332102
48	0.057674	0.090184	0.136420	0.200550	0.287582	0.308242	0.330106
49	0.056805	0.089035	0.134980	0.198841	0.285679	0.306316	0.328163
50	0.055965	0.087925	0.133584	0.197180	0.283827	0.304441	0.326271
51	0.055154	0.086849	0.132230	0.195566	0.282023	0.302613	0.324426
52	0.054371	0.085807	0.130915	0.193997	0.280266	0.300832	0.322627
53	0.053613	0.084797	0.129638	0.192469	0.278553	0.299095	0.320873
54	0.052879	0.083818	0.128398	0.190982	0.276881	0.297400	0.319160
55	0.052169	0.082868	0.127191	0.189533	0.275251	0.295746	0.317488
56	0.051481	0.081945	0.126017	0.188121	0.273659	0.294130	0.315854
57	0.050814	0.081048	0.124875	0.186744	0.272104	0.292552	0.314258
58	0.050177	0.080177	0.123762	0.185401	0.270585	0.291009	0.312697
59	0.049539	0.079330	0.122678	0.184090	0.269100	0.289501	0.311170
60	0.048929	0.078505	0.121622	0.182810	0.267648	0.288026	0.309676
61	0.048336	0.077703	0.120592	0.181560	0.266227	0.286582	0.308214
62	0.047761	0.076922	0.119587	0.180339	0.264837	0.285169	0.306783
63	0.047201	0.076161	0.118606	0.179146	0.263476	0.283785	0.305381
64	0.046656	0.075419	0.117649	0.177979	0.262144	0.282430	0.304007
65	0.046126	0.074696	0.116714	0.176837	0.260839	0.281101	0.302660

Unit	60	65	70	75	80	81	82
66	0.045610	0.073990	0.115801	0.175720	0.259560	0.279800	0.301340
67	0.045107	0.073302	0.114908	0.174627	0.258306	0.278524	0.300046
68	0.044617	0.072630	0.114036	0.173556	0.257077	0.277272	0.298776
69	0.044140	0.071974	0.113182	0.172508	0.255872	0.276044	0.297529
70	0.043674	0.071333	0.112347	0.171481	0.254690	0.274839	0.296306
71	0.043220	0.070707	0.111530	0.170474	0.253529	0.273657	0.295105
72	0.042777	0.070095	0.110730	0.169487	0.252390	0.272496	0.293926
73	0.042344	0.069497	0.109947	0.168520	0.251272	0.271355	0.292768
74	0.041922	0.068912	0.109180	0.167571	0.250174	0.270235	0.291629
75	0.041509	0.068339	0.108429	0.166640	0.249095	0.269135	0.290511
76	0.041106	0.067779	0.107692	0.165726	0.248035	0.268053	0.289411
77	0.040712	0.067231	0.106970	0.164830	0.246994	0.266990	0.288330
78	0.040327	0.066694	0.106262	0.163949	0.245970	0.265945	0.287267
79	0.039950	0.066168	0.105568	0.163085	0.244963	0.264917	0.286221
80	0.039581	0.065653	0.104887	0.162236	0.243973	0.263906	0.285192
81	0.039220	0.065148	0.104219	0.161401	0.242999	0.262911	0.284180
82	0.038867	0.064653	0.103563	0.160582	0.242041	0.261932	0.283183
83	0.038522	0.064168	0.102919	0.159776	0.241099	0.260969	0.282202
84	0.038183	0.063692	0.102286	0.158983	0.240171	0.260020	0.281236
85	0.037852	0.063225	0.101665	0.158205	0.239258	0.259086	0.280285
86	0.037527	0.062767	0.101055	0.157438	0.238359	0.258167	0.279348
87	0.037208	0.062318	0.100456	0.156685	0.237473	0.257261	0.278425
88	0.036896	0.061877	0.099867	0.155943	0.236601	0.256369	0.277515
89	0.036590	0.061444	0.099288	0.155214	0.235742	0.255490	0.276619
90	0.036290	0.061018	0.098719	0.154496	0.234895	0.254623	0.275735
91	0.035996	0.060601	0.098159	0.153789	0.234061	0.253769	0.274864
92	0.035707	0.060191	0.097608	0.153093	0.233239	0.252928	0.274006
93	0.035424	0.059788	0.097067	0.152407	0.232429	0.252098	0.273159
94	0.035146	0.059391	0.096534	0.151732	0.231630	0.251279	0.272324
95	0.034873	0.059002	0.096010	0.151067	0.230842	0.250472	0.271500
96	0.034605	0.058619	0.095494	0.150412	0.230065	0.249676	0.270687
97	0.034341	0.058243	0.094986	0.149767	0.229299	0.248891	0.269885
98	0.034083	0.057873	0.094486	0.149131	0.228543	0.248116	0.269094
99	0.033829	0.057509	0.093994	0.148503	0.227798	0.247352	0.268313
100	0.033579	0.057151	0.093509	0.147885	0.227062	0.246597	0.267542

Unit	60	65	70	75	80	81	82
101	0.033334	0.056799	0.093031	0.147276	0.226336	0.245852	0.266781
102	0.033093	0.056452	0.092561	0.146675	0.225619	0.245117	0.266029
103	0.032856	0.056111	0.092098	0.146082	0.224911	0.244391	0.265287
104	0.032622	0.055775	0.091641	0.145498	0.224213	0.243674	0.264554
105	0.032393	0.055444	0.091191	0.144921	0.223523	0.242966	0.263831
106	0.032168	0.055118	0.090747	0.144352	0.222842	0.242267	0.263116
107	0.031946	0.054798	0.090310	0.143790	0.222169	0.241577	0.262409
108	0.031728	0.054482	0.089878	0.143236	0.221505	0.240894	0.261711
109	0.031513	0.054171	0.089453	0.142689	0.220849	0.240220	0.261022
110	0.031301	0.053864	0.089034	0.142150	0.220201	0.239554	0.260340
111	0.031093	0.053562	0.088620	0.141617	0.219560	0.238896	0.259666
112	0.030889	0.053264	0.088212	0.141090	0.218927	0.238246	0.259000
113	0.030687	0.052971	0.087809	0.140571	0.218301	0.237603	0.258342
114	0.030488	0.052681	0.087412	0.140058	0.217683	0.236967	0.257691
115	0.030293	0.052396	0.087020	0.139551	0.217072	0.236339	0.257048
116	0.030100	0.052115	0.086633	0.139051	0.216468	0.235718	0.256411
117	0.029910	0.051838	0.086252	0.138556	0.215870	0.235103	0.255782
118	0.029723	0.051564	0.085875	0.138067	0.215280	0.234496	0.255159
119	0.029539	0.051295	0.085503	0.137585	0.214696	0.233895	0.254544
120	0.029357	0.051029	0.085135	0.137108	0.214118	0.233301	0.253935
121	0.029178	0.050766	0.084772	0.136636	0.213547	0.232713	0.253332
122	0.029002	0.050507	0.084414	0.136170	0.212982	0.232131	0.252736
123	0.028828	0.050251	0.084060	0.135710	0.212423	0.231556	0.252146
124	0.028656	0.049999	0.083711	0.135254	0.211870	0.230987	0.251562
125	0.028487	0.049750	0.083366	0.134804	0.211323	0.230423	0.250984
126	0.028320	0.049504	0.083024	0.134359	0.210781	0.229866	0.250412
127	0.028156	0.049262	0.082687	0.133919	0.210245	0.229314	0.249846
128	0.027994	0.049022	0.082354	0.133484	0.209715	0.228768	0.249285
129	0.027834	0.048786	0.082025	0.133053	0.209190	0.228227	0.248731
130	0.027676	0.048552	0.081700	0.132628	0.208671	0.227692	0.248181
131	0.027520	0.048322	0.081378	0.132207	0.208157	0.227162	0.247637
132	0.027366	0.048094	0.081061	0.131790	0.207648	0.226638	0.247099
133	0.027214	0.047869	0.080746	0.131378	0.207144	0.226118	0.246566
134	0.027064	0.047646	0.080436	0.130970	0.206645	0.225604	0.246037
135	0.026916	0.047427	0.080129	0.130566	0.206151	0.225095	0.245514

Unit	60	65	70	75	80	81	82
136	0.026770	0.047210	0.079825	0.130167	0.205662	0.224590	0.244996
137	0.026626	0.046995	0.079525	0.129772	0.205177	0.224091	0.244483
138	0.026484	0.046783	0.079227	0.129381	0.204698	0.223596	0.243974
139	0.026343	0.046574	0.078934	0.128994	0.204222	0.223105	0.243470
140	0.026205	0.046367	0.078643	0.128611	0.203752	0.222620	0.242971
141	0.026068	0.046162	0.078356	0.128231	0.203285	0.222139	0.242476
142	0.025932	0.045960	0.078071	0.127856	0.202823	0.221662	0.241986
143	0.025798	0.045760	0.077790	0.127484	0.202366	0.221190	0.241501
144	0.025666	0.045562	0.077511	0.127116	0.201912	0.220721	0.241019
145	0.025536	0.045366	0.077236	0.126751	0.201463	0.220258	0.240542
146	0.025407	0.045173	0.076963	0.126390	0.201018	0.219798	0.240069
147	0.025279	0.044982	0.076693	0.126032	0.200576	0.219342	0.239601
148	0.025153	0.044793	0.076426	0.125678	0.200139	0.218891	0.239136
149	0.025029	0.044606	0.076162	0.125327	0.199706	0.218443	0.238675
150	0.024906	0.044421	0.075900	0.124980	0.199276	0.217999	0.238219
151	0.024784	0.044238	0.075641	0.124636	0.198850	0.217559	0.237766
152	0.024664	0.044056	0.075384	0.124295	0.198428	0.217123	0.237317
153	0.024545	0.043877	0.075131	0.123957	0.198010	0.216691	0.236872
154	0.024427	0.043700	0.074879	0.123622	0.197595	0.216262	0.236431
155	0.024311	0.043525	0.074630	0.123291	0.197184	0.215837	0.235993
156	0.024196	0.043351	0.074384	0.122962	0.196776	0.215415	0.235559
157	0.024082	0.043179	0.074139	0.122636	0.196371	0.214997	0.235128
158	0.023970	0.043009	0.073898	0.122314	0.195970	0.214583	0.234701
159	0.023859	0.042841	0.073658	0.121994	0.195573	0.214171	0.234278
160	0.023749	0.042674	0.073421	0.121677	0.195178	0.213764	0.233857
161	0.023640	0.042509	0.073186	0.121363	0.194787	0.213359	0.233441
162	0.023532	0.042346	0.072953	0.121051	0.194399	0.212958	0.233027
163	0.023426	0.042184	0.072722	0.120742	0.194015	0.212560	0.232617
164	0.023320	0.042024	0.072494	0.120436	0.193633	0.212165	0.232210
165	0.023216	0.041866	0.072267	0.120133	0.193255	0.211773	0.231806
166	0.023113	0.041709	0.072043	0.119832	0.192879	0.211385	0.231406
167	0.023011	0.041553	0.071821	0.119533	0.192506	0.210999	0.231008
168	0.022910	0.041400	0.071600	0.119238	0.192137	0.210616	0.230613
169	0.022810	0.041247	0.071387	0.118944	0.191770	0.210237	0.230222
170	0.022711	0.041096	0.071166	0.118653	0.191406	0.209860	0.229833

Unit	60	65	70	75	80	81	82
171	0.022613	0.040947	0.070951	0.118365	0.191045	0.209486	0.229448
172	0.022516	0.040799	0.070739	0.118079	0.190687	0.209115	0.229065
173	0.022420	0.040652	0.070528	0.117795	0.190331	0.208747	0.228685
174	0.022325	0.040506	0.070319	0.117514	0.189978	0.208382	0.228308
175	0.022231	0.040362	0.070112	0.117234	0.189628	0.208019	0.227934
176	0.022138	0.040220	0.069907	0.116958	0.189281	0.207659	0.227562
177	0.022046	0.040078	0.069703	0.116683	0.188936	0.207301	0.227193
178	0.021954	0.039938	0.069502	0.116410	0.188593	0.206947	0.226827
179	0.021864	0.039800	0.069301	0.116140	0.188254	0.206595	0.226464
180	0.021774	0.039662	0.069103	0.115872	0.187916	0.206245	0.226103
181	0.021685	0.039526	0.068906	0.115606	0.187581	0.205898	0.225745
182	0.021598	0.039391	0.068711	0.115342	0.187249	0.205553	0.225389
183	0.021511	0.039257	0.068518	0.115080	0.186919	0.205211	0.225035
184	0.021424	0.039124	0.068326	0.114820	0.186591	0.204871	0.224685
185	0.021339	0.038992	0.068136	0.114562	0.186266	0.204534	0.224336
186	0.021254	0.038862	0.067947	0.114305	0.185943	0.204199	0.223990
187	0.021170	0.038733	0.067760	0.114051	0.185622	0.203867	0.223647
188	0.021087	0.038604	0.067574	0.113799	0.185304	0.203536	0.223305
189	0.021005	0.038477	0.067390	0.113549	0.184988	0.203208	0.222966
190	0.020924	0.038351	0.067207	0.113301	0.184674	0.202883	0.222630
191	0.020843	0.038226	0.067026	0.113054	0.184362	0.202559	0.222295
192	0.020763	0.038103	0.066846	0.112809	0.184052	0.202238	0.221963
193	0.020683	0.037980	0.066667	0.112566	0.183745	0.201919	0.221634
194	0.020605	0.037858	0.066490	0.112325	0.183439	0.201602	0.221306
195	0.020527	0.037737	0.066315	0.112086	0.183136	0.201287	0.220980
196	0.020450	0.037617	0.066140	0.111848	0.182835	0.200974	0.220657
197	0.020373	0.037499	0.065967	0.111612	0.182535	0.200663	0.220336
198	0.020297	0.037381	0.065796	0.111378	0.182238	0.200355	0.220016
199	0.020222	0.037264	0.065625	0.111145	0.181943	0.200048	0.219699
200	0.020147	0.037148	0.065456	0.110914	0.181649	0.199744	0.219384
201	0.020074	0.037033	0.065289	0.110685	0.181358	0.199441	0.219071
202	0.020000	0.036919	0.065122	0.110457	0.181068	0.199140	0.218760
203	0.019928	0.036806	0.064957	0.110231	0.180781	0.198841	0.218451
204	0.019856	0.036694	0.064793	0.110006	0.180495	0.198545	0.218144
205	0.019784	0.036582	0.064630	0.109783	0.180211	0.198250	0.217839

Unit	60	65	70	75	80	81	82
206	0.019713	0.036472	0.064468	0.109562	0.179929	0.197957	0.217536
207	0.019643	0.036362	0.064308	0.109342	0.179649	0.197665	0.217234
208	0.019573	0.036254	0.064149	0.109123	0.179370	0.197376	0.216935
209	0.019504	0.036146	0.063990	0.108906	0.179093	0.197088	0.216637
210	0.019436	0.036039	0.063833	0.108691	0.178818	0.196803	0.216341
211	0.019368	0.035932	0.063678	0.108477	0.178545	0.196519	0.216047
212	0.019301	0.035827	0.063523	0.108264	0.178274	0.196236	0.215755
213	0.019234	0.035722	0.063369	0.108053	0.178004	0.195956	0.215464
214	0.019167	0.035618	0.063217	0.107843	0.177736	0.195677	0.215176
215	0.019102	0.035515	0.063065	0.107634	0.177469	0.195400	0.214888
216	0.019037	0.035413	0.062915	0.107427	0.177204	0.195124	0.214603
217	0.018972	0.035312	0.062765	0.107221	0.176941	0.194851	0.214320
218	0.018908	0.035211	0.062617	0.107017	0.176679	0.194578	0.214038
219	0.018844	0.035111	0.062470	0.106814	0.176419	0.194308	0.213757
220	0.018781	0.035012	0.062324	0.106612	0.176160	0.194039	0.213479
221	0.018718	0.034913	0.062178	0.106412	0.175903	0.193772	0.213202
222	0.018656	0.034815	0.062034	0.106212	0.175648	0.193506	0.212926
223	0.018594	0.034718	0.061891	0.106015	0.175394	0.193242	0.212653
224	0.018533	0.034622	0.061748	0.105818	0.175142	0.192979	0.212380
225	0.018472	0.034526	0.061607	0.105622	0.174891	0.192718	0.212110
226	0.018412	0.034431	0.061467	0.105428	0.174641	0.192458	0.211840
227	0.018352	0.034337	0.061327	0.105235	0.174393	0.192200	0.211573
228	0.018293	0.034243	0.061189	0.105043	0.174146	0.191943	0.211307
229	0.018234	0.034150	0.061051	0.104853	0.173901	0.191688	0.211042
230	0.018176	0.034058	0.060914	0.104663	0.173657	0.191434	0.210779
231	0.018118	0.033966	0.060778	0.104475	0.173415	0.191182	0.210517
232	0.018060	0.033875	0.060643	0.104288	0.173174	0.190931	0.210257
233	0.018003	0.033784	0.060509	0.104102	0.172935	0.190682	0.209998
234	0.017946	0.033695	0.060376	0.103917	0.172696	0.190434	0.209741
235	0.017890	0.033605	0.060244	0.103733	0.172459	0.190187	0.209485
236	0.017834	0.033517	0.060112	0.103551	0.172224	0.189942	0.209231
237	0.017778	0.033429	0.059982	0.103369	0.171989	0.189698	0.208978
238	0.017723	0.033341	0.059852	0.103189	0.171756	0.189455	0.208726
239	0.017669	0.033255	0.059723	0.103009	0.171525	0.189214	0.208475
240	0.017614	0.033169	0.059595	0.102831	0.171294	0.188974	0.208226

Unit	60	65	70	75	80	81	82
241	0.017560	0.033083	0.059467	0.102653	0.171065	0.188735	0.207979
242	0.017507	0.032998	0.059341	0.102477	0.170837	0.188497	0.207732
243	0.017454	0.032913	0.059215	0.102302	0.170611	0.188261	0.207487
244	0.017401	0.032830	0.059090	0.102128	0.170385	0.188026	0.207243
245	0.017349	0.032746	0.058966	0.101955	0.170161	0.187793	0.207001
246	0.017297	0.032663	0.058842	0.101782	0.169938	0.187560	0.206759
247	0.017245	0.032581	0.058720	0.101611	0.169716	0.187329	0.206519
248	0.017194	0.032499	0.058598	0.101441	0.169496	0.187099	0.206281
249	0.017143	0.032418	0.058476	0.101272	0.169276	0.186870	0.206043
250	0.017092	0.032338	0.058356	0.101103	0.169058	0.186643	0.205807
251	0.017042	0.032257	0.058236	0.100936	0.168841	0.186417	0.205572
252	0.016992	0.032178	0.058117	0.100769	0.168625	0.186191	0.205338
253	0.016943	0.032099	0.057999	0.100604	0.168410	0.185967	0.205105
254	0.016894	0.032020	0.057881	0.100439	0.168196	0.185744	0.204874
255	0.016845	0.031942	0.057764	0.100276	0.167984	0.185523	0.204643
256	0.016796	0.031864	0.057648	0.100113	0.167772	0.185302	0.204414
257	0.016748	0.031787	0.057532	0.099951	0.167562	0.185083	0.204186
258	0.016700	0.031711	0.057418	0.099790	0.167352	0.184864	0.203959
259	0.016653	0.031635	0.057303	0.099630	0.167144	0.184647	0.203733
260	0.016605	0.031559	0.057190	0.099471	0.166937	0.184431	0.203509
261	0.016558	0.031484	0.057077	0.099312	0.166731	0.184216	0.203285
262	0.016512	0.031409	0.056965	0.099155	0.166526	0.184002	0.203063
263	0.016466	0.031335	0.056853	0.098998	0.166321	0.183789	0.202841
264	0.016420	0.031261	0.056742	0.098842	0.166118	0.183577	0.202621
265	0.016374	0.031188	0.056632	0.098688	0.165916	0.183366	0.202402
266	0.016328	0.031115	0.056522	0.098533	0.165715	0.183156	0.202184
267	0.016283	0.031042	0.056413	0.098380	0.165515	0.182947	0.201967
268	0.016239	0.030970	0.056305	0.098228	0.165316	0.182739	0.201751
269	0.016194	0.030898	0.056197	0.098076	0.165118	0.182533	0.201536
270	0.016150	0.030827	0.056090	0.097925	0.164921	0.182327	0.201322
271	0.016106	0.030757	0.055983	0.097775	0.164725	0.182122	0.201109
272	0.016062	0.030686	0.055877	0.097625	0.164530	0.181918	0.200897
273	0.016019	0.030616	0.055772	0.097477	0.164335	0.181715	0.200686
274	0.015976	0.030547	0.055667	0.097329	0.164142	0.181513	0.200476
275	0.015933	0.030478	0.055563	0.097182	0.163950	0.181313	0.200267

Unit	60	65	70	75	80	81	82
276	0.015890	0.030409	0.055459	0.097036	0.163758	0.181113	0.200059
277	0.015848	0.030341	0.055356	0.096890	0.163568	0.180914	0.199852
278	0.015806	0.030273	0.055254	0.096745	0.163378	0.180715	0.199646
279	0.015764	0.030205	0.055152	0.096601	0.163189	0.180518	0.199440
280	0.015723	0.030138	0.055050	0.096458	0.163001	0.180322	0.199236
281	0.015682	0.030072	0.054949	0.096315	0.162814	0.180127	0.199033
282	0.015641	0.030005	0.054849	0.096173	0.162628	0.179932	0.198831
283	0.015600	0.029939	0.054749	0.096032	0.162443	0.179739	0.198629
284	0.015559	0.029874	0.054650	0.095892	0.162259	0.179546	0.198429
285	0.015519	0.029809	0.054551	0.095752	0.162075	0.179354	0.198229
286	0.015479	0.029744	0.054453	0.095613	0.161893	0.179164	0.198031
287	0.015439	0.029679	0.054355	0.095474	0.161711	0.178973	0.197833
288	0.015400	0.029615	0.054258	0.095337	0.161530	0.178784	0.197636
289	0.015360	0.029552	0.054161	0.095200	0.161350	0.178596	0.197440
290	0.015321	0.029488	0.054065	0.095063	0.161170	0.178409	0.197245
291	0.015283	0.029425	0.053969	0.094928	0.160992	0.178222	0.197050
292	0.015244	0.029363	0.053874	0.094792	0.160814	0.178036	0.196857
293	0.015206	0.029300	0.053779	0.094658	0.160637	0.177851	0.196664
294	0.015167	0.029238	0.053685	0.094524	0.160461	0.177667	0.196473
295	0.015130	0.029177	0.053591	0.094391	0.160286	0.177484	0.196282
296	0.015092	0.029115	0.053498	0.094259	0.160111	0.177301	0.196092
297	0.015054	0.029054	0.053405	0.094127	0.159937	0.177120	0.195902
298	0.015017	0.028994	0.053313	0.093996	0.159765	0.176939	0.195714
299	0.014980	0.028933	0.053221	0.093865	0.159592	0.176759	0.195526
300	0.014943	0.028873	0.053130	0.093735	0.159421	0.176579	0.195339
301	0.014907	0.028814	0.053039	0.093606	0.159250	0.176401	0.195153
302	0.014870	0.028754	0.052949	0.093477	0.159080	0.176223	0.194968
303	0.014834	0.028695	0.052859	0.093349	0.158911	0.176046	0.194784
304	0.014798	0.028637	0.052769	0.093221	0.158743	0.175870	0.194600
305	0.014762	0.028578	0.052680	0.093094	0.158575	0.175694	0.194417
306	0.014727	0.028520	0.052591	0.092968	0.158408	0.175519	0.194235
307	0.014691	0.028462	0.052503	0.092842	0.158241	0.175345	0.194054
308	0.014656	0.028405	0.052415	0.092717	0.158076	0.175172	0.193873
309	0.014621	0.028348	0.052328	0.092592	0.157911	0.175000	0.193693
310	0.014587	0.028291	0.052241	0.092468	0.157747	0.174828	0.193514

Unit	.82	.81	.80	.75	.70	.65	.60
311	0.193336	0.174657	0.157583	0.092345	0.052155	0.028234	0.014552
312	0.193158	0.174486	0.157421	0.092222	0.052068	0.028178	0.014518
313	0.192981	0.174317	0.157259	0.092099	0.051983	0.028122	0.014483
314	0.192805	0.174148	0.157097	0.091977	0.051898	0.028066	0.014449
315	0.192630	0.173980	0.156936	0.091856	0.051813	0.028011	0.014416
316	0.192455	0.173812	0.156776	0.091735	0.051728	0.027956	0.014382
317	0.192281	0.173645	0.156617	0.091615	0.051644	0.027901	0.014348
318	0.192108	0.173479	0.156458	0.091495	0.051561	0.027847	0.014315
319	0.191935	0.173313	0.156300	0.091376	0.051477	0.027792	0.014282
320	0.191763	0.173149	0.156143	0.091258	0.051395	0.027738	0.014249
321	0.191592	0.172984	0.155986	0.091139	0.051312	0.027684	0.014216
322	0.191421	0.172821	0.155830	0.091022	0.051230	0.027631	0.014184
323	0.191252	0.172658	0.155674	0.090905	0.051148	0.027578	0.014152
324	0.191082	0.172496	0.155520	0.090788	0.051067	0.027525	0.014119
325	0.190914	0.172334	0.155365	0.090672	0.050986	0.027472	0.014087
326	0.190746	0.172174	0.155212	0.090557	0.050906	0.027420	0.014055
327	0.190579	0.172013	0.155059	0.090442	0.050825	0.027368	0.014024
328	0.190412	0.171854	0.154906	0.090327	0.050746	0.027316	0.013992
329	0.190246	0.171695	0.154755	0.090213	0.050666	0.027264	0.013961
330	0.190081	0.171536	0.154604	0.090099	0.050587	0.027213	0.013930
331	0.189917	0.171379	0.154453	0.089986	0.050508	0.027162	0.013899
332	0.189753	0.171222	0.154303	0.089874	0.050430	0.027111	0.013868
333	0.189589	0.171065	0.154154	0.089762	0.050352	0.027060	0.013837
334	0.189427	0.170909	0.154005	0.089650	0.050275	0.027010	0.013807
335	0.189264	0.170754	0.153857	0.089539	0.050197	0.026960	0.013776
336	0.189103	0.170599	0.153709	0.089428	0.050120	0.026910	0.013746
337	0.188942	0.170445	0.153562	0.089318	0.050044	0.026860	0.013716
338	0.188782	0.170292	0.153416	0.089208	0.049967	0.026811	0.013686
339	0.188622	0.170139	0.153270	0.089099	0.049892	0.026761	0.013656
340	0.188463	0.169987	0.153125	0.088990	0.049816	0.026713	0.013627
341	0.188305	0.169835	0.152980	0.088882	0.049741	0.026664	0.013597
342	0.188147	0.169684	0.152836	0.088774	0.049666	0.026615	0.013568
343	0.187990	0.169533	0.152692	0.088666	0.049591	0.026567	0.013539
344	0.187833	0.169383	0.152549	0.088559	0.049517	0.026519	0.013510
345	0.187677	0.169234	0.152407	0.088452	0.049443	0.026471	0.013481

Unit	60	65	70	75	80	81	82
346	0.013452	0.026424	0.049370	0.088346	0.152265	0.169085	0.187522
347	0.013423	0.026376	0.049296	0.088241	0.152124	0.168937	0.187367
348	0.013395	0.026329	0.049223	0.088135	0.151983	0.168789	0.187213
349	0.013367	0.026282	0.049151	0.088030	0.151842	0.168642	0.187059
350	0.013339	0.026236	0.049078	0.087926	0.151703	0.168495	0.186906
351	0.013311	0.026189	0.049006	0.087822	0.151563	0.168349	0.186753
352	0.013283	0.026143	0.048935	0.087718	0.151425	0.168204	0.186601
353	0.013255	0.026097	0.048863	0.087615	0.151286	0.168059	0.186450
354	0.013227	0.026051	0.048792	0.087512	0.151149	0.167914	0.186299
355	0.013200	0.026005	0.048722	0.087410	0.151011	0.167770	0.186148
356	0.013173	0.025960	0.048651	0.087308	0.150875	0.167627	0.185998
357	0.013145	0.025915	0.048581	0.087206	0.150739	0.167484	0.185849
358	0.013118	0.025870	0.048511	0.087105	0.150603	0.167342	0.185700
359	0.013091	0.025825	0.048441	0.087004	0.150468	0.167200	0.185552
360	0.013065	0.025780	0.048372	0.086904	0.150333	0.167058	0.185404
361	0.013038	0.025736	0.048303	0.086804	0.150199	0.166918	0.185257
362	0.013011	0.025692	0.048234	0.086704	0.150065	0.166777	0.185111
363	0.012985	0.025648	0.048166	0.086605	0.149932	0.166637	0.184964
364	0.012959	0.025604	0.048098	0.086506	0.149799	0.166498	0.184819
365	0.012932	0.025560	0.048030	0.086408	0.149667	0.166359	0.184674
366	0.012906	0.025517	0.047962	0.086310	0.149535	0.166221	0.184529
367	0.012880	0.025474	0.047895	0.086212	0.149404	0.166083	0.184385
368	0.012855	0.025431	0.047828	0.086115	0.149273	0.165946	0.184241
369	0.012829	0.025388	0.047761	0.086018	0.149143	0.165809	0.184098
370	0.012803	0.025345	0.047695	0.085921	0.149013	0.165673	0.183956
371	0.012778	0.025303	0.047629	0.085825	0.148883	0.165537	0.183814
372	0.012753	0.025260	0.047563	0.085729	0.148754	0.165401	0.183672
373	0.012727	0.025218	0.047497	0.085634	0.148626	0.165266	0.183531
374	0.012702	0.025176	0.047432	0.085539	0.148498	0.165132	0.183390
375	0.012677	0.025134	0.047367	0.085444	0.148370	0.164998	0.183250
376	0.012652	0.025093	0.047302	0.085349	0.148243	0.164864	0.183110
377	0.012628	0.025052	0.047237	0.085255	0.148116	0.164731	0.182971
378	0.012603	0.025010	0.047173	0.085162	0.147990	0.164599	0.182832
379	0.012579	0.024969	0.047109	0.085068	0.147864	0.164467	0.182694
380	0.012554	0.024928	0.047045	0.084975	0.147739	0.164335	0.182556

Unit	60	65	70	75	80	81	82
381	0.012530	0.024888	0.046981	0.084883	0.147614	0.164204	0.182419
382	0.012506	0.024847	0.046918	0.084790	0.147490	0.164073	0.182282
383	0.012482	0.024807	0.046855	0.084699	0.147365	0.163943	0.182146
384	0.012458	0.024767	0.046792	0.084607	0.147242	0.163813	0.182010
385	0.012434	0.024727	0.046730	0.084516	0.147119	0.163683	0.181874
386	0.012410	0.024687	0.046667	0.084425	0.146996	0.163554	0.181739
387	0.012386	0.024647	0.046605	0.084334	0.146873	0.163426	0.181605
388	0.012363	0.024608	0.046543	0.084244	0.146751	0.163297	0.181471
389	0.012339	0.024568	0.046482	0.084154	0.146630	0.163170	0.181337
390	0.012316	0.024529	0.046420	0.084064	0.146509	0.163042	0.181204
391	0.012293	0.024490	0.046359	0.083975	0.146388	0.162915	0.181071
392	0.012270	0.024451	0.046298	0.083886	0.146268	0.162789	0.180939
393	0.012247	0.024413	0.046238	0.083797	0.146148	0.162663	0.180807
394	0.012224	0.024374	0.046177	0.083709	0.146028	0.162537	0.180675
395	0.012201	0.024336	0.046117	0.083621	0.145909	0.162412	0.180544
396	0.012178	0.024298	0.046057	0.083533	0.145790	0.162287	0.180413
397	0.012156	0.024260	0.045997	0.083446	0.145672	0.162163	0.180283
398	0.012133	0.024222	0.045938	0.083359	0.145554	0.162039	0.180153
399	0.012111	0.024184	0.045878	0.083272	0.145437	0.161915	0.180024
400	0.012088	0.024146	0.045819	0.083186	0.145319	0.161792	0.179895
401	0.012066	0.024109	0.045761	0.083099	0.145203	0.161669	0.179767
402	0.012044	0.024072	0.045702	0.083013	0.145086	0.161547	0.179638
403	0.012022	0.024034	0.045644	0.082928	0.144970	0.161425	0.179511
404	0.012000	0.023997	0.045585	0.082843	0.144855	0.161304	0.179383
405	0.011978	0.023961	0.045527	0.082758	0.144739	0.161182	0.179256
406	0.011957	0.023924	0.045470	0.082673	0.144625	0.161062	0.179130
407	0.011935	0.023887	0.045412	0.082589	0.144510	0.160941	0.179004
408	0.011913	0.023851	0.045355	0.082505	0.144396	0.160821	0.178878
409	0.011892	0.023815	0.045298	0.082421	0.144282	0.160702	0.178753
410	0.011870	0.023779	0.045241	0.082337	0.144169	0.160582	0.178628
411	0.011849	0.023743	0.045184	0.082254	0.144056	0.160463	0.178503
412	0.011828	0.023707	0.045128	0.082171	0.143943	0.160345	0.178379
413	0.011807	0.023671	0.045072	0.082089	0.143831	0.160227	0.178255
414	0.011786	0.023635	0.045015	0.082006	0.143719	0.160109	0.178132
415	0.011765	0.023600	0.044960	0.081924	0.143607	0.159992	0.178009

Unit	60	65	70	75	80	81	82
416	0.011744	0.023565	0.044904	0.081842	0.143496	0.159875	0.177886
417	0.011723	0.023530	0.044849	0.081761	0.143385	0.159758	0.177764
418	0.011703	0.023495	0.044793	0.081680	0.143275	0.159642	0.177642
419	0.011682	0.023460	0.044738	0.081599	0.143165	0.159526	0.177521
420	0.011662	0.023425	0.044683	0.081518	0.143055	0.159410	0.177400
421	0.011641	0.023390	0.044629	0.081438	0.142945	0.159295	0.177279
422	0.011621	0.023356	0.044574	0.081357	0.142836	0.159180	0.177159
423	0.011601	0.023322	0.044520	0.081278	0.142727	0.159066	0.177039
424	0.011580	0.023287	0.044466	0.081198	0.142619	0.158951	0.176919
425	0.011560	0.023253	0.044412	0.081119	0.142511	0.158838	0.176800
426	0.011540	0.023219	0.044358	0.081039	0.042403	0.158724	0.176681
427	0.011520	0.023186	0.044305	0.080961	0.142296	0.158611	0.176552
428	0.011500	0.023152	0.044252	0.080882	0.142188	0.158498	0.176444
429	0.011481	0.023118	0.044199	0.080804	0.142082	0.158386	0.176326
430	0.011461	0.023085	0.044146	0.080726	0.141975	0.158274	0.176209
431	0.011441	0.023052	0.044093	0.080648	0.141869	0.158162	0.176091
432	0.011422	0.023019	0.044040	0.080570	0.141763	0.158051	0.175975
433	0.011402	0.022985	0.043988	0.080493	0.141658	0.157940	0.175858
434	0.011383	0.022953	0.043936	0.080416	0.141553	0.157829	0.175742
435	0.011364	0.022920	0.043884	0.080339	0.141448	0.157719	0.175626
436	0.011345	0.022887	0.043832	0.080263	0.141343	0.157609	0.175511
437	0.011325	0.022854	0.043780	0.080187	0.141239	0.157499	0.175396
438	0.011306	0.022822	0.043729	0.080110	0.141135	0.157389	0.175281
439	0.011287	0.022790	0.043678	0.080035	0.141032	0.157280	0.175167
440	0.011269	0.022758	0.043626	0.079959	0.140928	0.157172	0.175053
441	0.011250	0.022725	0.043576	0.079884	0.140825	0.157063	0.174939
442	0.011231	0.022693	0.043525	0.079809	0.140723	0.156955	0.174825
443	0.011212	0.022662	0.043474	0.079734	0.140620	0.156847	0.174712
444	0.011194	0.022630	0.043424	0.079659	0.140518	0.156740	0.174600
445	0.011175	0.022598	0.043374	0.079585	0.140417	0.156633	0.174487
446	0.011157	0.022567	0.043323	0.079511	0.140315	0.156526	0.174375
447	0.011138	0.022535	0.043274	0.079437	0.140214	0.156419	0.174263
448	0.011120	0.022504	0.043224	0.079363	0.140113	0.156313	0.174152
449	0.011102	0.022473	0.043174	0.079290	0.140013	0.156207	0.174041
450	0.011083	0.022442	0.043125	0.079217	0.139912	0.156101	0.173930

Unit	60	65	70	75	80	81	82
451	0.011065	0.022411	0.043076	0.079144	0.139813	0.155996	0.173819
452	0.011047	0.022380	0.043027	0.079071	0.139713	0.155891	0.173709
453	0.011029	0.022349	0.042978	0.078999	0.139614	0.155786	0.173599
454	0.011011	0.022319	0.042929	0.078926	0.139514	0.155682	0.173490
455	0.010994	0.022288	0.042880	0.078854	0.139416	0.155578	0.173381
456	0.010976	0.022258	0.042832	0.078783	0.139317	0.155474	0.173272
457	0.010958	0.022228	0.042784	0.078711	0.139219	0.155371	0.173163
458	0.010940	0.022197	0.042736	0.078640	0.139121	0.155267	0.173055
459	0.010923	0.022167	0.042688	0.078568	0.139023	0.155165	0.172947
460	0.010905	0.022137	0.042640	0.078497	0.138926	0.155062	0.172839
461	0.010888	0.022108	0.042592	0.078427	0.138829	0.154960	0.172731
462	0.010871	0.022078	0.042545	0.078356	0.138732	0.154858	0.172624
463	0.010853	0.022048	0.042498	0.078286	0.138636	0.154756	0.172517
464	0.010836	0.022019	0.042450	0.078216	0.138539	0.154654	0.172411
465	0.010819	0.021989	0.042403	0.078146	0.138443	0.154553	0.172305
466	0.010802	0.021960	0.042357	0.078076	0.138348	0.154452	0.172199
467	0.010785	0.021931	0.042310	0.078007	0.138252	0.154352	0.172093
468	0.010768	0.021901	0.042263	0.077938	0.138157	0.154251	0.171988
469	0.010751	0.021872	0.042217	0.077869	0.138062	0.154151	0.171883
470	0.010734	0.021844	0.042171	0.077800	0.137957	0.154051	0.171778
471	0.010717	0.021815	0.042125	0.077731	0.137873	0.153952	0.171673
472	0.010700	0.021786	0.042079	0.077663	0.137779	0.153853	0.171569
473	0.010684	0.021757	0.042033	0.077595	0.137685	0.153754	0.171465
474	0.010667	0.021729	0.041987	0.077527	0.137592	0.153655	0.171362
475	0.010650	0.021700	0.041942	0.077459	0.137498	0.153557	0.171258
476	0.010634	0.021672	0.041896	0.077391	0.137405	0.153458	0.171155
477	0.010618	0.021644	0.041851	0.077324	0.137312	0.153361	0.171052
478	0.010601	0.021616	0.041806	0.077257	0.137220	0.153263	0.170950
479	0.010585	0.021588	0.041761	0.077190	0.137128	0.153166	0.170848
480	0.010569	0.021560	0.041716	0.077123	0.137036	0.153069	0.170746
481	0.010552	0.021532	0.041672	0.077057	0.136944	0.152972	0.170644
482	0.010536	0.021504	0.041627	0.076990	0.136852	0.152875	0.170542
483	0.010520	0.021476	0.041583	0.076924	0.136761	0.152779	0.170441
484	0.010504	0.021449	0.041538	0.076858	0.136670	0.152683	0.170340
485	0.010488	0.021421	0.041494	0.076792	0.136579	0.152587	0.170240

Unit	60	65	70	75	80	81	82
486	0.010472	0.021394	0.041450	0.076726	0.136489	0.152492	0.170139
487	0.010456	0.021366	0.041407	0.076661	0.136398	0.152396	0.170039
488	0.010441	0.021339	0.041363	0.076596	0.136308	0.152301	0.169939
489	0.010425	0.021312	0.041319	0.076531	0.136218	0.152207	0.169840
490	0.010409	0.021285	0.041276	0.076466	0.136129	0.152112	0.169741
491	0.010394	0.021258	0.041233	0.076401	0.136040	0.152018	0.169642
492	0.010378	0.021231	0.041190	0.076337	0.135951	0.151924	0.169543
493	0.010362	0.021204	0.041147	0.076272	0.135862	0.151830	0.169444
494	0.010347	0.021178	0.041104	0.076208	0.135773	0.151737	0.169346
495	0.010332	0.021151	0.041061	0.076144	0.135685	0.151643	0.169248
496	0.010316	0.021125	0.041018	0.076081	0.135597	0.151550	0.169150
497	0.010301	0.021098	0.040976	0.076017	0.135509	0.151458	0.169053
498	0.010286	0.021072	0.040933	0.075954	0.135421	0.151365	0.168955
499	0.010271	0.021046	0.040891	0.075890	0.135334	0.151273	0.168858
500	0.010255	0.021019	0.040849	0.075827	0.135246	0.151181	0.168762
501	0.010240	0.020993	0.040807	0.075765	0.135159	0.151089	0.168665
502	0.010225	0.020967	0.040765	0.075702	0.135073	0.150997	0.168569
503	0.010210	0.020941	0.040724	0.075639	0.134986	0.150906	0.168473
504	0.010195	0.020916	0.040682	0.075577	0.134900	0.150815	0.168377
505	0.010180	0.020890	0.040640	0.075515	0.134814	0.150724	0.168282
506	0.010166	0.020864	0.040599	0.075453	0.134728	0.150633	0.168186
507	0.010151	0.020839	0.040558	0.075391	0.134642	0.150543	0.168091
508	0.010136	0.020813	0.040517	0.075330	0.134557	0.150453	0.167996
509	0.010121	0.020788	0.040476	0.075268	0.134472	0.150363	0.167902
510	0.010107	0.020762	0.040435	0.075207	0.134387	0.150273	0.167808
511	0.010092	0.020737	0.040394	0.075146	0.134302	0.150184	0.167713
512	0.010078	0.020712	0.040354	0.075085	0.134218	0.150095	0.167620
513	0.010063	0.020687	0.040313	0.075024	0.134133	0.150006	0.167526
514	0.010049	0.020662	0.040273	0.074963	0.134049	0.149917	0.167433
515	0.010034	0.020637	0.040232	0.074903	0.133966	0.149828	0.167339
516	0.010020	0.020612	0.040192	0.074843	0.133882	0.149740	0.167247
517	0.010006	0.020587	0.040152	0.074782	0.133798	0.149652	0.167154
518	0.009992	0.020562	0.040112	0.074723	0.133715	0.149564	0.167061
519	0.009977	0.020538	0.040073	0.074663	0.133632	0.149476	0.166969
520	0.009963	0.020513	0.040033	0.074603	0.133550	0.149389	0.166877

Unit	60	65	70	75	80	81	82
521	0.009949	0.020489	0.039993	0.074544	0.133467	0.149302	0.166785
522	0.009935	0.020464	0.039954	0.074484	0.133385	0.149215	0.166694
523	0.009921	0.020440	0.039915	0.074425	0.133302	0.149128	0.166603
524	0.009907	0.020416	0.039875	0.074366	0.133220	0.149041	0.166511
525	0.009893	0.020392	0.039836	0.074307	0.133139	0.148955	0.166421
526	0.009879	0.020368	0.039797	0.074249	0.133057	0.148869	0.166330
527	0.009866	0.020344	0.039758	0.074190	0.132976	0.148783	0.166240
528	0.009852	0.020320	0.039720	0.074132	0.032895	0.148697	0.166149
529	0.009838	0.020296	0.039681	0.074074	0.132814	0.148612	0.166059
530	0.009824	0.020272	0.039642	0.074016	0.132733	0.148526	0.165970
531	0.009811	0.020248	0.039604	0.073958	0.132653	0.148441	0.165880
532	0.009797	0.020224	0.039566	0.073900	0.132572	0.148356	0.165791
533	0.009784	0.020201	0.039527	0.073842	0.132492	0.148272	0.165702
534	0.009770	0.020177	0.039489	0.073785	0.132412	0.148187	0.165613
535	0.009757	0.020154	0.039451	0.073728	0.132332	0.148103	0.165524
536	0.009743	0.020131	0.039414	0.073671	0.132253	0.148019	0.165436
537	0.009730	0.020107	0.039376	0.073614	0.132174	0.147935	0.165347
538	0.009716	0.020084	0.039338	0.073557	0.132094	0.147851	0.165259
539	0.009703	0.020061	0.039300	0.073500	0.132015	0.147768	0.165171
540	0.039690	0.020038	0.039263	0.073444	0.131937	0.147685	0.165084
541	0.009677	0.020015	0.039226	0.073387	0.131858	0.147602	0.164996
542	0.009564	0.019992	0.039188	0.073331	0.131780	0.147519	0.164909
543	0.009650	0.019969	0.039151	0.073275	0.131702	0.147436	0.164822
544	0.009637	0.019946	0.039114	0.073219	0.131624	0.147354	0.164735
545	0.009624	0.019923	0.039077	0.073163	0.131546	0.147271	0.164649
546	0.009611	0.019901	0.039040	0.073108	0.131468	0.147189	0.164562
547	0.009598	0.019878	0.039004	0.073052	0.131391	0.147108	0.164476
548	0.009585	0.019855	0.038967	0.072997	0.131314	0.047026	0.164390
549	0.009573	0.019833	0.038930	0.072942	0.131237	0.146944	0.164304
550	0.009560	0.019811	0.038894	0.072886	0.131160	0.146863	0.164219
551	0.009547	0.019788	0.038858	0.072832	0.131083	0.146782	0.164133
552	0.009534	0.019766	0.038821	0.072777	0.131007	0.146701	0.164048
553	0.009522	0.019744	0.038785	0.072722	0.130930	0.146620	0.163963
554	0.009509	0.019722	0.038749	0.072668	0.130854	0.146540	0.163878
555	0.009496	0.019699	0.038713	0.072613	0.130778	0.146460	0.163794

Unit	60	65	70	75	80	81	82
556	0.009484	0.019677	0.038677	0.072559	0.130702	0.146380	0.163709
557	0.009471	0.019655	0.038642	0.072505	0.130627	0.146300	0.163625
558	0.009459	0.019634	0.038606	0.072451	0.130551	0.146220	0.163541
559	0.009446	0.019612	0.038571	0.072397	0.130476	0.146140	0.163457
560	0.009434	0.019590	0.038535	0.072343	0.130401	0.146061	0.163374
561	0.009421	0.019568	0.038500	0.072290	0.130326	0.145982	0.163290
562	0.009409	0.019547	0.038464	0.072236	0.130251	0.145903	0.163207
563	0.009397	0.019525	0.038429	0.072183	0.130177	0.145824	0.163124
564	0.009384	0.019503	0.038394	0.072130	0.130103	0.145745	0.163041
565	0.009372	0.019482	0.038359	0.072077	0.130028	0.145667	0.162959
566	0.009360	0.019461	0.038324	0.072024	0.129954	0.145588	0.162876
567	0.009348	0.019439	0.038290	0.071971	0.129881	0.145510	0.162794
568	0.009336	0.019418	0.038255	0.071919	0.129807	0.145432	0.162712
569	0.009323	0.019397	0.038220	0.071866	0.129733	0.145355	0.162630
570	0.009311	0.019376	0.038186	0.071814	0.129660	0.145277	0.162548
571	0.009299	0.019355	0.038151	0.071762	0.129587	0.145200	0.162466
572	0.009287	0.019333	0.038117	0.071710	0.129514	0.145122	0.162385
573	0.009275	0.019313	0.038083	0.071658	0.129441	0.145045	0.162304
574	0.009264	0.019292	0.038049	0.071606	0.129369	0.144969	0.162223
575	0.009252	0.019271	0.038014	0.071554	0.129296	0.144892	0.162142
576	0.009240	0.019250	0.037980	0.071503	0.129224	0.144815	0.162061
577	0.009228	0.019229	0.037947	0.071451	0.129152	0.144739	0.161981
578	0.009216	0.019209	0.037913	0.071400	0.129080	0.144663	0.161901
579	0.009205	0.019188	0.037879	0.071349	0.129008	0.144587	0.161821
580	0.009193	0.019167	0.037845	0.071297	0.128936	0.144511	0.161741
581	0.009181	0.019147	0.037812	0.071246	0.128865	0.144435	0.161661
582	0.009170	0.019126	0.037779	0.071196	0.128793	0.144360	0.161581
583	0.009158	0.019106	0.037745	0.071145	0.128722	0.144284	0.161502
584	0.009146	0.019086	0.037712	0.071094	0.128651	0.144209	0.161423
585	0.009135	0.019065	0.037679	0.071044	0.128580	0.144134	0.161344
586	0.009123	0.019045	0.037646	0.070994	0.128510	0.144060	0.161265
587	0.009112	0.019025	0.037613	0.070943	0.128439	0.143985	0.161186
588	0.009100	0.019005	0.037580	0.070893	0.128369	0.143910	0.161107
589	0.009089	0.018985	0.037547	0.070843	0.128299	0.143836	0.161029
590	0.009078	0.018965	0.037514	0.070793	0.128229	0.143762	0.160951

Unit	60	65	70	75	80	81	82
591	0.009066	0.018945	0.037481	0.070744	0.128159	0.143688	0.160873
592	0.009055	0.018925	0.037449	0.070694	0.128089	0.143614	0.160795
593	0.009044	0.018905	0.037416	0.070645	0.128019	0.143540	0.160717
594	0.009033	0.018885	0.037384	0.070595	0.127950	0.143467	0.160640
595	0.009021	0.018866	0.037351	0.070546	0.127881	0.143394	0.160563
596	0.009010	0.018846	0.037319	0.070497	0.127812	0.143320	0.160485
597	0.008999	0.018826	0.037287	0.070448	0.127743	0.143247	0.160408
598	0.008988	0.018807	0.037255	0.070399	0.127674	0.143174	0.160332
599	0.008977	0.018787	0.037223	0.070350	0.127605	0.143102	0.160255
600	0.008966	0.018768	0.037191	0.070301	0.127537	0.143029	0.160178
601	0.008955	0.018748	0.037159	0.070253	0.127468	0.142957	0.160102
602	0.008944	0.018729	0.037127	0.070204	0.127400	0.142885	0.160026
603	0.008933	0.018710	0.037096	0.070156	0.127332	0.142813	0.159950
604	0.008922	0.018690	0.037064	0.070108	0.127264	0.142741	0.159874
605	0.008911	0.018671	0.037033	0.070060	0.127196	0.142669	0.159798
606	0.008900	0.018652	0.037001	0.070012	0.127129	0.142597	0.159723
607	0.008890	0.018633	0.036970	0.069964	0.127061	0.142526	0.159647
608	0.008879	0.018614	0.036938	0.069916	0.126994	0.142454	0.159572
609	0.008868	0.018595	0.036907	0.069868	0.126927	0.142383	0.159497
610	0.008857	0.018576	0.036876	0.069821	0.126860	0.142312	0.159422
611	0.008847	0.018557	0.036845	0.069773	0.126793	0.142241	0.159347
612	0.008836	0.018538	0.036814	0.069726	0.126726	0.142171	0.159273
613	0.008825	0.018519	0.036783	0.069679	0.126660	0.142100	0.159198
614	0.008815	0.018501	0.036752	0.069631	0.126593	0.142030	0.159124
615	0.008804	0.018482	0.036721	0.069584	0.126527	0.141960	0.159050
616	0.008794	0.018463	0.036691	0.069538	0.126461	0.141889	0.158976
617	0.008783	0.018445	0.036660	0.069491	0.126395	0.141820	0.158902
618	0.008773	0.018426	0.036630	0.069444	0.126329	0.141750	0.158828
619	0.008762	0.018408	0.036599	0.069397	0.126263	0.141680	0.158755
620	0.008752	0.018389	0.036569	0.069351	0.126197	0.141611	0.158682
621	0.008742	0.018371	0.036538	0.069305	0.126132	0.141541	0.158608
622	0.008731	0.018352	0.036508	0.069258	0.126067	0.141472	0.158535
623	0.008721	0.018334	0.036478	0.069212	0.126002	0.141403	0.158462
624	0.008711	0.018316	0.036448	0.069166	0.125937	0.141334	0.158390
625	0.008700	0.018298	0.036418	0.069120	0.125872	0.141265	0.158317

Unit	60	65	70	75	80	81	82
626	0.008690	0.018279	0.036388	0.069074	0.125807	0.141197	0.158245
627	0.008680	0.018261	0.036358	0.069029	0.125742	0.141128	0.158172
628	0.008670	0.018243	0.036328	0.068983	0.125678	0.141060	0.158100
629	0.008659	0.018225	0.036299	0.068937	0.125613	0.140991	0.158028
630	0.008649	0.018207	0.036269	0.068892	0.125549	0.140923	0.157956
631	0.008639	0.018189	0.036239	0.068847	0.125485	0.140855	0.157885
632	0.008629	0.018171	0.036210	0.068801	0.125421	0.140788	0.157813
633	0.008619	0.018153	0.036180	0.068756	0.125357	0.140720	0.157742
634	0.008609	0.018136	0.036151	0.068711	0.125294	0.140653	0.157670
635	0.008599	0.018118	0.036122	0.068666	0.125230	0.140585	0.157599
636	0.008589	0.018100	0.036092	0.068622	0.125167	0.140518	0.157528
637	0.008579	0.018083	0.036063	0.068577	0.125103	0.140451	0.157457
638	0.008569	0.018065	0.036034	0.068532	0.125040	0.140384	0.157387
639	0.008559	0.018047	0.036005	0.068488	0.124977	0.140317	0.157316
640	0.008550	0.018030	0.035976	0.068443	0.124914	0.140250	0.157246
641	0.008540	0.018012	0.035947	0.068399	0.124851	0.140184	0.157175
642	0.008530	0.017995	0.035918	0.068355	0.124789	0.140117	0.157105
643	0.008520	0.017978	0.035890	0.068310	0.124726	0.140051	0.157035
644	0.008510	0.017960	0.035861	0.068266	0.124664	0.139985	0.156966
645	0.008501	0.017943	0.035832	0.068222	0.124602	0.139919	0.156896
646	0.008491	0.017926	0.035804	0.068179	0.124540	0.139853	0.156826
647	0.008481	0.017908	0.035775	0.068135	0.124478	0.139787	0.156757
648	0.008472	0.017891	0.035747	0.068091	0.124416	0.139722	0.156687
649	0.008462	0.017874	0.035719	0.068048	0.124354	0.139656	0.156618
650	0.008452	0.017857	0.035690	0.068004	0.124292	0.139591	0.156549
651	0.008443	0.017840	0.035662	0.067961	0.124231	0.139526	0.156480
652	0.008433	0.017823	0.035634	0.067918	0.124169	0.139461	0.156412
653	0.008424	0.017806	0.035606	0.067874	0.124108	0.139396	0.156343
654	0.008414	0.017789	0.035578	0.067831	0.124047	0.139331	0.156275
655	0.008405	0.017772	0.035550	0.067788	0.123986	0.139266	0.156206
656	0.008395	0.017755	0.035522	0.067745	0.123925	0.139201	0.156138
657	0.008386	0.017738	0.035494	0.067703	0.123864	0.139137	0.156070
658	0.008377	0.017722	0.035466	0.067660	0.123804	0.139073	0.156002
659	0.008367	0.017705	0.035439	0.067617	0.123743	0.139009	0.155934
660	0.008358	0.017688	0.035411	0.067575	0.123683	0.138944	0.155867

Unit	60	65	70	75	80	81	82
661	0.008349	0.017672	0.035383	0.067532	0.123623	0.138881	0.155799
662	0.008339	0.017655	0.035356	0.067490	0.123562	0.138817	0.155732
663	0.008330	0.017639	0.035328	0.067448	0.123502	0.138753	0.155664
664	0.008321	0.017622	0.035301	0.067405	0.123443	0.138689	0.155597
665	0.008311	0.017606	0.035274	0.067363	0.123383	0.138626	0.155530
666	0.008302	0.017589	0.035246	0.067321	0.123323	0.138563	0.155463
667	0.008293	0.017573	0.035219	0.067279	0.123264	0.138500	0.155396
668	0.008284	0.017556	0.035192	0.067238	0.123204	0.138436	0.155330
669	0.008275	0.017540	0.035165	0.067196	0.123145	0.138374	0.155263
670	0.008266	0.017524	0.035138	0.067154	0.123086	0.138311	0.155197
671	0.008257	0.017508	0.035111	0.067113	0.123027	0.138248	0.155131
672	0.008248	0.017491	0.035084	0.067071	0.122968	0.138185	0.155065
673	0.008239	0.017475	0.035057	0.067030	0.122909	0.138123	0.154999
674	0.008230	0.017459	0.035031	0.066988	0.122850	0.138061	0.154933
675	0.008221	0.017443	0.035004	0.066947	0.122791	0.137998	0.154867
676	0.008212	0.017427	0.034977	0.066906	0.122733	0.137936	0.154801
677	0.008203	0.017411	0.034951	0.066865	0.122674	0.137874	0.154736
678	0.008194	0.017395	0.034924	0.066824	0.122616	0.137813	0.154670
679	0.008185	0.017379	0.034898	0.066783	0.122558	0.137751	0.154605
680	0.008176	0.017363	0.034871	0.066743	0.122500	0.137689	0.154540
681	0.008167	0.017347	0.034845	0.066702	0.122442	0.137628	0.154475
682	0.008158	0.017331	0.034819	0.066661	0.122384	0.137566	0.154410
683	0.008149	0.017316	0.034792	0.066621	0.122326	0.137505	0.154345
684	0.008141	0.017300	0.034766	0.066580	0.122269	0.137444	0.154281
685	0.008132	0.017284	0.034740	0.066540	0.122211	0.137383	0.154216
686	0.008123	0.017269	0.034714	0.066500	0.122154	0.137322	0.154152
687	0.008114	0.017253	0.034688	0.066459	0.122097	0.137261	0.154088
688	0.008106	0.017237	0.034662	0.066419	0.122040	0.137200	0.154023
689	0.008097	0.017222	0.034636	0.066379	0.121983	0.137140	0.153959
690	0.008088	0.017206	0.034610	0.066339	0.121926	0.137079	0.153895
691	0.008080	0.017191	0.034584	0.066299	0.121869	0.137019	0.153832
692	0.008071	0.017175	0.034559	0.066260	0.121812	0.136959	0.153768
693	0.008063	0.017160	0.034533	0.066220	0.121755	0.136899	0.153704
694	0.008054	0.017145	0.034507	0.066180	0.121699	0.136839	0.153641
695	0.008046	0.017129	0.034482	0.066141	0.121642	0.136779	0.153578

Unit	60	65	70	75	80	81	82
696	0.008037	0.017114	0.034456	0.066101	0.121586	0.136719	0.153514
697	0.008029	0.017099	0.034431	0.066062	0.121530	0.136659	0.153451
698	0.008020	0.017084	0.034406	0.066023	0.121474	0.136600	0.153388
699	0.008012	0.017068	0.034380	0.065984	0.121418	0.136540	0.153325
700	0.008003	0.017053	0.034355	0.065944	0.121362	0.136481	0.153263
701	0.007995	0.017038	0.034330	0.065905	0.121306	0.136422	0.153200
702	0.007986	0.017023	0.034305	0.065866	0.121251	0.136363	0.153138
703	0.007978	0.017008	0.034279	0.065827	0.121195	0.136304	0.153075
704	0.007970	0.016993	0.034254	0.065789	0.121140	0.136245	0.153013
705	0.007961	0.016978	0.034229	0.065750	0.121084	0.136186	0.152951
706	0.007953	0.016963	0.034204	0.065711	0.121029	0.136127	0.152889
707	0.007945	0.016948	0.034179	0.065673	0.120974	0.136069	0.152827
708	0.007936	0.016933	0.034155	0.065634	0.120919	0.136010	0.152765
709	0.007928	0.016918	0.034130	0.065596	0.120864	0.135952	0.152703
710	0.007920	0.016903	0.034105	0.065557	0.120809	0.135894	0.152642
711	0.007912	0.016889	0.034080	0.065519	0.120754	0.135836	0.152580
712	0.007904	0.016874	0.034056	0.065481	0.120700	0.135778	0.152519
713	0.007895	0.016859	0.034031	0.065443	0.120645	0.135720	0.152457
714	0.007887	0.016845	0.034007	0.065405	0.120591	0.135662	0.152396
715	0.007879	0.016830	0.033982	0.065367	0.120537	0.135604	0.152335
716	0.007871	0.016815	0.033958	0.065329	0.120482	0.135547	0.152274
717	0.007863	0.016801	0.033933	0.065291	0.120428	0.135489	0.152213
718	0.007855	0.016786	0.033909	0.065253	0.120374	0.135432	0.152153
719	0.007847	0.016772	0.033885	0.065215	0.120320	0.135374	0.152092
720	0.007839	0.016757	0.033860	0.065178	0.120266	0.135317	0.152032
721	0.007831	0.016743	0.033836	0.065140	0.120213	0.135260	0.151971
722	0.007823	0.016728	0.033812	0.065103	0.120159	0.135203	0.151911
723	0.007815	0.016714	0.033788	0.065065	0.120106	0.135146	0.151851
724	0.007807	0.016700	0.033764	0.065028	0.120052	0.135090	0.151791
725	0.007799	0.016685	0.033740	0.064991	0.119999	0.135033	0.151731
726	0.007791	0.016671	0.033716	0.064954	0.119946	0.134976	0.151671
727	0.007783	0.016657	0.033692	0.064917	0.119892	0.134920	0.151611
728	0.007775	0.016643	0.033669	0.064880	0.119839	0.134863	0.151551
729	0.007767	0.016628	0.033645	0.064843	0.119786	0.134807	0.151492
730	0.007759	0.016614	0.033621	0.064806	0.119734	0.134751	0.151432

Unit	60	65	70	75	80	81	82
731	0.007752	0.016600	0.033597	0.064769	0.119681	0.134695	0.151373
732	0.007744	0.016586	0.033574	0.064732	0.119628	0.134639	0.151314
733	0.007736	0.016572	0.033550	0.064696	0.119576	0.134583	0.151255
734	0.007728	0.016558	0.033527	0.064659	0.119523	0.134527	0.151196
735	0.007720	0.016544	0.033503	0.064622	0.119471	0.134472	0.151137
736	0.007713	0.016530	0.033480	0.064586	0.119418	0.134416	0.151078
737	0.007705	0.016516	0.033456	0.064550	0.119366	0.134361	0.151019
738	0.007697	0.016502	0.033433	0.064513	0.119314	0.134305	0.150961
739	0.007690	0.016488	0.033410	0.064477	0.119262	0.134250	0.150902
740	0.007682	0.016474	0.033386	0.064441	0.119210	0.134195	0.150844
741	0.007674	0.016460	0.033363	0.064405	0.119158	0.134140	0.150785
742	0.007667	0.016447	0.033340	0.064369	0.119107	0.134085	0.150727
743	0.007659	0.016433	0.033317	0.064333	0.119055	0.134030	0.150669
744	0.007652	0.016419	0.033294	0.064297	0.119004	0.133975	0.150611
745	0.007644	0.016405	0.033271	0.064261	0.118952	0.133920	0.150553
746	0.007636	0.016392	0.033248	0.064225	0.118901	0.133866	0.150495
747	0.007629	0.016378	0.033225	0.064190	0.118850	0.133811	0.150438
748	0.007621	0.016365	0.033202	0.064154	0.118798	0.133757	0.150380
749	0.007614	0.016351	0.033179	0.064118	0.118747	0.133703	0.150322
750	0.007606	0.016337	0.033157	0.064083	0.118696	0.133648	0.150265
751	0.007599	0.016324	0.033134	0.064047	0.118645	0.133594	0.150208
752	0.007591	0.016310	0.033111	0.064012	0.118595	0.133540	0.150151
753	0.007584	0.016297	0.033089	0.063977	0.118544	0.133486	0.150093
754	0.007577	0.016283	0.033066	0.063942	0.118493	0.133432	0.150036
755	0.007569	0.016270	0.033043	0.063906	0.118443	0.133379	0.149979
756	0.007562	0.016257	0.033021	0.063871	0.118392	0.133325	0.149923
757	0.007554	0.016243	0.032999	0.063836	0.118342	0.133271	0.149866
758	0.007547	0.016230	0.032976	0.063801	0.118292	0.133218	0.149809
759	0.007540	0.016217	0.032954	0.063766	0.118241	0.133165	0.149753
760	0.007533	0.016203	0.032931	0.063732	0.118191	0.133111	0.149696
761	0.007525	0.016190	0.032909	0.063697	0.118141	0.133058	0.149640
762	0.007518	0.016177	0.032887	0.063662	0.118091	0.133005	0.149584
763	0.007511	0.016164	0.032865	0.063627	0.118041	0.132952	0.149528
764	0.007503	0.016151	0.032843	0.063593	0.117992	0.132899	0.149471
765	0.007496	0.016138	0.032821	0.063558	0.117942	0.132846	0.149416

Unit	60	65	70	75	80	81	82
766	0.007489	0.016124	0.032798	0.063524	0.117892	0.132793	0.149360
767	0.007482	0.016111	0.032776	0.063489	0.117843	0.132741	0.149304
768	0.007475	0.016098	0.032754	0.063455	0.117793	0.132688	0.149248
769	0.007467	0.016085	0.032733	0.063421	0.117744	0.132636	0.149193
770	0.007460	0.016072	0.032711	0.063387	0.117695	0.132583	0.149137
771	0.007453	0.016059	0.032689	0.063353	0.117646	0.132531	0.149082
772	0.007446	0.016046	0.032667	0.063318	0.117597	0.132479	0.149026
773	0.007439	0.016034	0.032645	0.063284	0.117548	0.132427	0.148971
774	0.007432	0.016021	0.032624	0.063251	0.117499	0.132375	0.148916
775	0.007425	0.016008	0.032602	0.063217	0.117450	0.132323	0.148861
776	0.007418	0.015995	0.032580	0.063183	0.117401	0.132271	0.148806
777	0.007411	0.015982	0.032559	0.063149	0.117353	0.132219	0.148751
778	0.007404	0.015969	0.032537	0.063115	0.117304	0.132167	0.148696
779	0.007397	0.015957	0.032516	0.063082	0.117255	0.132116	0.148642
780	0.007390	0.015944	0.032494	0.063048	0.117207	0.132064	0.148587
781	0.007383	0.015931	0.032473	0.063015	0.117159	0.132013	0.148533
782	0.007376	0.015919	0.032451	0.062981	0.117110	0.131962	0.148478
783	0.007369	0.015906	0.032430	0.062948	0.117062	0.131910	0.148424
784	0.007362	0.015893	0.032409	0.062914	0.117014	0.131859	0.148370
785	0.007355	0.015881	0.032388	0.062881	0.116966	0.131808	0.148316
786	0.007348	0.015868	0.032366	0.062848	0.116918	0.131757	0.148262
787	0.007341	0.015856	0.032345	0.062815	0.116870	0.131706	0.148208
788	0.007334	0.015843	0.032324	0.062782	0.116823	0.131655	0.148154
789	0.007327	0.015831	0.032303	0.062749	0.116775	0.131604	0.148100
790	0.007321	0.015818	0.032282	0.062716	0.116727	0.131554	0.148046
791	0.007314	0.015806	0.032261	0.062683	0.116680	0.131503	0.147993
792	0.007307	0.015793	0.032240	0.062650	0.116632	0.131453	0.147939
793	0.007300	0.015781	0.032219	0.062617	0.116585	0.131402	0.147886
794	0.007293	0.015769	0.032198	0.062584	0.116538	0.131352	0.147832
795	0.007287	0.015756	0.032177	0.062552	0.116490	0.131302	0.147779
796	0.007280	0.015744	0.032156	0.062519	0.116443	0.131252	0.147726
797	0.007273	0.015732	0.032136	0.062486	0.116396	0.131201	0.147673
798	0.007266	0.015720	0.032115	0.062454	0.116349	0.131151	0.147620
799	0.007260	0.015707	0.032094	0.062422	0.116302	0.131102	0.147567
800	0.007253	0.015695	0.032074	0.062389	0.116256	0.131052	0.147514

Unit	60	65	70	75	80	81	82
801	0.007246	0.015683	0.032053	0.062357	0.116209	0.131002	0.147461
802	0.007240	0.015671	0.032032	0.062325	0.116162	0.130952	0.147409
803	0.007233	0.015659	0.032012	0.062292	0.116116	0.130903	0.147356
804	0.007226	0.015646	0.031991	0.062260	0.116069	0.130853	0.147304
805	0.007220	0.015634	0.031971	0.062228	0.116023	0.130804	0.147251
806	0.007213	0.015622	0.031951	0.062196	0.115976	0.130754	0.147199
807	0.007207	0.015610	0.031930	0.062164	0.115930	0.130705	0.147147
808	0.007200	0.015598	0.031910	0.062132	0.115884	0.130656	0.147094
809	0.007194	0.015586	0.031890	0.062100	0.115838	0.130607	0.147042
810	0.007187	0.015574	0.031869	0.062068	0.115792	0.130558	0.146990
811	0.007180	0.015562	0.031849	0.062037	0.115746	0.130509	0.146938
812	0.007174	0.015551	0.031829	0.062005	0.115700	0.130460	0.146887
813	0.007167	0.015539	0.031809	0.061973	0.115654	0.130411	0.146835
814	0.007161	0.015527	0.031789	0.061942	0.115608	0.130362	0.146783
815	0.007154	0.015515	0.031768	0.061910	0.115562	0.130314	0.146732
816	0.007148	0.015503	0.031748	0.061878	0.115517	0.130265	0.146680
817	0.007142	0.015491	0.031728	0.061847	0.115471	0.130217	0.146629
818	0.007135	0.015480	0.031708	0.061816	0.115426	0.130168	0.146577
819	0.007129	0.015468	0.031689	0.061784	0.115380	0.130120	0.146526
820	0.007122	0.015456	0.031669	0.061753	0.115335	0.130072	0.146475
821	0.007116	0.015444	0.031649	0.061722	0.115290	0.130023	0.146424
822	0.007110	0.015433	0.031629	0.061691	0.115245	0.129975	0.146373
823	0.007103	0.015421	0.031609	0.061659	0.115200	0.129927	0.146322
824	0.007097	0.015409	0.031589	0.061628	0.115155	0.129879	0.146271
825	0.007090	0.015398	0.031570	0.061597	0.115110	0.129831	0.146220
826	0.007084	0.015386	0.031550	0.061566	0.115065	0.129784	0.146169
827	0.007078	0.015375	0.031530	0.061536	0.115020	0.129736	0.146119
828	0.007072	0.015363	0.031511	0.061505	0.114975	0.129688	0.146068
829	0.007065	0.015352	0.031491	0.061474	0.114931	0.129641	0.146018
830	0.007059	0.015340	0.031472	0.061443	0.114886	0.129593	0.145967
831	0.007053	0.015329	0.031452	0.061412	0.114841	0.129546	0.145917
832	0.007046	0.015317	0.031433	0.061382	0.114797	0.129498	0.145867
833	0.007040	0.015306	0.031413	0.061351	0.114753	0.129451	0.145817
834	0.007034	0.015294	0.031394	0.061321	0.114708	0.129404	0.145767
835	0.007028	0.015283	0.031375	0.061290	0.114664	0.129357	0.145717

Unit	60	65	70	75	80	81	82
836	0.007022	0.015272	0.031355	0.061260	0.114620	0.129310	0.145667
837	0.007015	0.015260	0.031336	0.061229	0.114576	0.129263	0.145617
838	0.007009	0.015249	0.031317	0.061199	0.114532	0.129216	0.145567
839	0.007003	0.015238	0.031298	0.061169	0.114488	0.129169	0.145517
840	0.006997	0.015226	0.031278	0.061138	0.114444	0.129122	0.145468
841	0.006991	0.015215	0.031259	0.061108	0.114400	0.129076	0.145418
842	0.006985	0.015204	0.031240	0.061078	0.114356	0.129029	0.145369
843	0.006979	0.015193	0.031221	0.061048	0.114313	0.128982	0.145319
844	0.006972	0.015181	0.031202	0.061018	0.114269	0.128936	0.145270
845	0.006966	0.015170	0.031183	0.060988	0.114225	0.128889	0.145221
846	0.006960	0.015159	0.031164	0.060958	0.114182	0.128843	0.145172
847	0.006954	0.015148	0.031145	0.060928	0.114138	0.128797	0.145123
848	0.006948	0.015137	0.031126	0.060898	0.114095	0.128751	0.145073
849	0.006942	0.015126	0.031107	0.060869	0.114052	0.128705	0.145025
850	0.006936	0.015115	0.031088	0.060839	0.114009	0.128659	0.144976
851	0.006930	0.015104	0.031070	0.060809	0.113966	0.128613	0.144927
852	0.006924	0.015093	0.031051	0.060780	0.113922	0.128567	0.144878
853	0.006918	0.015082	0.031032	0.060750	0.113879	0.128521	0.144830
854	0.006912	0.015071	0.031013	0.060720	0.113836	0.128475	0.144781
855	0.006906	0.015060	0.030995	0.060691	0.113794	0.128429	0.144732
856	0.006900	0.015049	0.030976	0.060662	0.113751	0.128384	0.144684
857	0.006894	0.015038	0.030958	0.060632	0.113708	0.128338	0.144636
858	0.006888	0.015027	0.030939	0.060603	0.113665	0.128293	0.144587
859	0.006883	0.015016	0.030920	0.060574	0.113623	0.128247	0.144539
860	0.006877	0.015005	0.030902	0.060544	0.113580	0.128202	0.144491
861	0.006871	0.014994	0.030883	0.060515	0.113538	0.128157	0.144443
862	0.006865	0.014984	0.030865	0.060486	0.113495	0.128111	0.144395
863	0.006859	0.014973	0.030847	0.060457	0.113453	0.128066	0.144347
864	0.006853	0.014962	0.030828	0.060428	0.113411	0.128021	0.144299
865	0.006847	0.014951	0.030810	0.060399	0.113368	0.127976	0.144251
866	0.006841	0.014941	0.030792	0.060370	0.113326	0.127931	0.144204
867	0.006836	0.014930	0.030773	0.060341	0.113284	0.127886	0.144156
868	0.006830	0.014919	0.030755	0.060312	0.113242	0.127842	0.144108
869	0.006824	0.014908	0.030737	0.060283	0.113200	0.127797	0.144061
870	0.006818	0.014898	0.030719	0.060254	0.113158	0.127752	0.144014

Unit	60	65	70	75	80	81	82
871	0.006813	0.014887	0.030701	0.060226	0.113116	0.127707	0.143966
872	0.006807	0.014877	0.030682	0.060197	0.113075	0.127663	0.143919
873	0.006801	0.014866	0.030664	0.060168	0.113033	0.127618	0.143872
874	0.006795	0.014855	0.030646	0.060140	0.112991	0.127574	0.143825
875	0.006790	0.014845	0.030628	0.060111	0.112950	0.127530	0.143777
876	0.006784	0.014834	0.030610	0.060083	0.112908	0.127485	0.143730
877	0.006778	0.014824	0.030592	0.060054	0.112867	0.127441	0.143684
878	0.006772	0.014813	0.030574	0.060026	0.112825	0.127397	0.143637
879	0.006767	0.014803	0.030556	0.059998	0.112784	0.127353	0.143590
880	0.006761	0.014792	0.030539	0.059969	0.112743	0.127309	0.143543
881	0.006755	0.014782	0.030521	0.059941	0.112701	0.127265	0.143496
882	0.006750	0.014772	0.030503	0.059913	0.112660	0.127221	0.143450
883	0.006744	0.014761	0.030485	0.059885	0.112619	0.127177	0.143403
884	0.006739	0.014751	0.030467	0.059857	0.112578	0.127134	0.143357
885	0.006733	0.014740	0.030450	0.059829	0.112537	0.127090	0.143310
886	0.006727	0.014730	0.030432	0.059800	0.112496	0.127046	0.143264
887	0.006722	0.014720	0.030414	0.059772	0.112455	0.127003	0.143218
888	0.006716	0.014709	0.030397	0.059745	0.112415	0.126959	0.143172
889	0.006711	0.014699	0.030379	0.059717	0.112374	0.126916	0.143126
890	0.006705	0.014689	0.030361	0.059689	0.112333	0.126872	0.143079
891	0.006699	0.014679	0.030344	0.059661	0.112293	0.126829	0.143033
892	0.006694	0.014668	0.030326	0.059633	0.112252	0.126786	0.142988
893	0.006688	0.014658	0.030309	0.059605	0.112212	0.126743	0.142942
894	0.006683	0.014648	0.030292	0.059578	0.112171	0.126700	0.142896
895	0.006677	0.014638	0.030274	0.059550	0.112131	0.126657	0.142850
896	0.006672	0.014628	0.030257	0.059523	0.112091	0.126614	0.142805
897	0.006666	0.014618	0.030239	0.059495	0.112050	0.126571	0.142759
898	0.006661	0.014607	0.030222	0.059468	0.112010	0.126528	0.142713
899	0.006655	0.014597	0.030205	0.059440	0.111970	0.126485	0.142668
900	0.006650	0.014587	0.030187	0.059413	0.111930	0.126442	0.142623
901	0.006645	0.014577	0.030170	0.059385	0.111890	0.126400	0.142577
902	0.006639	0.014567	0.030153	0.059358	0.111850	0.126357	0.142532
903	0.006634	0.014557	0.030136	0.059331	0.111810	0.126314	0.142487
904	0.006628	0.014547	0.030119	0.059303	0.111770	0.126272	0.142442
905	0.006623	0.014537	0.030101	0.059276	0.111731	0.126229	0.142396

Unit	60	65	70	75	80	81	82
906	0.006618	0.014527	0.030084	0.059249	0.111691	0.126187	0.142351
907	0.006612	0.014517	0.030067	0.059222	0.111651	0.126145	0.142306
908	0.006607	0.014507	0.030050	0.059195	0.111612	0.126102	0.142262
909	0.006601	0.014497	0.030033	0.059168	0.111572	0.126060	0.142217
910	0.006596	0.014487	0.030016	0.059141	0.111533	0.126018	0.142172
911	0.006591	0.014478	0.029999	0.059114	0.111493	0.125976	0.142127
912	0.006585	0.014468	0.029982	0.059087	0.111454	0.125934	0.142083
913	0.006580	0.014458	0.029965	0.059060	0.111414	0.125892	0.142038
914	0.006575	0.014448	0.029949	0.059033	0.111375	0.125850	0.141994
915	0.006570	0.014438	0.029932	0.059006	0.111336	0.125808	0.141949
916	0.006564	0.014428	0.029915	0.058980	0.111297	0.125767	0.141905
917	0.006559	0.014419	0.029898	0.058953	0.111258	0.125725	0.141860
918	0.006554	0.014409	0.029881	0.058926	0.111219	0.125683	0.141816
919	0.006548	0.014399	0.029865	0.058900	0.111180	0.125642	0.141772
920	0.006543	0.014389	0.029848	0.058873	0.111141	0.125600	0.141728
921	0.006538	0.014380	0.029831	0.058847	0.111102	0.125559	0.141684
922	0.006533	0.014370	0.029815	0.058820	0.111063	0.125517	0.141640
923	0.006528	0.014360	0.029798	0.058794	0.111024	0.125476	0.141596
924	0.006522	0.014351	0.029781	0.058767	0.110986	0.125435	0.141552
925	0.006517	0.014341	0.029765	0.058741	0.110947	0.125393	0.141508
926	0.006512	0.014331	0.029748	0.058714	0.110908	0.125352	0.141464
927	0.006507	0.014322	0.029732	0.058688	0.110870	0.125311	0.141421
928	0.006502	0.014312	0.029715	0.058662	0.110831	0.125270	0.141377
929	0.006496	0.014303	0.029699	0.058636	0.110793	0.125229	0.141333
930	0.006491	0.014293	0.029682	0.058610	0.110755	0.125188	0.141290
931	0.006486	0.014283	0.029666	0.058583	0.110716	0.125147	0.141246
932	0.006481	0.014274	0.029650	0.058557	0.110678	0.125106	0.141203
933	0.006476	0.014264	0.029633	0.058531	0.110640	0.125066	0.141160
934	0.006471	0.014255	0.029617	0.058505	0.110602	0.125025	0.141116
935	0.006466	0.014245	0.029601	0.058479	0.110564	0.124984	0.141073
936	0.006461	0.014236	0.029584	0.058453	0.110526	0.124944	0.141030
937	0.006456	0.014227	0.029568	0.058427	0.110488	0.124903	0.140987
938	0.006450	0.014217	0.029552	0.058402	0.110450	0.124862	0.140944
939	0.006445	0.014208	0.029536	0.058376	0.110412	0.124822	0.140901
940	0.006440	0.014198	0.029519	0.058350	0.110374	0.124782	0.140858

Unit	60	65	70	75	80	81	82
941	0.006435	0.014189	0.029503	0.058324	0.110336	0.124741	0.140815
942	0.006430	0.014180	0.029487	0.058299	0.110298	0.124701	0.140772
943	0.006425	0.014170	0.029471	0.058273	0.110261	0.124661	0.140729
944	0.006420	0.014161	0.029455	0.058247	0.110223	0.124621	0.140687
945	0.006415	0.014152	0.029439	0.058222	0.110186	0.124581	0.140644
946	0.006410	0.014142	0.029423	0.058196	0.110148	0.124541	0.140602
947	0.006405	0.014133	0.029407	0.058171	0.110111	0.124501	0.140559
948	0.006400	0.014124	0.029391	0.058145	0.110073	0.124461	0.140517
949	0.006395	0.014114	0.029375	0.058120	0.110036	0.124421	0.140474
950	0.006390	0.014105	0.029359	0.058094	0.109999	0.124381	0.140432
951	0.006385	0.014096	0.029343	0.058069	0.109961	0.124341	0.140389
952	0.006380	0.014087	0.029327	0.058044	0.109924	0.124301	0.140347
953	0.006375	0.014078	0.029312	0.058018	0.109887	0.124262	0.140305
954	0.006371	0.014068	0.029296	0.057993	0.109850	0.124222	0.140263
955	0.006366	0.014059	0.029280	0.057968	0.109813	0.124183	0.140221
956	0.006361	0.014050	0.029264	0.057943	0.109776	0.124143	0.140179
957	0.006356	0.014041	0.029248	0.057918	0.109739	0.124104	0.140137
958	0.006351	0.014032	0.029233	0.057892	0.109702	0.124064	0.140095
959	0.006346	0.014023	0.029217	0.057867	0.109665	0.124025	0.140053
960	0.006341	0.014014	0.029201	0.057842	0.109628	0.123986	0.140011
961	0.006336	0.014005	0.029186	0.057817	0.109592	0.123946	0.139970
962	0.006331	0.013996	0.029170	0.057792	0.109555	0.123907	0.139928
963	0.006327	0.013987	0.029155	0.057767	0.109518	0.123868	0.139886
964	0.006322	0.013978	0.029139	0.057743	0.109482	0.123829	0.139845
965	0.006317	0.013969	0.029123	0.057718	0.109445	0.123790	0.139803
966	0.006312	0.013960	0.029108	0.057693	0.109409	0.123751	0.139762
967	0.006307	0.013951	0.029092	0.057668	0.109372	0.123712	0.139720
968	0.006302	0.013942	0.029077	0.057643	0.109336	0.123673	0.139679
969	0.006298	0.013933	0.029061	0.057619	0.109300	0.123634	0.139638
970	0.006293	0.013924	0.029046	0.057594	0.109263	0.123596	0.139597
971	0.006288	0.013915	0.029031	0.057569	0.109227	0.123557	0.139555
972	0.006283	0.013906	0.029015	0.057545	0.109191	0.123518	0.139514
973	0.006279	0.013897	0.029000	0.057520	0.109155	0.123480	0.139473
974	0.006274	0.013888	0.028985	0.057496	0.109119	0.123441	0.139432
975	0.006269	0.013879	0.028969	0.057471	0.109083	0.123403	0.139391

Unit	60	65	70	75	80	81	82
976	0.006264	0.013870	0.028954	0.057447	0.109047	0.123364	0.139350
977	0.006260	0.013862	0.028939	0.057422	0.109011	0.123326	0.139309
978	0.006255	0.013853	0.028924	0.057398	0.108975	0.123287	0.139269
979	0.006250	0.013844	0.028908	0.057374	0.108939	0.123249	0.139228
980	0.006246	0.013835	0.028893	0.057349	0.108903	0.123211	0.139187
981	0.006241	0.013827	0.028878	0.057325	0.108867	0.123173	0.139147
982	0.006236	0.013818	0.028863	0.057301	0.108832	0.123134	0.139106
983	0.006231	0.013809	0.028848	0.057277	0.108796	0.123096	0.139066
984	0.006227	0.013800	0.028833	0.057253	0.108760	0.123058	0.139025
985	0.006222	0.013792	0.028818	0.057228	0.108725	0.123020	0.138985
986	0.006217	0.013783	0.028803	0.057204	0.108689	0.122982	0.138944
987	0.006213	0.013774	0.028788	0.057180	0.108654	0.122944	0.138904
988	0.006208	0.013766	0.028773	0.057156	0.108618	0.122907	0.138864
989	0.006204	0.013757	0.028758	0.057132	0.108583	0.122869	0.138823
990	0.006199	0.013748	0.028743	0.057108	0.108548	0.122831	0.138783
991	0.006194	0.013740	0.028728	0.057084	0.108513	0.122793	0.138743
992	0.006190	0.013731	0.028713	0.057060	0.108477	0.122756	0.138703
993	0.006185	0.013722	0.028698	0.057037	0.108442	0.122718	0.138663
994	0.006181	0.013714	0.028683	0.057013	0.108407	0.122681	0.138623
995	0.006176	0.013705	0.028668	0.056989	0.108372	0.122643	0.138583
996	0.006171	0.013697	0.028653	0.056965	0.108337	0.122606	0.138543
997	0.006167	0.013688	0.028639	0.056942	0.108302	0.122568	0.138504
998	0.006162	0.013680	0.028624	0.056918	0.108267	0.122531	0.138464
999	0.006158	0.013671	0.028609	0.056894	0.108232	0.122494	0.138424
1000	0.006153	0.013663	0.028594	0.056871	0.108197	0.122456	0.138385

Unit	60	65	70	75	80	81	82
1010	0.006108	0.013578	0.028448	0.056636	0.107851	0.122087	0.137991
1020	0.006064	0.013496	0.028304	0.056405	0.107510	0.121721	0.137602
1030	0.006021	0.013414	0.028163	0.056177	0.107172	0.121361	0.137218
1040	0.005978	0.013334	0.028023	0.055952	0.106840	0.121005	0.136839
1050	0.005936	0.013255	0.027885	0.055731	0.106511	0.120653	0.136465
1060	0.005895	0.013177	0.027750	0.055512	0.106186	0.120306	0.136095
1070	0.005854	0.013100	0.027616	0.055296	0.105866	0.119963	0.135730
1080	0.005814	0.013025	0.027484	0.055083	0.105549	0.119625	0.135369
1090	0.005775	0.012950	0.027354	0.054872	0.105237	0.119290	0.135012
1100	0.005736	0.012877	0.027226	0.054665	0.104928	0.118959	0.134659
1110	0.005698	0.012805	0.027099	0.054460	0.104622	0.118632	0.134311
1120	0.005660	0.012733	0.026975	0.054258	0.104321	0.118309	0.133966
1130	0.005623	0.012663	0.026851	0.054058	0.104023	0.117990	0.133626
1140	0.005587	0.012594	0.026730	0.053860	0.103728	0.117674	0.133289
1150	0.005551	0.012526	0.026610	0.053666	0.103437	0.117362	0.132956
1160	0.005516	0.012459	0.026492	0.053473	0.103149	0.117054	0.132627
1170	0.005481	0.012392	0.026375	0.053283	0.102864	0.116749	0.132302
1180	0.005447	0.012327	0.026260	0.053095	0.102583	0.116447	0.131980
1190	0.005413	0.012263	0.026146	0.052909	0.102305	0.116149	0.131661
1200	0.005380	0.012199	0.026034	0.052726	0.102029	0.115854	0.131346
1210	0.005347	0.012136	0.025923	0.052545	0.101757	0.115562	0.131035
1220	0.005314	0.012074	0.025813	0.052365	0.101488	0.115273	0.130726
1230	0.005283	0.012013	0.025705	0.052188	0.101222	0.114987	0.130421
1240	0.005251	0.011953	0.025598	0.052013	0.100958	0.114705	0.130119
1250	0.005220	0.011893	0.025493	0.051840	0.100697	0.114425	0.129820
1260	0.005190	0.011835	0.025388	0.051669	0.100439	0.114148	0.129524
1270	0.005159	0.011777	0.025285	0.051500	0.100184	0.113874	0.129231
1280	0.005130	0.011719	0.025183	0.051332	0.099931	0.113603	0.128942
1290	0.005100	0.011663	0.025083	0.051167	0.099681	0.113334	0.128655
1300	0.005071	0.011607	0.024983	0.051003	0.099434	0.113069	0.128370
1310	0.005043	0.011552	0.024885	0.050841	0.099189	0.112806	0.128089
1320	0.005015	0.011497	0.024788	0.050681	0.098946	0.112545	0.127811
1330	0.004987	0.011444	0.024692	0.050522	0.098706	0.112287	0.127535
1340	0.004959	0.011390	0.024597	0.050366	0.098468	0.112032	0.127261
1350	0.004932	0.011338	0.024503	0.050210	0.098233	0.111779	0.126991

Unit	60	65	70	75	80	81	82
1360	0.004906	0.011286	0.024410	0.050057	0.098000	0.111528	0.126723
1370	0.004879	0.011235	0.024318	0.049905	0.097769	0.111280	0.126457
1380	0.004853	0.011184	0.024227	0.049755	0.097540	0.111034	0.126194
1390	0.004827	0.011134	0.024137	0.049606	0.097314	0.110791	0.125934
1400	0.004802	0.011085	0.024048	0.049458	0.097090	0.110550	0.125675
1410	0.004777	0.011036	0.023961	0.049312	0.096867	0.110311	0.125420
1420	0.004752	0.010987	0.023874	0.049168	0.096647	0.110074	0.125166
1430	0.004727	0.010939	0.023787	0.049025	0.096429	0.109839	0.124915
1440	0.004703	0.010892	0.023702	0.048883	0.096213	0.109607	0.124666
1450	0.004679	0.010845	0.023618	0.048743	0.095999	0.109377	0.124419
1460	0.004656	0.010799	0.023535	0.048604	0.095787	0.109148	0.124175
1470	0.004632	0.010753	0.023452	0.048467	0.095577	0.108922	0.123932
1480	0.004609	0.010708	0.023371	0.048331	0.095368	0.108698	0.123692
1490	0.004586	0.010664	0.023290	0.048196	0.095162	0.108476	0.123454
1500	0.004564	0.010619	0.023210	0.048062	0.094957	0.108255	0.123217
1510	0.004542	0.010576	0.023130	0.047930	0.094754	0.108037	0.122983
1520	0.004519	0.010532	0.023052	0.047799	0.094553	0.107820	0.122751
1530	0.004498	0.010489	0.022974	0.047669	0.094354	0.107605	0.122521
1540	0.004476	0.010447	0.022897	0.047540	0.094156	0.107393	0.122292
1550	0.004455	0.010405	0.022821	0.047412	0.093960	0.107181	0.122066
1560	0.004434	0.010364	0.022746	0.047286	0.093766	0.106972	0.121841
1570	0.004413	0.010323	0.022671	0.047161	0.093573	0.106764	0.121619
1580	0.004392	0.010282	0.022597	0.047037	0.093382	0.106559	0.121398
1590	0.004372	0.010242	0.022524	0.046914	0.093192	0.106354	0.121179
1600	0.004352	0.010202	0.022452	0.046792	0.093004	0.106152	0.120961
1610	0.004332	0.010162	0.022380	0.046671	0.092818	0.105951	0.120746
1620	0.004312	0.010123	0.022308	0.046551	0.092633	0.105752	0.120532
1630	0.004293	0.010085	0.022238	0.046432	0.092450	0.105554	0.120320
1640	0.004273	0.010046	0.022168	0.046315	0.092268	0.105358	0.120109
1650	0.004254	0.010009	0.022099	0.046198	0.092088	0.105163	0.119900
1660	0.004235	0.009971	0.022030	0.046082	0.091909	0.104970	0.119693
1670	0.004217	0.009934	0.021962	0.045968	0.091731	0.104779	0.119488
1680	0.004198	0.009897	0.021895	0.045854	0.091555	0.104589	0.119284
1690	0.004180	0.009861	0.021828	0.045741	0.091380	0.104400	0.119081
1700	0.004162	0.009825	0.021762	0.045629	0.091207	0.104213	0.118880

Unit	60	65	70	75	80	81	82
1710	0.004144	0.009789	0.021696	0.045518	0.091035	0.104028	0.118681
1720	0.004126	0.009753	0.021631	0.045408	0.090864	0.103844	0.118483
1730	0.004108	0.009718	0.021567	0.045299	0.090695	0.103661	0.118286
1740	0.004091	0.009684	0.021503	0.045191	0.090527	0.103479	0.118091
1750	0.004074	0.009649	0.021440	0.045084	0.090360	0.103299	0.117898
1760	0.004057	0.009615	0.021377	0.044977	0.090194	0.103120	0.117705
1770	0.004040	0.009581	0.021315	0.044871	0.090030	0.102943	0.117515
1780	0.004023	0.009548	0.021253	0.044767	0.089867	0.102767	0.117325
1790	0.004006	0.009515	0.021192	0.044663	0.089705	0.102592	0.117137
1800	0.003990	0.009482	0.021131	0.044559	0.089544	0.102418	0.116950
1810	0.003974	0.009449	0.021071	0.044457	0.089384	0.102246	0.116765
1820	0.003958	0.009417	0.021011	0.044356	0.089226	0.102075	0.116581
1830	0.003942	0.009385	0.020952	0.044255	0.089069	0.101905	0.116398
1840	0.003926	0.009353	0.020894	0.044155	0.088913	0.101736	0.116217
1850	0.003910	0.009322	0.020835	0.044056	0.088758	0.101569	0.116037
1860	0.003895	0.009290	0.020778	0.043957	0.088604	0.101402	0.115858
1870	0.003879	0.009260	0.020720	0.043859	0.088451	0.101237	0.115680
1880	0.003864	0.009229	0.020664	0.043762	0.088299	0.101073	0.115503
1890	0.003849	0.009199	0.020607	0.043666	0.088149	0.100910	0.115328
1900	0.003834	0.009168	0.020551	0.043571	0.087999	0.100749	0.115154
1910	0.003819	0.009139	0.020496	0.043476	0.087850	0.100588	0.114981
1920	0.003805	0.009109	0.020441	0.043382	0.087703	0.100428	0.114809
1930	0.003790	0.009080	0.020386	0.043288	0.087556	0.100270	0.114639
1940	0.003776	0.009050	0.020332	0.043196	0.087411	0.100112	0.114469
1950	0.003761	0.009022	0.020279	0.043103	0.087266	0.099956	0.114301
1960	0.003747	0.008993	0.020225	0.043012	0.087123	0.099801	0.114134
1970	0.003733	0.008965	0.020172	0.042921	0.086980	0.099646	0.113967
1980	0.003719	0.008936	0.020120	0.042831	0.086838	0.099493	0.113802
1990	0.003706	0.008908	0.020068	0.042742	0.086698	0.099341	0.113638
2000	0.003692	0.008881	0.020016	0.042653	0.086558	0.099190	0.113475
2010	0.003678	0.008853	0.019965	0.042565	0.086419	0.099039	0.113313
2020	0.003665	0.008826	0.019914	0.042477	0.086281	0.098890	0.113152
2030	0.003652	0.008799	0.019863	0.042390	0.086144	0.098742	0.112993
2040	0.003638	0.008772	0.019813	0.042304	0.086008	0.098594	0.112834
2050	0.003625	0.008745	0.019763	0.042218	0.085872	0.098448	0.112676

Unit	60	65	70	75	80	81	82
2060	0.003612	0.008719	0.019714	0.042133	0.085738	0.098302	0.112519
2070	0.003600	0.008693	0.019665	0.042048	0.085604	0.098158	0.112363
2080	0.003587	0.008667	0.019616	0.041964	0.085472	0.098014	0.112208
2090	0.003574	0.008641	0.019568	0.041881	0.085340	0.097871	0.112054
2100	0.003562	0.008615	0.019520	0.041798	0.085209	0.097729	0.111901
2110	0.003549	0.008590	0.019472	0.041716	0.085079	0.097588	0.111749
2120	0.003537	0.008565	0.019425	0.041634	0.084949	0.097448	0.111598
2130	0.003525	0.008540	0.019378	0.041553	0.084821	0.097309	0.111448
2140	0.003512	0.008515	0.019331	0.041472	0.084693	0.097170	0.111298
2150	0.003500	0.008490	0.019285	0.041392	0.084566	0.097033	0.111150
2160	0.003488	0.008466	0.019239	0.041312	0.084440	0.096896	0.111002
2170	0.003477	0.008442	0.019193	0.041233	0.084314	0.096760	0.110856
2180	0.003465	0.008418	0.019148	0.041154	0.084189	0.096625	0.110710
2190	0.003453	0.008394	0.019103	0.041076	0.084065	0.096490	0.110565
2200	0.003442	0.008370	0.019058	0.040999	0.083942	0.096357	0.110421
2210	0.003430	0.008346	0.019014	0.040922	0.083820	0.096224	0.110277
2220	0.003419	0.008323	0.018970	0.040845	0.083698	0.096092	0.110135
2230	0.003407	0.008300	0.018926	0.040769	0.083577	0.095961	0.109993
2240	0.003396	0.008277	0.018882	0.040693	0.083457	0.095831	0.109853
2250	0.003385	0.008254	0.018839	0.040618	0.083337	0.095701	0.109713
2260	0.003374	0.008231	0.018796	0.040543	0.083218	0.095572	0.109573
2270	0.003363	0.008209	0.018753	0.040469	0.083100	0.095444	0.109435
2280	0.003352	0.008186	0.018711	0.040395	0.082983	0.095316	0.109297
2290	0.003341	0.008164	0.018669	0.040322	0.082866	0.095190	0.109160
2300	0.003331	0.008142	0.018627	0.040249	0.082750	0.095064	0.109024
2310	0.003320	0.008120	0.018586	0.040177	0.082634	0.094938	0.108889
2320	0.003309	0.008098	0.018544	0.040105	0.082519	0.094814	0.108754
2330	0.003299	0.008077	0.018503	0.040033	0.082405	0.094690	0.108621
2340	0.003289	0.008055	0.018463	0.039962	0.082291	0.094567	0.108487
2350	0.003278	0.008034	0.018422	0.039892	0.082179	0.094444	0.108355
2360	0.003268	0.008013	0.018382	0.039821	0.082066	0.094322	0.108223
2370	0.003258	0.007992	0.018342	0.039751	0.081955	0.094201	0.108092
2380	0.003248	0.007971	0.018302	0.039682	0.081844	0.094081	0.107962
2390	0.003238	0.007950	0.018263	0.039613	0.081733	0.093961	0.107833
2400	0.003228	0.007929	0.018224	0.039544	0.081623	0.093841	0.107704

Unit	60	65	70	75	80	81	82
2410	0.003218	0.007909	0.018185	0.039476	0.081514	0.093723	0.107576
2420	0.003208	0.007889	0.018146	0.039408	0.081406	0.093605	0.107448
2430	0.003198	0.007868	0.018107	0.039341	0.081298	0.093488	0.107322
2440	0.003189	0.007848	0.018069	0.039274	0.081190	0.093371	0.107195
2450	0.003179	0.007828	0.018031	0.039207	0.081083	0.093255	0.107070
2460	0.003170	0.007809	0.017994	0.039141	0.080977	0.093140	0.106945
2470	0.003160	0.007789	0.017956	0.039075	0.080872	0.093025	0.106821
2480	0.003151	0.007769	0.017919	0.039010	0.080766	0.092911	0.106698
2490	0.003141	0.007750	0.017882	0.038945	0.080662	0.092797	0.106575
2500	0.003132	0.007731	0.017845	0.038880	0.080558	0.092684	0.106452
2510	0.003123	0.007712	0.017808	0.038816	0.080454	0.092572	0.106331
2520	0.003114	0.007693	0.017772	0.038752	0.080351	0.092460	0.106210
2530	0.003105	0.007674	0.017736	0.038688	0.080249	0.092349	0.106089
2540	0.003096	0.007655	0.017700	0.038625	0.080147	0.092238	0.105970
2550	0.003087	0.007636	0.017664	0.038562	0.080046	0.092128	0.105851
2560	0.003078	0.007618	0.017628	0.038499	0.079945	0.092018	0.105732
2570	0.003069	0.007599	0.017593	0.038437	0.079845	0.091909	0.105614
2580	0.003060	0.007581	0.017558	0.038375	0.079745	0.091801	0.105497
2590	0.003052	0.007563	0.017523	0.038314	0.079646	0.091693	0.105380
2600	0.003043	0.007545	0.017488	0.038252	0.079547	0.091586	0.105264
2610	0.003034	0.007527	0.017454	0.038191	0.079449	0.091479	0.105148
2620	0.003026	0.007509	0.017419	0.038131	0.079351	0.091372	0.105033
2630	0.003017	0.007491	0.017385	0.038071	0.079254	0.091267	0.104919
2640	0.003009	0.007473	0.017351	0.038011	0.079157	0.091161	0.104805
2650	0.003000	0.007456	0.017318	0.037951	0.079061	0.091057	0.104691
2660	0.002992	0.007438	0.017284	0.037892	0.078965	0.090953	0.104578
2670	0.002984	0.007421	0.017251	0.037833	0.078870	0.090849	0.104466
2680	0.002976	0.007404	0.017218	0.037774	0.078775	0.090746	0.104354
2690	0.002967	0.007387	0.017185	0.037716	0.078680	0.090643	0.104243
2700	0.002959	0.007370	0.017152	0.037658	0.078586	0.090541	0.104132
2710	0.002951	0.007353	0.017119	0.037600	0.078493	0.090439	0.104022
2720	0.002943	0.007336	0.017087	0.037543	0.078400	0.090338	0.103913
2730	0.002935	0.007319	0.017055	0.037486	0.078307	0.090237	0.103804
2740	0.002927	0.007303	0.017023	0.037429	0.078215	0.090137	0.103695
2750	0.002920	0.007286	0.016991	0.037372	0.078124	0.090037	0.103587

Unit	60	65	70	75	80	81	82
2760	0.002912	0.007270	0.016959	0.037316	0.078032	0.089938	0.103479
2770	0.002904	0.007253	0.016927	0.037260	0.077942	0.089839	0.103372
2780	0.002896	0.007237	0.016896	0.037204	0.077851	0.089741	0.103266
2790	0.002889	0.007221	0.016865	0.037149	0.077761	0.089643	0.103159
2800	0.002881	0.007205	0.016834	0.037094	0.077672	0.089545	0.103054
2810	0.002874	0.007189	0.016803	0.037039	0.077583	0.089448	0.102949
2820	0.002866	0.007173	0.016772	0.036984	0.077494	0.089352	0.102844
2830	0.002859	0.007157	0.016742	0.036930	0.077406	0.089256	0.102740
2840	0.002851	0.007142	0.016711	0.036876	0.077318	0.089160	0.102636
2850	0.002844	0.007126	0.016681	0.036822	0.077230	0.089065	0.102533
2860	0.002836	0.007111	0.016651	0.036769	0.077143	0.088970	0.102430
2870	0.002829	0.007095	0.016621	0.036716	0.077057	0.088876	0.102328
2880	0.002822	0.007080	0.016592	0.036663	0.076971	0.088782	0.102226
2890	0.002815	0.007065	0.016562	0.036610	0.076885	0.088688	0.102125
2900	0.002808	0.007050	0.016533	0.036557	0.076799	0.088595	0.102024
2910	0.002800	0.007034	0.016503	0.036505	0.076714	0.088502	0.101923
2920	0.002793	0.007019	0.016474	0.036453	0.076630	0.088410	0.101823
2930	0.002786	0.007005	0.016445	0.036402	0.076545	0.088318	0.101724
2940	0.002779	0.006990	0.016417	0.036350	0.076461	0.088227	0.101624
2950	0.002772	0.006975	0.016388	0.036299	0.076378	0.088136	0.101526
2960	0.002766	0.006960	0.016359	0.036248	0.076295	0.088045	0.101427
2970	0.002759	0.006946	0.016331	0.036197	0.076212	0.087955	0.101329
2980	0.002752	0.006931	0.016303	0.036147	0.076129	0.087865	0.101232
2990	0.002745	0.006917	0.016275	0.036097	0.076047	0.087776	0.101135
3000	0.002738	0.006903	0.016247	0.036047	0.075966	0.087687	0.101038
3010	0.002732	0.006888	0.016219	0.035997	0.075884	0.087598	0.100942
3020	0.002725	0.006874	0.016191	0.035947	0.075803	0.087510	0.100846
3030	0.002718	0.006860	0.016164	0.035898	0.075723	0.087422	0.100751
3040	0.002712	0.006846	0.016136	0.035849	0.075642	0.087334	0.100656
3050	0.002705	0.006832	0.016109	0.035800	0.075562	0.087247	0.100561
3060	0.002699	0.006818	0.016082	0.035752	0.075483	0.087160	0.100467
3070	0.002692	0.006804	0.016055	0.035703	0.075404	0.087074	0.100373
3080	0.002686	0.006791	0.016028	0.035655	0.075325	0.086988	0.100280
3090	0.002679	0.006777	0.016002	0.035607	0.075246	0.086902	0.100187
3100	0.002673	0.006763	0.015975	0.035559	0.075168	0.086817	0.100094

Unit	60	65	70	75	80	81	82
3110	0.002667	0.006750	0.015948	0.035512	0.075090	0.086732	0.100002
3120	0.002660	0.006736	0.015922	0.035465	0.075012	0.086647	0.099910
3130	0.002654	0.006723	0.015896	0.035418	0.074935	0.086563	0.099819
3140	0.002648	0.006710	0.015870	0.035371	0.074858	0.086479	0.099727
3150	0.002642	0.006696	0.015844	0.035324	0.074782	0.086396	0.099637
3160	0.002635	0.006683	0.015818	0.035278	0.074705	0.086312	0.099546
3170	0.002629	0.006670	0.015792	0.035231	0.074630	0.086230	0.099456
3180	0.002623	0.006657	0.015767	0.035185	0.074554	0.086147	0.099367
3190	0.002617	0.006644	0.015741	0.035140	0.074479	0.086065	0.099277
3200	0.002611	0.006631	0.015716	0.035094	0.074404	0.085983	0.099188
3210	0.002605	0.006618	0.015691	0.035048	0.074329	0.085902	0.099100
3220	0.002599	0.006606	0.015666	0.035003	0.074254	0.085820	0.099012
3230	0.002593	0.006593	0.015641	0.034958	0.074180	0.085739	0.098924
3240	0.002587	0.006580	0.015616	0.034913	0.074107	0.085659	0.098836
3250	0.002581	0.006568	0.015591	0.034869	0.074033	0.085579	0.098749
3260	0.002576	0.006555	0.015567	0.034824	0.073960	0.085499	0.098662
3270	0.002570	0.006543	0.015542	0.034780	0.073887	0.085419	0.098576
3280	0.002564	0.006530	0.015518	0.034736	0.073814	0.085340	0.098490
3290	0.002558	0.006518	0.015493	0.034692	0.073742	0.085261	0.098404
3300	0.002553	0.006506	0.015469	0.034649	0.073670	0.085182	0.098318
3310	0.002547	0.006493	0.015445	0.034605	0.073598	0.085104	0.098233
3320	0.002541	0.006481	0.015421	0.034562	0.073527	0.085026	0.098148
3330	0.002536	0.006469	0.015397	0.034519	0.073456	0.084948	0.098064
3340	0.002530	0.006457	0.015374	0.034476	0.073385	0.084871	0.097980
3350	0.002524	0.006445	0.015350	0.034433	0.073314	0.084794	0.097896
3360	0.002519	0.006433	0.015326	0.034390	0.073244	0.084717	0.097813
3370	0.002513	0.006421	0.015303	0.034348	0.073174	0.084641	0.097729
3380	0.002508	0.006409	0.015280	0.034306	0.073104	0.084564	0.097646
3390	0.002502	0.006398	0.015256	0.034264	0.073035	0.084488	0.097564
3400	0.002497	0.006386	0.015233	0.034222	0.072966	0.084413	0.097482
3410	0.002492	0.006374	0.015210	0.034180	0.072897	0.084338	0.097400
3420	0.002486	0.006363	0.015187	0.034139	0.072828	0.084262	0.097318
3430	0.002481	0.006351	0.015165	0.034097	0.072759	0.084188	0.097237
3440	0.002476	0.006340	0.015142	0.034056	0.072691	0.084113	0.097156
3450	0.002470	0.006328	0.015119	0.034015	0.072623	0.084039	0.097075

Unit	60	65	70	75	80	81	82
3460	0.002465	0.006317	0.015097	0.033974	0.072556	0.083965	0.096995
3470	0.002460	0.006306	0.015074	0.033934	0.072488	0.083892	0.096915
3480	0.002455	0.006294	0.015052	0.033893	0.072421	0.083818	0.096835
3490	0.002449	0.006283	0.015030	0.033853	0.072354	0.083745	0.096755
3500	0.002444	0.006272	0.015008	0.033813	0.072288	0.083672	0.096676
3510	0.002439	0.006261	0.014986	0.033773	0.072221	0.083600	0.096597
3520	0.002434	0.006250	0.014964	0.033733	0.072155	0.083527	0.096518
3530	0.002429	0.006239	0.014942	0.033693	0.072089	0.083455	0.096440
3540	0.002424	0.006228	0.014920	0.033654	0.072024	0.083384	0.096362
3550	0.002419	0.006217	0.014899	0.033614	0.071958	0.083312	0.096284
3560	0.002414	0.006206	0.014877	0.033575	0.071893	0.083241	0.096207
3570	0.002409	0.006195	0.014856	0.033536	0.071828	0.083170	0.096129
3580	0.002404	0.006184	0.014834	0.033497	0.071764	0.083099	0.096052
3590	0.002399	0.006174	0.014813	0.033458	0.071699	0.083029	0.095976
3600	0.002394	0.006163	0.014792	0.033420	0.071635	0.082959	0.095899
3610	0.002389	0.006152	0.014771	0.033381	0.071571	0.082889	0.095823
3620	0.002384	0.006142	0.014750	0.033343	0.071508	0.082819	0.095747
3630	0.002379	0.006131	0.014729	0.033305	0.071444	0.082750	0.095672
3640	0.002375	0.006121	0.014708	0.033267	0.071381	0.082681	0.095596
3650	0.002370	0.006110	0.014687	0.033229	0.071318	0.082612	0.095521
3660	0.002365	0.006100	0.014667	0.033191	0.071255	0.082543	0.095447
3670	0.002360	0.006090	0.014646	0.033154	0.071192	0.082474	0.095372
3680	0.002356	0.006079	0.014625	0.033116	0.071130	0.082406	0.095298
3690	0.002351	0.006069	0.014605	0.033079	0.071068	0.082338	0.095224
3700	0.002346	0.006059	0.014585	0.033042	0.071006	0.082271	0.095150
3710	0.002342	0.006049	0.014565	0.033005	0.070944	0.082203	0.095077
3720	0.002337	0.006039	0.014544	0.032968	0.070883	0.082136	0.095003
3730	0.002332	0.006029	0.014524	0.032931	0.070822	0.082069	0.094930
3740	0.002328	0.006019	0.014504	0.032895	0.070761	0.082002	0.094858
3750	0.002323	0.006009	0.014484	0.032858	0.070700	0.081936	0.094785
3760	0.002319	0.005999	0.014465	0.032822	0.070639	0.081869	0.094713
3770	0.002314	0.005989	0.014445	0.032786	0.070579	0.081803	0.094641
3780	0.002309	0.005979	0.014425	0.032750	0.070519	0.081737	0.094569
3790	0.002305	0.005969	0.014405	0.032714	0.070459	0.081672	0.094498
3800	0.002301	0.005959	0.014386	0.032678	0.070399	0.081606	0.094426

Unit	60	65	70	75	80	81	82
3810	0.002296	0.005950	0.014367	0.032642	0.070340	0.081541	0.094355
3820	0.002292	0.005940	0.014347	0.032607	0.070280	0.081476	0.094285
3830	0.002287	0.005930	0.014328	0.032572	0.070221	0.081411	0.094214
3840	0.002283	0.005921	0.014309	0.032536	0.070162	0.081347	0.094144
3850	0.002278	0.005911	0.014290	0.032501	0.070103	0.081283	0.094074
3860	0.002274	0.005902	0.014270	0.032466	0.070045	0.081219	0.094004
3870	0.002270	0.005892	0.014251	0.032431	0.069987	0.081155	0.093934
3880	0.002265	0.005883	0.014233	0.032397	0.069929	0.081091	0.093865
3890	0.002261	0.005873	0.014214	0.032362	0.069871	0.081028	0.093796
3900	0.002257	0.005864	0.014195	0.032328	0.069813	0.080964	0.093727
3910	0.002253	0.005855	0.014176	0.032293	0.069755	0.080901	0.093658
3920	0.002248	0.005845	0.014158	0.032259	0.069698	0.080839	0.093590
3930	0.002244	0.005836	0.014139	0.032225	0.069641	0.080776	0.093521
3940	0.002240	0.005827	0.014121	0.032191	0.069584	0.080714	0.093453
3950	0.002236	0.005818	0.014102	0.032157	0.069527	0.080651	0.093385
3960	0.002232	0.005809	0.014084	0.032123	0.069471	0.080589	0.093318
3970	0.002227	0.005800	0.014066	0.032090	0.069414	0.080528	0.093251
3980	0.002223	0.005790	0.014047	0.032056	0.069358	0.080466	0.093183
3990	0.002219	0.005781	0.014029	0.032023	0.069302	0.080405	0.093116
4000	0.002215	0.005772	0.014011	0.031990	0.069246	0.080344	0.093050
4010	0.002211	0.005764	0.013993	0.031957	0.069191	0.080283	0.092983
4020	0.002207	0.005755	0.013975	0.031924	0.069135	0.080222	0.092917
4030	0.002203	0.005746	0.013957	0.031891	0.069080	0.080161	0.092851
4040	0.002199	0.005737	0.013940	0.031858	0.069025	0.080101	0.092785
4050	0.002195	0.005728	0.013922	0.031825	0.068970	0.080041	0.092719
4060	0.002191	0.005719	0.013904	0.031793	0.068915	0.079981	0.092654
4070	0.002187	0.005711	0.013887	0.031760	0.068861	0.079921	0.092589
4080	0.002183	0.005702	0.013869	0.031728	0.068806	0.079861	0.092524
4090	0.002179	0.005693	0.013852	0.031696	0.068752	0.079802	0.092459
4100	0.002175	0.005685	0.013834	0.031664	0.068698	0.079743	0.092394
4110	0.002171	0.005676	0.013817	0.031632	0.068644	0.079684	0.092330
4120	0.002167	0.005667	0.013800	0.031600	0.068590	0.079625	0.092266
4130	0.002164	0.005659	0.013783	0.031568	0.068537	0.079566	0.092202
4140	0.002160	0.005650	0.013765	0.031536	0.068484	0.079508	0.092138
4150	0.002156	0.005642	0.013748	0.031505	0.068430	0.079449	0.092074

Unit	60	65	70	75	80	81	82
4160	0.002152	0.005633	0.013731	0.031473	0.068377	0.079391	0.092011
4170	0.002148	0.005625	0.013714	0.031442	0.068325	0.079333	0.091948
4180	0.002144	0.005617	0.013697	0.031411	0.068272	0.079276	0.091884
4190	0.002141	0.005608	0.013681	0.031379	0.068219	0.079218	0.091822
4200	0.002137	0.005600	0.013664	0.031348	0.068167	0.079161	0.091759
4210	0.002133	0.005592	0.013647	0.031318	0.068115	0.079104	0.091697
4220	0.002129	0.005584	0.013630	0.031287	0.068063	0.079046	0.091634
4230	0.002126	0.005575	0.013614	0.031256	0.068011	0.078990	0.091572
4240	0.002122	0.005567	0.013597	0.031225	0.067959	0.078933	0.091510
4250	0.002118	0.005559	0.013581	0.031195	0.067908	0.078876	0.091449
4260	0.002115	0.005551	0.013564	0.031164	0.067856	0.078820	0.091387
4270	0.002111	0.005543	0.013548	0.031134	0.067805	0.078764	0.091326
4280	0.002107	0.005535	0.013532	0.031104	0.067754	0.078708	0.091265
4290	0.002104	0.005527	0.013516	0.031074	0.067703	0.078652	0.091204
4300	0.002100	0.005519	0.013499	0.031044	0.067653	0.078596	0.091143
4310	0.002097	0.005511	0.013483	0.031014	0.067602	0.078541	0.091082
4320	0.002093	0.005503	0.013467	0.030984	0.067552	0.078486	0.091022
4330	0.002089	0.005495	0.013451	0.030954	0.067501	0.078431	0.090962
4340	0.002086	0.005487	0.013435	0.030925	0.067451	0.078376	0.090902
4350	0.002082	0.005479	0.013419	0.030895	0.067401	0.078321	0.090842
4360	0.002079	0.005471	0.013403	0.030866	0.067351	0.078266	0.090782
4370	0.002075	0.005464	0.013388	0.030836	0.067302	0.078212	0.090722
4380	0.002072	0.005456	0.013372	0.030807	0.067252	0.078157	0.090663
4390	0.002068	0.005448	0.013356	0.030778	0.067203	0.078103	0.090604
4400	0.002065	0.005440	0.013341	0.030749	0.067154	0.078049	0.090545
4410	0.002061	0.005433	0.013325	0.030720	0.067105	0.077995	0.090486
4420	0.002058	0.005425	0.013310	0.030691	0.067056	0.077942	0.090427
4430	0.002055	0.005418	0.013294	0.030662	0.067007	0.077888	0.090369
4440	0.002051	0.005410	0.013279	0.030634	0.066958	0.077835	0.090311
4450	0.002048	0.005402	0.013263	0.030605	0.066910	0.077781	0.090253
4460	0.002044	0.005395	0.013248	0.030577	0.066862	0.077728	0.090195
4470	0.002041	0.005387	0.013233	0.030548	0.066813	0.077675	0.090137
4480	0.002038	0.005380	0.013218	0.030520	0.066765	0.077623	0.090079
4490	0.002034	0.005372	0.013202	0.030492	0.066717	0.077570	0.090022
4500	0.002031	0.005365	0.013187	0.030464	0.066670	0.077518	0.089964

Unit	60	65	70	75	90	81	82
4510	0.002028	0.005358	0.013172	0.030435	0.066622	0.077465	0.089907
4520	0.002024	0.005350	0.013157	0.030407	0.066575	0.077413	0.089850
4530	0.002021	0.005343	0.013142	0.030380	0.066527	0.077361	0.089793
4540	0.002018	0.005336	0.013127	0.030352	0.066480	0.077309	0.089737
4550	0.002015	0.005328	0.013113	0.030324	0.066433	0.077258	0.089680
4560	0.002011	0.005321	0.013098	0.030297	0.066386	0.077206	0.089624
4570	0.002008	0.005314	0.013083	0.030269	0.066339	0.077155	0.089568
4580	0.002005	0.005307	0.013068	0.030242	0.066293	0.077104	0.089512
4590	0.002002	0.005299	0.013054	0.030214	0.066246	0.077052	0.089456
4600	0.001998	0.005292	0.013039	0.030187	0.066200	0.077001	0.089400
4610	0.001995	0.005285	0.013024	0.030160	0.066153	0.076951	0.089344
4620	0.001992	0.005278	0.013010	0.030133	0.066107	0.076900	0.089289
4630	0.001939	0.005271	0.012995	0.030106	0.066061	0.076849	0.089234
4640	0.001986	0.005264	0.012981	0.030079	0.066015	0.076799	0.089179
4650	0.001982	0.005257	0.012967	0.030052	0.065970	0.076749	0.089124
4660	0.001979	0.005250	0.012952	0.030025	0.065924	0.076699	0.089069
4670	0.001976	0.005243	0.012938	0.029998	0.065879	0.076649	0.089014
4680	0.001973	0.005236	0.012924	0.029972	0.065833	0.076599	0.088960
4690	0.001970	0.005229	0.012910	0.029945	0.065788	0.076549	0.088905
4700	0.001967	0.005222	0.012895	0.029919	0.065743	0.076500	0.088851
4710	0.031964	0.005215	0.012881	0.029892	0.065698	0.076450	0.088797
4720	0.001961	0.005208	0.012867	0.029866	0.065653	0.076401	0.088743
4730	0.031958	0.005201	0.012853	0.029840	0.065608	0.076352	0.088689
4740	0.001955	0.005195	0.012839	0.029814	0.065564	0.076303	0.088636
4750	0.001952	0.005188	0.012825	0.029788	0.065519	0.076254	0.088582
4760	0.001949	0.005181	0.012812	0.029762	0.065475	0.076205	0.088529
4770	0.001946	0.005174	0.012798	0.029736	0.065431	0.076157	0.088476
4780	0.001943	0.005167	0.012784	0.029710	0.065387	0.076108	0.088423
4790	0.001940	0.005161	0.012770	0.029684	0.065343	0.076060	0.088370
4800	0.031937	0.005154	0.012757	0.029658	0.065299	0.076012	0.088317
4810	0.001934	0.005147	0.012743	0.029633	0.065255	0.075964	0.088265
4820	0.001931	0.005141	0.012729	0.029607	0.065211	0.075916	0.088212
4830	0.001928	0.005134	0.012716	0.029582	0.065168	0.075868	0.088160
4840	0.001925	0.005128	0.012702	0.029556	0.065125	0.075820	0.088108
4850	0.001922	0.005121	0.012689	0.029531	0.065081	0.075773	0.088056

Unit	60	65	70	75	80	81	82
4860	0.001919	0.005114	0.012675	0.029506	0.065038	0.075725	0.088004
4870	0.001916	0.005108	0.012662	0.029481	0.064995	0.075678	0.087952
4880	0.001913	0.005101	0.012648	0.029456	0.064952	0.075631	0.087900
4890	0.001910	0.005095	0.012635	0.029431	0.064909	0.075584	0.087849
4900	0.001907	0.005088	0.012622	0.029406	0.064867	0.075537	0.087797
4910	0.001905	0.005082	0.012609	0.029381	0.064824	0.075490	0.087746
4920	0.001902	0.005076	0.012595	0.029356	0.064782	0.075443	0.087695
4930	0.001899	0.005069	0.012582	0.029331	0.064739	0.075397	0.087644
4940	0.001896	0.005063	0.012569	0.029307	0.064697	0.075350	0.087593
4950	0.001893	0.005056	0.012556	0.029282	0.064655	0.075304	0.087543
4960	0.001890	0.005050	0.012543	0.029257	0.064613	0.075258	0.087492
4970	0.001888	0.005044	0.012530	0.029233	0.064571	0.075212	0.087442
4980	0.001885	0.005037	0.012517	0.029209	0.064529	0.075166	0.087391
4990	0.001882	0.005031	0.012504	0.029184	0.064488	0.075120	0.087341
5000	0.001879	0.005025	0.012491	0.029160	0.064446	0.075074	0.087291
5010	0.001876	0.005019	0.012479	0.029136	0.064405	0.075029	0.087241
5020	0.001874	0.005013	0.012466	0.029112	0.064363	0.074983	0.087191
5030	0.001871	0.005006	0.012453	0.029088	0.064322	0.074938	0.087142
5040	0.001868	0.005000	0.012440	0.029064	0.064281	0.074892	0.087092
5050	0.001866	0.004994	0.012428	0.029040	0.064240	0.074847	0.087043
5060	0.001863	0.004988	0.012415	0.029016	0.064199	0.074802	0.086993
5070	0.001860	0.004982	0.012402	0.028992	0.064158	0.074757	0.086944
5080	0.001857	0.004976	0.012390	0.028969	0.064118	0.074713	0.086895
5090	0.001855	0.004970	0.012377	0.028945	0.064077	0.074668	0.086846
5100	0.001852	0.004964	0.012365	0.028921	0.064037	0.074624	0.086797
5110	0.001849	0.004957	0.012352	0.028898	0.063996	0.074579	0.086749
5120	0.001847	0.004951	0.012340	0.028874	0.063955	0.074535	0.086700
5130	0.001844	0.004945	0.012327	0.028851	0.063916	0.074491	0.086652
5140	0.001841	0.004939	0.012315	0.028828	0.063876	0.074446	0.086604
5150	0.001839	0.004933	0.012303	0.028805	0.063836	0.074403	0.086555
5160	0.001836	0.004928	0.012291	0.028781	0.063796	0.074359	0.086507
5170	0.001834	0.004922	0.012278	0.028758	0.063756	0.074315	0.086459
5180	0.001831	0.004916	0.012266	0.028735	0.063717	0.074271	0.086412
5190	0.001828	0.004910	0.012254	0.028712	0.063677	0.074228	0.086364
5200	0.001826	0.004904	0.012242	0.028689	0.063638	0.074184	0.086316

Unit	60	65	70	75	80	81	82
5210	0.001823	0.004898	0.012230	0.028666	0.063598	0.074141	0.086269
5220	0.001821	0.004892	0.012218	0.028644	0.063559	0.074098	0.086221
5230	0.001818	0.004886	0.012206	0.028621	0.063520	0.074055	0.086174
5240	0.001815	0.004881	0.012194	0.028598	0.063481	0.074012	0.086127
5250	0.001813	0.004875	0.012182	0.028576	0.063442	0.073969	0.086080
5260	0.001810	0.004869	0.012170	0.028553	0.063403	0.073926	0.086033
5270	0.001808	0.004863	0.012158	0.028530	0.063364	0.073883	0.085986
5280	0.001805	0.004858	0.012146	0.028508	0.063326	0.073841	0.085940
5290	0.001803	0.004852	0.012134	0.028486	0.063287	0.073798	0.085893
5300	0.001800	0.004846	0.012122	0.028463	0.063249	0.073756	0.085847
5310	0.001798	0.004841	0.012111	0.028441	0.063210	0.073714	0.085801
5320	0.001795	0.004835	0.012099	0.028419	0.063172	0.073672	0.085754
5330	0.001793	0.004829	0.012087	0.028397	0.063134	0.073630	0.085708
5340	0.001790	0.004824	0.012076	0.028375	0.063096	0.073588	0.085662
5350	0.001788	0.004818	0.012064	0.028353	0.063058	0.073546	0.085616
5360	0.001785	0.004812	0.012052	0.028331	0.063020	0.073504	0.085571
5370	0.001783	0.004807	0.012041	0.028309	0.062982	0.073462	0.085525
5380	0.001780	0.004801	0.012029	0.028287	0.062944	0.073421	0.085479
5390	0.001778	0.004796	0.012018	0.028265	0.062907	0.073379	0.085434
5400	0.001776	0.004790	0.012006	0.028243	0.062869	0.073338	0.085389
5410	0.001773	0.004785	0.011995	0.028222	0.062832	0.073297	0.085343
5420	0.001771	0.004779	0.011984	0.028200	0.062794	0.073256	0.085298
5430	0.001768	0.004774	0.011972	0.028179	0.062757	0.073215	0.085253
5440	0.001766	0.004768	0.011961	0.028157	0.062720	0.073174	0.085208
5450	0.001764	0.004763	0.011950	0.028136	0.062683	0.073133	0.085164
5460	0.001761	0.004757	0.011938	0.028114	0.062646	0.073092	0.085119
5470	0.001759	0.004752	0.011927	0.028093	0.062609	0.073051	0.085074
5480	0.001756	0.004747	0.011916	0.028072	0.062572	0.073011	0.085030
5490	0.001754	0.004741	0.011905	0.028050	0.062536	0.072970	0.084986
5500	0.001752	0.004736	0.011893	0.028029	0.062499	0.072930	0.084941
5510	0.001749	0.004731	0.011882	0.028008	0.062462	0.072890	0.084897
5520	0.001747	0.004725	0.011871	0.027987	0.062426	0.072850	0.084853
5530	0.001745	0.004720	0.011860	0.027966	0.062390	0.072810	0.084809
5540	0.001742	0.004715	0.011849	0.027945	0.062353	0.072770	0.084765
5550	0.001740	0.004709	0.011838	0.027924	0.062317	0.072730	0.084721

Unit	60	65	70	75	80	81	82
5560	0.001738	0.004704	0.011827	0.027903	0.062281	0.072690	0.084678
5570	0.001736	0.004699	0.011816	0.027882	0.062245	0.072650	0.084634
5580	0.001733	0.004694	0.011805	0.027862	0.062209	0.072611	0.084591
5590	0.001731	0.004688	0.011795	0.027841	0.062173	0.072571	0.084547
5600	0.001729	0.004683	0.011784	0.027820	0.062137	0.072532	0.084504
5610	0.001726	0.004678	0.011773	0.027800	0.062102	0.072492	0.084461
5620	0.001724	0.004673	0.011762	0.027779	0.062066	0.072453	0.084418
5630	0.001722	0.004668	0.011751	0.027759	0.062031	0.072414	0.084375
5640	0.001720	0.004663	0.011741	0.027738	0.061995	0.072375	0.084332
5650	0.001717	0.004657	0.011730	0.027718	0.061960	0.072336	0.084289
5660	0.001715	0.004652	0.011719	0.027697	0.061925	0.072297	0.084247
5670	0.001713	0.004647	0.011709	0.027677	0.061889	0.072258	0.084204
5680	0.001711	0.004642	0.011698	0.027657	0.061854	0.072220	0.084162
5690	0.001708	0.004637	0.011687	0.027637	0.061819	0.072181	0.084119
5700	0.001706	0.004632	0.011677	0.027617	0.061784	0.072142	0.084077
5710	0.001704	0.004627	0.011666	0.027597	0.061749	0.072104	0.084035
5720	0.001702	0.004622	0.011656	0.027577	0.061715	0.072066	0.083993
5730	0.001700	0.004617	0.011645	0.027557	0.061680	0.072027	0.083951
5740	0.001698	0.004612	0.011635	0.027537	0.061645	0.071989	0.083909
5750	0.001695	0.004607	0.011625	0.027517	0.061611	0.071951	0.083867
5760	0.001693	0.004602	0.011614	0.027497	0.061576	0.071913	0.083825
5770	0.001691	0.004597	0.011604	0.027477	0.061542	0.071875	0.083784
5780	0.001689	0.004592	0.011593	0.027457	0.061508	0.071837	0.083742
5790	0.001687	0.004587	0.011583	0.027438	0.061474	0.071800	0.083701
5800	0.001685	0.004582	0.011573	0.027418	0.061439	0.071762	0.083659
5810	0.001682	0.004577	0.011563	0.027398	0.061405	0.071724	0.083618
5820	0.001680	0.004572	0.011552	0.027379	0.061371	0.071687	0.083577
5830	0.001678	0.004568	0.011542	0.027359	0.061337	0.071650	0.083536
5840	0.001676	0.004563	0.011532	0.027340	0.061304	0.071612	0.083495
5850	0.001674	0.004558	0.011522	0.027321	0.061270	0.071575	0.083454
5860	0.001672	0.004553	0.011512	0.027301	0.061236	0.071538	0.083413
5870	0.001670	0.004548	0.011502	0.027282	0.061203	0.071501	0.083373
5880	0.001668	0.004543	0.011492	0.027263	0.061169	0.071464	0.083332
5890	0.001666	0.004539	0.011482	0.027243	0.061136	0.071427	0.083291
5900	0.001663	0.004534	0.011472	0.027224	0.061102	0.071390	0.083251

Unit	60	65	70	75	80	81	82
5910	0.001661	0.004529	0.011462	0.027205	0.061069	0.071353	0.083211
5920	0.001659	0.004524	0.011452	0.027186	0.061036	0.071317	0.083170
5930	0.001657	0.004519	0.011442	0.027167	0.061003	0.071280	0.083130
5940	0.001655	0.004515	0.011432	0.027148	0.060969	0.071244	0.083090
5950	0.001653	0.004510	0.011422	0.027129	0.060936	0.071207	0.083050
5960	0.001651	0.004505	0.011412	0.027110	0.060904	0.071171	0.083010
5970	0.001649	0.004501	0.011402	0.027091	0.060871	0.071135	0.082970
5980	0.001647	0.004496	0.011392	0.027072	0.060838	0.071098	0.082931
5990	0.001645	0.004491	0.011382	0.027054	0.060805	0.071062	0.082891
6000	0.001643	0.004487	0.011373	0.027035	0.060772	0.071026	0.082851
6010	0.001641	0.004482	0.011363	0.027016	0.060740	0.070990	0.082812
6020	0.001639	0.004477	0.011353	0.026998	0.060707	0.070954	0.082772
6030	0.001637	0.004473	0.011344	0.026979	0.060675	0.070919	0.082733
6040	0.001635	0.004468	0.011334	0.026960	0.060643	0.070883	0.082694
6050	0.001633	0.004464	0.011324	0.026942	0.060610	0.070847	0.082655
6060	0.001631	0.004459	0.011315	0.026924	0.060578	0.070812	0.082616
6070	0.001629	0.004454	0.011305	0.026905	0.060546	0.070776	0.082577
6080	0.001627	0.004450	0.011295	0.026887	0.060514	0.070741	0.082538
6090	0.001625	0.004445	0.011286	0.026868	0.060482	0.070705	0.082499
6100	0.001623	0.004441	0.011276	0.026850	0.060450	0.070670	0.082460
6110	0.001621	0.004436	0.011267	0.026832	0.060418	0.070635	0.082422
6120	0.001619	0.004432	0.011257	0.026814	0.060386	0.070600	0.082383
6130	0.001617	0.004427	0.011248	0.026796	0.060355	0.070565	0.082344
6140	0.001615	0.004423	0.011239	0.026777	0.060323	0.070530	0.082306
6150	0.001613	0.004418	0.011229	0.026759	0.060291	0.070495	0.082268
6160	0.001611	0.004414	0.011220	0.026741	0.060260	0.070460	0.082229
6170	0.001609	0.004409	0.011210	0.026723	0.060228	0.070425	0.082191
6180	0.001608	0.004405	0.011201	0.026705	0.060197	0.070391	0.082153
6190	0.001606	0.004401	0.011192	0.026687	0.060166	0.070356	0.082115
6200	0.001604	0.004396	0.011182	0.026670	0.060134	0.070322	0.082077
6210	0.001602	0.004392	0.011173	0.026652	0.060103	0.070287	0.082039
6220	0.001600	0.004387	0.011164	0.026634	0.060072	0.070253	0.082002
6230	0.001598	0.004383	0.011155	0.026616	0.060041	0.070219	0.081964
6240	0.001596	0.004379	0.011146	0.026598	0.060010	0.070184	0.081926
6250	0.001594	0.004374	0.011136	0.026581	0.059979	0.070150	0.081889

Unit	60	65	70	75	80	81	82
6260	0.001592	0.004370	0.011127	0.026563	0.059948	0.070116	0.081851
6270	0.001591	0.004366	0.011118	0.026546	0.059917	0.070082	0.081814
6280	0.001589	0.004361	0.011109	0.026528	0.059887	0.070048	0.081776
6290	0.001587	0.004357	0.011100	0.026510	0.059856	0.070014	0.081739
6300	0.001585	0.004353	0.011091	0.026493	0.059825	0.069980	0.081702
6310	0.001583	0.004348	0.011082	0.026476	0.059795	0.069947	0.081665
6320	0.001581	0.004344	0.011073	0.026458	0.059764	0.069913	0.081628
6330	0.001579	0.004340	0.011064	0.026441	0.059734	0.069880	0.081591
6340	0.001578	0.004336	0.011055	0.026424	0.059704	0.069846	0.081554
6350	0.001576	0.004331	0.011046	0.026406	0.059673	0.069813	0.081517
6360	0.001574	0.004327	0.011037	0.026389	0.059643	0.069779	0.081481
6370	0.001572	0.004323	0.011028	0.026372	0.059613	0.069746	0.081444
6380	0.001570	0.004319	0.011019	0.026355	0.059583	0.069713	0.081407
6390	0.001568	0.004314	0.011010	0.026337	0.059553	0.069679	0.081371
6400	0.001567	0.004310	0.011001	0.026320	0.059523	0.069646	0.081335
6410	0.001565	0.004306	0.010992	0.026303	0.059493	0.069613	0.081298
6420	0.001563	0.004302	0.010984	0.026286	0.059463	0.069580	0.081262
6430	0.001561	0.004298	0.010975	0.026269	0.059433	0.069547	0.081226
6440	0.001559	0.004294	0.010966	0.026252	0.059404	0.069514	0.081190
6450	0.001558	0.004289	0.010957	0.026236	0.059374	0.069482	0.081153
6460	0.001556	0.004285	0.010949	0.026219	0.059344	0.069449	0.081117
6470	0.001554	0.004281	0.010940	0.026202	0.059315	0.069416	0.081082
6480	0.001552	0.004277	0.010931	0.026185	0.059285	0.069384	0.081046
6490	0.001551	0.004273	0.010922	0.026168	0.059256	0.069351	0.081010
6500	0.001549	0.004269	0.010914	0.026152	0.059227	0.069319	0.080974
6510	0.001547	0.004265	0.010905	0.026135	0.059197	0.069286	0.080939
6520	0.001545	0.004261	0.010897	0.026118	0.059168	0.069254	0.080903
6530	0.001544	0.004257	0.010888	0.026102	0.059139	0.069222	0.080868
6540	0.001542	0.004253	0.010879	0.026085	0.059110	0.069190	0.080832
6550	0.001540	0.004249	0.010871	0.026069	0.059081	0.069157	0.080797
6560	0.001538	0.004245	0.010862	0.026052	0.059052	0.069125	0.080762
6570	0.001537	0.004241	0.010854	0.026036	0.059023	0.069093	0.080726
6580	0.001535	0.004237	0.010845	0.026019	0.058994	0.069061	0.080691
6590	0.001533	0.004233	0.010837	0.026003	0.058965	0.069030	0.080656
6600	0.001532	0.004229	0.010828	0.025986	0.058936	0.068998	0.080621

Unit	60	65	70	75	80	81	82
6610	0.001530	0.004225	0.010820	0.025970	0.058907	0.068966	0.080586
6620	0.001528	0.004221	0.010812	0.025954	0.058879	0.068934	0.080551
6630	0.001526	0.004217	0.010803	0.025938	0.058850	0.068903	0.080516
6640	0.001525	0.004213	0.010795	0.025921	0.058822	0.068871	0.080482
6650	0.001523	0.004209	0.010786	0.025905	0.058793	0.068840	0.080447
6660	0.001521	0.004205	0.010778	0.025889	0.058765	0.068808	0.080412
6670	0.001520	0.004201	0.010770	0.025873	0.058736	0.068777	0.080378
6680	0.001518	0.004197	0.010761	0.025857	0.058708	0.068746	0.080343
6690	0.001516	0.004193	0.010753	0.025841	0.058680	0.068714	0.080309
6700	0.001515	0.004189	0.010745	0.025825	0.058651	0.068683	0.080275
6710	0.001513	0.004185	0.010737	0.025809	0.058623	0.068652	0.080240
6720	0.001511	0.004182	0.010728	0.025793	0.058595	0.068621	0.080206
6730	0.001510	0.004178	0.010720	0.025777	0.058567	0.068590	0.080172
6740	0.001508	0.004174	0.010712	0.025761	0.058539	0.068559	0.080138
6750	0.001506	0.004170	0.010704	0.025745	0.058511	0.068528	0.080104
6760	0.001505	0.004166	0.010696	0.025729	0.058483	0.068497	0.080070
6770	0.001503	0.004162	0.010688	0.025714	0.058456	0.068466	0.080036
6780	0.001501	0.004158	0.010680	0.025698	0.058428	0.068436	0.080002
6790	0.001500	0.004155	0.010671	0.025682	0.058400	0.068405	0.079969
6800	0.001498	0.004151	0.010663	0.025666	0.058372	0.068374	0.079935
6810	0.001497	0.004147	0.010655	0.025651	0.058345	0.068344	0.079901
6820	0.001495	0.004143	0.010647	0.025635	0.058317	0.068313	0.079868
6830	0.001493	0.004140	0.010639	0.025620	0.058290	0.068283	0.079834
6840	0.001492	0.004136	0.010631	0.025604	0.058262	0.068253	0.079801
6850	0.001490	0.004132	0.010623	0.025588	0.058235	0.068222	0.079767
6860	0.001489	0.004128	0.010615	0.025573	0.058208	0.068192	0.079734
6870	0.001487	0.004125	0.010607	0.025558	0.058180	0.068162	0.079701
6880	0.001485	0.004121	0.010599	0.025542	0.058153	0.068132	0.079668
6890	0.001484	0.004117	0.010591	0.025527	0.058126	0.068102	0.079635
6900	0.001482	0.004113	0.010584	0.025511	0.058099	0.068072	0.079602
6910	0.001481	0.004110	0.010576	0.025496	0.058072	0.068042	0.079569
6920	0.001479	0.004106	0.010568	0.025481	0.058045	0.068012	0.079536
6930	0.001477	0.004102	0.010560	0.025465	0.058018	0.067982	0.079503
6940	0.001476	0.004099	0.010552	0.025450	0.057991	0.067952	0.079470
6950	0.001474	0.004095	0.010544	0.025435	0.057964	0.067922	0.079437

Unit	60	65	70	75	80	81	82
6960	0.001473	0.004091	0.010536	0.025420	0.057937	01067893	0.079404
6970	0.001471	0.004088	0.010529	0.025405	0.057910	0.067863	0.079372
6980	0.001470	0.004084	0.010521	0.025390	0.057884	0.067833	0.079339
6990	0.001468	0.004080	0.010513	0.025375	0.057857	0.067804	0.079307
7000	0.001467	0.004077	0.010505	0.025359	0.057830	0.067775	0.079274
7010	0.001465	0.004073	0.010498	0.025344	0.057804	0.067745	0.079242
7020	0.001463	0.004070	0.010490	0.025329	0.057777	0.067716	0.079210
7030	0.001462	0.004066	0.010482	0.025315	0.057751	0.067686	0.079177
7040	0.001460	0.004062	0.010475	0.025300	0.057724	0.067657	0.079145
7050	0.001459	0.004059	0.010467	0.025285	0.057698	0.067628	0.079113
7060	0.001457	0.004055	0.010459	0.025270	0.057672	0.067599	0.079081
7070	0.001456	0.004052	0.010452	0.025255	0.057645	0.067570	0.079049
7080	0.001454	0.004048	0.010444	0.025240	0.057619	0.067541	0.079017
7090	0.001453	0.004045	0.010437	0.025225	0.057593	0.067512	0.078985
7100	0.001451	0.004041	0.010429	0.025211	0.057567	0.067483	0.078953
7110	0.001450	0.004037	0.010422	0.025196	0.057541	0.067454	0.078921
7120	0.001448	0.004034	0.010414	0.025181	0.057515	0.067425	0.078889
7130	0.001447	0.004030	0.010406	0.025167	0.057489	0.067396	0.078858
7140	0.001445	0.004027	0.010399	0.025152	0.057463	0.067368	0.078826
7150	0.001444	0.004023	0.010391	0.025137	0.057437	0.067339	0.078795
7160	0.001442	0.004020	0.010384	0.025123	0.057411	0.067310	0.078763
7170	0.001441	0.004016	0.010377	0.025108	0.057385	0.067282	0.078732
7180	0.001439	0.004013	0.010369	0.025094	0.057359	0.067253	0.078700
7190	0.001438	0.004009	0.010362	0.025079	0.057334	0.067225	0.078669
7200	0.001436	0.004006	0.010354	0.025065	0.057308	0.067197	0.078637
7210	0.001435	0.004003	0.010347	0.025050	0.057283	0.067168	0.078606
7220	0.001433	0.003999	0.010340	0.025036	0.057257	0.067140	0.078575
7230	0.001432	0.003996	0.010332	0.025021	0.057231	0.067112	0.078544
7240	0.001431	0.003992	0.010325	0.025007	0.057206	0.067083	0.078513
7250	0.001429	0.003989	0.010317	0.024993	0.057181	0.067055	0.078482
7260	0.001428	0.003985	0.010310	0.024979	0.057155	0.067027	0.078451
7270	0.001426	0.003982	0.010303	0.024964	0.057130	0.066999	0.078420
7280	0.001425	0.003979	0.010296	0.024950	0.057105	0.066971	0.078389
7290	0.001423	0.003975	0.010288	0.024936	0.057079	0.066943	0.078358
7300	0.001422	0.003972	0.010281	0.024922	0.057054	0.066915	0.078328

Unit	60	65	70	75	80	81	82
7310	0.001420	0.003968	0.010274	0.024907	0.057029	0.066888	0.078297
7320	0.001419	0.003965	0.010267	0.024893	0.057004	0.066860	0.078266
7330	0.001418	0.003962	0.010259	0.024879	0.056979	0.066832	0.078236
7340	0.001416	0.003958	0.010252	0.024865	0.056954	0.066804	0.078205
7350	0.001415	0.003955	0.010245	0.024851	0.056929	0.066777	0.078175
7360	0.001413	0.003952	0.010238	0.024837	0.056904	0.066749	0.078144
7370	0.001412	0.003948	0.010231	0.024823	0.056879	0.066722	0.078114
7380	0.001411	0.003945	0.010224	0.024809	0.056854	0.066694	0.078084
7390	0.001409	0.003942	0.010216	0.024795	0.056830	0.066667	0.078053
7400	0.001408	0.003938	0.010209	0.024781	0.056805	0.066639	0.078023
7410	0.001406	0.003935	0.010202	0.024767	0.056780	0.066612	0.077993
7420	0.001405	0.003932	0.010195	0.024754	0.056756	0.066585	0.077963
7430	0.001404	0.003928	0.010188	0.024740	0.056731	0.066557	0.077933
7440	0.001402	0.003925	0.010181	0.024726	0.056706	0.066530	0.077903
7450	0.001401	0.003922	0.010174	0.024712	0.056682	0.066503	0.077873
7460	0.001399	0.003919	0.010167	0.024698	0.056657	0.066476	0.077843
7470	0.001398	0.003915	0.010160	0.024685	0.056633	0.066449	0.077813
7480	0.001397	0.003912	0.010153	0.024671	0.056609	0.066422	0.077783
7490	0.001395	0.003909	0.010146	0.024657	0.056584	0.066395	0.077753
7500	0.001394	0.003906	0.010139	0.024644	0.056560	0.066368	0.077724
7510	0.001392	0.003902	0.010132	0.024630	0.056536	0.066341	0.077694
7520	0.001391	0.003899	0.010125	0.024616	0.056511	0.066314	0.077665
7530	0.001390	0.003896	0.010118	0.024603	0.056487	0.066287	0.077635
7540	0.001388	0.003893	0.010111	0.024589	0.056463	0.066261	0.077605
7550	0.001387	0.003890	0.010104	0.024576	0.056439	0.066234	0.077576
7560	0.001386	0.003886	0.010098	0.024562	0.056415	0.066207	0.077547
7570	0.001384	0.003883	0.010091	0.024549	0.056391	0.066181	0.077517
7580	0.001383	0.003880	0.010084	0.024535	0.056367	0.066154	0.077488
7590	0.001382	0.003877	0.010077	0.024522	0.056343	0.066128	0.077459
7600	0.001380	0.003874	0.010070	0.024509	0.056319	0.066101	0.077430
7610	0.001379	0.003870	0.010063	0.024495	0.056295	0.066075	0.077400
7620	0.001378	0.003867	0.010057	0.024482	0.056272	0.066048	0.077371
7630	0.001376	0.003864	0.010050	0.024468	0.056248	0.066022	0.077342
7640	0.001375	0.003861	0.010043	0.024455	0.056224	0.065996	0.077313
7650	0.001374	0.003858	0.010036	0.024442	0.056201	0.065969	0.077284

Unit	60	65	70	75	80	81	82
7660	0.001372	0.003855	0.010030	0.024429	0.056177	0.065943	0.077255
7670	0.001371	0.003852	0.010023	0.024415	0.056153	0.065917	0.077227
7680	0.001370	0.003849	0.010016	0.024402	0.056130	0.065891	0.077198
7690	0.001368	0.003845	0.010009	0.024389	0.056106	0.065865	0.077169
7700	0.001367	0.003842	0.010003	0.024376	0.056083	0.065839	0.077140
7710	0.001366	0.003839	0.009996	0.024363	0.056059	0.065813	0.077112
7720	0.001364	0.003836	0.009989	0.024350	0.056036	0.065787	0.077083
7730	0.001363	0.003833	0.009983	0.024337	0.056013	0.065761	0.077055
7740	0.001362	0.003830	0.009976	0.024324	0.055989	0.065735	0.077026
7750	0.001361	0.003827	0.009969	0.024311	0.055966	0.065710	0.076998
7760	0.001359	0.003824	0.009963	0.024297	0.055943	0.065684	0.076969
7770	0.001358	0.003821	0.009956	0.024285	0.055920	0.065658	0.076941
7780	0.001357	0.003818	0.009950	0.024272	0.055896	0.065632	0.076912
7790	0.001355	0.003815	0.009943	0.024259	0.055873	0.065607	0.076884
7800	0.001354	0.003812	0.009936	0.024246	0.055850	0.065581	0.076856
7810	0.001353	0.003809	0.009930	0.024233	0.055827	0.065556	0.076828
7820	0.001352	0.003806	0.009923	0.024220	0.055804	0.065530	0.076800
7830	0.001350	0.003803	0.009917	0.024207	0.055781	0.065505	0.076771
7840	0.001349	0.003800	0.009910	0.024194	0.055758	0.065479	0.076743
7850	0.001348	0.003797	0.009904	0.024181	0.055736	0.065454	0.076715
7860	0.001346	0.003794	0.009897	0.024169	0.055713	0.065429	0.076687
7870	0.001345	0.003790	0.009891	0.024156	0.055690	0.065403	0.076660
7880	0.001344	0.003788	0.009884	0.024143	0.055667	0.065378	0.076632
7890	0.001343	0.003785	0.009878	0.024131	0.055644	0.065353	0.076604
7900	0.001341	0.003782	0.009872	0.024118	0.055622	0.065328	0.076576
7910	0.001340	0.003779	0.009865	0.024105	0.055599	0.065303	0.076548
7920	0.001339	0.003776	0.009859	0.024093	0.055576	0.065277	0.076521
7930	0.001338	0.003773	0.009852	0.024080	0.055554	0.065252	0.076493
7940	0.001336	0.003770	0.009846	0.024067	0.055531	0.065227	0.076465
7950	0.001335	0.003767	0.009840	0.024055	0.055509	0.065203	0.076438
7960	0.001334	0.003764	0.009833	0.024042	0.055486	0.065178	0.076410
7970	0.001333	0.003761	0.009827	0.024030	0.055464	0.065153	0.076383
7980	0.001332	0.003758	0.009821	0.024017	0.055442	0.065128	0.076355
7990	0.001330	0.003755	0.009814	0.024005	0.055419	0.065103	0.076328
8000	0.001329	0.003752	0.009808	0.023992	0.055397	0.065078	0.076301

Unit	83	84	85	86	87	88	89
1	1.000000	1.000000	1.000000	1.000000	1.000000	1.000000	1.000000
2	0.830000	0.840000	0.850000	0.860000	0.870000	0.880000	0.890000
3	0.744289	0.758552	0.772915	0.787377	0.801937	0.816596	0.831352
4	0.688900	0.705600	0.722500	0.739600	0.756900	0.774400	0.792100
5	0.648791	0.667086	0.685671	0.704547	0.723716	0.743178	0.762934
6	0.617760	0.637184	0.656978	0.677144	0.697685	0.718604	0.739903
7	0.592684	0.612950	0.633656	0.654808	0.676408	0.698463	0.720974
8	0.571787	0.592704	0.614125	0.636056	0.658503	0.681472	0.704969
9	0.553967	0.575402	0.597397	0.619962	0.643103	0.666829	0.691146
10	0.538497	0.560352	0.582820	0.605911	0.629633	0.653997	0.679012
11	0.524875	0.547078	0.569941	0.593474	0.617691	0.642601	0.668218
12	0.512741	0.535234	0.558431	0.582344	0.606986	0.632372	0.658514
13	0.501826	0.524566	0.548049	0.572289	0.597303	0.623105	0.649712
14	0.491928	0.514878	0.538608	0.563135	0.588475	0.614647	0.641667
15	0.482889	0.506020	0.529965	0.554744	0.580374	0.606876	0.634267
16	0.474583	0.497871	0.522006	0.547008	0.572898	0.599695	0.627422
17	0.466912	0.490337	0.514639	0.539840	0.565962	0.593028	0.621060
18	0.459792	0.483337	0.507788	0.533167	0.559500	0.586809	0.615120
19	0.453158	0.476808	0.501391	0.526932	0.553455	0.580987	0.609554
20	0.446952	0.470696	0.495397	0.521083	0.547780	0.575517	0.604320
21	0.441129	0.464955	0.489762	0.515580	0.542437	0.570362	0.599384
22	0.435647	0.459546	0.484450	0.510388	0.537391	0.565489	0.594714
23	0.430472	0.454436	0.479427	0.505475	0.532613	0.560872	0.590286
24	0.425575	0.449597	0.474666	0.500816	0.528078	0.556487	0.586078
25	0.420930	0.445004	0.470145	0.496387	0.523765	0.552313	0.582069
26	0.416516	0.440635	0.465841	0.492169	0.519653	0.548333	0.578243
27	0.412311	0.436472	0.461737	0.488143	0.515728	0.544529	0.574586
28	0.408300	0.432498	0.457817	0.484296	0.511974	0.540889	0.571084
29	0.404467	0.428697	0.454065	0.480612	0.508377	0.537400	0.567724
30	0.400798	0.425057	0.450471	0.477080	0.504926	0.534051	0.564498
31	0.397280	0.421565	0.447021	0.473688	0.501610	0.530831	0.561394
32	0.393904	0.418212	0.443705	0.470427	0.498421	0.527732	0.558406
33	0.390659	0.414987	0.440516	0.467288	0.495349	0.524745	0.555525
34	0.387537	0.411883	0.437443	0.464262	0.492387	0.521864	0.552743
35	0.384529	0.408891	0.434480	0.461343	0.489527	0.519082	0.550056

Unit	83	84	85	86	87	88	89
36	0.381628	0.406003	0.431620	0.458524	0.486765	0.516392	0.547457
37	0.378827	0.403215	0.428856	0.455798	0.484092	0.513789	0.544941
38	0.376121	0.400519	0.426183	0.453161	0.481506	0.511269	0.542503
39	0.373504	0.397911	0.423595	0.450607	0.478999	0.508825	0.540139
40	0.370971	0.395385	0.421088	0.448132	0.476569	0.506455	0.537845
41	0.368516	0.392936	0.418657	0.445730	0.474211	0.504154	0.535617
42	0.366137	0.390562	0.416298	0.443399	0.471920	0.501918	0.533451
43	0.363828	0.388257	0.414008	0.441135	0.469694	0.499745	0.531345
44	0.361587	0.386018	0.411782	0.438934	0.467530	0.497630	0.529295
45	0.359409	0.383842	0.409618	0.436792	0.465424	0.495572	0.527299
46	0.357292	0.381726	0.407513	0.434709	0.463373	0.493568	0.525355
47	0.355232	0.379667	0.405463	0.432679	0.461375	0.491614	0.523459
48	0.353227	0.377661	0.403466	0.430701	0.459428	0.489709	0.521609
49	0.351275	0.375708	0.401521	0.428773	0.457528	0.487850	0.519804
50	0.349372	0.373803	0.399623	0.426893	0.455675	0.486036	0.518041
51	0.347517	0.371946	0.397772	0.425057	0.453866	0.484264	0.516320
52	0.345708	0.370134	0.395965	0.423265	0.452099	0.482533	0.514637
53	0.343942	0.368365	0.394201	0.421514	0.450372	0.480841	0.512991
54	0.342219	0.366637	0.392477	0.419803	0.448683	0.479186	0.511382
55	0.340535	0.364948	0.390792	0.418131	0.447032	0.477567	0.509807
56	0.338889	0.363298	0.389144	0.416494	0.445417	0.475983	0.508265
57	0.337281	0.361684	0.387533	0.414894	0.443836	0.474432	0.506754
58	0.335707	0.360105	0.385956	0.413326	0.442288	0.472912	0.505275
59	0.334168	0.358560	0.384412	0.411792	0.440771	0.471424	0.503825
60	0.332662	0.357048	0.382900	0.410289	0.439285	0.469965	0.502403
61	0.331187	0.355566	0.381419	0.408816	0.437829	0.468534	0.501009
62	0.329743	0.354115	0.379967	0.407372	0.436401	0.467131	0.499641
63	0.328327	0.352692	0.378545	0.405956	0.435000	0.465755	0.498299
64	0.326940	0.351298	0.377150	0.404567	0.433626	0.464404	0.496981
65	0.325581	0.349931	0.375781	0.403205	0.432278	0.463078	0.495688
66	0.324247	0.348589	0.374438	0.401867	0.430954	0.461776	0.494417
67	0.322939	0.347273	0.373120	0.400555	0.429653	0.460497	0.493168
68	0.321655	0.345982	0.371827	0.399265	0.428377	0.459241	0.491942
69	0.320396	0.344713	0.370556	0.397999	0.427122	0.458006	0.490736
70	0.319159	0.343468	0.369308	0.396755	0.425889	0.456792	0.489550

Unit	83	84	85	86	87	88	89
71	0.317944	0.342245	0.368082	0.395532	0.424677	0.455599	0.488384
72	0.316751	0.341043	0.366877	0.394330	0.423485	0.454425	0.487237
73	0.315579	0.339862	0.365692	0.393149	0.422313	0.453271	0.486108
74	0.314427	0.338700	0.364527	0.391987	0.421160	0.452135	0.484998
75	0.313294	0.337559	0.363382	0.390843	0.420026	0.451017	0.483904
76	0.312181	0.336436	0.362255	0.389719	0.418910	0.449916	0.482828
77	0.311084	0.335332	0.361147	0.388612	0.417811	0.448833	0.481768
78	0.310008	0.334245	0.360056	0.387522	0.416729	0.447766	0.480724
79	0.308948	0.333176	0.358982	0.386449	0.415664	0.446715	0.479696
80	0.307906	0.332123	0.357925	0.385393	0.414615	0.445680	0.478682
81	0.306879	0.331087	0.356884	0.384353	0.413581	0.444660	0.477683
82	0.305869	0.330067	0.355858	0.383328	0.412563	0.443655	0.476699
83	0.304873	0.329062	0.354848	0.382318	0.411560	0.442665	0.475729
84	0.303894	0.328072	0.353853	0.381323	0.410571	0.441688	0.474772
85	0.302928	0.327097	0.352873	0.380343	0.409596	0.440725	0.473828
86	0.301977	0.326136	0.351907	0.379376	0.408634	0.439775	0.472897
87	0.301040	0.325189	0.350954	0.378423	0.407686	0.438839	0.471979
88	0.300117	0.324255	0.350015	0.377483	0.406751	0.437915	0.471073
89	0.299207	0.323335	0.349089	0.376556	0.405829	0.437003	0.470179
90	0.298309	0.322428	0.348175	0.375642	0.404919	0.436104	0.469297
91	0.297425	0.321533	0.347274	0.374739	0.404021	0.435216	0.468425
92	0.296552	0.320650	0.346386	0.373849	0.403135	0.434339	0.467566
93	0.295691	0.319779	0.345509	0.372971	0.402260	0.433474	0.466717
94	0.294843	0.318920	0.344643	0.372104	0.401396	0.432620	0.465878
95	0.294005	0.318072	0.343789	0.371248	0.400544	0.431777	0.465050
96	0.293179	0.317236	0.342946	0.370403	0.399702	0.430944	0.464232
97	0.292363	0.316410	0.342114	0.369569	0.398871	0.430121	0.463424
98	0.291558	0.315595	0.341292	0.368745	0.398050	0.429308	0.462625
99	0.290763	0.314790	0.340481	0.367931	0.397239	0.428505	0.461837
100	0.289979	0.313995	0.339680	0.367128	0.396437	0.427711	0.461057
101	0.289204	0.313210	0.338888	0.366334	0.395646	0.426927	0.460286
102	0.288439	0.312435	0.338106	0.365549	0.394863	0.426152	0.459524
103	0.287684	0.311669	0.337334	0.364774	0.394090	0.425386	0.458771
104	0.286938	0.310912	0.336570	0.364008	0.393326	0.424629	0.458027
105	0.286201	0.310165	0.335816	0.363251	0.392570	0.423880	0.457290

Unit	83	84	85	86	87	88	89
106	0.285472	0.309426	0.335070	0.362502	0.391823	0.423140	0.456562
107	0.284753	0.308696	0.334334	0.361762	0.391085	0.422408	0.455842
108	0.284041	0.307975	0.333605	0.361031	0.390355	0.421684	0.455130
109	0.283339	0.307262	0.332885	0.360308	0.389632	0.420967	0.454425
110	0.282644	0.306557	0.332173	0.359592	0.388918	0.420259	0.453728
111	0.281957	0.305860	0.331469	0.358885	0.388212	0.419558	0.453038
112	0.281278	0.305170	0.330773	0.358185	0.387513	0.418865	0.452355
113	0.280607	0.304489	0.330084	0.357493	0.386821	0.418179	0.451680
114	0.279943	0.303815	0.329403	0.356808	0.386137	0.417500	0.451011
115	0.279286	0.303148	0.328729	0.356131	0.385460	0.416828	0.450350
116	0.278637	0.302488	0.328062	0.355461	0.384790	0.416163	0.449695
117	0.277995	0.301836	0.327403	0.354797	0.384127	0.415504	0.449046
118	0.277360	0.301191	0.326750	0.354141	0.383471	0.414853	0.448404
119	0.276731	0.300552	0.326104	0.353491	0.382821	0.414208	0.447768
120	0.276109	0.299920	0.325465	0.352848	0.382178	0.413569	0.447139
121	0.275494	0.299295	0.324832	0.352212	0.381542	0.412936	0.446515
122	0.274885	0.298676	0.324206	0.351581	0.380911	0.412310	0.445898
123	0.274283	0.298063	0.323586	0.350958	0.380287	0.411690	0.445286
124	0.273686	0.297456	0.322972	0.350340	0.379669	0.411076	0.444681
125	0.273096	0.296856	0.322365	0.349728	0.379057	0.410467	0.444080
126	0.272512	0.296262	0.321763	0.349122	0.378450	0.409864	0.443486
127	0.271933	0.295673	0.321167	0.348522	0.377850	0.409267	0.442897
128	0.271361	0.295090	0.320577	0.347928	0.377255	0.408676	0.442313
129	0.270793	0.294513	0.319993	0.347339	0.376665	0.408089	0.441735
130	0.270232	0.293942	0.319414	0.346756	0.376081	0.407509	0.441162
131	0.269676	0.293376	0.318840	0.346178	0.375503	0.406933	0.440594
132	0.269125	0.292815	0.318272	0.345606	0.374930	0.406363	0.440031
133	0.268580	0.292260	0.317710	0.345039	0.374362	0.405798	0.439473
134	0.268039	0.291710	0.317152	0.344477	0.373799	0.405237	0.438920
135	0.267504	0.291165	0.316600	0.343920	0.373241	0.404682	0.438372
136	0.266974	0.290625	0.316053	0.343368	0.372688	0.404132	0.437828
137	0.266449	0.290089	0.315510	0.342821	0.372139	0.403586	0.437289
138	0.265928	0.289559	0.314973	0.342279	0.371596	0.403045	0.436755
139	0.265413	0.289034	0.314440	0.341742	0.371057	0.402509	0.436225
140	0.264902	0.288513	0.313912	0.341209	0.370523	0.401977	0.435699

Unit	83	84	85	86	87	88	89
141	0.264395	0.287997	0.313388	0.340681	0.369994	0.401450	0.435178
142	0.263894	0.287486	0.312869	0.340158	0.369469	0.400927	0.434662
143	0.263396	0.286979	0.312355	0.339639	0.368948	0.400408	0.434149
144	0.262903	0.286476	0.311845	0.339124	0.368432	0.399894	0.433641
145	0.262415	0.285978	0.311340	0.338614	0.367920	0.399384	0.433137
146	0.261930	0.285484	0.310838	0.338108	0.367413	0.398878	0.432636
147	0.261450	0.284994	0.310341	0.337606	0.366909	0.398376	0.432140
148	0.260974	0.284508	0.309848	0.337108	0.366410	0.397878	0.431648
149	0.260502	0.284027	0.309359	0.336615	0.365914	0.397385	0.431159
150	0.260034	0.283549	0.308875	0.336125	0.365423	0.396895	0.430675
151	0.259570	0.283076	0.308394	0.335640	0.364935	0.396409	0.430194
152	0.259110	0.282606	0.307917	0.335158	0.364452	0.395926	0.429717
153	0.258653	0.282141	0.307444	0.334680	0.363972	0.395448	0.429243
154	0.258201	0.281679	0.306975	0.334206	0.363496	0.394973	0.428774
155	0.257752	0.281220	0.306509	0.333736	0.363023	0.394502	0.428307
156	0.257307	0.280766	0.306047	0.333269	0.362555	0.394034	0.427844
157	0.256865	0.280315	0.305589	0.332806	0.362089	0.393570	0.427385
158	0.256427	0.279868	0.305135	0.332346	0.361628	0.393110	0.426929
159	0.255993	0.279424	0.304683	0.331891	0.361170	0.392652	0.426476
160	0.255562	0.278983	0.304236	0.331438	0.360715	0.392199	0.426027
161	0.255134	0.278547	0.303792	0.330989	0.360264	0.391748	0.425581
162	0.254710	0.278113	0.303351	0.330543	0.359816	0.391301	0.425138
163	0.254289	0.277683	0.302914	0.330101	0.359371	0.390857	0.424699
164	0.253871	0.277256	0.302480	0.329662	0.358930	0.390417	0.424262
165	0.253456	0.276832	0.302049	0.329226	0.358492	0.389979	0.423829
166	0.253045	0.276412	0.301621	0.328794	0.358057	0.389545	0.423398
167	0.252637	0.275995	0.301197	0.328364	0.357625	0.389114	0.422971
168	0.252232	0.275580	0.300775	0.327938	0.357196	0.388685	0.422547
169	0.251830	0.275169	0.300357	0.327515	0.356771	0.388260	0.422125
170	0.251430	0.274761	0.299942	0.327095	0.356348	0.387838	0.421707
171	0.251034	0.274356	0.299530	0.326677	0.355928	0.387419	0.421291
172	0.250641	0.273954	0.299121	0.326263	0.355512	0.387002	0.420879
173	0.250251	0.273555	0.298714	0.325852	0.355098	0.386589	0.420469
174	0.249863	0.273159	0.298311	0.325444	0.354687	0.386178	0.420061
175	0.249479	0.272765	0.297910	0.325038	0.354279	0.385770	0.419657

Unit	83	84	85	86	87	88	89
176	0.249097	0.272375	0.297513	0.324635	0.353873	0.385365	0.419255
177	0.248718	0.271987	0.297118	0.324235	0.353471	0.384963	0.418856
178	0.248342	0.271601	0.296725	0.323838	0.353071	0.384563	0.418459
179	0.247968	0.271219	0.296336	0.323444	0.352674	0.384166	0.418065
180	0.247597	0.270839	0.295949	0.323052	0.352279	0.383771	0.417674
181	0.247228	0.270462	0.295565	0.322662	0.351887	0.383379	0.417285
182	0.246862	0.270087	0.295183	0.322276	0.351498	0.382990	0.416899
183	0.246499	0.269715	0.294804	0.321892	0.351111	0.382603	0.416515
184	0.246138	0.269346	0.294428	0.321510	0.350727	0.382219	0.416133
185	0.245780	0.268979	0.294054	0.321131	0.350345	0.381837	0.415754
186	0.245424	0.268615	0.293683	0.320755	0.349966	0.381457	0.415378
187	0.245070	0.268253	0.293314	0.320381	0.349589	0.381080	0.415003
188	0.244719	0.267893	0.292947	0.320009	0.349215	0.380706	0.414631
189	0.244371	0.267536	0.292583	0.319640	0.348843	0.380333	0.414262
190	0.244024	0.267181	0.292221	0.319273	0.348473	0.379963	0.413894
191	0.243680	0.266828	0.291862	0.318909	0.348106	0.379596	0.413529
192	0.243338	0.266478	0.291504	0.318547	0.347741	0.379230	0.413166
193	0.242999	0.266130	0.291150	0.318187	0.347378	0.378867	0.412806
194	0.242661	0.265784	0.290797	0.317829	0.347018	0.378506	0.412447
195	0.242326	0.265441	0.290447	0.317474	0.346659	0.378148	0.412091
196	0.241993	0.265099	0.290099	0.317121	0.346303	0.377791	0.411737
197	0.241662	0.264760	0.289753	0.316770	0.345949	0.377437	0.411385
198	0.241334	0.264423	0.289409	0.316421	0.345598	0.377084	0.411035
199	0.241007	0.264088	0.289067	0.316074	0.345248	0.376734	0.410687
200	0.240683	0.263756	0.288728	0.315730	0.344900	0.376386	0.410341
201	0.240360	0.263425	0.288390	0.315387	0.344555	0.376040	0.409997
202	0.240040	0.263096	0.288055	0.315047	0.344212	0.375696	0.409655
203	0.239721	0.262770	0.287722	0.314709	0.343870	0.375354	0.409315
204	0.239405	0.262445	0.287390	0.314372	0.343531	0.375014	0.408977
205	0.239090	0.262123	0.287061	0.314038	0.343194	0.374676	0.408641
206	0.238778	0.261802	0.286734	0.313706	0.342858	0.374340	0.408306
207	0.238467	0.261483	0.286408	0.313375	0.342525	0.374006	0.407974
208	0.238158	0.261166	0.286085	0.313047	0.342193	0.373673	0.407644
209	0.237851	0.260851	0.285763	0.312720	0.341864	0.373343	0.407315
210	0.237546	0.260538	0.285444	0.312396	0.341536	0.373014	0.406988

Unit	83	84	85	86	87	88	89
211	0.237243	0.260227	0.285126	0.312073	0.341210	0.372688	0.406663
212	0.236942	0.259918	0.284810	0.311752	0.340886	0.372363	0.406340
213	0.236642	0.259611	0.284496	0.311433	0.340564	0.372040	0.406019
214	0.236345	0.259305	0.284184	0.311116	0.340244	0.371719	0.405699
215	0.236049	0.259001	0.283873	0.310800	0.339925	0.371399	0.405382
216	0.235754	0.258699	0.283564	0.310487	0.339608	0.371082	0.405065
217	0.235462	0.258398	0.283257	0.310175	0.339293	0.370766	0.404751
218	0.235171	0.258100	0.282952	0.309865	0.338980	0.370451	0.404438
219	0.234882	0.257803	0.282649	0.309556	0.338669	0.370139	0.404127
220	0.234594	0.257508	0.282347	0.309249	0.338359	0.369828	0.403818
221	0.234309	0.257214	0.282047	0.308944	0.338051	0.369519	0.403510
222	0.234024	0.256922	0.281749	0.308641	0.337744	0.369211	0.403204
223	0.233742	0.256632	0.281452	0.308339	0.337439	0.368905	0.402899
224	0.233461	0.256343	0.281157	0.308039	0.337136	0.368601	0.402596
225	0.233181	0.256056	0.280863	0.307741	0.336835	0.368298	0.402295
226	0.232904	0.255771	0.280571	0.307444	0.336535	0.367997	0.401995
227	0.232627	0.255487	0.280281	0.307149	0.336236	0.367698	0.401697
228	0.232353	0.255204	0.279992	0.306855	0.335939	0.367400	0.401400
229	0.232079	0.254924	0.279705	0.306563	0.335644	0.367103	0.401105
230	0.231808	0.254644	0.279420	0.306273	0.335350	0.366808	0.400811
231	0.231538	0.254367	0.279136	0.305984	0.335058	0.366515	0.400519
232	0.231269	0.254090	0.278853	0.305696	0.334768	0.366223	0.400228
233	0.231002	0.253816	0.278572	0.305410	0.334478	0.365933	0.399939
234	0.230736	0.253542	0.278292	0.305126	0.334191	0.365644	0.399651
235	0.230471	0.253270	0.278014	0.304843	0.333905	0.365356	0.399365
236	0.230209	0.253000	0.277738	0.304561	0.333620	0.365070	0.399080
237	0.229947	0.252731	0.277462	0.304281	0.333336	0.364786	0.398796
238	0.229687	0.252464	0.277189	0.304003	0.333055	0.364503	0.398514
239	0.229428	0.252197	0.276916	0.303725	0.332774	0.364221	0.398233
240	0.229171	0.251933	0.276645	0.303449	0.332495	0.363941	0.397953
241	0.228915	0.251669	0.276376	0.303175	0.332217	0.363662	0.397675
242	0.228660	0.251407	0.276107	0.302902	0.331941	0.363384	0.397399
243	0.228407	0.251147	0.275841	0.302630	0.331666	0.363108	0.397123
244	0.228155	0.250887	0.275575	0.302360	0.331393	0.362833	0.396849
245	0.227904	0.250629	0.275311	0.302091	0.331121	0.362559	0.396576

Unit	83	84	85	86	87	88	89
246	0.227655	0.250373	0.275048	0.301823	0.330850	0.362287	0.396305
247	0.227407	0.250117	0.274787	0.301557	0.330580	0.362016	0.396035
248	0.227160	0.249863	0.274527	0.301292	0.330312	0.361746	0.395766
249	0.226914	0.249611	0.274268	0.301028	0.330045	0.361478	0.395498
250	0.226670	0.249359	0.274010	0.300766	0.329779	0.361211	0.395232
251	0.226427	0.249109	0.273754	0.300505	0.329515	0.360945	0.394966
252	0.226185	0.248860	0.273499	0.300245	0.329252	0.360681	0.394703
253	0.225944	0.248612	0.273245	0.299986	0.328990	0.360417	0.394440
254	0.225705	0.248365	0.272992	0.299729	0.328729	0.360155	0.394178
255	0.225466	0.248120	0.272741	0.299473	0.328470	0.359894	0.393918
256	0.225229	0.247876	0.272491	0.299218	0.328212	0.359635	0.393659
257	0.224993	0.247633	0.272242	0.298964	0.327955	0.359376	0.393401
258	0.224759	0.247391	0.271994	0.298712	0.327699	0.359119	0.393144
259	0.224525	0.247151	0.271747	0.298460	0.327444	0.358863	0.392889
260	0.224292	0.246911	0.271502	0.298210	0.327191	0.358608	0.392634
261	0.224061	0.246673	0.271258	0.297961	0.326939	0.358354	0.392381
262	0.223831	0.246436	0.271014	0.297713	0.326687	0.358101	0.392129
263	0.223602	0.246200	0.270772	0.297467	0.326438	0.357850	0.391878
264	0.223374	0.245965	0.270532	0.297221	0.326189	0.357599	0.391628
265	0.223147	0.245731	0.270292	0.296977	0.325941	0.357350	0.391379
266	0.222921	0.245498	0.270053	0.296733	0.325694	0.357102	0.391131
267	0.222696	0.245267	0.269816	0.296491	0.325449	0.356855	0.390884
268	0.222473	0.245036	0.269579	0.296250	0.325205	0.356609	0.390639
269	0.222250	0.244807	0.269344	0.296010	0.324961	0.356364	0.390394
270	0.222028	0.244578	0.269110	0.295771	0.324719	0.356120	0.390151
271	0.221808	0.244351	0.268877	0.295534	0.324478	0.355878	0.389908
272	0.221588	0.244125	0.268645	0.295297	0.324238	0.355636	0.389667
273	0.221370	0.243899	0.268414	0.295061	0.323999	0.355395	0.389427
274	0.221152	0.243675	0.268184	0.294826	0.323761	0.355156	0.389187
275	0.220936	0.243452	0.267955	0.294593	0.323524	0.354917	0.388949
276	0.220721	0.243230	0.267727	0.294360	0.323289	0.354680	0.388712
277	0.220506	0.243009	0.267500	0.294129	0.323054	0.354443	0.388475
278	0.220293	0.242788	0.267274	0.293898	0.322820	0.354208	0.388240
279	0.220080	0.242569	0.267049	0.293669	0.322587	0.353973	0.388006
280	0.219868	0.242351	0.266825	0.293440	0.322355	0.353740	0.387772

Unit	83	84	85	86	87	88	89
281	0.219658	0.242134	0.266602	0.293213	0.322124	0.353507	0.387540
282	0.219448	0.241918	0.266380	0.292986	0.321895	0.353276	0.387309
283	0.219239	0.241702	0.266159	0.292760	0.321666	0.353045	0.387078
284	0.219032	0.241488	0.265939	0.292536	0.321438	0.352816	0.386849
285	0.218825	0.241274	0.265720	0.292312	0.321211	0.352587	0.386620
286	0.218619	0.241062	0.265502	0.292089	0.320985	0.352359	0.386393
287	0.218414	0.240850	0.265285	0.291868	0.320760	0.352133	0.386166
288	0.218210	0.240640	0.265068	0.291647	0.320536	0.351907	0.385940
289	0.218006	0.240430	0.264853	0.291427	0.320313	0.351682	0.385715
290	0.217804	0.240221	0.264639	0.291208	0.320091	0.351458	0.385492
291	0.217603	0.240013	0.264425	0.290990	0.319869	0.351235	0.385268
292	0.217402	0.239806	0.264213	0.290773	0.319649	0.351013	0.385046
293	0.217202	0.239600	0.264001	0.290557	0.319429	0.350791	0.384825
294	0.217004	0.239395	0.263790	0.290341	0.319211	0.350571	0.384605
295	0.216806	0.239191	0.263580	0.290127	0.318993	0.350352	0.384385
296	0.216608	0.238987	0.263371	0.289913	0.318776	0.350133	0.384167
297	0.216412	0.238784	0.263163	0.289701	0.318560	0.349915	0.383949
298	0.216217	0.238583	0.262956	0.289489	0.318345	0.349698	0.383732
299	0.216022	0.238382	0.262749	0.289278	0.318131	0.349482	0.383516
300	0.215828	0.238181	0.262543	0.289068	0.317918	0.349267	0.383301
301	0.215635	0.237982	0.262339	0.288859	0.317705	0.349053	0.383086
302	0.215443	0.237784	0.262135	0.288650	0.317494	0.348840	0.382873
303	0.215252	0.237586	0.261932	0.288443	0.317283	0.348627	0.382660
304	0.215061	0.237389	0.261729	0.288236	0.317073	0.348415	0.382448
305	0.214871	0.237193	0.261528	0.288030	0.316864	0.348204	0.382237
306	0.214682	0.236998	0.261327	0.287825	0.316655	0.347994	0.382027
307	0.214494	0.236804	0.261127	0.287621	0.316448	0.347785	0.381817
308	0.214307	0.236610	0.260928	0.287417	0.316241	0.347576	0.381608
309	0.214120	0.236417	0.260730	0.287215	0.316035	0.347369	0.381401
310	0.213934	0.236225	0.260533	0.287013	0.315830	0.347162	0.381193
311	0.213749	0.236034	0.260336	0.286812	0.315626	0.346955	0.380987
312	0.213565	0.235843	0.260140	0.286611	0.315422	0.346750	0.380781
313	0.213381	0.235653	0.259945	0.286412	0.315220	0.346546	0.380577
314	0.213198	0.235464	0.259751	0.286213	0.315018	0.346342	0.380373
315	0.213016	0.235276	0.259557	0.286015	0.314817	0.346139	0.380169

Unit	83	84	85	86	87	88	89
316	0.212835	0.235089	0.259364	0.285818	0.314616	0.345936	0.379967
317	0.212654	0.234902	0.259172	0.285622	0.314417	0.345735	0.379765
318	0.212474	0.234716	0.258981	0.285426	0.314218	0.345534	0.379564
319	0.212295	0.234531	0.258790	0.285231	0.314019	0.345334	0.379364
320	0.212116	0.234346	0.258601	0.285037	0.313822	0.345135	0.379164
321	0.211938	0.234162	0.258411	0.284843	0.313625	0.344936	0.378965
322	0.211761	0.233979	0.258223	0.284651	0.313429	0.344738	0.378767
323	0.211585	0.233797	0.258035	0.284459	0.313234	0.344541	0.378570
324	0.211409	0.233615	0.257848	0.284267	0.313040	0.344345	0.378373
325	0.211234	0.233434	0.257662	0.284077	0.312846	0.344149	0.378177
326	0.211060	0.233254	0.257477	0.283887	0.312653	0.343954	0.377982
327	0.210886	0.233074	0.257292	0.283698	0.312461	0.343760	0.377787
328	0.210713	0.232895	0.257108	0.283509	0.312269	0.343567	0.377593
329	0.210540	0.232717	0.256924	0.283322	0.312078	0.343374	0.377400
330	0.210369	0.232539	0.256741	0.283135	0.311888	0.343182	0.377208
331	0.210198	0.232362	0.256559	0.282948	0.311698	0.342990	0.377016
332	0.210027	0.232186	0.256378	0.282763	0.311509	0.342800	0.376825
333	0.209858	0.232010	0.256197	0.282578	0.311321	0.342609	0.376634
334	0.209689	0.231836	0.256017	0.282393	0.311134	0.342420	0.376444
335	0.209520	0.231661	0.255838	0.282210	0.310947	0.342231	0.376255
336	0.209352	0.231488	0.255659	0.282027	0.310761	0.342043	0.376067
337	0.209185	0.231315	0.255481	0.281844	0.310575	0.341856	0.375879
338	0.209019	0.231142	0.255304	0.281663	0.310391	0.341669	0.375692
339	0.208853	0.230971	0.255127	0.281482	0.310206	0.341483	0.375505
340	0.208687	0.230800	0.254951	0.281301	0.310023	0.341297	0.375319
341	0.208523	0.230629	0.254775	0.281122	0.309840	0.341113	0.375134
342	0.208359	0.230459	0.254600	0.280943	0.309658	0.340929	0.374949
343	0.208195	0.230290	0.254426	0.280764	0.309476	0.340745	0.374765
344	0.208032	0.230122	0.254252	0.280586	0.309295	0.340562	0.374582
345	0.207870	0.229954	0.254079	0.280409	0.309115	0.340380	0.374399
346	0.207708	0.229786	0.253907	0.280233	0.308935	0.340198	0.374217
347	0.207547	0.229619	0.253735	0.280057	0.308756	0.340017	0.374035
348	0.207387	0.229453	0.253564	0.279881	0.308578	0.339837	0.373855
349	0.207227	0.229288	0.253394	0.279707	0.308400	0.339657	0.373674
350	0.207067	0.229123	0.253224	0.279533	0.308223	0.339478	0.373495

Unit	83	84	85	86	87	88	89
351	0.206909	0.228958	0.253054	0.279359	0.308046	0.339299	0.373315
352	0.206751	0.228795	0.252886	0.279186	0.307870	0.339121	0.373137
353	0.206593	0.228631	0.252718	0.279014	0.307694	0.338944	0.372959
354	0.206436	0.228469	0.252550	0.278842	0.307520	0.338767	0.372782
355	0.206279	0.228307	0.252383	0.278671	0.307345	0.338591	0.372605
356	0.206123	0.228145	0.252217	0.278501	0.307172	0.338415	0.372429
357	0.205968	0.227984	0.252051	0.278331	0.306999	0.338240	0.372253
358	0.205813	0.227824	0.251886	0.278161	0.306826	0.338066	0.372078
359	0.205659	0.227664	0.251721	0.277993	0.306654	0.337892	0.371904
360	0.205505	0.227505	0.251557	0.277824	0.306483	0.337719	0.371730
361	0.205352	0.227346	0.251393	0.277657	0.306312	0.337546	0.371556
362	0.205199	0.227188	0.251230	0.277490	0.306142	0.337374	0.371384
363	0.205047	0.227031	0.251068	0.277323	0.305972	0.337202	0.371211
364	0.204896	0.226873	0.250906	0.277157	0.305803	0.337031	0.371040
365	0.204745	0.226717	0.250744	0.276992	0.305635	0.336861	0.370869
366	0.204594	0.226561	0.250584	0.276827	0.305467	0.336691	0.370698
367	0.204444	0.226406	0.250423	0.276663	0.305299	0.336521	0.370528
368	0.204295	0.226251	0.250264	0.276499	0.305133	0.336352	0.370359
369	0.204146	0.226096	0.250105	0.276336	0.304966	0.336184	0.370190
370	0.203997	0.225942	0.249946	0.276173	0.304800	0.336016	0.370021
371	0.203849	0.225789	0.249788	0.276011	0.304635	0.335849	0.369854
372	0.203702	0.225636	0.249630	0.275849	0.304470	0.335683	0.369686
373	0.203555	0.225484	0.249473	0.275688	0.304306	0.335516	0.369519
374	0.203408	0.225332	0.249316	0.275528	0.304143	0.335351	0.369353
375	0.203262	0.225181	0.249160	0.275368	0.303980	0.335186	0.369187
376	0.203117	0.225030	0.249005	0.275208	0.303817	0.335021	0.369022
377	0.202972	0.224880	0.248850	0.275049	0.303655	0.334857	0.368857
378	0.202828	0.224730	0.248695	0.274891	0.303493	0.334693	0.368693
379	0.202684	0.224581	0.248541	0.274733	0.303332	0.334530	0.368529
380	0.202540	0.224432	0.248388	0.274575	0.303172	0.334368	0.368366
381	0.202397	0.224284	0.248235	0.274418	0.303012	0.334206	0.368203
382	0.202254	0.224136	0.248082	0.274262	0.302852	0.334044	0.368041
383	0.202112	0.223988	0.247930	0.274106	0.302693	0.333883	0.367879
384	0.201971	0.223841	0.247779	0.273950	0.302535	0.333723	0.367718
385	0.201830	0.223695	0.247628	0.273795	0.302377	0.333563	0.367557

Unit	83	84	85	86	87	88	89
386	0.201689	0.223549	0.247477	0.273641	0.302219	0.333403	0.367397
387	0.201549	0.223404	0.247327	0.273487	0.302062	0.333244	0.367237
388	0.201409	0.223259	0.247177	0.273333	0.301905	0.333086	0.367078
389	0.201270	0.223114	0.247028	0.273180	0.301749	0.332927	0.366919
390	0.201131	0.222970	0.246880	0.273028	0.301594	0.332770	0.366761
391	0.200992	0.222827	0.246732	0.272876	0.301438	0.332613	0.366603
392	0.200854	0.222684	0.246584	0.272724	0.301284	0.332456	0.366446
393	0.200717	0.222541	0.246437	0.272573	0.301130	0.332300	0.366289
394	0.200580	0.222399	0.246290	0.272422	0.300976	0.332144	0.366132
395	0.200443	0.222257	0.246143	0.272272	0.300823	0.331989	0.365976
396	0.200307	0.222116	0.245998	0.272122	0.300670	0.331834	0.365821
397	0.200171	0.221975	0.245852	0.271973	0.300518	0.331680	0.365666
398	0.200036	0.221834	0.245707	0.271824	0.300366	0.331526	0.365511
399	0.199901	0.221694	0.245563	0.271676	0.300214	0.331373	0.365357
400	0.199766	0.221555	0.245419	0.271528	0.300063	0.331220	0.365203
401	0.199632	0.221416	0.245275	0.271380	0.229913	0.331067	0.365050
402	0.199499	0.221277	0.245132	0.271233	0.299763	0.330915	0.364897
403	0.199366	0.221139	0.244989	0.271087	0.299613	0.330764	0.364745
404	0.199233	0.221001	0.244847	0.270940	0.299464	0.330612	0.364593
405	0.199101	0.220864	0.244705	0.270795	0.299315	0.330462	0.364441
406	0.198969	0.220727	0.244563	0.270649	0.299167	0.330312	0.364290
407	0.198837	0.220590	0.244422	0.270505	0.299019	0.330162	0.364139
408	0.198706	0.220454	0.244282	0.270360	0.298872	0.330012	0.363989
409	0.198575	0.220318	0.244142	0.270216	0.298725	0.329863	0.363839
410	0.198445	0.220183	0.244002	0.270073	0.298578	0.329715	0.363690
411	0.198315	0.220048	0.243862	0.269930	0.298432	0.329567	0.363541
412	0.198185	0.219914	0.243724	0.269787	0.298287	0.329419	0.363393
413	0.198056	0.219779	0.243585	0.269645	0.298141	0.329272	0.363245
414	0.197928	0.219646	0.243447	0.269503	0.297997	0.329125	0.363097
415	0.197799	0.219513	0.243309	0.269361	0.297852	0.328979	0.362950
416	0.197671	0.219380	0.243172	0.269220	0.297708	0.328833	0.362803
417	0.197544	0.219247	0.243035	0.269080	0.297565	0.328687	0.362656
418	0.197417	0.219115	0.242899	0.268939	0.297421	0.328542	0.362510
419	0.197290	0.218984	0.242763	0.268800	0.297279	0.328397	0.362365
420	0.197164	0.218852	0.242627	0.268660	0.297136	0.328253	0.362220

Unit	83	84	85	86	87	88	89
421	0.197038	0.218721	0.242492	0.268521	0.296994	0.328109	0.362075
422	0.196912	0.218591	0.242357	0.268383	0.296853	0.327965	0.361931
423	0.196787	3.218461	0.242222	0.268245	0.296712	0.327822	0.361787
424	0.196662	0.218331	0.242088	0.268107	0.296571	0.327679	0.361643
425	0.196537	0.218202	0.241955	0.267969	0.296431	0.327537	0.361500
426	0.196413	0.218073	0.241821	0.267832	0.296291	0.327395	0.361357
427	0.196289	0.217944	0.241689	0.267696	0.296151	0.327254	0.361214
428	0.196166	0.217816	0.241556	0.267560	0.296012	0.327112	0.361072
429	0.196043	0.217688	0.241424	0.267424	0.295873	0.326972	0.360931
430	0.195920	0.217561	0.241292	0.267288	0.295735	0.326831	0.360790
431	0.195798	0.217434	0.241161	0.267153	0.295597	0.326691	0.360649
432	0.195676	0.217307	0.241030	0.267018	0.295459	0.326552	0.360508
433	0.195555	0.217181	0.240899	0.266884	0.295322	0.326413	0.360368
434	0.195433	0.217055	0.240769	0.266750	0.295185	0.326274	0.360228
435	0.195312	0.216929	0.240639	0.266617	0.295049	0.326135	0.360089
436	0.195192	0.216804	0.240509	0.266484	0.294913	0.325997	0.359950
437	0.195072	0.216679	0.240380	0.266351	0.294777	0.325859	0.359811
438	0.194952	0.216554	0.240252	0.266218	0.294642	0.325722	0.359673
439	0.194832	0.216430	0.240123	0.266086	0.294507	0.325585	0.359535
440	0.194713	0.216306	0.239995	0.265955	0.294372	0.325449	0.359398
441	0.194595	0.216183	0.239867	0.265823	0.294238	0.325312	0.359261
442	0.194476	0.216060	0.239740	0.265692	0.294104	0.325176	0.359124
443	0.194358	0.215937	0.239613	0.265562	0.293971	0.325041	0.358987
444	0.194240	0.215814	0.239486	0.265431	0.293837	0.324906	0.358851
445	0.194123	0.215692	0.239360	0.265301	0.293705	0.324771	0.358716
446	0.194006	0.215571	0.239234	0.265172	0.293572	0.324637	0.358580
447	0.193889	0.215449	0.239108	0.265043	0.293440	0.324503	0.358445
448	0.193772	0.215328	0.238983	0.264914	0.293308	0.324369	0.358311
449	0.193656	0.215207	0.238858	0.264785	0.293177	0.324236	0.358176
450	0.193541	0.215087	0.238734	0.264657	0.293046	0.324103	0.358042
451	0.193425	0.214967	0.238610	0.264529	0.292915	0.323970	0.357909
452	0.193310	0.214847	0.238486	0.264402	0.292785	0.323838	0.357776
453	0.193195	0.214728	0.238362	0.264275	0.292655	0.323706	0.357643
454	0.193081	0.214609	0.238239	0.264148	0.292525	0.323574	0.357510
455	0.192967	0.214490	0.238116	0.264022	0.292396	0.323443	0.357378

Unit	83	84	85	86	87	88	89
456	0.192853	0.214372	0.237994	0.263896	0.292267	0.323312	0.357246
457	0.192739	0.214254	0.237871	0.263770	0.292139	0.323181	0.357115
458	0.192626	0.214136	0.237749	0.263644	0.292010	0.323051	0.356983
459	0.192513	0.214018	0.237628	0.263519	0.291882	0.322921	0.356852
460	0.192400	0.213901	0.237507	0.263395	0.291755	0.322791	0.356722
461	0.192288	0.213784	0.237386	0.263270	0.291628	0.322662	0.356592
462	0.192176	0.213668	0.237265	0.263146	0.291501	0.322533	0.356462
463	0.192065	0.213552	0.237145	0.263022	0.291374	0.322405	0.356332
464	0.191953	0.213436	0.237025	0.262899	0.291248	0.322276	0.356203
465	0.191842	0.213320	0.236905	0.262776	0.291122	0.322149	0.356074
466	0.191731	0.213205	0.236786	0.262653	0.290996	0.322021	0.355946
467	0.191621	0.213090	0.236667	0.262530	0.290871	0.321894	0.355817
468	0.191511	0.212976	0.236548	0.262408	0.290746	0.321767	0.355689
469	0.191401	0.212861	0.236430	0.262286	0.290621	0.321640	0.355562
470	0.191291	0.212747	0.236312	0.262165	0.290497	0.321514	0.355434
471	0.191182	0.212633	0.236194	0.262044	0.290373	0.321388	0.355307
472	0.191073	0.212520	0.236077	0.261923	0.290249	0.321262	0.355181
473	0.190964	0.212407	0.235960	0.261802	0.290126	0.321137	0.355054
474	0.190856	0.212294	0.235843	0.261682	0.290003	0.321012	0.354928
475	0.190748	0.212182	0.235726	0.261562	0.289880	0.320887	0.354803
476	0.190640	0.212069	0.235610	0.261442	0.289758	0.320762	0.354677
477	0.190533	0.211958	0.235494	0.261323	0.289635	0.320638	0.354552
478	0.190425	0.211846	0.235379	0.261204	0.289514	0.320514	0.354427
479	0.190318	0.211735	0.235263	0.261085	0.289392	0.320391	0.354303
480	0.190212	0.211624	0.235148	0.260967	0.289271	0.320268	0.354179
481	0.190105	0.211513	0.235034	0.260848	0.289150	0.320145	0.354055
482	0.189999	0.211402	0.234919	0.260731	0.289029	0.320022	0.353931
483	0.189893	0.211292	0.234805	0.260613	0.288909	0.319900	0.353808
484	0.189788	0.211182	0.234691	0.260496	0.288789	0.319778	0.353685
485	0.189683	0.211073	0.234578	0.260379	0.288669	0.319656	0.353562
486	0.189578	0.210963	0.234465	0.260262	0.288550	0.319535	0.353440
487	0.189473	0.210854	0.234352	0.260146	0.288431	0.319414	0.353318
488	0.189368	0.210745	0.234239	0.260030	0.288312	0.319293	0.353196
489	0.189264	0.210637	0.234126	0.259914	0.288193	0.319172	0.353074
490	0.189160	0.210529	0.234014	0.259798	0.288075	0.319052	0.352953

Unit	83	84	85	86	87	88	89
491	0.189057	0.210421	0.233903	0.259683	0.287957	0.318932	0.352832
492	0.188953	0.210313	0.233791	0.259568	0.287839	0.318813	0.352711
493	0.188850	0.210206	0.233680	0.259454	0.287722	0.318693	0.352591
494	0.188747	0.210099	0.233569	0.259339	0.287605	0.318574	0.352471
495	0.188645	0.209992	0.233458	0.259225	0.287488	0.318455	0.352351
496	0.188543	0.209885	0.233348	0.259111	0.287371	0.318337	0.352231
497	0.188440	0.209779	0.233237	0.258998	0.287255	0.318219	0.352112
498	0.188339	0.209673	0.233127	0.258884	0.287139	0.318101	0.351993
499	0.188237	0.209567	0.233018	0.258771	0.287023	0.317983	0.351875
500	0.188136	0.209462	0.232908	0.258659	0.286908	0.317866	0.351756
501	0.188035	0.209356	0.232799	0.258546	0.286793	0.317749	0.351638
502	0.187934	0.209251	0.232691	0.258434	0.286678	0.317632	0.351520
503	0.187834	0.209147	0.232582	0.258322	0.286563	0.317515	0.351403
504	0.187733	0.209042	0.232474	0.258211	0.286449	0.317399	0.351285
505	0.187633	0.208938	0.232366	0.258099	0.286335	0.317283	0.351168
506	0.187534	0.208834	0.232258	0.257988	0.286221	0.317167	0.351051
507	0.187434	0.208730	0.232151	0.257877	0.286108	0.317052	0.350935
508	0.187335	0.208627	0.232043	0.257767	0.285994	0.316936	0.350819
509	0.187236	0.208524	0.231936	0.257657	0.285881	0.316822	0.350703
510	0.187137	0.208421	0.231830	0.257547	0.285769	0.316707	0.350587
511	0.187039	0.208318	0.231723	0.257437	0.285656	0.316593	0.350472
512	0.186940	0.208216	0.231617	0.257327	0.285544	0.316478	0.350356
513	0.186842	0.208114	0.231511	0.257218	0.285432	0.316365	0.350241
514	0.186744	0.208012	0.231405	0.257109	0.285321	0.316251	0.350127
515	0.186647	0.207910	0.231300	0.257001	0.285209	0.316138	0.350012
516	0.186550	0.207809	0.231195	0.256892	0.285098	0.316024	0.349898
517	0.186453	0.207707	0.231090	0.256784	0.284987	0.315912	0.349784
518	0.186356	0.207606	0.230985	0.256676	0.284876	0.315799	0.349671
519	0.186259	0.207506	0.230881	0.256568	0.284766	0.315687	0.349557
520	0.186163	0.207405	0.230777	0.256461	0.284656	0.315575	0.349444
521	0.186067	0.207305	0.230673	0.256354	0.284546	0.315463	0.349331
522	0.185971	0.207205	0.230569	0.256247	0.284437	0.315351	0.349219
523	0.185875	0.207105	0.230465	0.256140	0.284327	0.315240	0.349107
524	0.185780	0.207006	0.230362	0.256034	0.284218	0.315129	0.348994
525	0.185684	0.206907	0.230259	0.255927	0.284109	0.315018	0.348883

Unit	83	84	85	86	87	88	89
526	0.185590	0.206808	0.230157	0.255821	0.284001	0.314908	0.348771
527	0.185495	0.206709	0.230054	0.255716	0.283892	0.314797	0.348660
528	0.185400	0.206610	0.229952	0.255610	0.283784	0.314687	0.348549
529	0.185306	0.206512	0.229850	0.255505	0.283676	0.314578	0.348438
530	0.185212	0.206414	0.229748	0.255400	0.283569	0.314468	0.348327
531	0.185118	0.206316	0.229647	0.255295	0.283461	0.314359	0.348217
532	0.185024	0.206218	0.229545	0.255191	0.283354	0.314250	0.348107
533	0.184931	0.206121	0.229444	0.255087	0.283247	0.314141	0.347997
534	0.184838	0.206024	0.229343	0.254983	0.283141	0.314032	0.347887
535	0.184745	0.205927	0.229243	0.254879	0.283034	0.313924	0.347778
536	0.184652	0.205830	0.229143	0.254775	0.282928	0.313816	0.347668
537	0.184560	0.205734	0.229042	0.254672	0.282822	0.313708	0.347559
538	0.184468	0.205638	0.228943	0.254569	0.282716	0.313600	0.347451
539	0.184375	0.205542	0.228843	0.254466	0.282611	0.313493	0.347342
540	0.184284	0.205446	0.228743	0.254363	0.282506	0.313386	0.347234
541	0.184192	0.205350	0.228644	0.254261	0.282401	0.313279	0.347126
542	0.184101	0.205255	0.228545	0.254159	0.282296	0.313172	0.347018
543	0.184009	0.205160	0.228446	0.254057	0.282191	0.313066	0.346911
544	0.183918	0.205065	0.228348	0.253955	0.282087	0.312960	0.346804
545	0.183828	0.204970	0.228250	0.253854	0.281983	0.312854	0.346696
546	0.183737	0.204875	0.228152	0.253752	0.281879	0.312748	0.346590
547	0.183647	0.204781	0.228054	0.253651	0.281776	0.312642	0.346483
548	0.183557	0.204687	0.227956	0.253551	0.281672	0.312537	0.346377
549	0.183467	0.204593	0.227859	0.253450	0.281569	0.312432	0.346271
550	0.183377	0.204500	0.227761	0.253350	0.281466	0.312327	0.346165
551	0.183287	0.204406	0.227664	0.253250	0.281364	0.312223	0.346059
552	0.183198	0.204313	0.227568	0.253150	0.281261	0.312118	0.345953
553	0.183109	0.204220	0.227471	0.253050	0.281159	0.312014	0.345848
554	0.183020	0.204127	0.227375	0.252951	0.281057	0.311910	0.345743
555	0.182931	0.204035	0.227279	0.252851	0.280955	0.311806	0.345638
556	0.182843	0.203942	0.227183	0.252752	0.280853	0.311703	0.345534
557	0.182755	0.203850	0.227087	0.252654	0.280752	0.311600	0.345429
558	0.182666	0.203758	0.226992	0.252555	0.280651	0.311496	0.345325
559	0.182578	0.203666	0.226896	0.252457	0.280550	0.311394	0.345221
560	0.182491	0.203575	0.226801	0.252358	0.280449	0.311291.	0.345118

Unit	83	84	85	86	87	88	89
561	0.182403	0.203484	0.226706	0.252260	0.280349	0.311189	0.345014
562	0.182316	0.203392	0.226612	0.252163	0.280248	0.311086	0.344911
563	0.182229	0.203301	0.226517	0.252065	0.280148	0.310984	0.344808
564	0.182142	0.203211	0.226423	0.251968	0.280048	0.310883	0.344705
565	0.182055	0.203120	0.226329	0.251871	0.279949	0.310781	0.344602
566	0.181969	0.203030	0.226235	0.251774	0.279849	0.310680	0.344500
567	0.181882	0.202940	0.226142	0.251677	0.279750	0.310579	0.344397
568	0.181796	0.202850	0.226048	0.251581	0.279651	0.310478	0.344295
569	0.181710	0.202760	0.225955	0.251484	0.279552	0.310377	0.344194
570	0.181625	0.202671	0.225862	0.251388	0.279454	0.310277	0.344092
571	0.181539	0.202581	0.225769	0.251293	0.279355	0.310176	0.343991
572	0.181454	0.202492	0.225677	0.251197	0.279257	0.310076	0.343890
573	0.181368	0.202403	0.225584	0.251101	0.279159	0.309976	0.343789
574	0.181283	0.202314	0.225492	0.251006	0.279061	0.309877	0.343688
575	0.181199	0.202226	0.225400	0.250911	0.278964	0.309777	0.343587
576	0.181114	0.202137	0.225308	0.250816	0.278866	0.309678	0.343487
577	0.181030	0.202049	0.225217	0.250722	0.278769	0.309579	0.343387
578	0.180945	0.201961	0.225125	0.250627	0.278672	0.309480	0.343287
579	0.180861	0.201873	0.225034	0.250533	0.278575	0.309381	0.343187
580	0.180777	0.201786	0.224943	0.250439	0.278479	0.309283	0.343087
581	0.180694	0.201698	0.224852	0.250345	0.278382	0.309185	0.342988
582	0.180610	0.201611	0.224761	0.250251	0.278286	0.309087	0.342889
583	0.180527	0.201524	0.224671	0.250158	0.278190	0.308989	0.342790
584	0.180444	0.201437	0.224581	0.250065	0.278095	0.308891	0.342691
585	0.180361	0.201351	0.224491	0.249972	0.277999	0.308794	0.342593
586	0.180278	0.201264	0.224401	0.249879	0.277904	0.308696	0.342494
587	0.180195	0.201178	0.224311	0.249786	0.277808	0.308599	0.342396
588	0.180113	0.201092	0.224221	0.249693	0.277713	0.308503	0.342298
589	0.180031	0.201006	0.224132	0.249601	0.277619	0.308406	0.342200
590	0.179949	0.200920	0.224043	0.249509	0.277524	0.308309	0.342103
591	0.179867	0.200834	0.223954	0.249417	0.277430	0.308213	0.342005
592	0.179785	0.200749	0.223865	0.249325	0.277335	0.308117	0.341908
593	0.179703	0.200664	0.223777	0.249234	0.277241	0.308021	0.341811
594	0.179622	0.200579	0.223688	0.249142	0.277148	0.307925	0.341714
595	0.179541	0.200494	0.223600	0.249051	0.277054	0.307830	0.341618

Unit	83	84	85	86	87	88	89
596	0.179460	0.200409	0.223512	0.248960	0.276960	0.307735	0.341521
597	0.179379	0.200325	0.223424	0.248870	0.276867	0.307640	0.341425
598	0.179298	0.200241	0.223337	0.248779	0.276774	0.307545	0.341329
599	0.179218	0.200156	0.223249	0.248688	0.276681	0.307450	0.341233
600	0.179137	0.200072	0.223162	0.248598	0.276588	0.307355	0.341138
601	0.179057	0.199989	0.223075	0.248508	0.276496	0.307261	0.341042
602	0.178977	0.199905	0.222988	0.248418	0.276404	0.307167	0.340947
603	0.178897	0.199822	0.222901	0.248329	0.276311	0.307073	0.340852
604	0.178818	0.199738	0.222815	0.248239	0.276219	0.306979	0.340757
605	0.178738	0.199655	0.222728	0.248150	0.276128	0.306885	0.340662
606	0.178659	0.199572	0.222642	0.248061	0.276036	0.306792	0.340567
607	0.178580	0.199490	0.222556	0.247972	0.275945	0.306698	0.340473
608	0.178501	0.199407	0.222470	0.247883	0.275853	0.306605	0.340379
609	0.178422	0.199325	0.222384	0.247794	0.275762	0.306512	0.340285
610	0.178343	0.199242	0.222299	0.247706	0.275671	0.306420	0.340191
611	0.178265	0.199160	0.222213	0.247617	0.275581	0.306327	0.340097
612	0.178186	0.199078	0.222128	0.247529	0.275490	0.306235	0.340004
613	0.178108	0.198997	0.222043	0.247441	0.275400	0.306143	0.339910
614	0.178030	0.198915	0.221958	0.247354	0.275310	0.306051	0.339817
615	0.177952	0.198834	0.221874	0.247266	0.275220	0.305959	0.339724
616	0.177875	0.198752	0.221789	0.247179	0.275130	0.305867	0.339631
617	0.177797	0.198671	0.221705	0.247092	0.275040	0.305776	0.339539
618	0.177720	0.198590	0.221621	0.247004	0.274951	0.305684	0.339446
619	0.177642	0.198510	0.221537	0.246918	0.274861	0.305593	0.339354
620	0.177565	0.198429	0.221453	0.246831	0.274772	0.305502	0.339262
621	0.177488	0.198349	0.221369	0.246744	0.274683	0.305411	0.339170
622	0.177412	0.198268	0.221286	0.246658	0.274595	0.305321	0.339078
623	0.177335	0.198188	0.221202	0.246572	0.274506	0.305230	0.338987
624	0.177259	0.198108	0.221119	0.246486	0.274418	0.305140	0.338896
625	0.177182	0.198029	0.221036	0.246400	0.274329	0.305050	0.338804
626	0.177106	0.197949	0.220953	0.246314	0.274241	0.304960	0.338713
627	0.177030	0.197869	0.220871	0.246229	0.274153	0.304870	0.338622
628	0.176954	0.197790	0.220788	0.246143	0.274065	0.304781	0.338532
629	0.176879	0.197711	0.220705	0.246058	0.273978	0.304691	0.338441
630	0.176803	0.197632	0.220624	0.245972	0.273890	0.304603	0.338351

Unit	83	84	85	86	87	88	89
631	0.176728	0.197553	0.220542	0.245888	0.273803	0.304513	0.338261
632	0.176653	0.197475	0.220460	0.245803	0.273716	0.304424	0.338170
633	0.176578	0.197396	0.220378	0.245719	0.273629	0.304335	0.338081
634	0.176503	0.197318	0.220296	0.245635	0.273542	0.304247	0.337991
635	0.176428	0.197239	0.220215	0.245550	0.273456	0.304158	0.337901
636	0.176353	0.197161	0.220134	0.245466	0.273369	0.304070	0.337812
637	0.176279	0.197083	0.220053	0.245382	0.273283	0.303982	0.337723
638	0.176205	0.197006	0.219972	0.245299	0.273197	0.303894	0.337634
639	0.176130	0.196928	0.219891	0.245215	0.273111	0.303806	0.337545
640	0.176056	0.196851	0.219810	0.245132	0.273025	0.303719	0.337456
641	0.175983	0.196773	0.219730	0.245048	0.272940	0.303631	0.337367
642	0.175909	0.196696	0.219650	0.244965	0.272854	0.303544	0.337279
643	0.175835	0.196619	0.219570	0.244882	0.272769	0.303457	0.337191
644	0.175762	0.196542	0.219490	0.244799	0.272684	0.303370	0.337103
645	0.175688	0.196466	0.219410	0.244717	0.272599	0.303283	0.337015
646	0.175615	0.196389	0.219330	0.244634	0.272514	0.303196	0.336927
647	0.175542	0.196313	0.219251	0.244552	0.272429	0.303110	0.336839
648	0.175469	0.196237	0.219171	0.244470	0.272345	0.303024	0.336752
649	0.175397	0.196160	0.219092	0.244388	0.272260	0.302937	0.336665
650	0.175324	0.196084	0.219013	0.244306	0.272176	0.302851	0.336578
651	0.175252	0.196009	0.218934	0.244224	0.272092	0.302766	0.336491
652	0.175179	0.195933	0.218855	0.244143	0.272008	0.302680	0.336404
653	0.175107	0.195858	0.218777	0.244061	0.271924	0.302594	0.336317
654	0.175035	0.195782	0.218698	0.243980	0.271841	0.302509	0.336231
655	0.174963	0.195707	0.218620	0.243899	0.271757	0.302424	0.336144
656	0.174892	0.195632	0.218542	0.243818	0.271674	0.302339	0.336058
657	0.174820	0.195557	0.218463	0.243737	0.271591	0.302254	0.335972
658	0.174749	0.195482	0.218386	0.243657	0.271508	0.302169	0.335886
659	0.174677	0.195407	0.218308	0.243576	0.271425	0.302084	0.335800
660	0.174606	0.195333	0.218230	0.243496	0.271342	0.302000	0.335715
661	0.174535	0.195259	0.218153	0.243416	0.271260	0.301916	0.335629
662	0.174464	0.195184	0.218075	0.243335	0.271178	0.301831	0.335544
663	0.174393	0.195110	0.217998	0.243256	0.271095	0.301747	0.335459
664	0.174323	0.195036	0.217921	0.243176	0.271013	0.301664	0.335374
665	0.174252	0.194962	0.217844	0.243096	0.270931	0.301580	0.335289

Unit	83	84	85	86	87	88	89
666	0.174182	0.194889	0.217768	0.243017	0.270850	0.301496	0.335204
667	0.174112	0.194815	0.217691	0.242937	0.270768	0.301413	0.335120
668	0.174041	0.194742	0.217615	0.242858	0.270686	0.301330	0.335035
669	0.173971	0.194669	0.217538	0.242779	0.270605	0.301246	0.334951
670	0.173902	0.194595	0.217462	0.242700	0.270524	0.301164	0.334867
671	0.173832	0.194522	0.217386	0.242622	0.270443	0.301081	0.334783
672	0.173762	0.194450	0.217310	0.242543	0.270362	0.300998	0.334699
673	0.173693	0.194377	0.217234	0.242464	0.270281	0.300915	0.334616
674	0.173624	0.194304	0.217159	0.242386	0.270201	0.300833	0.334532
675	0.173554	0.194232	0.217083	0.242308	0.270120	0.300751	0.334449
676	0.173485	0.194160	0.217008	0.242230	0.270040	0.300669	0.334366
677	0.173416	0.194087	0.216933	0.242152	0.269960	0.300587	0.334282
678	0.173348	0.194015	0.216858	0.242074	0.269880	0.300505	0.334200
679	0.173279	0.193943	0.216783	0.241997	0.269800	0.300423	0.334117
680	0.173210	0.193872	0.216708	0.241919	0.269720	0.300342	0.334034
681	0.173142	0.193800	0.216633	0.241842	0.269640	0.300260	0.333952
682	0.173074	0.193728	0.216559	0.241765	0.269561	0.300179	0.333869
683	0.173006	0.193657	0.216485	0.241688	0.269481	0.300098	0.333787
684	0.172938	0.193586	0.216410	0.241611	0.269402	0.300017	0.333705
685	0.172870	0.193515	0.216336	0.241534	0.269323	0.299936	0.333623
686	0.172802	0.193444	0.216262	0.241457	0.269244	0.299856	0.333541
687	0.172734	0.193373	0.216188	0.241381	0.269165	0.299775	0.333459
688	0.172667	0.193302	0.216115	0.241304	0.269087	0.299695	0.333378
689	0.172599	0.193231	0.216041	0.241228	0.269008	0.299614	0.333296
690	0.172532	0.193161	0.215968	0.241152	0.268930	0.299534	0.333215
691	0.172465	0.193091	0.215894	0.241076	0.268852	0.299454	0.333134
692	0.172398	0.193020	0.215821	0.241000	0.268774	0.299374	0.333053
693	0.172331	0.192950	0.215748	0.240924	0.268696	0.299295	0.332972
694	0.172264	0.192880	0.215675	0.240849	0.268618	0.299215	0.332892
695	0.172197	0.192810	0.215602	0.240773	0.268540	0.299136	0.332811
696	0.172131	0.192741	0.215530	0.240698	0.268462	0.299056	0.332731
697	0.172065	0.192671	0.215457	0.240623	0.268385	0.298977	0.332650
698	0.171998	0.192602	0.215385	0.240548	0.268308	0.298898	0.332570
699	0.171932	0.192532	0.215312	0.240473	0.268231	0.298819	0.332490
700	0.171866	0.192463	0.215240	0.240398	0.268154	0.298740	0.332410

Unit	83	84	85	86	87	88	89
701	0.171800	0.192394	0.215168	0.240323	0.268077	0.298662	0.332330
702	0.171734	0.192325	0.215096	0.240249	0.268000	0.298583	0.332251
703	0.171669	0.192256	0.215024	0.240175	0.267923	0.298505	0.332171
704	0.171603	0.192187	0.214953	0.240100	0.267847	0.298427	0.332092
705	0.171537	0.192119	0.214881	0.240026	0.267770	0.298349	0.332013
706	0.171472	0.192050	0.214810	0.239952	0.267694	0.298271	0.331933
707	0.171407	0.191982	0.214739	0.239878	0.267618	0.298193	0.331854
708	0.171342	0.191914	0.214667	0.239804	0.267542	0.298115	0.331776
709	0.171277	0.191846	0.214596	0.239731	0.267466	0.298037	0.331697
710	0.171212	0.191778	0.214526	0.239657	0.267390	0.297960	0.331618
711	0.171147	0.191710	0.214455	0.239584	0.267315	0.297883	0.331540
712	0.171082	0.191642	0.214384	0.239511	0.267239	0.297805	0.331462
713	0.171018	0.191574	0.214314	0.239437	0.267164	0.297728	0.331383
714	0.170954	0.191507	0.214243	0.239364	0.267089	0.297651	0.331305
715	0.170889	0.191439	0.214173	0.239292	0.267014	0.297575	0.331227
716	0.170825	0.191372	0.214103	0.239219	0.266939	0.297498	0.331150
717	0.170761	0.191305	0.214033	0.239146	0.266864	0.297421	0.331072
718	0.170697	0.191238	0.213963	0.239074	0.266789	0.297345	0.330994
719	0.170633	0.191171	0.213893	0.239001	0.266715	0.297269	0.330917
720	0.170569	0.191104	0.213823	0.238929	0.266640	0.297192	0.330839
721	0.170506	0.191037	0.213754	0.238857	0.266566	0.297116	0.330762
722	0.170442	0.190971	0.213684	0.238785	0.266492	0.297040	0.330685
723	0.170379	0.190904	0.213615	0.238713	0.266417	0.296965	0.330608
724	0.170316	0.190838	0.213546	0.238641	0.266344	0.296889	0.330531
725	0.170252	0.190772	0.213477	0.238570	0.266270	0.296813	0.330455
726	0.170189	0.190706	0.213408	0.238498	0.266196	0.296738	0.330378
727	0.170126	0.190640	0.213339	0.238427	0.266122	0.296663	0.330302
728	0.170063	0.190574	0.213270	0.238355	0.266049	0.296587	0.330225
729	0.170001	0.190508	0.213201	0.238284	0.265975	0.296512	0.330149
730	0.169938	0.190442	0.213133	0.238213	0.265902	0.296437	0.330073
731	0.169876	0.190377	0.213064	0.238142	0.265829	0.296363	0.329997
732	0.169813	0.190311	0.212996	0.238071	0.265756	0.296288	0.329921
733	0.169751	0.190246	0.212928	0.238001	0.265683	0.296213	0.329846
734	0.169689	0.190181	0.212860	0.237930	0.265610	0.296139	0.329770
735	0.169627	0.190116	0.212792	0.237859	0.265538	0.296064	0.329695

Unit	83	84	85	86	87	88	89
736	0.169565	0.190051	0.212724	0.237789	0.265465	0.295990	0.329619
737	0.169503	0.189986	0.212656	0.237719	0.265393	0.295916	0.329544
738	0.169441	0.189921	0.212589	0.237649	0.265321	0.295842	0.329469
739	0.169379	0.189856	0.212521	0.237579	0.265248	0.295768	0.329394
740	0.169318	0.189792	0.212454	0.237509	0.265176	0.295694	0.329319
741	0.169256	0.189727	0.212387	0.237439	0.265104	0.295621	0.329244
742	0.169195	0.189663	0.212320	0.237369	0.265033	0.295547	0.329170
743	0.169134	0.189599	0.212253	0.237300	0.264961	0.295474	0.329095
744	0.169073	0.189534	0.212186	0.237230	0.264889	0.295401	0.329021
745	0.169011	0.189470	0.212119	0.237161	0.264818	0.295327	0.328946
746	0.168951	0.189406	0.212052	0.237092	0.264746	0.295254	0.328872
747	0.168890	0.189343	0.211986	0.237023	0.264675	0.295181	0.328798
748	0.168829	0.189279	0.211919	0.236954	0.264604	0.295109	0.328724
749	0.168768	0.189215	0.211853	0.236885	0.264533	0.295036	0.328650
750	0.168708	0.189152	0.211786	0.236816	0.264462	0.294963	0.328577
751	0.168647	0.189088	0.211720	0.236747	0.264391	0.294891	0.328503
752	0.168587	0.189025	0.211654	0.236679	0.264321	0.294819	0.328430
753	0.168527	0.188962	0.211588	0.236611	0.264250	0.294746	0.328356
754	0.168467	0.188899	0.211522	0.236542	0.264180	0.294674	0.328283
755	0.168407	0.188836	0.211457	0.236474	0.264109	0.294602	0.328210
756	0.168347	0.188773	0.211391	0.236406	0.264039	0.294530	0.328137
757	0.168287	0.188710	0.211326	0.236338	0.263969	0.294458	0.328064
758	0.168227	0.188648	0.211260	0.236270	0.263899	0.294387	0.327991
759	0.168168	0.188585	0.211195	0.236202	0.263829	0.294315	0.327918
760	0.168108	0.188523	0.211130	0.236135	0.263759	0.294244	0.327846
761	0.168049	0.188460	0.211065	0.236067	0.263690	0.294172	0.327773
762	0.167990	0.188398	0.211000	0.236000	0.263620	0.294101	0.327701
763	0.167930	0.188336	0.210935	0.235932	0.263551	0.294030	0.327629
764	0.167871	0.188274	0.210870	0.235865	0.263481	0.293959	0.327557
765	0.167812	0.188212	0.210805	0.235798	0.263412	0.293888	0.327485
766	0.167753	0.188150	0.210741	0.235731	0.263343	0.293817	0.327413
767	0.167694	0.188088	0.210676	0.235664	0.263274	0.293747	0.327341
768	0.167636	0.188027	0.210612	0.235597	0.263205	0.293676	0.327269
769	0.167577	0.187965	0.210548	0.235530	0.263136	0.293606	0.327198
770	0.167519	0.187904	0.210484	0.235464	0.263068	0.293535	0.327126

Unit	83	84	85	86	87	88	89
771	0.167460	0.187843	0.210420	0.235397	0.262999	0.293465	0.327055
772	0.167402	0.187781	0.210356	0.235331	0.262930	0.293395	0.326983
773	0.167344	0.187720	0.210292	0.235265	0.262862	0.293325	0.326912
774	0.167285	0.187659	0.210228	0.235199	0.262794	0.293255	0.326841
775	0.167227	0.187598	0.210164	0.235133	0.262726	0.293185	0.326770
776	0.167169	0.187537	0.210101	0.235067	0.262658	0.293115	0.326699
777	0.167112	0.187477	0.210037	0.235001	0.262590	0.293046	0.326629
778	0.167054	0.187416	0.209974	0.234935	0.262522	0.292976	0.326558
779	0.166996	0.187355	0.209911	0.234869	0.262454	0.292907	0.326488
780	0.166938	0.187295	0.209848	0.234804	0.262386	0.292837	0.326417
781	0.166881	0.187235	0.209785	0.234738	0.262319	0.292768	0.326347
782	0.166824	0.187174	0.209722	0.234673	0.262251	0.292699	0.326277
783	0.166766	0.187114	0.209659	0.234608	0.262184	0.292630	0.326207
784	0.166709	0.187054	0.209596	0.234543	0.262117	0.292561	0.326137
785	0.166652	0.186994	0.209534	0.234477	0.262050	0.292493	0.326067
786	0.166595	0.186934	0.209471	0.234413	0.261983	0.292424	0.325997
787	0.166538	0.186875	0.209409	0.234348	0.261916	0.292355	0.325927
788	0.166481	0.186815	0.209346	0.234283	0.261849	0.292287	0.325858
789	0.166424	0.186755	0.209284	0.234218	0.261782	0.292219	0.325788
790	0.166368	0.186696	0.209222	0.234154	0.261716	0.292150	0.325719
791	0.166311	0.186636	0.209160	0.234089	0.261649	0.292082	0.325650
792	0.166255	0.186577	0.209098	0.234025	0.261583	0.292014	0.325580
793	0.166198	0.186518	0.209036	0.233961	0.261517	0.291946	0.325511
794	0.166142	0.186459	0.208974	0.233897	0.261450	0.291878	0.325442
795	0.166086	0.186400	0.208913	0.233833	0.261384	0.291811	0.325374
796	0.166030	0.186341	0.208851	0.233769	0.261318	0.291743	0.325305
797	0.165974	0.186282	0.208790	0.233705	0.261252	0.291675	0.325236
798	0.165918	0.186223	0.208728	0.233641	0.261186	0.291608	0.325168
799	0.165862	0.186165	0.208667	0.233577	0.261121	0.291541	0.325099
800	0.165806	0.186106	0.208606	0.233514	0.261055	0.291473	0.325031
801	0.165751	0.186048	0.208545	0.233450	0.260990	0.291406	0.324962
802	0.165695	0.185989	0.208484	0.233387	0.260924	0.291339	0.324894
803	0.165639	0.185931	0.208423	0.233324	0.260859	0.291272	0.324826
804	0.165584	0.185873	0.208362	0.233260	0.260794	0.291205	0.324758
805	0.165529	0.185815	0.208301	0.233197	0.260729	0.291139	0.324690

Unit	83	84	85	86	87	88	89
806	0.165473	0.185757	0.208241	0.233134	0.260664	0.291072	0.324623
807	0.165418	0.185699	0.208180	0.233072	0.260599	0.291005	0.324555
808	0.165363	0.185641	0.208120	0.233009	0.260534	0.290939	0.324487
809	0.165308	0.185583	0.208059	0.232946	0.260469	0.290873	0.324420
810	0.165253	0.185525	0.207999	0.232883	0.260404	0.290806	0.324353
811	0.165199	0.185468	0.207939	0.232821	0.260340	0.290740	0.324285
812	0.165144	0.185410	0.207879	0.232758	0.260275	0.290674	0.324218
813	0.165089	0.185353	0.207819	0.232696	0.260211	0.290608	0.324151
814	0.165035	0.185296	0.207759	0.232634	0.260147	0.290542	0.324084
815	0.164980	0.185238	0.207699	0.232572	0.260083	0.290477	0.324017
816	0.164926	0.185181	0.207639	0.232510	0.260019	0.290411	0.323950
817	0.164872	0.185124	0.207580	0.232448	0.259955	0.290345	0.323884
818	0.164817	0.185067	0.207520	0.232386	0.259891	0.290280	0.323817
819	0.164763	0.185010	0.207461	0.232324	0.259827	0.290214	0.323751
820	0.164709	0.184954	0.207402	0.232262	0.259763	0.290149	0.323684
821	0.164655	0.184897	0.207342	0.232201	0.259700	0.290084	0.323618
822	0.164601	0.184840	0.207283	0.232139	0.259636	0.290019	0.323552
823	0.164548	0.184784	0.207224	0.232078	0.259573	0.289954	0.323486
824	0.164494	0.184727	0.207165	0.232017	0.259509	0.289889	0.323420
825	0.164440	0.184671	0.207106	0.231955	0.259446	0.289824	0.323354
826	0.164387	0.184615	0.207047	0.231894	0.259383	0.289759	0.323288
827	0.164333	0.184559	0.206989	0.231833	0.259320	0.289695	0.323222
828	0.164280	0.184503	0.206930	0.231772	0.259257	0.289630	0.323156
829	0.164227	0.184446	0.206871	0.231711	0.259194	0.289566	0.323091
830	0.164173	0.184391	0.206813	0.231651	0.259131	0.289501	0.323025
831	0.164120	0.184335	0.206755	0.231590	0.259069	0.289437	0.322960
832	0.164067	0.184279	0.206696	0.231529	0.259006	0.289373	0.322895
833	0.164014	0.184223	0.206638	0.231469	0.258944	0.289309	0.322829
834	0.163961	0.184168	0.206580	0.231408	0.258881	0.289245	0.322764
835	0.163909	0.184112	0.206522	0.231348	0.258819	0.289181	0.322699
836	0.163856	0.184057	0.206464	0.231288	0.258757	0.289117	0.322634
837	0.163803	0.184001	0.206406	0.231228	0.258695	0.289053	0.322569
838	0.163751	0.183946	0.206348	0.231168	0.258632	0.288989	0.322505
839	0.163698	0.183891	0.206291	0.231108	0.258571	0.288926	0.322440
840	0.163646	0.183836	0.206233	0.231048	0.258509	0.288862	0.322376

Unit	83	84	85	86	87	88	89
841	0.163593	0.183781	0.206175	0.230988	0.258447	0.288799	0.322311
842	0.163541	0.183726	0.206118	0.230928	0.258385	0.288736	0.322247
843	0.163489	0.183671	0.206061	0.230869	0.258324	0.288673	0.322182
844	0.163437	0.183616	0.206003	0.230809	0.258262	0.288609	0.322118
845	0.163385	0.183562	0.205946	0.230750	0.258201	0.288546	0.322054
846	0.163333	0.183507	0.205889	0.230690	0.258139	0.288483	0.321990
847	0.163281	0.183453	0.205832	0.230631	0.258078	0.288421	0.321926
848	0.163229	0.183398	0.205775	0.230572	0.258017	0.288358	0.321862
849	0.163178	0.183344	0.205718	0.230513	0.257956	0.288295	0.321798
850	0.163126	0.183290	0.205662	0.230454	0.257895	0.288233	0.321735
851	0.163074	0.183235	0.205605	0.230395	0.257834	0.288170	0.321671
852	0.163023	0.183181	0.205548	0.230336	0.257773	0.288108	0.321608
853	0.162972	0.183127	0.205492	0.230277	0.257712	0.288045	0.321544
854	0.162920	0.183073	0.205435	0.230218	0.257652	0.287983	0.321481
855	0.162869	0.183019	0.205379	0.230160	0.257591	0.287921	0.321418
856	0.162818	0.182965	0.205323	0.230101	0.257531	0.287859	0.321354
857	0.162767	0.182912	0.205266	0.230043	0.257470	0.287797	0.321291
858	0.162716	0.182858	0.205210	0.229984	0.257410	0.287735	0.321228
859	0.162665	0.182805	0.205154	0.229926	0.257350	0.287673	0.321166
860	0.162614	0.182751	0.205098	0.229868	0.257289	0.287612	0.321103
861	0.162563	0.182698	0.205042	0.229810	0.257229	0.287550	0.321040
862	0.162512	0.182644	0.204987	0.229752	0.257169	0.287488	0.320977
863	0.162462	0.182591	0.204931	0.229694	0.257109	0.287427	0.320915
864	0.162411	0.182538	0.204875	0.229636	0.257050	0.287366	0.320852
865	0.162361	0.182485	0.204820	0.229578	0.256990	0.287304	0.320790
866	0.162310	0.182432	0.204764	0.229520	0.256930	0.287243	0.320728
867	0.162260	0.182379	0.204709	0.229463	0.256871	0.287182	0.320665
868	0.162210	0.182326	0.204654	0.229405	0.256811	0.287121	0.320603
869	0.162159	0.182273	0.204598	0.229348	0.256752	0.287060	0.320541
870	0.162109	0.182220	0.204543	0.229290	0.256692	0.286999	0.320479
871	0.162059	0.182168	0.204488	0.229233	0.256633	0.286938	0.320417
872	0.162009	0.182115	0.204433	0.229176	0.256574	0.286878	0.320356
873	0.161959	0.182063	0.204378	0.229119	0.256515	0.286817	0.320294
874	0.161910	0.182010	0.204323	0.229062	0.256456	0.286756	0.320232
875	0.161860	0.181958	0.204268	0.229005	0.256397	0.286696	0.320171

Unit	83	84	85	86	87	88	89
876	0.161810	0.181906	0.204214	0.228948	0.256338	0.286635	0.320109
877	0.161760	0.181853	0.204159	0.228891	0.256280	0.286575	0.320048
878	0.161711	0.181801	0.204105	0.228834	0.256221	0.286515	0.319986
879	0.161661	0.181749	0.204050	0.228777	0.256162	0.286455	0.319925
880	0.161612	0.181697	0.203996	0.228721	0.256104	0.286395	0.319864
881	0.161563	0.181645	0.203941	0.228664	0.256045	0.286335	0.319803
882	0.161513	0.181594	0.203887	0.228608	0.255987	0.286275	0.319742
883	0.161464	0.181542	0.203833	0.228552	0.255929	0.286215	0.319681
884	0.161415	0.181490	0.203779	0.228495	0.255871	0.286155	0.319620
885	0.161366	0.181439	0.203725	0.228439	0.255812	0.286096	0.319559
886	0.161317	0.181387	0.203671	0.228383	0.255754	0.286036	0.319499
887	0.161268	0.181336	0.203617	0.228327	0.255696	0.285977	0.319438
888	0.161219	0.181284	0.203563	0.228271	0.255639	0.285917	0.319378
889	0.161171	0.181233	0.203510	0.228215	0.255581	0.285858	0.319317
890	0.161122	0.181182	0.203456	0.228159	0.255523	0.285799	0.319257
891	0.161073	0.181130	0.203402	0.228103	0.255465	0.285739	0.319197
892	0.161025	0.181079	0.203349	0.228048	0.255408	0.285680	0.319137
893	0.160976	0.181028	0.203296	0.227992	0.255350	0.285621	0.319076
894	0.160928	0.180977	0.203242	0.227937	0.255293	0.285562	0.319016
895	0.160879	0.180926	0.203189	0.227881	0.255236	0.285503	0.318956
896	0.160831	0.180876	0.203136	0.227826	0.255178	0.285445	0.318897
897	0.160783	0.180825	0.203083	0.227771	0.255121	0.285386	0.318837
898	0.160735	0.180774	0.203030	0.227715	0.255064	0.285327	0.318777
899	0.160687	0.180724	0.202977	0.227660	0.255007	0.285269	0.318717
900	0.160639	0.180673	0.202924	0.227605	0.254950	0.285210	0.318658
901	0.160591	0.180623	0.202871	0.227550	0.254893	0.285152	0.318598
902	0.160543	0.180572	0.202818	0.227495	0.254836	0.285093	0.318539
903	0.160495	0.180522	0.202765	0.227440	0.254780	0.285035	0.318480
904	0.160447	0.180472	0.202713	0.227386	0.254723	0.284977	0.318420
905	0.160400	0.180422	0.202660	0.227331	0.254666	0.284919	0.318361
906	0.160352	0.180371	0.202608	0.227276	0.254610	0.284861	0.318302
907	0.160304	0.180321	0.202555	0.227222	0.254553	0.284803	0.318243
908	0.160257	0.180271	0.202503	0.227167	0.254497	0.284745	0.318184
909	0.160210	0.180221	0.202451	0.227113	0.254441	0.284687	0.318125
910	0.160162	0.180172	0.202399	0.227059	0.254385	0.284630	0.318066

Unit	83	84	85	86	87	88	89
911	0.160115	0.180122	0.202347	0.227004	0.254329	0.284572	0.318008
912	0.160068	0.180072	0.202294	0.226950	0.254272	0.284514	0.317949
913	0.160021	0.180023	0.202243	0.226896	0.254217	0.284457	0.317890
914	0.159973	0.179973	0.202191	0.226842	0.254161	0.284399	0.317832
915	0.159926	0.179923	0.202139	0.226788	0.254105	0.284342	0.317773
916	0.159880	0.179874	0.202087	0.226734	0.254049	0.284285	0.317715
917	0.159833	0.179825	0.202035	0.226680	0.253993	0.284228	0.317657
918	0.159786	0.179775	0.201984	0.226627	0.253938	0.284171	0.317599
919	0.159739	0.179726	0.201932	0.226573	0.253882	0.284113	0.317541
920	0.159692	0.179677	0.201881	0.226519	0.253827	0.284056	0.317482
921	0.159646	0.179628	0.201829	0.226466	0.253771	0.284000	0.317425
922	0.159599	0.179579	0.201778	0.226412	0.253716	0.283943	0.317367
923	0.159553	0.179530	0.201727	0.226359	0.253661	0.283886	0.317309
924	0.159506	0.179481	0.201675	0.226305	0.253606	0.283829	0.317251
925	0.159460	0.179432	0.201624	0.226252	0.253550	0.283773	0.317193
926	0.159414	0.179383	0.201573	0.226199	0.253495	0.283716	0.317136
927	0.159367	0.179335	0.201522	0.226146	0.253440	0.283660	0.317078
928	0.159321	0.179286	0.201471	0.226093	0.253386	0.283603	0.317021
929	0.159275	0.179238	0.201420	0.226040	0.253331	0.283547	0.316963
930	0.159229	0.179189	0.201370	0.225987	0.253276	0.283491	0.316906
931	0.159183	0.179141	0.201319	0.225934	0.253221	0.283435	0.316849
932	0.159137	0.179092	0.201268	0.225881	0.253167	0.283378	0.316792
933	0.159091	0.179044	0.201218	0.225829	0.253112	0.283322	0.316734
934	0.159045	0.178996	0.201167	0.225776	0.253058	0.283266	0.316677
935	0.159000	0.178948	0.201117	0.225724	0.253003	0.283210	0.316620
936	0.158954	0.178899	0.201066	0.225671	0.252949	0.283155	0.316564
937	0.158908	0.178851	0.201016	0.225619	0.252895	0.283099	0.316507
938	0.158863	0.178803	0.200956	0.225566	0.252840	0.283043	0.316450
939	0.158817	0.178755	0.200915	0.225514	0.252786	0.282988	0.316393
940	0.158772	0.178708	0.200865	0.225462	0.252732	0.282932	0.316337
941	0.158726	0.178660	0.200815	0.225410	0.252678	0.282877	0.316280
942	0.158681	0.178612	0.200765	0.225357	0.252624	0.282821	0.316224
943	0.158636	0.178564	0.200715	0.225305	0.252571	0.282766	0.316167
944	0.158591	0.178517	0.200665	0.225254	0.252517	0.282711	0.316111
945	0.158546	0.178469	0.200616	0.225202	0.252463	0.282655	0.316055

Unit	83	84	85	86	87	88	89
946	0.158500	0.178422	0.200566	0.225150	0.252409	0.282600	0.315998
947	0.158455	0.178374	0.200516	0.225098	0.252356	0.282545	0.315942
948	0.158411	0.178327	0.200467	0.225046	0.252302	0.282490	0.315886
949	0.158366	0.178280	0.200417	0.224995	0.252249	0.282435	0.315830
950	0.158321	0.178233	0.200368	0.224943	0.252196	0.282380	0.315774
951	0.158276	0.178185	0.200318	0.224892	0.252142	0.282326	0.315719
952	0.158231	0.178138	0.200269	0.224840	0.252089	0.282271	0.315663
953	0.158187	0.178091	0.200219	0.224789	0.252036	0.282216	0.315607
954	0.158142	0.178044	0.200170	0.224738	0.251983	0.282162	0.315551
955	0.158098	0.177997	0.200121	0.224686	0.251930	0.282107	0.315496
956	0.158053	0.177951	0.200072	0.224635	0.251877	0.282053	0.315440
957	0.158009	0.177904	0.200023	0.224584	0.251824	0.281998	0.315385
958	0.157964	0.177857	0.199974	0.224533	0.251771	0.281944	0.315329
959	0.157920	0.177810	0.199925	0.224482	0.251718	0.281890	0.315274
960	0.157876	0.177764	0.199876	0.224431	0.251666	0.281836	0.315219
961	0.157832	0.177717	0.199827	0.224380	0.251613	0.281782	0.315164
962	0.157787	0.177671	0.199779	0.224330	0.251560	0.281727	0.315109
963	0.157743	0.177624	0.199730	0.224279	0.251508	0.281674	0.315054
964	0.157699	0.177578	0.199681	0.224228	0.251455	0.281620	0.314999
965	0.157655	0.177532	0.199633	0.224178	0.251403	0.281566	0.314944
956	0.157612	0.177485	0.199584	0.224127	0.251351	0.281512	0.314889
967	0.157558	0.177439	0.199536	0.224077	0.251298	0.281458	0.314834
968	0.157524	0.177393	0.199488	0.224026	0.251246	0.281405	0.314779
969	0.157480	0.177347	0.199439	0.223976	0.251194	0.281351	0.314725
970	0.157437	0.177301	0.199391	0.223926	0.251142	0.281298	0.314670
971	0.157393	0.177255	0.199343	0.223876	0.251090	0.281244	0.314616
972	0.157349	0.177209	0.199295	0.223825	0.251038	0.281191	0.314561
973	0.157306	0.177163	0.199247	0.223775	0.250986	0.281137	0.314507
974	0.157263	0.177118	0.199199	0.223725	0.250935	0.281084	0.314453
975	0.157219	0.177072	0.199151	0.223675	0.250883	0.281031	0.314398
976	0.157176	0.177026	0.199103	0.223626	0.250831	0.280978	0.314344
977	0.157133	0.176981	0.199055	0.223576	0.250780	0.280925	0.314290
978	0.157089	0.176935	0.199008	0.223526	0.250728	0.280872	0.314236
979	0.157046	0.176890	0.198960	0.223476	0.250677	0.280819	0.314192
980	0.157003	0.176844	0.198912	0.223425	0.250627	0.280766	0.314138

Unit	83	84	85	86	87	88	89
981	0.156960	0.176799	0.198865	0.223377	0.250574	0.280713	0.314074
982	0.156917	0.176753	0.198817	0.223327	0.250522	0.280660	0.314020
983	0.156874	0.176708	0.198770	0.223278	0.250471	0.280608	0.313967
984	0.156831	0.176663	0.198722	0.223229	0.250420	0.280555	0.313913
985	0.156788	0.176618	0.198675	0.223179	0.250369	0.280503	0.313859
986	0.156746	0.176573	0.198628	0.223130	0.250318	0.280450	0.313806
937	0.156703	0.176528	0.198581	0.223081	0.250267	0.280398	0.313752
988	0.156660	0.176483	0.198533	0.223032	0.250216	0.280345	0.313699
989	0.156618	0.176438	0.198486	0.222983	0.250165	0.280293	0.313646
990	0.156575	0.176393	0.198439	0.222934	0.250114	0.280241	0.313592
991	0.156533	0.176348	0.198392	0.222885	0.250064	0.280189	0.313539
992	0.156490	0.176304	0.198345	0.222836	0.250013	0.280136	0.313486
993	0.156448	0.176259	0.198299	0.222787	0.249962	0.280084	0.313433
974	0.156406	0.176214	0.198252	0.222738	0.249912	0.280032	0.313380
995	0.156363	0.176170	0.198205	0.222689	0.249861	0.279980	0.313327
996	0.156321	0.176125	0.198158	0.222641	0.249811	0.279929	0.313274
997	0.156279	0.176081	0.198112	0.222592	0.249761	0.279877	0.313221
998	0.156237	0.176036	0.198065	0.222543	0.249710	0.279825	0.313168
999	0.156195	0.175992	0.198019	0.222495	0.249660	0.279773	0.313116
1000	0.156153	0.175498	0.197972	0.222447	0.249610	0.279722	0.313063

Unit	83	84	85	86	87	88	89
1010	0.155736	0.175508	0.197511	0.221965	0.249111	0.279209	0.312540
1020	0.155324	0.175074	0.197055	0.221490	0.248619	0.278702	0.312022
1030	0.154917	0.174644	0.196605	0.221020	0.248132	0.278201	0.311511
1040	0.154515	0.174220	0.196160	0.220556	0.247651	0.277706	0.311005
1050	0.154118	0.173802	0.195720	0.220097	0.247175	0.277216	0.310505
1060	0.153726	0.173388	0.195286	0.219644	0.246705	0.276732	0.310011
1070	0.153338	0.172979	0.194856	0.219196	0.246240	0.276253	0.309522
1080	0.152955	0.172574	0.194432	0.218752	0.245780	0.275780	0.309038
1090	0.152577	0.172175	0.194012	0.218314	0.245325	0.275311	0.308560
1100	0.152203	0.171780	0.193597	0.217881	0.244876	0.274848	0.308086
1110	0.151833	0.171389	0.193187	0.217452	0.244431	0.274390	0.307618
1120	0.151467	0.171003	0.192781	0.217028	0.243991	0.273936	0.307155
1130	0.151106	0.170621	0.192380	0.216609	0.243555	0.273487	0.306696
1140	0.150748	0.170243	0.191983	0.216194	0.243125	0.273043	0.306242
1150	0.150395	0.169870	0.191590	0.215784	0.242698	0.272604	0.305793
1160	0.150045	0.169500	0.191201	0.215377	0.242277	0.272169	0.305348
1170	0.149699	0.169135	0.190817	0.214976	0.241859	0.271738	0.304907
1180	0.149357	0.168773	0.190437	0.214578	0.241446	0.271312	0.304472
1190	0.149019	0.168415	0.190060	0.214184	0.241037	0.270890	0.304040
1200	0.148684	0.168061	0.189688	0.213794	0.240632	0.270473	0.303612
1210	0.148353	0.167710	0.189319	0.213409	0.240231	0.270059	0.303189
1220	0.148025	0.167364	0.188954	0.213027	0.239834	0.269649	0.302770
1230	0.147700	0.167020	0.188593	0.212649	0.239441	0.269244	0.302355
1240	0.147379	0.166680	0.188235	0.212275	0.239052	0.268842	0.301943
1250	0.147061	0.166344	0.187881	0.211904	0.238666	0.268444	0.301536
1260	0.146747	0.166011	0.187530	0.211537	0.238285	0.268050	0.301132
1270	0.146435	0.165681	0.187183	0.211173	0.237907	0.267659	0.300732
1280	0.146127	0.165355	0.186839	0.210813	0.237532	0.267272	0.300336
1290	0.145821	0.165031	0.186498	0.210456	0.237161	0.266889	0.299943
1300	0.145519	0.164711	0.186161	0.210103	0.236793	0.266509	0.299554
1310	0.145220	0.164394	0.185827	0.209753	0.236429	0.266133	0.299168
1320	0.144923	0.164080	0.185496	0.209406	0.236068	0.265760	0.298786
1330	0.144629	0.163768	0.185168	0.209063	0.235710	0.265390	0.298407
1340	0.144338	0.163460	0.184843	0.208722	0.235356	0.265024	0.298032
1350	0.144050	0.163155	0.184521	0.208385	0.235004	0.264661	0.297659

Unit	83	84	85	86	87	88	89
1360	0.143765	0.162852	0.184202	0.208051	0.234656	0.264301	0.297290
1370	0.143482	0.162552	0.183886	0.207719	0.234311	0.263944	0.296924
1380	0.143202	0.162255	0.183572	0.207391	0.233969	0.263590	0.296562
1390	0.142924	0.161961	0.183262	0.207065	0.233630	0.263239	0.296202
1400	0.142649	0.161669	0.182954	0.206742	0.233294	0.262892	0.295845
1410	0.142376	0.161380	0.182649	0.206422	0.232960	0.262547	0.295491
1420	0.142106	0.161093	0.182347	0.206105	0.232630	0.262205	0.295140
1430	0.141838	0.160809	0.182047	0.205791	0.232302	0.261866	0.294792
1440	0.141573	0.160527	0.181750	0.205479	0.231977	0.261529	0.294447
1450	0.141309	0.160248	0.181455	0.205170	0.231655	0.261196	0.294105
1460	0.141049	0.159971	0.181163	0.204863	0.231335	0.260865	0.293765
1470	0.140790	0.159697	0.180873	0.204559	0.231018	0.260537	0.293428
1480	0.140534	0.159425	0.180586	0.204258	0.230703	0.260211	0.293094
1490	0.140280	0.159155	0.180301	0.203959	0.230392	0.259888	0.292762
1500	0.140028	0.158888	0.180018	0.203662	0.230082	0.259568	0.292433
1510	0.139778	0.158622	0.179738	0.203368	0.229775	0.259250	0.292107
1520	0.139530	0.158359	0.179460	0.203076	0.229471	0.258934	0.291783
1530	0.139284	0.158098	0.179185	0.202786	0.229169	0.258622	0.291461
1540	0.139040	0.157839	0.178911	0.202499	0.228869	0.258311	0.291142
1550	0.138799	0.157582	0.178640	0.202214	0.228571	0.258003	0.290826
1560	0.138559	0.157328	0.178371	0.201931	0.228276	0.257697	0.290511
1570	0.138321	0.157075	0.178104	0.201651	0.227983	0.257394	0.290199
1580	0.138085	0.156824	0.177839	0.201372	0.227693	0.257092	0.289890
1590	0.137851	0.156576	0.177576	0.201096	0.227404	0.256793	0.289582
1600	0.137619	0.156329	0.177315	0.200822	0.227118	0.256497	0.289277
1610	0.137389	0.156084	0.177056	0.200550	0.226834	0.256202	0.288975
1620	0.137160	0.155841	0.176799	0.200280	0.226552	0.255910	0.288674
1630	0.136934	0.155600	0.176544	0.200012	0.226272	0.255619	0.288375
1640	0.136709	0.155361	0.176291	0.199746	0.225994	0.255331	0.288079
1650	0.136485	0.155124	0.176040	0.199482	0.225718	0.255045	0.287785
1660	0.136264	0.154888	0.175791	0.199220	0.225444	0.254761	0.287492
1670	0.136044	0.154654	0.175544	0.198959	0.225172	0.254479	0.287202
1680	0.135826	0.154422	0.175298	0.198701	0.224903	0.254199	0.286914
1690	0.135609	0.154192	0.175054	0.198445	0.224635	0.253921	0.286628
1700	0.135395	0.153963	0.174812	0.198190	0.224368	0.253645	0.286344

Unit	83	84	85	86	87	88	89
1710	0.135181	0.153736	0.174572	0.197937	0.224104	0.253371	0.286062
1720	0.134970	0.153511	0.174334	0.197686	0.223842	0.253098	0.285781
1730	0.134759	0.153287	0.174097	0.197437	0.223581	0.252828	0.285503
1740	0.134551	0.153065	0.173862	0.197190	0.223322	0.252559	0.285227
1750	0.134344	0.152845	0.173628	0.196944	0.223065	0.252292	0.284952
1760	0.134138	0.152626	0.173396	0.196700	0.222810	0.252027	0.284679
1770	0.133934	0.152408	0.173166	0.196458	0.222557	0.251764	0.284408
1780	0.133731	0.152193	0.172938	0.196217	0.222305	0.251503	0.284139
1790	0.133530	0.151978	0.172711	0.195978	0.222055	0.251243	0.283871
1800	0.133330	0.151765	0.172485	0.195740	0.221807	0.250985	0.283605
1810	0.133132	0.151554	0.172261	0.195505	0.221560	0.250729	0.283341
1820	0.132935	0.151344	0.172039	0.195270	0.221315	0.250474	0.283079
1830	0.132739	0.151136	0.171818	0.195038	0.221071	0.250221	0.282818
1840	0.132545	0.150929	0.171599	0.194807	0.220829	0.249970	0.282559
1850	0.132352	0.150723	0.171381	0.194577	0.220589	0.249720	0.282302
1860	0.132160	0.150519	0.171164	0.194349	0.220350	0.249472	0.282046
1870	0.131970	0.150316	0.170949	0.194122	0.220113	0.249225	0.281792
1880	0.131781	0.150114	0.170735	0.193897	0.219877	0.248980	0.281540
1890	0.131593	0.149914	0.170523	0.193673	0.219643	0.248737	0.281289
1900	0.131406	0.149715	0.170312	0.193451	0.219410	0.248495	0.281039
1910	0.131221	0.149518	0.170103	0.193230	0.219179	0.248254	0.280791
1920	0.131037	0.149322	0.169895	0.193011	0.218949	0.248015	0.280545
1930	0.130854	0.149127	0.169688	0.192793	0.218721	0.247778	0.280300
1940	0.130672	0.148933	0.169482	0.192576	0.218494	0.247542	0.280056
1950	0.130492	0.148740	0.169278	0.192361	0.218268	0.247307	0.279815
1960	0.130313	0.148549	0.169075	0.192147	0.218044	0.247074	0.279574
1970	0.130134	0.148359	0.168874	0.191934	0.217821	0.246842	0.279335
1980	0.129957	0.148170	0.168673	0.191723	0.217600	0.246612	0.279097
1990	0.129782	0.147983	0.168474	0.191513	0.217379	0.246383	0.278861
2000	0.129607	0.147796	0.168276	0.191304	0.217161	0.246155	0.278626
2010	0.129433	0.147611	0.168080	0.191097	0.216943	0.245929	0.278392
2020	0.129261	0.147427	0.167884	0.190890	0.216727	0.245704	0.278160
2030	0.129089	0.147244	0.167690	0.190685	0.216512	0.245480	0.277929
2040	0.128919	0.147062	0.167497	0.190482	0.216298	0.245258	0.277700
2050	0.128749	0.146881	0.167305	0.190279	0.216086	0.245037	0.277472

Unit	83	84	85	86	87	88	89
2060	0.128581	0.146701	0.167114	0.190078	0.215875	0.244817	0.277245
2070	0.128414	0.146523	0.166925	0.189877	0.215665	0.244598	0.277019
2080	0.128248	0.146345	0.166736	0.189678	0.215456	0.244381	0.276795
2090	0.128082	0.146169	0.166549	0.189481	0.215249	0.244165	0.276572
2100	0.127918	0.145993	0.166362	0.189284	0.215042	0.243950	0.276350
2110	0.127755	0.145819	0.166177	0.189088	0.214837	0.243737	0.276129
2120	0.127592	0.145646	0.165993	0.188894	0.214633	0.243524	0.275910
2130	0.127431	0.145473	0.165810	0.188701	0.214430	0.243313	0.275692
2140	0.127271	0.145302	0.165628	0.188508	0.214229	0.243103	0.275475
2150	0.127111	0.145132	0.165447	0.188317	0.214028	0.242894	0.275259
2160	0.126953	0.144962	0.165267	0.188127	0.213829	0.242686	0.275044
2170	0.126795	0.144794	0.165088	0.187938	0.213630	0.242479	0.274831
2180	0.126639	0.144627	0.164910	0.187750	0.213433	0.242274	0.274618
2190	0.126483	0.144460	0.164733	0.187563	0.213237	0.242069	0.274407
2200	0.126328	0.144295	0.164558	0.187378	0.213042	0.241866	0.274197
2210	0.126174	0.144130	0.164383	0.187193	0.212848	0.241664	0.273988
2220	0.126021	0.143967	0.164209	0.187009	0.212655	0.241463	0.273780
2230	0.125869	0.143804	0.164036	0.186826	0.212463	0.241263	0.273573
2240	0.125718	0.143642	0.163864	0.186644	0.212272	0.241064	0.273368
2250	0.125567	0.143482	0.163693	0.186463	0.212082	0.240866	0.273163
2260	0.125418	0.143322	0.163523	0.186284	0.211893	0.240669	0.272959
2270	0.125269	0.143163	0.163354	0.186105	0.211705	0.240473	0.272757
2280	0.125121	0.143004	0.163185	0.185927	0.211518	0.240278	0.272555
2290	0.124974	0.142847	0.163018	0.185750	0.211332	0.240084	0.272355
2300	0.124828	0.142691	0.162851	0.185574	0.211148	0.239891	0.272155
2310	0.124682	0.142535	0.162686	0.185399	0.210964	0.239700	0.271957
2320	0.124538	0.142380	0.162521	0.185225	0.210781	0.239509	0.271760
2330	0.124394	0.142226	0.162357	0.185051	0.210599	0.239319	0.271563
2340	0.124251	0.142073	0.162194	0.184879	0.210417	0.239130	0.271368
2350	0.124108	0.141921	0.162032	0.184707	0.210237	0.238942	0.271173
2360	0.123967	0.141769	0.161871	0.184537	0.210058	0.238755	0.270980
2370	0.123826	0.141618	0.161711	0.184367	0.209880	0.238569	0.270787
2380	0.123686	0.141469	0.161551	0.184198	0.209702	0.238384	0.270595
2390	0.123546	0.141319	0.161392	0.184030	0.209525	0.238199	0.270405
2400	0.123408	0.141171	0.161234	0.183863	0.209350	0.238016	0.270215

Unit	83	84	85	86	87	88	89
2410	0.123270	0.141024	0.161077	0.183697	0.209175	0.237833	0.270026
2420	0.123133	0.140877	0.160921	0.183532	0.209001	0.237652	0.269838
2430	0.122996	0.140731	0.160766	0.183367	0.208828	0.237471	0.269651
2440	0.122861	0.140585	0.160611	0.183203	0.208656	0.237291	0.269465
2450	0.122726	0.140441	0.160457	0.183040	0.208484	0.237113	0.269280
2460	0.122591	0.140297	0.160304	0.182878	0.208314	0.236934	0.269096
2470	0.122458	0.140154	0.160151	0.182717	0.208144	0.236757	0.268912
2480	0.122325	0.140012	0.160000	0.182556	0.207975	0.236581	0.268730
2490	0.122193	0.139870	0.159849	0.182396	0.207807	0.236405	0.268548
2500	0.122061	0.139729	0.159699	0.182237	0.207640	0.236231	0.268367
2510	0.121930	0.139589	0.159549	0.182079	0.207473	0.236057	0.268187
2520	0.121800	0.139449	0.159401	0.181922	0.207308	0.235884	0.268008
2530	0.121670	0.139310	0.159253	0.181765	0.207143	0.235712	0.267829
2540	0.121541	0.139172	0.159105	0.181609	0.206979	0.235540	0.267652
2550	0.121413	0.139035	0.158959	0.181454	0.206815	0.235370	0.267475
2560	0.121285	0.138898	0.158813	0.181299	0.206653	0.235200	0.267299
2570	0.121158	0.138762	0.158668	0.181146	0.206491	0.235031	0.267124
2580	0.121032	0.138626	0.158524	0.180993	0.206330	0.234862	0.266949
2590	0.120906	0.138491	0.158380	0.180840	0.206170	0.234695	0.266776
2600	0.120781	0.138357	0.158237	0.180689	0.206010	0.234528	0.266603
2610	0.120656	0.138224	0.158094	0.180538	0.205851	0.234362	0.266431
2620	0.120532	0.138091	0.157953	0.180388	0.205693	0.234197	0.266260
2630	0.120409	0.137959	0.157812	0.180238	0.205536	0.234032	0.266089
2640	0.120286	0.137827	0.157671	0.180089	0.205379	0.233869	0.265920
2650	0.120164	0.137696	0.157532	0.179941	0.205223	0.233706	0.265751
2660	0.120042	0.137566	0.157393	0.179794	0.205068	0.233543	0.265582
2670	0.119921	0.137436	0.157254	0.179647	0.204913	0.233382	0.265415
2680	0.119801	0.137307	0.157116	0.179501	0.204760	0.233221	0.265248
2690	0.119681	0.137178	0.156979	0.179356	0.204606	0.233061	0.265082
2700	0.119562	0.137050	0.156843	0.179211	0.204454	0.232901	0.264917
2710	0.119443	0.136923	0.156707	0.179067	0.204302	0.232743	0.264752
2720	0.119325	0.136796	0.156572	0.178923	0.204151	0.232585	0.264588
2730	0.119207	0.136670	0.156437	0.178781	0.204000	0.232427	0.264425
2740	0.119090	0.136544	0.156303	0.178638	0.203851	0.232271	0.264263
2750	0.118973	0.136419	0.156169	0.178497	0.203702	0.232115	0.264101

Unit	83	84	85	86	87	88	89
2760	0.118857	0.136294	0.156037	0.178356	0.203553	0.231959	0.263940
2770	0.118742	0.136170	0.155904	0.178216	0.203405	0.231805	0.263779
2780	0.118627	0.136047	0.155773	0.178076	0.203258	0.231651	0.263620
2790	0.118512	0.135924	0.155642	0.177937	0.203111	0.231497	0.263460
2800	0.118398	0.135802	0.155511	0.177798	0.202965	0.231345	0.263302
2810	0.118285	0.135680	0.155381	0.177661	0.202820	0.231193	0.263144
2820	0.118172	0.135559	0.155252	0.177523	0.202675	0.231041	0.262987
2830	0.118060	0.135438	0.155123	0.177387	0.202531	0.230890	0.262831
2840	0.117948	0.135318	0.154995	0.177251	0.202388	0.230740	0.262675
2850	0.117836	0.135199	0.154867	0.177115	0.202245	0.230591	0.262520
2860	0.117726	0.135080	0.154740	0.176980	0.202103	0.230442	0.262365
2870	0.117615	0.134961	0.154613	0.176846	0.201961	0.230293	0.262211
2880	0.117505	0.134843	0.154487	0.176712	0.201820	0.230146	0.262058
2890	0.117396	0.134726	0.154362	0.176579	0.201679	0.229999	0.261905
2900	0.117287	0.134609	0.154237	0.176446	0.201540	0.229852	0.261753
2910	0.117178	0.134492	0.154112	0.176314	0.201400	0.229706	0.261602
2920	0.117070	0.134376	0.153988	0.176182	0.201261	0.229561	0.261451
2930	0.116963	0.134261	0.153865	0.176051	0.201123	0.229416	0.261301
2940	0.116856	0.134146	0.153742	0.175921	0.200986	0.229272	0.261151
2950	0.116749	0.134031	0.153620	0.175791	0.200848	0.229129	0.261002
2960	0.116643	0.133917	0.153498	0.175662	0.200712	0.228986	0.260854
2970	0.116537	0.133803	0.153377	0.175533	0.200576	0.228843	0.260706
2980	0.116432	0.133690	0.153256	0.175404	0.200441	0.228702	0.260558
2990	0.116327	0.133578	0.153136	0.175277	0.200306	0.228560	0.260412
3000	0.116223	0.133466	0.153016	0.175149	0.200171	0.228420	0.260266
3010	0.116119	0.133354	0.152896	0.175022	0.200038	0.228279	0.260120
3020	0.116015	0.133243	0.152777	0.174896	0.199904	0.228140	0.259975
3030	0.115912	0.133132	0.152659	0.174770	0.199772	0.228001	0.259831
3040	0.115810	0.133022	0.152541	0.174645	0.199639	0.227862	0.259687
3050	0.115708	0.132912	0.152424	0.174520	0.199508	0.227724	0.259543
3060	0.115606	0.132802	0.152307	0.174396	0.199377	0.227587	0.259401
3070	0.115504	0.132693	0.152190	0.174272	0.199246	0.227450	0.259258
3080	0.115404	0.132585	0.152074	0.174149	0.199116	0.227314	0.259117
3090	0.115303	0.132477	0.151959	0.174026	0.198986	0.227178	0.258975
3100	0.115203	0.132369	0.151844	0.173904	0.198857	0.227042	0.258835

Unit	83	84	85	86	87	88	89
3110	0.115103	0.132262	0.151729	0.173782	0.198728	0.226908	0.258695
3120	0.115004	0.132155	0.151615	0.173661	0.198600	0.226773	0.258555
3130	0.114905	0.132049	0.151501	0.173540	0.198473	0.226640	0.258416
3140	0.114807	0.131943	0.151388	0.173420	0.198345	0.226506	0.258277
3150	0.114708	0.131838	0.151275	0.173300	0.198219	0.226373	0.258139
3160	0.114611	0.131733	0.151163	0.173180	0.198093	0.226241	0.258002
3170	0.114513	0.131628	0.151051	0.173061	0.197967	0.226109	0.257865
3180	0.114417	0.131524	0.150939	0.172943	0.197842	0.225978	0.257728
3190	0.114320	0.131420	0.150828	0.172824	0.197717	0.225847	0.257592
3200	0.114224	0.131316	0.150718	0.172707	0.197593	0.225717	0.257457
3210	0.114128	0.131213	0.150607	0.172590	0.197469	0.225587	0.257322
3220	0.114033	0.131111	0.150498	0.172473	0.197345	0.225458	0.257187
3230	0.113938	0.131009	0.150388	0.172356	0.197223	0.225329	0.257053
3240	0.113843	0.130907	0.150279	0.172241	0.197100	0.225200	0.256920
3250	0.113749	0.130805	0.150171	0.172125	0.196978	0.225072	0.256787
3260	0.113655	0.130704	0.150063	0.172010	0.196857	0.224945	0.256654
3270	0.113561	0.130604	0.149955	0.171896	0.196735	0.224818	0.256522
3280	0.113468	0.130503	0.149848	0.171781	0.196615	0.224691	0.256390
3290	0.113375	0.130403	0.149741	0.171668	0.196495	0.224565	0.256259
3300	0.113283	0.130304	0.149634	0.171554	0.196375	0.224440	0.256128
3310	0.113191	0.130205	0.149528	0.171441	0.196255	0.224314	0.255998
3320	0.113099	0.130106	0.149422	0.171329	0.196137	0.224190	0.255868
3330	0.113008	0.130008	0.149317	0.171217	0.196018	0.224065	0.255739
3340	0.112917	0.129910	0.149212	0.171105	0.195900	0.223941	0.255610
3350	0.112826	0.129812	0.149108	0.170994	0.195782	0.223818	0.255482
3360	0.112736	0.129715	0.149003	0.170883	0.195665	0.223695	0.255354
3370	0.112646	0.129618	0.148900	0.170773	0.195548	0.223572	0.255226
3380	0.112556	0.129521	0.148796	0.170662	0.195432	0.223450	0.255099
3390	0.112466	0.129425	0.148693	0.170553	0.195316	0.223329	0.254972
3400	0.112377	0.129329	0.148590	0.170443	0.195201	0.223207	0.254846
3410	0.112289	0.129234	0.148488	0.170335	0.195085	0.223086	0.254720
3420	0.112200	0.129138	0.148386	0.170226	0.194971	0.222966	0.254595
3430	0.112112	0.129044	0.148285	0.170118	0.194856	0.222846	0.254470
3440	0.112025	0.128949	0.148184	0.170010	0.194742	0.222726	0.254345
3450	0.111937	0.128855	0.148083	0.169903	0.194629	0.222607	0.254221

Unit	83	84	85	86	87	88	89
3460	0.111850	0.128761	0.147982	0.169796	0.194516	0.222488	0.254098
3470	0.111764	0.128668	0.147882	0.169689	0.194403	0.222370	0.253974
3480	0.111677	0.128575	0.147782	0.169583	0.194291	0.222252	0.253852
3490	0.111591	0.128482	0.147683	0.169477	0.194179	0.222134	0.253729
3500	0.111505	0.128390	0.147584	0.169372	0.194067	0.222017	0.253607
3510	0.111420	0.128297	0.147485	0.169267	0.193956	0.221900	0.253486
3520	0.111335	0.128206	0.147387	0.169162	0.193845	0.221784	0.253364
3530	0.111250	0.128114	0.147289	0.169058	0.193734	0.221668	0.253243
3540	0.111165	0.128023	0.147191	0.168954	0.193624	0.221552	0.253123
3550	0.111081	0.127932	0.147094	0.168850	0.193515	0.221437	0.253003
3560	0.110997	0.127842	0.146997	0.168747	0.193405	0.221322	0.252883
3570	0.110913	0.127752	0.146900	0.168644	0.193296	0.221208	0.252764
3580	0.110830	0.127662	0.146804	0.168541	0.193188	0.221094	0.252645
3590	0.110747	0.127572	0.146708	0.168439	0.193080	0.220980	0.252527
3600	0.110664	0.127483	0.146612	0.168337	0.192972	0.220867	0.252409
3610	0.110581	0.127394	0.146517	0.168235	0.192864	0.220754	0.252291
3620	0.110499	0.127305	0.146422	0.168134	0.192757	0.220641	0.252174
3630	0.110417	0.127217	0.146327	0.168033	0.192650	0.220529	0.252057
3640	0.110336	0.127129	0.146233	0.167933	0.192544	0.220417	0.251940
3650	0.110254	0.127041	0.146139	0.167832	0.192438	0.220306	0.251824
3660	0.110173	0.126954	0.146045	0.167732	0.192332	0.220195	0.251708
3670	0.110093	0.126867	0.145952	0.167633	0.192226	0.220084	0.251593
3680	0.110012	0.126780	0.145859	0.167534	0.192121	0.219973	0.251478
3690	0.109932	0.126694	0.145766	0.167435	0.192017	0.219863	0.251363
3700	0.109852	0.126607	0.145674	0.167336	0.191912	0.219754	0.251249
3710	0.109772	0.126521	0.145581	0.167238	0.191808	0.219644	0.251135
3720	0.109693	0.126436	0.145490	0.167140	0.191705	0.219535	0.251021
3730	0.109614	0.126350	0.145398	0.167042	0.191601	0.219427	0.250908
3740	0.109535	0.126265	0.145307	0.166945	0.191498	0.219318	0.250795
3750	0.109456	0.126181	0.145216	0.166848	0.191395	0.219210	0.250682
3760	0.109378	0.126096	0.145125	0.166752	0.191293	0.219103	0.250570
3770	0.109300	0.126012	0.145035	0.166655	0.191191	0.218995	0.250458
3780	0.109222	0.125928	0.144945	0.166559	0.191089	0.218888	0.250347
3790	0.109144	0.125844	0.144855	0.166463	0.190988	0.218782	0.250236
3800	0.109067	0.125761	0.144766	0.166368	0.190887	0.218675	0.250125

Unit	83	84	85	86	87	88	89
3810	0.108990	0.125678	0.144676	0.166273	0.190786	0.218569	0.250014
3820	0.108913	0.125595	0.144587	0.166178	0.190686	0.218464	0.249904
3830	0.108837	0.125512	0.144499	0.166084	0.190585	0.218358	0.249794
3840	0.108761	0.125430	0.144411	0.165989	0.190486	0.218254	0.249685
3850	0.108685	0.125348	0.144323	0.165895	0.190386	0.218149	0.249576
3860	0.108609	0.125266	0.144235	0.165802	0.190287	0.218045	0.249467
3870	0.108533	0.125185	0.144147	0.165709	0.190188	0.217940	0.249358
3880	0.108458	0.125104	0.144060	0.165615	0.190089	0.217837	0.249250
3890	0.108383	0.125023	0.143973	0.165523	0.189991	0.217733	0.249142
3900	0.108308	0.124942	0.143887	0.165430	0.189893	0.217630	0.249035
3910	0.108234	0.124861	0.143800	0.165338	0.189796	0.217528	0.248928
3920	0.108159	0.124781	0.143714	0.165246	0.189698	0.217425	0.248821
3930	0.108085	0.124701	0.143628	0.165155	0.189601	0.217323	0.248714
3940	0.108012	0.124622	0.143543	0.165063	0.189504	0.217221	0.248608
3950	0.107938	0.124542	0.143457	0.164972	0.189408	0.217120	0.248502
3960	0.107865	0.124463	0.143372	0.164882	0.189312	0.217018	0.248397
3970	0.107792	0.124384	0.143288	0.164791	0.189216	0.216917	0.248291
3980	0.107719	0.124305	0.143203	0.164701	0.189120	0.216817	0.248186
3990	0.107646	0.124227	0.143119	0.164611	0.189025	0.216717	0.248082
4000	0.107574	0.124149	0.143035	0.164521	0.188930	0.216617	0.247977
4010	0.107501	0.124071	0.142951	0.164432	0.188835	0.216517	0.247873
4020	0.107430	0.123993	0.142868	0.164343	0.188741	0.216417	0.247769
4030	0.107358	0.123916	0.142785	0.164254	0.188646	0.216318	0.247666
4040	0.107286	0.123838	0.142702	0.164166	0.188552	0.216219	0.247563
4050	0.107215	0.123761	0.142619	0.164077	0.188459	0.216121	0.247460
4060	0.107144	0.123685	0.142536	0.163989	0.188365	0.216023	0.247357
4070	0.107073	0.123608	0.142454	0.163902	0.188272	0.215925	0.247255
4080	0.107003	0.123532	0.142372	0.163814	0.188180	0.215827	0.247153
4090	0.106932	0.123456	0.142291	0.163727	0.188087	0.215729	0.247051
4100	0.106862	0.123380	0.142209	0.163640	0.187995	0.215632	0.246950
4110	0.106792	0.123304	0.142128	0.163553	0.187903	0.215535	0.246849
4120	0.106722	0.123229	0.142047	0.163467	0.187811	0.215439	0.246748
4130	0.106653	0.123154	0.141966	0.163381	0.187720	0.215343	0.246647
4140	0.106583	0.123079	0.141886	0.163295	0.187628	0.215247	0.246547
4150	0.106514	0.123004	0.141806	0.163209	0.187537	0.215151	0.246447

Unit	83	84	85	86	87	88	89
4160	0.106445	0.122930	0.141726	0.163123	0.187447	0.215055	0.246347
4170	0.106377	0.122856	0.141646	0.163038	0.187356	0.214960	0.246248
4180	0.106308	0.122782	0.141566	0.162953	0.187266	0.214865	0.246149
4190	0.106240	0.122708	0.141487	0.162869	0.187176	0.214771	0.246050
4200	0.106172	0.122634	0.141408	0.162784	0.187087	0.214676	0.245951
4210	0.106104	0.122561	0.141329	0.162700	0.186997	0.214582	0.245853
4220	0.106036	0.122488	0.141251	0.162616	0.186908	0.214488	0.245755
4230	0.105969	0.122415	0.141172	0.162532	0.186819	0.214395	0.245657
4240	0.105902	0.122342	0.141094	0.162449	0.186731	0.214301	0.245560
4250	0.105835	0.122270	0.141016	0.162365	0.186642	0.214208	0.245463
4260	0.105768	0.122198	0.140938	0.162282	0.186554	0.214115	0.245366
4270	0.105701	0.122126	0.140861	0.162200	0.186467	0.214023	0.245269
4280	0.105635	0.122054	0.140784	0.162117	0.186379	0.213930	0.245172
4290	0.105569	0.121982	0.140707	0.162035	0.186292	0.213838	0.245076
4300	0.105503	0.121911	0.140630	0.161953	0.186204	0.213747	0.244980
4310	0.105437	0.121840	0.140553	0.161871	0.186118	0.213655	0.244885
4320	0.105371	0.121768	0.140477	0.161789	0.186031	0.213564	0.244789
4330	0.105306	0.121698	0.140401	0.161708	0.185944	0.213473	0.244694
4340	0.105240	0.121627	0.140325	0.161627	0.185858	0.213382	0.244599
4350	0.105175	0.121557	0.140249	0.161546	0.185772	0.213291	0.244505
4360	0.105110	0.121487	0.140174	0.161465	0.185687	0.213201	0.244410
4370	0.105046	0.121417	0.140099	0.161385	0.185601	0.213111	0.244316
4380	0.104981	0.121347	0.140023	0.161304	0.185516	0.213021	0.244222
4390	0.104917	0.121277	0.139949	0.161224	0.185431	0.212932	0.244129
4400	0.104853	0.121208	0.139874	0.161145	0.185346	0.212842	0.244035
4410	0.104789	0.121139	0.139800	0.161065	0.185262	0.212753	0.243942
4420	0.104725	0.121070	0.139725	0.160986	0.185178	0.212664	0.243849
4430	0.104661	0.121001	0.139651	0.160907	0.185093	0.212576	0.243757
4440	0.104598	0.120932	0.139578	0.160828	0.185010	0.212487	0.243664
4450	0.104534	0.120864	0.139504	0.160749	0.184926	0.212399	0.243572
4460	0.104471	0.120796	0.139431	0.160670	0.184843	0.212311	0.243480
4470	0.104409	0.120727	0.139357	0.160592	0.184759	0.212224	0.243389
4480	0.104346	0.120660	0.139284	0.160514	0.184677	0.212136	0.243297
4490	0.104283	0.120592	0.139212	0.160436	0.184594	0.212049	0.243206
4500	0.104221	0.120525	0.139139	0.160359	0.184511	0.211962	0.243115

Unit	83	84	85	86	87	88	89
4510	0.104159	0.120457	0.139067	0.160281	0.184429	0.211875	0.243024
4520	0.104097	0.120390	0.138994	0.160204	0.184347	0.211789	0.242934
4530	0.104035	0.120323	0.138922	0.160127	0.184265	0.211702	0.242844
4540	0.103973	0.120257	0.138851	0.160050	0.184184	0.211616	0.242754
4550	0.103912	0.120190	0.138779	0.159974	0.184102	0.211530	0.242664
4560	0.103851	0.120124	0.138707	0.159897	0.184021	0.211445	0.242574
4570	0.103789	0.120057	0.138636	0.159821	0.183940	0.211359	0.242485
4580	0.103728	0.119991	0.138565	0.159745	0.183859	0.211274	0.242396
4590	0.103668	0.119926	0.138494	0.159669	0.183779	0.211189	0.242307
4600	0.103607	0.119860	0.138424	0.159594	0.183698	0.211104	0.242218
4610	0.103547	0.119795	0.138353	0.159518	0.183618	0.211020	0.242130
4620	0.103486	0.119729	0.138283	0.159443	0.183538	0.210936	0.242042
4630	0.103426	0.119664	0.138213	0.159368	0.183459	0.210852	0.241954
4640	0.103366	0.119599	0.138143	0.159293	0.183379	0.210768	0.241866
4650	0.103306	0.119535	0.138073	0.159219	0.183300	0.210684	0.241778
4660	0.103247	0.119470	0.138004	0.159144	0.183221	0.210601	0.241691
4670	0.103187	0.119406	0.137934	0.159070	0.183142	0.210517	0.241604
4680	0.103128	0.119341	0.137865	0.158996	0.183063	0.210434	0.241517
4690	0.103069	0.119277	0.137796	0.158922	0.182985	0.210351	0.241431
4700	0.103010	0.119213	0.137727	0.158848	0.182906	0.210269	0.241344
4710	0.102951	0.119150	0.137659	0.158775	0.182828	0.210186	0.241258
4720	0.102892	0.119086	0.137590	0.158702	0.182750	0.210104	0.241172
4730	0.102834	0.119023	0.137522	0.158629	0.182673	0.210022	0.241086
4740	0.102775	0.118960	0.137454	0.158556	0.182595	0.209940	0.241000
4750	0.102717	0.118896	0.137386	0.158483	0.182518	0.209859	0.240915
4760	0.102659	0.118834	0.137318	0.158411	0.182441	0.209777	0.240830
4770	0.102601	0.118771	0.137251	0.158338	0.182364	0.209696	0.240745
4780	0.102543	0.118708	0.137184	0.158266	0.182287	0.209615	0.240660
4790	0.102486	0.118646	0.137116	0.158194	0.182211	0.209535	0.240576
4800	0.102428	0.118584	0.137049	0.158122	0.182134	0.209454	0.240491
4810	0.102371	0.118522	0.136982	0.158051	0.182058	0.209374	0.240407
4820	0.102314	0.118460	0.136916	0.157979	0.181982	0.209293	0.240323
4830	0.102257	0.118398	0.136849	0.157908	0.181906	0.209213	0.240240
4840	0.102200	0.118336	0.136783	0.157837	0.181831	0.209134	0.240156
4850	0.102144	0.118275	0.136717	0.157766	0.181756	0.209054	0.240073

Unit	83	84	85	86	87	88	89
4860	0.102087	0.118214	0.136651	0.157696	0.181680	0.208975	0.239990
4870	0.102031	0.118153	0.136585	0.157625	0.181605	0.208895	0.239907
4880	0.101974	0.118092	0.136519	0.157555	0.181530	0.208816	0.239824
4890	0.101918	0.118031	0.136454	0.157485	0.181456	0.208738	0.239741
4900	0.101862	0.117970	0.136388	0.157415	0.181381	0.208659	0.239659
4910	0.101806	0.117910	0.136323	0.157345	0.181307	0.208581	0.239577
4920	0.101751	0.117849	0.136258	0.157275	0.181233	0.208502	0.239495
4930	0.101695	0.117789	0.136193	0.157206	0.181159	0.208424	0.239413
4940	0.101640	0.117729	0.136129	0.157136	0.181085	0.208346	0.239332
4950	0.101585	0.117669	0.136064	0.157067	0.181012	0.208269	0.239250
4960	0.101530	0.117610	0.136000	0.156998	0.180938	0.208191	0.239169
4970	0.101475	0.117550	0.135935	0.156929	0.180865	0.208114	0.239088
4980	0.101420	0.117491	0.135871	0.156861	0.180792	0.208037	0.239008
4990	0.101365	0.117431	0.135808	0.156792	0.180719	0.207960	0.238927
5000	0.101311	0.117372	0.135744	0.156724	0.180647	0.207883	0.238847
5010	0.101256	0.117313	0.135680	0.156656	0.180574	0.207806	0.238766
5020	0.101202	0.117255	0.135617	0.156588	0.180502	0.207730	0.238686
5030	0.101148	0.117196	0.135554	0.156520	0.180430	0.207654	0.238606
5040	0.101094	0.117137	0.135490	0.156453	0.180358	0.207578	0.238527
5050	0.101040	0.117079	0.135427	0.156385	0.180286	0.207502	0.238447
5060	0.100986	0.117021	0.135365	0.156318	0.180214	0.207426	0.238368
5070	0.100933	0.116963	0.135302	0.156251	0.180143	0.207351	0.238289
5080	0.100879	0.116905	0.135240	0.156184	0.180071	0.207275	0.238210
5090	0.100826	0.116847	0.135177	0.156117	0.180000	0.207200	0.238131
5100	0.100773	0.116789	0.135115	0.156050	0.179929	0.207125	0.238053
5110	0.100720	0.116732	0.135053	0.155984	0.179859	0.207050	0.237974
5120	0.100667	0.116674	0.134991	0.155917	0.179788	0.206976	0.237896
5130	0.100614	0.116617	0.134929	0.155851	0.179717	0.206901	0.237818
5140	0.100561	0.116560	0.134868	0.155785	0.179647	0.206827	0.237740
5150	0.100509	0.116503	0.134806	0.155719	0.179577	0.206753	0.237663
5160	0.100456	0.116446	0.134745	0.155654	0.179507	0.206679	0.237585
5170	0.100404	0.116389	0.134684	0.155588	0.179437	0.206605	0.237508
5180	0.100352	0.116333	0.134623	0.155523	0.179368	0.206532	0.237431
5190	0.100300	0.116276	0.134562	0.155457	0.179298	0.206458	0.237354
5200	0.100248	0.116220	0.134501	0.155392	0.179229	0.206385	0.237277

Unit	83	84	85	86	87	88	89
5210	0.100196	0.116164	0.134441	0.155327	0.179160	0.206312	0.237200
5220	0.100145	0.116108	0.134380	0.155263	0.179091	0.206239	0.237124
5230	0.100093	0.116052	0.134320	0.155198	0.179022	0.206166	0.237047
5240	0.100042	0.115996	0.134260	0.155133	0.178953	0.206093	0.236971
5250	0.099991	0.115941	0.134200	0.155069	0.178884	0.206021	0.236895
5260	0.099939	0.115885	0.134140	0.155005	0.178816	0.205949	0.236820
5270	0.099888	0.115830	0.134080	0.154941	0.178748	0.205876	0.236744
5280	0.099837	0.115775	0.134021	0.154877	0.178680	0.205804	0.236668
5290	0.099787	0.115720	0.133961	0.154813	0.178612	0.205733	0.236593
5300	0.099736	0.115665	0.133902	0.154750	0.178544	0.205661	0.236518
5310	0.099686	0.115610	0.133843	0.154686	0.178477	0.205590	0.236443
5320	0.099635	0.115555	0.133784	0.154623	0.178409	0.205518	0.236368
5330	0.099585	0.115500	0.133725	0.154560	0.178342	0.205447	0.236294
5340	0.099535	0.115446	0.133666	0.154497	0.178275	0.205376	0.236219
5350	0.099485	0.115392	0.133607	0.154434	0.178208	0.205305	0.236145
5360	0.099435	0.115337	0.133549	0.154371	0.178141	0.205234	0.236071
5370	0.099385	0.115283	0.133491	0.154308	0.178074	0.205164	0.235997
5380	0.099335	0.115229	0.133432	0.154246	0.178008	0.205094	0.235923
5390	0.099286	0.115176	0.133374	0.154184	0.177941	0.205023	0.235849
5400	0.099236	0.115122	0.133316	0.154121	0.177875	0.204953	0.235776
5410	0.099187	0.115068	0.133259	0.154059	0.177809	0.204883	0.235703
5420	0.099138	0.115015	0.133201	0.153998	0.177743	0.204814	0.235630
5430	0.099088	0.114962	0.133143	0.153936	0.177677	0.204744	0.235556
5440	0.099039	0.114908	0.133086	0.153874	0.177611	0.204675	0.235484
5450	0.098991	0.114855	0.133029	0.153813	0.177546	0.204605	0.235411
5460	0.098942	0.114802	0.132971	0.153751	0.177480	0.204536	0.235338
5470	0.098893	0.114750	0.132914	0.153690	0.177415	0.204467	0.235266
5480	0.098845	0.114697	0.132857	0.153629	0.177350	0.204398	0.235194
5490	0.098796	0.114644	0.132801	0.153568	0.177285	0.204329	0.235122
5500	0.098748	0.114592	0.132744	0.153507	0.177220	0.204261	0.235050
5510	0.098700	0.114540	0.132687	0.153447	0.177156	0.204192	0.234978
5520	0.098652	0.114487	0.132631	0.153386	0.177091	0.204124	0.234906
5530	0.098604	0.114435	0.132575	0.153326	0.177027	0.204056	0.234835
5540	0.098556	0.114383	0.132519	0.153265	0.176962	0.203988	0.234764
5550	0.098508	0.114331	0.132463	0.153205	0.176898	0.203920	0.234692

Unit	83	84	85	86	87	88	89
5560	0.098460	0.114280	0.132407	0.153145	0.176834	0.203853	0.234621
5570	0.098413	0.114228	0.132351	0.153085	0.176771	0.203785	0.234551
5580	0.098365	0.114176	0.132295	0.153026	0.176707	0.203718	0.234480
5590	0.098318	0.114125	0.132240	0.152966	0.176643	0.203650	0.234409
5600	0.098271	0.114074	0.132184	0.152907	0.176580	0.203583	0.234339
5610	0.098224	0.114022	0.132129	0.152847	0.176517	0.203516	0.234269
5620	0.098177	0.113971	0.132074	0.152788	0.176453	0.203449	0.234198
5630	0.098130	0.113920	0.132019	0.152729	0.176390	0.203383	0.234128
5640	0.098083	0.113870	0.131964	0.152670	0.176328	0.203316	0.234059
5650	0.098036	0.113819	0.131909	0.152611	0.176265	0.203250	0.233989
5660	0.097990	0.113768	0.131854	0.152552	0.176202	0.203183	0.233919
5670	0.097943	0.113718	0.131800	0.152494	0.176140	0.203117	0.233850
5680	0.097897	0.113667	0.131745	0.152435	0.176077	0.203051	0.233781
5690	0.097850	0.113617	0.131691	0.152377	0.176015	0.202986	0.233712
5700	0.097804	0.113567	0.131637	0.152319	0.175953	0.202920	0.233643
5710	0.097758	0.113517	0.131583	0.152261	0.175891	0.202854	0.233574
5720	0.097712	0.113467	0.131529	0.152203	0.175829	0.202789	0.233505
5730	0.097666	0.113417	0.131475	0.152145	0.175768	0.202723	0.233436
5740	0.097621	0.113367	0.131421	0.152087	0.175706	0.202658	0.233368
5750	0.097575	0.113318	0.131368	0.152030	0.175645	0.202593	0.233300
5760	0.097529	0.113268	0.131314	0.151972	0.175583	0.202528	0.233232
5770	0.097484	0.113219	0.131261	0.151915	0.175522	0.202464	0.233164
5780	0.097439	0.113169	0.131207	0.151858	0.175461	0.202399	0.233096
5790	0.097393	0.113120	0.131154	0.151801	0.175400	0.202334	0.233028
5800	0.097348	0.113071	0.131101	0.151744	0.175339	0.202270	0.232960
5810	0.097303	0.113022	0.131048	0.151687	0.175279	0.202206	0.232893
5820	0.097258	0.112973	0.130996	0.151630	0.175218	0.202142	0.232826
5830	0.097213	0.112925	0.130943	0.151573	0.175158	0.202078	0.232758
5840	0.097168	0.112876	0.130890	0.151517	0.175097	0.202014	0.232691
5850	0.097124	0.112827	0.130838	0.151460	0.175037	0.201950	0.232624
5860	0.097079	0.112779	0.130785	0.151404	0.174977	0.201886	0.232558
5870	0.097035	0.112731	0.130733	0.151348	0.174917	0.201823	0.232491
5880	0.096990	0.112682	0.130681	0.151292	0.174857	0.201760	0.232424
5890	0.096946	0.112634	0.130629	0.151236	0.174798	0.201696	0.232358
5900	0.096902	0.112586	0.130577	0.151180	0.174738	0.201633	0.232292

Unit	83	84	85	86	87	88	89
5910	0.096858	0.112538	0.130525	0.151124	0.174679	0.201570	0.232226
5920	0.096814	0.112490	0.130473	0.151069	0.174619	0.201507	0.232160
5930	0.096770	0.112443	0.130422	0.151013	0.174560	0.201445	0.232094
5940	0.096726	0.112395	0.130370	0.150958	0.174501	0.201382	0.232028
5950	0.096682	0.112347	0.130319	0.150903	0.174442	0.201320	0.231962
5960	0.096639	0.112300	0.130267	0.150848	0.174383	0.201257	0.231897
5970	0.096595	0.112253	0.130216	0.150793	0.174325	0.201195	0.231832
5980	0.096552	0.112205	0.130165	0.150738	0.174266	0.201133	0.231766
5990	0.096508	0.112158	0.130114	0.150683	0.174208	0.201071	0.231701
6000	0.096465	0.112111	0.130063	0.150628	0.174149	0.201009	0.231636
6010	0.096422	0.112064	0.130013	0.150574	0.174091	0.200948	0.231572
6020	0.096379	0.112017	0.129962	0.150519	0.174033	0.200886	0.231507
6030	0.096336	0.111971	0.129911	0.150465	0.173975	0.200824	0.231442
6040	0.096293	0.111924	0.129861	0.150411	0.173917	0.200763	0.231378
6050	0.096250	0.111877	0.129810	0.150357	0.173859	0.200702	0.231313
6060	0.096207	0.111831	0.129760	0.150303	0.173801	0.200641	0.231249
6070	0.096165	0.111784	0.129710	0.150249	0.173744	0.200580	0.231185
6080	0.096122	0.111738	0.129660	0.150195	0.173686	0.200519	0.231121
6090	0.096080	0.111692	0.129610	0.150141	0.173629	0.200458	0.231057
6100	0.096037	0.111646	0.129560	0.150088	0.173572	0.200397	0.230994
6110	0.095995	0.111600	0.129510	0.150034	0.173515	0.200337	0.230930
6120	0.095953	0.111554	0.129461	0.149981	0.173458	0.200276	0.230866
6130	0.095911	0.111508	0.129411	0.149927	0.173401	0.200216	0.230803
6140	0.095869	0.111463	0.129362	0.149874	0.173344	0.200156	0.230740
6150	0.095827	0.111417	0.129312	0.149821	0.173287	0.200096	0.230677
6160	0.095785	0.111371	0.129263	0.149768	0.173231	0.200036	0.230614
6170	0.095743	0.111326	0.129214	0.149715	0.173174	0.199976	0.230551
6180	0.095702	0.111281	0.129165	0.149663	0.173118	0.199916	0.230488
6190	0.095660	0.111235	0.129116	0.149610	0.173062	0.199857	0.230425
6200	0.095618	0.111190	0.129067	0.149557	0.173006	0.199797	0.230363
6210	0.095577	0.111145	0.129018	0.149505	0.172950	0.199738	0.230301
6220	0.095536	0.111100	0.128970	0.149453	0.172894	0.199679	0.230238
6230	0.095494	0.111055	0.128921	0.149400	0.172838	0.199620	0.230176
6240	0.095453	0.111010	0.128873	0.149348	0.172782	0.199561	0.230114
6250	0.095412	0.110966	0.128824	0.149296	0.172727	0.199502	0.230052

Unit	83	84	85	86	87	88	89
6260	0.095371	0.110921	0.128776	0.149244	0.172671	0.199443	0.229990
6270	0.095330	0.110877	0.128728	0.149193	0.172616	0.199384	0.229929
6280	0.095289	0.110832	0.128680	0.149141	0.172561	0.199326	0.229867
6290	0.095249	0.110788	0.128632	0.149089	0.172505	0.199267	0.229805
6300	0.095208	0.110744	0.128584	0.149038	0.172450	0.199209	0.229744
6310	0.095167	0.110699	0.128536	0.148986	0.172395	0.199150	0.229683
6320	0.095127	0.110655	0.128488	0.148935	0.172341	0.199092	0.229622
6330	0.095087	0.110611	0.128441	0.148884	0.172286	0.199034	0.229561
6340	0.095046	0.110567	0.128393	0.148833	0.172231	0.198976	0.229500
6350	0.095006	0.110524	0.128346	0.148782	0.172177	0.198918	0.229439
6360	0.094966	0.110480	0.128298	0.148731	0.172122	0.198861	0.229378
6370	0.094926	0.110436	0.128251	0.148680	0.172068	0.198803	0.229318
6380	0.094886	0.110393	0.128204	0.148629	0.172014	0.198746	0.229257
6390	0.094846	0.110349	0.128157	0.148578	0.171960	0.198688	0.229197
6400	0.094806	0.110306	0.128110	0.148528	0.171906	0.198631	0.229137
6410	0.094766	0.110262	0.128063	0.148477	0.171852	0.198574	0.229076
6420	0.094726	0.110219	0.128016	0.148427	0.171798	0.198517	0.229016
6430	0.094687	0.110176	0.127970	0.148377	0.171744	0.198460	0.228957
6440	0.094647	0.110133	0.127923	0.148327	0.171691	0.198403	0.228897
6450	0.094608	0.110090	0.127876	0.148277	0.171637	0.198346	0.228837
6460	0.094568	0.110047	0.127830	0.148227	0.171584	0.198289	0.228777
6470	0.094529	0.110004	0.127784	0.148177	0.171530	0.198233	0.228718
6480	0.094490	0.109962	0.127737	0.148127	0.171477	0.198176	0.228659
6490	0.094451	0.109919	0.127691	0.148077	0.171424	0.198120	0.228599
6500	0.094412	0.109876	0.127645	0.148028	0.171371	0.198064	0.228540
6510	0.094373	0.109834	0.127599	0.147978	0.171318	0.198008	0.228481
6520	0.094334	0.109792	0.127553	0.147929	0.171265	0.197952	0.228422
6530	0.094295	0.109749	0.127507	0.147879	0.171212	0.197896	0.228363
6540	0.094256	0.109707	0.127462	0.147830	0.171160	0.197840	0.228305
6550	0.094217	0.109665	0.127416	0.147781	0.171107	0.197784	0.228246
6560	0.094179	0.109623	0.127370	0.147732	0.171055	0.197728	0.228187
6570	0.094140	0.109581	0.127325	0.147683	0.171003	0.197673	0.228129
6580	0.094102	0.109539	0.127280	0.147634	0.170950	0.197617	0.228071
6590	0.094063	0.109497	0.127234	0.147585	0.170898	0.197562	0.228012
6600	0.094025	0.109455	0.127189	0.147537	0.170846	0.197507	0.227954

Unit	83	84	85	86	87	88	89
6610	0.093987	0.109414	0.127144	0.147488	0.170794	0.197452	0.227896
6620	0.093948	0.109372	0.127099	0.147440	0.170742	0.197397	0.227838
6630	0.093910	0.109330	0.127054	0.147391	0.170690	0.197342	0.227780
6640	0.093872	0.109289	0.127009	0.147343	0.170639	0.197287	0.227723
6650	0.093834	0.109248	0.126964	0.147295	0.170587	0.197232	0.227665
6660	0.093796	0.109206	0.126919	0.147246	0.170536	0.197178	0.227608
6670	0.093759	0.109165	0.126875	0.147198	0.170484	0.197123	0.227550
6680	0.093721	0.109124	0.126830	0.147150	0.170433	0.197069	0.227493
6690	0.093683	0.109083	0.126786	0.147102	0.170382	0.197014	0.227436
6700	0.093646	0.109042	0.126741	0.147055	0.170331	0.196960	0.227379
6710	0.093608	0.109001	0.126697	0.147007	0.170280	0.196906	0.227322
6720	0.093571	0.108960	0.126653	0.146959	0.170229	0.196852	0.227265
6730	0.093533	0.108920	0.126609	0.146912	0.170178	0.196798	0.227208
6740	0.093496	0.108879	0.126565	0.146864	0.170127	0.196744	0.227151
6750	0.093459	0.108838	0.126521	0.146817	0.170076	0.196690	0.227095
6760	0.093421	0.108798	0.126477	0.146770	0.170026	0.196636	0.227038
6770	0.093384	0.108757	0.126433	0.146722	0.169975	0.196583	0.226982
6780	0.093347	0.108717	0.126389	0.146675	0.169925	0.196529	0.226925
6790	0.093310	0.108677	0.126345	0.146628	0.169875	0.196476	0.226869
6800	0.093273	0.108636	0.126302	0.146581	0.169824	0.196422	0.226813
6810	0.093236	0.108596	0.126258	0.146535	0.169774	0.196369	0.226757
6820	0.093200	0.108556	0.126215	0.146488	0.169724	0.196316	0.226701
6830	0.093163	0.108516	0.126172	0.146441	0.169674	0.196263	0.226645
6840	0.093126	0.108476	0.126128	0.146394	0.169624	0.196210	0.226589
6850	0.093090	0.108436	0.126085	0.146348	0.169575	0.196157	0.226534
6860	0.093053	0.108397	0.126042	0.146301	0.169525	0.196104	0.226478
6870	0.093017	0.108357	0.125999	0.146255	0.169475	0.196052	0.226423
6880	0.092981	0.108317	0.125956	0.146209	0.169426	0.195999	0.226367
6890	0.092944	0.108278	0.125913	0.146163	0.169376	0.195947	0.226312
6900	0.092908	0.108238	0.125870	0.146117	0.169327	0.195894	0.226257
6910	0.092872	0.108199	0.125828	0.146070	0.169278	0.195842	0.226202
6920	0.092836	0.108159	0.125785	0.146025	0.169229	0.195790	0.226202
6930	0.092800	0.108120	0.125742	0.145979	0.169180	0.195738	0.226092
6940	0.092764	0.108081	0.125700	0.145933	0.169131	0.195686	0.226037
6950	0.092728	0.108042	0.125657	0.145887	0.169082	0.195634	0.225983

Unit	83	84	85	86	87	88	89
6960	0.092692	0.108003	0.125615	0.145842	0.169033	0.195582	0.225928
6970	0.092656	0.107964	0.125573	0.145796	0.168984	0.195530	0.225873
6980	0.092621	0.107925	0.125531	0.145750	0.168935	0.195478	0.225819
6990	0.092585	0.107886	0.125488	0.145705	0.168887	0.195427	0.225765
7000	0.092549	0.107847	0.125446	0.145660	0.168838	0.195375	0.225710
7010	0.092514	0.107808	0.125404	0.145615	0.168790	0.195324	0.225656
7020	0.092478	0.107770	0.125362	0.145569	0.168742	0.195272	0.225602
7030	0.092443	0.107731	0.125321	0.145524	0.168693	0.195221	0.225548
7040	0.092408	0.107693	0.125279	0.145479	0.168645	0.195170	0.225494
7050	0.092372	0.107654	0.125237	0.145434	0.168597	0.195119	0.225440
7060	0.092337	0.107616	0.125196	0.145390	0.168549	0.195068	0.225387
7070	0.092302	0.107578	0.125154	0.145345	0.168501	0.195017	0.225333
7080	0.092267	0.107539	0.125113	0.145300	0.168453	0.194966	0.225280
7090	0.092232	0.107501	0.125071	0.145255	0.168405	0.194915	0.225226
7100	0.092197	0.107463	0.125030	0.145211	0.168358	0.194865	0.225173
7110	0.092162	0.107425	0.124989	0.145166	0.168310	0.194814	0.225119
7120	0.092127	0.107387	0.124947	0.145122	0.168263	0.194764	0.225066
7130	0.092093	0.107349	0.124906	0.145078	0.168215	0.194713	0.225013
7140	0.092058	0.107311	0.124865	0.145033	0.168168	0.194663	0.224960
7150	0.092023	0.107274	0.124824	0.144989	0.168121	0.194613	0.224907
7160	0.091989	0.107236	0.124783	0.144945	0.168073	0.194563	0.224854
7170	0.091954	0.107198	0.124743	0.144901	0.168026	0.194513	0.224802
7180	0.091920	0.107161	0.124702	0.144857	0.167979	0.194463	0.224749
7190	0.091885	0.107123	0.124661	0.144813	0.167932	0.194413	0.224696
7200	0.091851	0.107086	0.124621	0.144770	0.167885	0.194363	0.224644
7210	0.091817	0.107048	0.124580	0.144726	0.167839	0.194313	0.224591
7220	0.091783	0.107011	0.124540	0.144682	0.167792	0.194263	0.224539
7230	0.091748	0.106974	0.124499	0.144639	0.167745	0.194214	0.224487
7240	0.091714	0.106937	0.124459	0.144595	0.167699	0.194164	0.224435
7250	0.091680	0.106899	0.124418	0.144552	0.167652	0.194115	0.224383
7260	0.091646	0.106862	0.124378	0.144508	0.167606	0.194066	0.224331
7270	0.091613	0.106825	0.124338	0.144465	0.167559	0.194016	0.224279
7280	0.091579	0.106788	0.124298	0.144422	0.167513	0.193967	0.224227
7290	0.091545	0.106752	0.124258	0.144379	0.167467	0.193918	0.224175
7300	0.091511	0.106715	0.124218	0.144336	0.167421	0.193869	0.224124

Unit	83	84	85	86	87	88	89
7310	0.091477	0.106678	0.124178	0.144293	0.167375	0.193820	0.224072
7320	0.091444	0.106641	0.124138	0.144250	0.167329	0.193771	0.224020
7330	0.091410	0.106605	0.124099	0.144207	0.167283	0.193722	0.223969
7340	0.091377	0.106568	0.124059	0.144164	0.167237	0.193674	0.223918
7350	0.091343	0.106532	0.124020	0.144122	0.167191	0.193625	0.223866
7360	0.091310	0.106495	0.123980	0.144079	0.167146	0.193577	0.223815
7370	0.091277	0.106459	0.123941	0.144036	0.167100	0.193528	0.223764
7380	0.091243	0.106423	0.123901	0.143994	0.167055	0.193480	0.223713
7390	0.091210	0.106386	0.123862	0.143951	0.167009	0.193431	0.223662
7400	0.091177	0.106350	0.123823	0.143909	0.166964	0.193383	0.223611
7410	0.091144	0.106314	0.123783	0.143867	0.166918	0.193335	0.223561
7420	0.091111	0.106278	0.123744	0.143825	0.166873	0.193287	0.223510
7430	0.091078	0.106242	0.123705	0.143782	0.166828	0.193239	0.223459
7440	0.091045	0.106206	0.123666	0.143740	0.166783	0.193191	0.223409
7450	0.091012	0.106170	0.123627	0.143698	0.166738	0.193143	0.223358
7460	0.090979	0.106134	0.123588	0.143656	0.166693	0.193095	0.223308
7470	0.090947	0.106099	0.123549	0.143615	0.166648	0.193048	0.223258
7480	0.090914	0.106063	0.123511	0.143573	0.166603	0.193000	0.223208
7490	0.090881	0.106027	0.123472	0.143531	0.166559	0.192952	0.223157
7500	0.090849	0.105992	0.123433	0.143489	0.166514	0.192905	0.223107
7510	0.090816	0.105956	0.123395	0.143448	0.166469	0.192858	0.223057
7520	0.090784	0.105921	0.123356	0.143406	0.166425	0.192810	0.223008
7530	0.090751	0.105885	0.123318	0.143365	0.166381	0.192763	0.222958
7540	0.090719	0.105850	0.123280	0.143323	0.166336	0.192716	0.222908
7550	0.090687	0.105815	0.123241	0.143282	0.166292	0.192669	0.222858
7560	0.090654	0.105779	0.123203	0.143241	0.166248	0.192622	0.222809
7570	0.090622	0.105744	0.123165	0.143200	0.166204	0.192575	0.222759
7580	0.090590	0.105709	0.123127	0.143159	0.166159	0.192528	0.222710
7590	0.090558	0.105674	0.123089	0.143117	0.166115	0.192481	0.222660
7600	0.090526	0.105639	0.123051	0.143076	0.166072	0.192434	0.222611
7610	0.090494	0.105604	0.123013	0.143036	0.166028	0.192388	0.222562
7620	0.090462	0.105569	0.122975	0.142995	0.165984	0.192341	0.222513
7630	0.090430	0.105535	0.122937	0.142954	0.165940	0.192295	0.222464
7640	0.090398	0.105500	0.122899	0.142913	0.165896	0.192248	0.222415
7650	0.090366	0.105465	0.122862	0.142872	0.165853	0.192202	0.222366

Unit	83	84	85	86	87	88	89
7660	0.090335	0.105430	0.122824	0.142832	0.165809	0.192155	0.222317
7670	0.090303	0.105396	0.122786	0.142791	0.165766	0.192109	0.222268
7680	0.090271	0.105361	0.122749	0.142751	0.165723	0.192063	0.222220
7690	0.090240	0.105327	0.122712	0.142710	0.165679	0.192017	0.222171
7700	0.090208	0.105292	0.122674	0.142670	0.165636	0.191971	0.222122
7710	0.090177	0.105258	0.122637	0.142630	0.165593	0.191925	0.222074
7720	0.090145	0.105224	0.122600	0.142590	0.165550	0.191879	0.222026
7730	0.090114	0.105189	0.122562	0.142549	0.165507	0.191833	0.221977
7740	0.090083	0.105155	0.122525	0.142509	0.165464	0.191788	0.221929
7750	0.090051	0.105121	0.122488	0.142469	0.165421	0.191742	0.221881
7760	0.090020	0.105087	0.122451	0.142429	0.165378	0.191696	0.221833
7770	0.089989	0.105053	0.122414	0.142389	0.165335	0.191651	0.221785
7780	0.089958	0.105019	0.122377	0.142350	0.165292	0.191605	0.221737
7790	0.089927	0.104985	0.122340	0.142310	0.165250	0.191560	0.221689
7800	0.089896	0.104951	0.122304	0.142270	0.165207	0.191515	0.221641
7810	0.089865	0.104917	0.122267	0.142230	0.165165	0.191469	0.221593
7820	0.089834	0.104884	0.122230	0.142191	0.165122	0.191424	0.221546
7830	0.089803	0.104850	0.122194	0.142151	0.165080	0.191379	0.221498
7840	0.089772	0.104816	0.122157	0.142112	0.165037	0.191334	0.221451
7850	0.089742	0.104783	0.122120	0.142072	0.164995	0.191289	0.221403
7860	0.089711	0.104749	0.122084	0.142033	0.164953	0.191244	0.221356
7870	0.089680	0.104716	0.122048	0.141994	0.164911	0.191199	0.221308
7880	0.089650	0.104682	0.122011	0.141955	0.164869	0.191155	0.221261
7890	0.089619	0.104649	0.121975	0.141915	0.164827	0.191110	0.221214
7900	0.089589	0.104615	0.121939	0.141876	0.164785	0.191065	0.221167
7910	0.089558	0.104582	0.121903	0.141837	0.164743	0.191021	0.221120
7920	0.089528	0.104549	0.121867	0.141798	0.164701	0.190976	0.221073
7930	0.089497	0.104516	0.121830	0.141759	0.164659	0.190932	0.221026
7940	0.089467	0.104483	0.121794	0.141720	0.164618	0.190887	0.220979
7950	0.089437	0.104450	0.121759	0.141682	0.164576	0.190843	0.220932
7960	0.089407	0.104417	0.121723	0.141643	0.164534	0.190799	0.220886
7970	0.089376	0.104384	0.121687	0.141604	0.164493	0.190755	0.220839
7980	0.089346	0.104351	0.121651	0.141566	0.164452	0.190711	0.220793
7990	0.089316	0.104318	0.121615	0.141527	0.164410	0.190667	0.220746
8000	0.089286	0.104285	0.121580	0.141488	0.164369	0.190623	0.220700

Unit	90	91	92	93	94	95	96
1	1.000000	1.000000	1.000000	1.000000	1.000000	1.000000	1.000000
2	0.900000	0.910000	0.920000	0.930000	0.940000	0.950000	0.960000
3	0.846206	0.861157	0.876204	0.891347	0.906585	0.921919	0.937347
4	0.810000	0.828100	0.846400	0.864900	0.883600	0.902500	0.921600
5	0.782987	0.803336	0.823982	0.844928	0.866173	0.887720	0.909568
6	0.761585	0.783653	0.806107	0.828952	0.852190	0.875823	0.899854
7	0.743948	0.767387	0.791297	0.815681	0.840544	0.865889	0.891721
8	0.729000	0.753571	0.778688	0.804357	0.830584	0.857375	0.884736
9	0.716065	0.741591	0.767733	0.794499	0.821897	0.849935	0.878620
10	0.704688	0.731035	0.758064	0.785783	0.814203	0.843334	0.873185
11	0.694553	0.721617	0.749422	0.777981	0.807305	0.837407	0.868298
12	0.685427	0.713124	0.741619	0.770926	0.801059	0.832032	0.863859
13	0.677138	0.705399	0.734512	0.764492	0.795355	0.827118	0.859797
14	0.669553	0.698323	0.727993	0.758584	0.790111	0.822595	0.856052
15	0.662568	0.691798	0.721976	0.753124	0.785260	0.818406	0.852581
16	0.656100	0.685750	0.716393	0.748052	0.780749	0.814506	0.849347
17	0.650082	0.680116	0.711187	0.743319	0.776535	0.810860	0.846320
18	0.644458	0.674848	0.706314	0.738884	0.772583	0.807438	0.843475
19	0.639183	0.669901	0.701735	0.734713	0.768863	0.804214	0.840794
20	0.634219	0.665242	0.697419	0.730778	0.765351	0.801167	0.838258
21	0.629533	0.660841	0.693337	0.727055	0.762025	0.798280	0.835853
22	0.625097	0.656671	0.689468	0.723522	0.758867	0.795536	0.833566
23	0.620888	0.652711	0.685791	0.720163	0.755861	0.792924	0.831386
24	0.616884	0.648943	0.682289	0.716961	0.752995	0.790430	0.829305
25	0.613068	0.645348	0.678947	0.713903	0.750256	0.788046	0.827314
26	0.609424	0.641914	0.675751	0.710978	0.747634	0.785762	0.825405
27	0.605938	0.638626	0.672690	0.708174	0.745120	0.783571	0.823572
28	0.602598	0.635473	0.669754	0.705483	0.742705	0.781465	0.821810
29	0.599392	0.632447	0.666933	0.702896	0.740382	0.779438	0.820114
30	0.596311	0.629536	0.664218	0.700405	0.738144	0.777485	0.818478
31	0.593347	0.626734	0.661603	0.698005	0.735987	0.775601	0.816899
32	0.590490	0.624032	0.659081	0.695688	0.733904	0.773781	0.815373
33	0.587734	0.621425	0.656646	0.693451	0.731891	0.772021	0.813897
34	0.585074	0.618906	0.654292	0.691287	0.729943	0.770317	0.812467
35	0.582501	0.616470	0.652015	0.689192	0.728057	0.768667	0.811081

Unit	90	91	92	93	94	95	96
36	0.580012	0.614111	0.649809	0.687162	0.726228	0.767066	0.809736
37	0.577602	0.611826	0.647671	0.685194	0.724454	0.765512	0.808431
38	0.575265	0.609610	0.645596	0.683283	0.722731	0.764003	0.807162
39	0.572998	0.607459	0.643582	0.681428	0.721058	0.762536	0.805928
40	0.570797	0.605370	0.641625	0.679624	0.719430	0.761109	0.804728
41	0.568659	0.603340	0.639722	0.677869	0.717846	0.759719	0.803558
42	0.566580	0.601365	0.637870	0.676161	0.716303	0.758366	0.802419
43	0.564557	0.599443	0.636067	0.674497	0.714800	0.757046	0.801307
44	0.562588	0.597571	0.634311	0.672876	0.713335	0.755759	0.800223
45	0.560669	0.595746	0.632598	0.671294	0.711905	0.754504	0.799165
46	0.558799	0.593967	0.630928	0.669751	0.710510	0.753277	0.798131
47	0.556975	0.592232	0.629298	0.668245	0.709147	0.752080	0.797121
48	0.555196	0.590538	0.627706	0.666774	0.707816	0.750909	0.796133
49	0.553458	0.588883	0.626151	0.665336	0.706514	0.749764	0.795167
50	0.551761	0.587267	0.624631	0.663930	0.705241	0.748644	0.794221
51	0.550103	0.585687	0.623145	0.662555	0.703995	0.747548	0.793295
52	0.548482	0.584141	0.621691	0.661209	0.702776	0.746474	0.792389
53	0.546896	0.582629	0.620268	0.659892	0.701582	0.745423	0.791500
54	0.545344	0.581149	0.618875	0.658602	0.700412	0.744392	0.790630
55	0.543825	0.579700	0.617511	0.657338	0.699266	0.743382	0.789776
56	0.542338	0.578281	0.616174	0.656099	0.698142	0.742392	0.788938
57	0.540881	0.576890	0.614863	0.654884	0.697040	0.741420	0.788116
58	0.539453	0.575526	0.613578	0.653693	0.695959	0.740466	0.787309
59	0.538053	0.574189	0.612318	0.652524	0.694898	0.739530	0.786517
60	0.536680	0.572878	0.611081	0.651377	0.693856	0.738611	0.785739
61	0.535333	0.571591	0.609867	0.650251	0.692833	0.737708	0.784974
62	0.534012	0.570328	0.608675	0.649144	0.691828	0.736821	0.784223
63	0.532715	0.569087	0.607505	0.648058	0.690840	0.735949	0.783484
64	0.531441	0.567869	0.606355	0.646990	0.689870	0.735092	0.782758
65	0.530190	0.566673	0.605225	0.645941	0.688916	0.734249	0.782044
66	0.528961	0.565497	0.604115	0.644909	0.687977	0.733420	0.781341
67	0.527753	0.564341	0.603023	0.643895	0.687055	0.732604	0.780649
68	0.526566	0.563204	0.601949	0.642897	0.686147	0.731802	0.779968
69	0.525399	0.562087	0.600893	0.641915	0.685253	0.731011	0.779298
70	0.524251	0.560987	0.599854	0.640948	0.684373	0.730233	0.778638

Unit	90	91	92	93	94	95	96
71	0.523122	0.559906	0.598831	0.639997	0.683507	0.729467	0.777988
72	0.522011	0.558841	0.597824	0.639061	0.682654	0.728713	0.777347
73	0.520918	0.557793	0.596833	0.638139	0.681814	0.727969	0.776716
74	0.519842	0.556762	0.595857	0.637230	0.680987	0.727237	0.776094
75	0.518782	0.555746	0.594896	0.636335	0.680171	0.726515	0.775480
76	0.517739	0.554745	0.593949	0.635454	0.679368	0.725803	0.774876
77	0.516711	0.553759	0.593015	0.634584	0.678575	0.725101	0.774279
78	0.515698	0.552788	0.592096	0.633728	0.677794	0.724409	0.773691
79	0.514701	0.551831	0.591189	0.632883	0.677024	0.723727	0.773111
80	0.513718	0.550887	0.590295	0.632050	0.676264	0.723053	0.772538
81	0.512748	0.549957	0.589414	0.631229	0.675515	0.722389	0.771973
82	0.511793	0.549039	0.588544	0.630418	0.674775	0.721733	0.771416
83	0.510851	0.548135	0.587687	0.629619	0.674045	0.721086	0.770865
84	0.509922	0.547242	0.586841	0.628830	0.673325	0.720447	0.770322
85	0.509005	0.546362	0.586006	0.628051	0.672614	0.719817	0.769785
86	0.508101	0.545493	0.585182	0.627282	0.671912	0.719194	0.769255
87	0.507209	0.544636	0.584369	0.626524	0.671219	0.718579	0.768731
88	0.506329	0.543789	0.583566	0.625774	0.670535	0.717971	0.768214
89	0.505460	0.542954	0.582773	0.625035	0.669859	0.717371	0.767703
90	0.504602	0.542129	0.581990	0.624304	0.669191	0.716778	0.767198
91	0.503755	0.541315	0.581217	0.623582	0.668531	0.716193	0.766699
92	0.502919	0.540510	0.580454	0.622869	0.667879	0.715614	0.766206
93	0.502093	0.539716	0.579699	0.622164	0.667235	0.715041	0.765718
94	0.501278	0.538931	0.578954	0.621468	0.666598	0.714476	0.765236
95	0.500472	0.538156	0.578217	0.620780	0.665969	0.713916	0.764759
96	0.499676	0.537389	0.577490	0.620100	0.665347	0.713363	0.764288
97	0.498890	0.536632	0.576770	0.619427	0.664731	0.712817	0.763821
98	0.498113	0.535884	0.576059	0.618762	0.664123	0.712276	0.763360
99	0.497344	0.535144	0.575356	0.618105	0.663522	0.711741	0.762904
100	0.496585	0.534413	0.574661	0.617455	0.662927	0.711212	0.762452
101	0.495835	0.533690	0.573973	0.616812	0.662338	0.710688	0.762006
102	0.495093	0.532975	0.573293	0.616176	0.661756	0.710170	0.761564
103	0.494359	0.532268	0.572621	0.615547	0.661180	0.709658	0.761126
104	0.493634	0.531569	0.571956	0.614925	0.660610	0.709150	0.760693
105	0.492916	0.530877	0.571298	0.613309	0.660046	0.708648	0.760265

Unit	90	91	92	93	94	95	96
106	0.492206	0.530193	0.570647	0.613700	0.659487	0.708152	0.759840
107	0.491504	0.529516	0.570003	0.613097	0.658935	0.707660	0.759420
108	0.490810	0.528846	0.569365	0.612500	0.658388	0.707173	0.759004
109	0.490123	0.528183	0.568734	0.611909	0.657846	0.706691	0.758593
110	0.489443	0.527527	0.568110	0.611324	0.657310	0.706213	0.758185
111	0.488770	0.526878	0.567492	0.610745	0.656779	0.705740	0.757781
112	0.488104	0.526236	0.566880	0.610172	0.656254	0.705272	0.757380
113	0.487445	0.525600	0.566274	0.609604	0.655733	0.704808	0.756984
114	0.486793	0.524970	0.565674	0.609042	0.655218	0.704349	0.756591
115	0.486147	0.524346	0.565080	0.608486	0.654707	0.703894	0.756202
116	0.485508	0.523729	0.564492	0.607934	0.654201	0.703443	0.755817
117	0.484875	0.523118	0.563909	0.607388	0.653700	0.702996	0.755435
118	0.484248	0.522512	0.563332	0.606847	0.653204	0.702554	0.755056
119	0.483627	0.521913	0.562761	0.606311	0.652712	0.702115	0.754681
120	0.483012	0.521319	0.562194	0.605780	0.652224	0.701681	0.754309
121	0.482403	0.520730	0.561633	0.605254	0.651741	0.701250	0.753941
122	0.481800	0.520148	0.561078	0.604733	0.651263	0.700823	0.753575
123	0.481203	0.519570	0.560527	0.604216	0.650788	0.700400	0.753213
124	0.480611	0.518998	0.559981	0.603704	0.650318	0.699980	0.752854
125	0.480024	0.518431	0.559440	0.603197	0.649852	0.699564	0.752498
126	0.479443	0.517870	0.558904	0.602694	0.649390	0.699152	0.752145
127	0.478867	0.517313	0.558373	0.602195	0.648932	0.698743	0.751795
128	0.478297	0.516761	0.557847	0.601701	0.648478	0.698337	0.751448
129	0.477731	0.516214	0.557325	0.601211	0.648027	0.697935	0.751103
130	0.477171	0.515672	0.556807	0.600725	0.647581	0.697537	0.750762
131	0.476616	0.515135	0.556294	0.600243	0.647138	0.697141	0.750423
132	0.476065	0.514602	0.555785	0.599766	0.646699	0.696749	0.750087
133	0.475519	0.514074	0.555281	0.599292	0.646263	0.696360	0.749754
134	0.474978	0.513550	0.554781	0.598822	0.645831	0.695974	0.749423
135	0.474441	0.513031	0.554285	0.598356	0.645403	0.695591	0.749095
136	0.473910	0.512516	0.553793	0.597894	0.644978	0.695211	0.748769
137	0.473382	0.512005	0.553305	0.597435	0.644556	0.694835	0.748446
138	0.472859	0.511499	0.552821	0.596981	0.644138	0.694461	0.748126
139	0.472340	0.510997	0.552341	0.596530	0.643723	0.694090	0.747808
140	0.471826	0.510499	0.551865	0.596082	0.643311	0.693722	0.747492

Unit	90	91	92	93	94	95	96
141	0.471316	0.510004	0.551393	0.595638	0.642902	0.693356	0.747179
142	0.470810	0.509514	0.550925	0.595198	0.642497	0.692994	0.746868
143	0.470308	0.509028	0.550460	0.594760	0.642095	0.692634	0.746557
144	0.469810	0.508546	0.549998	0.594327	0.641695	0.692277	0.746253
145	0.469316	0.508067	0.549541	0.593896	0.641299	0.691923	0.745949
146	0.468826	0.507592	0.549087	0.593469	0.640906	0.691571	0.745647
147	0.468340	0.507121	0.548636	0.593045	0.640515	0.691222	0.745347
148	0.467857	0.506653	0.548189	0.592624	0.640128	0.690875	0.745050
149	0.467379	0.506189	0.547745	0.592206	0.639743	0.690531	0.744755
150	0.466904	0.505729	0.547304	0.591792	0.639361	0.690189	0.744461
151	0.466432	0.505272	0.546867	0.591380	0.638982	0.689850	0.744170
152	0.465965	0.504818	0.546433	0.590972	0.638606	0.689513	0.743881
153	0.465500	0.504368	0.546002	0.590566	0.638232	0.689178	0.743593
154	0.465040	0.503921	0.545574	0.590164	0.637861	0.688846	0.743308
155	0.464582	0.503478	0.545150	0.589764	0.637492	0.688516	0.743025
156	0.464129	0.503037	0.544728	0.589367	0.637127	0.688189	0.742744
157	0.463678	0.502600	0.544309	0.588973	0.636763	0.687863	0.742464
158	0.463231	0.502166	0.543894	0.588581	0.636402	0.687540	0.742187
159	0.462787	0.501735	0.543481	0.588193	0.636044	0.687219	0.741911
160	0.462346	0.501307	0.543072	0.587807	0.635688	0.686901	0.741637
161	0.461908	0.500883	0.542665	0.587423	0.635335	0.686584	0.741365
162	0.461474	0.500461	0.542261	0.587043	0.634984	0.686269	0.741095
163	0.461042	0.500042	0.541859	0.586665	0.634635	0.685957	0.740826
164	0.460614	0.499626	0.541461	0.586289	0.634289	0.685647	0.740559
165	0.460188	0.499213	0.541065	0.585916	0.633944	0.685338	0.740294
166	0.459766	0.498803	0.540672	0.585545	0.633603	0.685032	0.740031
167	0.459346	0.498395	0.540281	0.585177	0.633263	0.684727	0.739769
168	0.458930	0.497990	0.539893	0.584812	0.632926	0.684425	0.739509
169	0.458516	0.497588	0.539508	0.584448	0.632590	0.684124	0.739251
170	0.458105	0.497189	0.539125	0.584087	0.632257	0.683826	0.738994
171	0.457697	0.496793	0.538745	0.583729	0.631926	0.683529	0.738739
172	0.457291	0.496399	0.538367	0.583373	0.631597	0.683234	0.738485
173	0.456888	0.496007	0.537992	0.583019	0.631271	0.682941	0.738233
174	0.456488	0.495618	0.537619	0.582667	0.630946	0.682650	0.737982
175	0.456091	0.495232	0.537249	0.582318	0.630623	0.682361	0.737733

Unit	90	91	92	93	94	95	96
176	0.455696	0.494848	0.536881	0.581970	0.630303	0.682073	0.737486
177	0.455304	0.494467	0.536515	0.581625	0.629984	0.681787	0.737240
178	0.454914	0.494088	0.536151	0.581282	0.629667	0.681503	0.736995
179	0.454527	0.493712	0.535790	0.580941	0.629352	0.681220	0.736752
180	0.454142	0.493337	0.535431	0.580603	0.629039	0.680940	0.736510
181	0.453760	0.492966	0.535075	0.580266	0.628728	0.680660	0.736270
182	0.453380	0.492596	0.534720	0.579931	0.628419	0.680383	0.736031
183	0.453002	0.492229	0.534368	0.579599	0.628112	0.680107	0.735794
184	0.452627	0.491864	0.534017	0.579268	0.627806	0.679833	0.735558
185	0.452254	0.491502	0.533669	0.578939	0.627503	0.679560	0.735323
186	0.451884	0.491141	0.533323	0.578613	0.627201	0.679289	0.735089
187	0.451516	0.490783	0.532980	0.578288	0.626901	0.679020	0.734857
188	0.451150	0.490427	0.532638	0.577965	0.626602	0.678752	0.734626
189	0.450786	0.490073	0.532298	0.577644	0.626306	0.678485	0.734397
190	0.450425	0.489722	0.531960	0.577325	0.626011	0.678221	0.734169
191	0.450066	0.489372	0.531624	0.577008	0.625717	0.677957	0.733942
192	0.449709	0.489024	0.531290	0.576693	0.625426	0.677695	0.733716
193	0.449354	0.488679	0.530959	0.576379	0.625136	0.677435	0.733492
194	0.449001	0.488335	0.530629	0.576067	0.624848	0.677176	0.733268
195	0.448650	0.487994	0.530300	0.575757	0.624561	0.676918	0.733047
196	0.448301	0.487654	0.529974	0.575449	0.624276	0.676662	0.732826
197	0.447955	0.487317	0.529650	0.575143	0.623992	0.676407	0.732606
198	0.447610	0.486981	0.529327	0.574838	0.623710	0.676154	0.732388
199	0.447267	0.486647	0.529007	0.574535	0.623430	0.675902	0.732170
200	0.446927	0.486316	0.528688	0.574233	0.623151	0.675651	0.731954
201	0.446588	0.485986	0.528371	0.573933	0.622874	0.675402	0.731739
202	0.446251	0.485658	0.528055	0.573635	0.622598	0.675154	0.731526
203	0.445916	0.485332	0.527742	0.573339	0.622323	0.674907	0.731313
204	0.445583	0.485007	0.527430	0.573044	0.622050	0.674662	0.731101
205	0.445252	0.484685	0.527120	0.572751	0.621779	0.674418	0.730891
206	0.444923	0.484364	0.526811	0.572459	0.621509	0.674175	0.730681
207	0.444596	0.484045	0.526505	0.572169	0.621240	0.673933	0.730473
208	0.444270	0.483727	0.526199	0.571880	0.620973	0.673693	0.730266
209	0.443946	0.483412	0.525896	0.571593	0.620707	0.673454	0.730059
210	0.443624	0.483098	0.525594	0.571307	0.620443	0.673216	0.729854

Unit	90	91	92	93	94	95	96
211	0.443304	0.482786	0.525294	0.571023	0.620180	0.672979	0.729650
212	0.442986	0.482475	0.524995	0.570741	0.619918	0.672744	0.729447
213	0.442669	0.482167	0.524698	0.570460	0.619658	0.672510	0.729245
214	0.442354	0.481859	0.524402	0.570180	0.619399	0.672277	0.729044
215	0.442041	0.481554	0.524108	0.569902	0.619141	0.672045	0.728843
216	0.441729	0.481250	0.523816	0.569625	0.618884	0.671814	0.728644
217	0.441419	0.480948	0.523525	0.569349	0.618629	0.671585	0.728446
218	0.441110	0.480647	0.523235	0.569075	0.618376	0.671356	0.728249
219	0.440804	0.480348	0.522947	0.568803	0.618123	0.671129	0.728053
220	0.440499	0.480050	0.522661	0.568532	0.617872	0.670902	0.727857
221	0.440195	0.479754	0.522376	0.568262	0.617622	0.670677	0.727663
222	0.439893	0.479459	0.522092	0.567993	0.617373	0.670453	0.727469
223	0.439593	0.479166	0.521810	0.567726	0.617125	0.670230	0.727277
224	0.439294	0.478874	0.521529	0.567460	0.616879	0.670009	0.727085
225	0.438996	0.478584	0.521250	0.567195	0.616633	0.669788	0.726895
226	0.438701	0.478296	0.520972	0.566932	0.616389	0.669568	0.726705
227	0.438406	0.478008	0.520695	0.566670	0.616146	0.669349	0.726516
228	0.438113	0.477723	0.520420	0.566409	0.615905	0.669132	0.726328
229	0.437822	0.477438	0.520146	0.566150	0.615664	0.668915	0.726141
230	0.437532	0.477155	0.519874	0.565892	0.615425	0.668699	0.725954
231	0.437244	0.476874	0.519602	0.565635	0.615186	0.668485	0.725769
232	0.436957	0.476593	0.519332	0.565379	0.614949	0.668271	0.725584
233	0.436671	0.476315	0.519064	0.565124	0.614713	0.668058	0.725400
234	0.436387	0.476037	0.518796	0.564871	0.614478	0.667847	0.725217
235	0.436104	0.475761	0.518530	0.564619	0.614244	0.667636	0.725035
236	0.435823	0.475486	0.518266	0.564368	0.614012	0.667426	0.724854
237	0.435543	0.475213	0.518002	0.564118	0.613780	0.667217	0.724674
238	0.435264	0.474941	0.517740	0.563870	0.613549	0.667009	0.724494
239	0.434987	0.474670	0.517479	0.563622	0.613320	0.666802	0.724315
240	0.434711	0.474400	0.517219	0.563376	0.613091	0.666596	0.724137
241	0.434436	0.474132	0.516960	0.563131	0.612863	0.666391	0.723960
242	0.434163	0.473865	0.516703	0.562887	0.612637	0.666187	0.723783
243	0.433891	0.473599	0.516446	0.562644	0.612412	0.665984	0.723607
244	0.433620	0.473334	0.516191	0.562402	0.612187	0.665782	0.723432
245	0.433351	0.473071	0.515937	0.562161	0.611964	0.665580	0.723258

Unit	90	91	92	93	94	95	96
246	0.433082	0.472809	0.515685	0.561921	0.611741	0.665380	0.723085
247	0.432815	0.472548	0.515433	0.561683	0.611520	0.665180	0.722912
248	0.432550	0.472288	0.515183	0.561445	0.611299	0.664981	0.722740
249	0.432285	0.472030	0.514933	0.561209	0.611080	0.664783	0.722569
250	0.432022	0.471772	0.514685	0.560973	0.610861	0.664586	0.722398
251	0.431760	0.471516	0.514438	0.560739	0.610643	0.664390	0.722228
252	0.431499	0.471261	0.514192	0.560505	0.610427	0.664194	0.722059
253	0.431239	0.471007	0.513947	0.560273	0.610211	0.663999	0.721891
254	0.430981	0.470755	0.513703	0.560042	0.609996	0.663806	0.721723
255	0.430723	0.470503	0.513461	0.559811	0.609782	0.663613	0.721556
256	0.430467	0.470253	0.513219	0.559582	0.609569	0.663420	0.721390
257	0.430212	0.470003	0.512978	0.559354	0.609357	0.663229	0.721224
258	0.429958	0.469755	0.512739	0.559126	0.609146	0.663039	0.721059
259	0.429706	0.469508	0.512500	0.558900	0.608935	0.662849	0.720895
260	0.429454	0.469262	0.512263	0.558674	0.608726	0.662660	0.720731
261	0.429203	0.469017	0.512026	0.558450	0.608517	0.662472	0.720568
262	0.428954	0.468773	0.511791	0.558226	0.608310	0.662284	0.720406
263	0.428706	0.468530	0.511556	0.558004	0.608103	0.662097	0.720245
264	0.428458	0.468288	0.511323	0.557782	0.607897	0.661912	0.720084
265	0.428212	0.468047	0.511090	0.557561	0.607692	0.661726	0.719923
266	0.427967	0.467807	0.510859	0.557341	0.607487	0.661542	0.719764
267	0.427723	0.467568	0.510628	0.557122	0.607284	0.661358	0.719605
268	0.427480	0.467331	0.510398	0.556904	0.607081	0.661175	0.719446
269	0.427238	0.467094	0.510170	0.556687	0.606880	0.660993	0.719288
270	0.426997	0.466858	0.509942	0.556471	0.606679	0.660812	0.719131
271	0.426757	0.466623	0.509715	0.556256	0.606478	0.660631	0.718975
272	0.426519	0.466390	0.509490	0.556041	0.606279	0.660451	0.718819
273	0.426281	0.466157	0.509265	0.555828	0.606081	0.660272	0.718663
274	0.426044	0.465925	0.509041	0.555615	0.605883	0.660093	0.718509
275	0.425808	0.465694	0.508818	0.555403	0.605686	0.659915	0.718355
276	0.425573	0.465464	0.508596	0.555192	0.605489	0.659738	0.718201
277	0.425339	0.465235	0.508374	0.554982	0.605294	0.659561	0.718048
278	0.425106	0.465007	0.508154	0.554773	0.605099	0.659385	0.717896
279	0.424874	0.464780	0.507935	0.554564	0.604905	0.659210	0.717744
280	0.424643	0.464554	0.507716	0.554356	0.604712	0.659036	0.717593

Unit	90	91	92	93	94	95	96
281	0.424413	0.464328	0.507498	0.554149	0.604520	0.658862	0.717442
282	0.424184	0.464104	0.507282	0.553943	0.604328	0.658689	0.717292
283	0.423956	0.463881	0.507066	0.553738	0.604137	0.658516	0.717142
284	0.423729	0.463658	0.506851	0.553534	0.603947	0.658344	0.716993
285	0.423502	0.463436	0.506636	0.553330	0.603758	0.658173	0.716845
286	0.423277	0.463215	0.506423	0.553127	0.603569	0.658002	0.716697
287	0.423053	0.462996	0.506210	0.552925	0.603381	0.657833	0.716550
288	0.422829	0.462776	0.505999	0.552724	0.603194	0.657663	0.716403
289	0.422606	0.462558	0.505788	0.552523	0.603007	0.657495	0.716257
290	0.422384	0.462341	0.505577	0.552323	0.602821	0.657327	0.716111
291	0.422163	0.462124	0.505368	0.552124	0.602636	0.657159	0.715966
292	0.421943	0.461909	0.505160	0.551926	0.602451	0.656992	0.715821
293	0.421724	0.461694	0.504952	0.551729	0.602267	0.656826	0.715677
294	0.421506	0.461480	0.504745	0.551532	0.602084	0.656661	0.715534
295	0.421288	0.461267	0.504539	0.551336	0.601902	0.656496	0.715391
296	0.421072	0.461054	0.504334	0.551140	0.601720	0.656331	0.715248
297	0.420856	0.460843	0.504129	0.550946	0.601539	0.656167	0.715106
298	0.420641	0.460632	0.503925	0.550752	0.601358	0.656004	0.714964
299	0.420427	0.460422	0.503722	0.550559	0.601179	0.655842	0.714823
300	0.420213	0.460213	0.503520	0.550366	0.600999	0.655680	0.714683
301	0.420001	0.460005	0.503318	0.550175	0.600821	0.655518	0.714543
302	0.419789	0.459797	0.503118	0.549984	0.600643	0.655357	0.714403
303	0.419578	0.459591	0.502917	0.549793	0.600466	0.655197	0.714264
304	0.419368	0.459385	0.502718	0.549604	0.600289	0.655037	0.714125
305	0.419159	0.459179	0.502520	0.549415	0.600113	0.654878	0.713987
306	0.418950	0.458975	0.502322	0.549227	0.599938	0.654719	0.713850
307	0.418743	0.458771	0.502125	0.549039	0.599763	0.654561	0.713713
308	0.418536	0.458568	0.501928	0.548852	0.599589	0.654404	0.713576
309	0.418330	0.458366	0.501733	0.548666	0.599416	0.654247	0.713440
310	0.418124	0.458165	0.501538	0.548480	0.599243	0.654090	0.713304
311	0.417920	0.457964	0.501343	0.548295	0.599071	0.653935	0.713169
312	0.417716	0.457764	0.501150	0.548111	0.598899	0.653779	0.713034
313	0.417513	0.457565	0.500957	0.547928	0.598728	0.653624	0.712900
314	0.417310	0.457366	0.500765	0.547745	0.598557	0.653470	0.712766
315	0.417109	0.457168	0.500573	0.547562	0.598388	0.653316	0.712632

Unit	90	91	92	93	94	95	96
316	0.416908	0.456971	0.500382	0.547381	0.598218	0.653163	0.712499
317	0.416707	0.456775	0.500192	0.547200	0.598050	0.653011	0.712367
318	0.416508	0.456579	0.500003	0.547019	0.597881	0.652858	0.712234
319	0.416309	0.456384	0.499814	0.546839	0.597714	0.652707	0.712103
320	0.416111	0.456190	0.499626	0.546660	0.597547	0.652556	0.711971
321	0.415914	0.455996	0.499438	0.546482	0.597381	0.652405	0.711841
322	0.415717	0.455803	0.499251	0.546304	0.597215	0.652255	0.711710
323	0.415521	0.455611	0.499065	0.546126	0.597049	0.652105	0.711580
324	0.415326	0.455419	0.498880	0.545950	0.596885	0.651956	0.711451
325	0.415132	0.455228	0.498695	0.545774	0.596720	0.651807	0.711322
326	0.414938	0.455038	0.498511	0.545598	0.596557	0.651659	0.711193
327	0.414745	0.454848	0.498327	0.545423	0.596394	0.651511	0.711065
328	0.414552	0.454660	0.498144	0.545249	0.596231	0.651364	0.710937
329	0.414361	0.454471	0.497962	0.545075	0.596069	0.651218	0.710809
330	0.414169	0.454284	0.497780	0.544902	0.595908	0.651071	0.710682
331	0.413979	0.454097	0.497599	0.544729	0.595747	0.650926	0.710556
332	0.413789	0.453910	0.497418	0.544557	0.595586	0.650780	0.710430
333	0.413600	0.453725	0.497238	0.544386	0.595427	0.650635	0.710304
334	0.413412	0.453540	0.497059	0.544215	0.595267	0.650491	0.710178
335	0.413224	0.453355	0.496880	0.544045	0.595108	0.650347	0.710053
336	0.413037	0.453171	0.496702	0.543875	0.594950	0.650204	0.709929
337	0.412850	0.452988	0.496524	0.543706	0.594792	0.650061	0.709804
338	0.412664	0.452805	0.496348	0.543537	0.594635	0.649918	0.709681
339	0.412479	0.452624	0.496171	0.543369	0.594478	0.649776	0.709557
340	0.412294	0.452442	0.495995	0.543201	0.594322	0.649635	0.709434
341	0.412110	0.452261	0.495820	0.543034	0.594166	0.649493	0.709311
342	0.411927	0.452081	0.495646	0.542868	0.594011	0.649353	0.709189
343	0.411744	0.451902	0.495472	0.542702	0.593856	0.649212	0.709067
344	0.411562	0.451723	0.495298	0.542537	0.593702	0.649073	0.708945
345	0.411380	0.451544	0.495125	0.542372	0.593548	0.648933	0.708824
346	0.411199	0.451367	0.494953	0.542207	0.593395	0.648794	0.708703
347	0.411019	0.451189	0.494781	0.542044	0.593242	0.648656	0.708583
348	0.410839	0.451013	0.494610	0.541880	0.593089	0.648517	0.708463
349	0.410660	0.450837	0.494439	0.541718	0.592937	0.648380	0.708343
350	0.410482	0.450661	0.494269	0.541555	0.592786	0.648243	0.708224

Unit	90	91	92	93	94	95	96
351	0.410304	0.450486	0.494099	0.541394	0.592635	0.648106	0.708105
352	0.410126	0.450312	0.493930	0.541232	0.592485	0.647969	0.707986
353	0.409949	0.450138	0.493762	0.541072	0.592334	0.647833	0.707868
354	0.409773	0.449965	0.493594	0.540911	0.592185	0.647698	0.707750
355	0.409598	0.449792	0.493426	0.540752	0.592036	0.647562	0.707632
356	0.409422	0.449620	0.493259	0.540592	0.591887	0.647428	0.707515
357	0.409248	0.449449	0.493093	0.540434	0.591739	0.647293	0.707398
358	0.409074	0.449278	0.492927	0.540275	0.591591	0.647159	0.707282
359	0.408901	0.449107	0.492762	0.540118	0.591444	0.647026	0.707166
360	0.408728	0.448937	0.492597	0.539960	0.591297	0.646893	0.707050
361	0.408555	0.448768	0.492432	0.539804	0.591151	0.646760	0.706934
362	0.408384	0.448599	0.492269	0.539647	0.591005	0.646627	0.706819
363	0.408212	0.448431	0.492105	0.539491	0.590859	0.646495	0.706704
364	0.408042	0.448263	0.491942	0.539336	0.590714	0.646364	0.706590
365	0.407872	0.448095	0.491780	0.539181	0.590570	0.646233	0.706476
366	0.407702	0.447929	0.491618	0.539027	0.590425	0.646102	0.706362
367	0.407533	0.447762	0.491457	0.538873	0.590281	0.645971	0.706248
368	0.407365	0.447597	0.491296	0.538719	0.590138	0.645841	0.706135
369	0.407197	0.447431	0.491136	0.538566	0.589995	0.645712	0.706022
370	0.407029	0.447267	0.490976	0.538414	0.589853	0.645582	0.705910
371	0.406862	0.447102	0.490816	0.538262	0.589711	0.645453	0.705798
372	0.406696	0.446939	0.490658	0.538110	0.589569	0.645325	0.705686
373	0.406530	0.446775	0.490499	0.537959	0.589428	0.645197	0.705574
374	0.406364	0.446613	0.490341	0.537808	0.589287	0.645069	0.705463
375	0.406199	0.446451	0.490184	0.537658	0.589146	0.644941	0.705352
376	0.406035	0.446289	0.490027	0.537508	0.589006	0.644814	0.705241
377	0.405871	0.446128	0.489870	0.537358	0.588867	0.644688	0.705131
378	0.405708	0.445967	0.489714	0.537209	0.588727	0.644561	0.705021
379	0.405545	0.445806	0.489558	0.537061	0.588589	0.644435	0.704911
380	0.405382	0.445647	0.489403	0.536912	0.588450	0.644310	0.704802
381	0.405221	0.445487	0.489249	0.536765	0.588312	0.644184	0.704693
382	0.405059	0.445328	0.489094	0.536617	0.588174	0.644059	0.704584
383	0.404898	0.445170	0.488941	0.536471	0.588037	0.643935	0.704476
384	0.404738	0.445012	0.488787	0.536324	0.587900	0.643810	0.704368
385	0.404578	0.444855	0.488634	0.536178	0.587764	0.643687	0.704260

Unit	90	91	92	93	94	95	96
386	0.404418	0.444698	0.488482	0.536033	0.587628	0.643563	0.704152
387	0.404259	0.444541	0.488330	0.535887	0.587492	0.643440	0.704045
388	0.404101	0.444385	0.488178	0.535743	0.587357	0.643317	0.703938
389	0.403943	0.444230	0.488027	0.535598	0.587222	0.643194	0.703831
390	0.403785	0.444074	0.487876	0.535454	0.587087	0.643072	0.703725
391	0.403628	0.443920	0.487726	0.535311	0.586953	0.642950	0.703619
392	0.403471	0.443765	0.487576	0.535168	0.586819	0.642829	0.703513
393	0.403315	0.443612	0.487427	0.535025	0.586686	0.642708	0.703407
394	0.403159	0.443458	0.487278	0.534883	0.586553	0.642587	0.703302
395	0.403004	0.443305	0.487129	0.534741	0.586420	0.642466	0.703197
396	0.402849	0.443153	0.486981	0.534599	0.586288	0.642346	0.703092
397	0.402695	0.443001	0.486833	0.534458	0.586156	0.642226	0.702988
398	0.402541	0.442849	0.486686	0.534317	0.586024	0.642107	0.702884
399	0.402387	0.442698	0.486539	0.534177	0.585893	0.641987	0.702780
400	0.402234	0.442547	0.486393	0.534037	0.585762	0.641869	0.702676
401	0.402081	0.442397	0.486247	0.533897	0.585631	0.641750	0.702573
402	0.401929	0.442247	0.486101	0.533758	0.585501	0.641632	0.702470
403	0.401777	0.442098	0.485956	0.533619	0.585371	0.641514	0.702367
404	0.401626	0.441949	0.485811	0.533481	0.585242	0.641396	0.702265
405	0.401475	0.441800	0.485667	0.533343	0.585113	0.641279	0.702162
406	0.401325	0.441652	0.485522	0.533205	0.584984	0.641162	0.702060
407	0.401175	0.441504	0.485379	0.533068	0.584855	0.641045	0.701959
408	0.401025	0.441357	0.485236	0.532931	0.584727	0.640929	0.701857
409	0.400876	0.441210	0.485093	0.532794	0.584600	0.640813	0.701756
410	0.400727	0.441063	0.484950	0.532658	0.584472	0.640697	0.701655
411	0.400579	0.440917	0.484808	0.532522	0.584345	0.640581	0.701554
412	0.400431	0.440771	0.484666	0.532387	0.584218	0.640466	0.701454
413	0.400283	0.440626	0.484525	0.532252	0.584092	0.640351	0.701354
414	0.400136	0.440481	0.484384	0.532117	0.583966	0.640237	0.701254
415	0.399989	0.440336	0.484244	0.531982	0.583840	0.640122	0.701154
416	0.399843	0.440192	0.484103	0.531848	0.583715	0.640008	0.701055
417	0.399697	0.440048	0.483964	0.531715	0.583590	0.639895	0.700956
418	0.399552	0.439905	0.483824	0.531581	0.583465	0.639781	0.700857
419	0.399407	0.439762	0.483685	0.531448	0.583340	0.639668	0.700758
420	0.399262	0.439619	0.483546	0.531316	0.583216	0.639555	0.700660

Unit	90	91	92	93	94	95	96
421	0.399118	0.439477	0.483408	0.531184	0.583092	0.639443	0.700562
422	0.398974	0.439335	0.483270	0.531052	0.582969	0.639330	0.700464
423	0.398830	0.439194	0.483133	0.530920	0.582846	0.639218	0.700366
424	0.398687	0.439053	0.482995	0.530789	0.582723	0.639107	0.700269
425	0.398544	0.438912	0.482859	0.530658	0.582600	0.638995	0.700172
426	0.398402	0.438772	0.482722	0.530527	0.582478	0.638884	0.700075
427	0.398260	0.438632	0.482586	0.530397	0.582356	0.638773	0.699978
428	0.398119	0.438492	0.482450	0.530267	0.582235	0.638663	0.699882
429	0.397977	0.438353	0.482315	0.530138	0.582113	0.638553	0.699786
430	0.397837	0.438214	0.482180	0.530008	0.581992	0.638443	0.699690
431	0.397696	0.438075	0.482045	0.529880	0.581872	0.638333	0.699594
432	0.397556	0.437937	0.481911	0.529751	0.581751	0.638223	0.699498
433	0.397416	0.437800	0.481777	0.529623	0.581631	0.638114	0.699403
434	0.397277	0.437662	0.481643	0.529495	0.581512	0.638005	0.699308
435	0.397138	0.437525	0.481510	0.529367	0.581392	0.637897	0.699213
436	0.396999	0.437389	0.481377	0.529240	0.581273	0.637788	0.699119
437	0.396861	0.437252	0.481244	0.529113	0.581154	0.637680	0.699025
438	0.396723	0.437116	0.481112	0.528987	0.581036	0.637572	0.698930
439	0.396586	0.436981	0.480980	0.528860	0.580917	0.637465	0.698837
440	0.396449	0.436845	0.480848	0.528734	0.580799	0.637357	0.698743
441	0.396312	0.436710	0.480717	0.528609	0.580682	0.637250	0.698650
442	0.396176	0.436576	0.480586	0.528483	0.580564	0.637144	0.698556
443	0.396039	0.436442	0.480455	0.528358	0.580447	0.637037	0.698463
444	0.395904	0.436308	0.480325	0.528234	0.580330	0.636931	0.698371
445	0.395768	0.436174	0.480195	0.528109	0.580214	0.636825	0.698278
446	0.395633	0.436041	0.480065	0.527985	0.580098	0.636719	0.698186
447	0.395499	0.435908	0.479936	0.527861	0.579982	0.636613	0.698094
448	0.395364	0.435776	0.479807	0.527738	0.579866	0.636508	0.698002
449	0.395230	0.435644	0.479678	0.527615	0.579750	0.636403	0.697910
450	0.395097	0.435512	0.479550	0.527492	0.579635	0.636298	0.697819
451	0.394963	0.435380	0.479422	0.527369	0.579521	0.636194	0.697728
452	0.394831	0.435249	0.479294	0.527247	0.579406	0.636090	0.697637
453	0.394698	0.435118	0.479167	0.527125	0.579292	0.635986	0.697546
454	0.394566	0.434988	0.479040	0.527003	0.579178	0.635882	0.697455
455	0.394434	0.434857	0.478913	0.526882	0.579064	0.635778	0.697365

Computed Values of X^b

Unit	90	91	92	93	94	95	96
456	0.394302	0.434728	0.478786	0.526761	0.578950	0.635675	0.697275
457	0.394171	0.434598	0.478660	0.526640	0.578837	0.635572	0.697185
458	0.394040	0.434469	0.478534	0.526519	0.578724	0.635469	0.697095
459	0.393909	0.434340	0.478409	0.526399	0.578612	0.635367	0.697005
460	0.393779	0.434211	0.478284	0.526279	0.578499	0.635264	0.696916
461	0.393649	0.434083	0.478159	0.526160	0.578387	0.635162	0.696827
462	0.393519	0.433955	0.478034	0.526040	0.578275	0.635060	0.696738
463	0.393390	0.433827	0.477910	0.525921	0.578164	0.634959	0.696649
464	0.393261	0.433700	0.477786	0.525802	0.578052	0.634857	0.696561
465	0.393132	0.433573	0.477662	0.525684	0.577941	0.634756	0.696473
466	0.393004	0.433446	0.477539	0.525566	0.577830	0.634655	0.696384
467	0.392876	0.433320	0.477416	0.525448	0.577720	0.634555	0.696297
468	0.392748	0.433194	0.477293	0.525330	0.577610	0.634454	0.696209
469	0.392621	0.433068	0.477170	0.525213	0.577499	0.634354	0.696121
470	0.392494	0.432943	0.477048	0.525096	0.577390	0.634254	0.696034
471	0.392367	0.432817	0.476926	0.524979	0.577280	0.634154	0.695947
472	0.392241	0.432692	0.476804	0.524862	0.577171	0.634055	0.695860
473	0.392114	0.432568	0.476683	0.524746	0.577062	0.633955	0.695773
474	0.391989	0.432444	0.476562	0.524630	0.576953	0.633856	0.695687
475	0.391863	0.432320	0.476441	0.524514	0.576845	0.633758	0.695600
476	0.391738	0.432196	0.476321	0.524399	0.576736	0.633659	0.695514
477	0.391613	0.432073	0.476200	0.524284	0.576628	0.633561	0.695428
478	0.391488	0.431949	0.476080	0.524169	0.576520	0.633462	0.695342
479	0.391364	0.431827	0.475961	0.524054	0.576413	0.633364	0.695257
480	0.391240	0.431704	0.475841	0.523940	0.576306	0.633267	0.695171
481	0.391116	0.431582	0.475722	0.523825	0.576199	0.633169	0.695086
482	0.390993	0.431460	0.475603	0.523711	0.576092	0.633072	0.695001
483	0.390869	0.431338	0.475485	0.523598	0.575985	0.632975	0.694916
484	0.390747	0.431217	0.475366	0.523484	0.575879	0.632878	0.694832
485	0.390624	0.431096	0.475248	0.523371	0.575773	0.632781	0.694747
486	0.390502	0.430975	0.475131	0.523259	0.575667	0.632685	0.694663
487	0.390380	0.430855	0.475013	0.523146	0.575561	0.632589	0.694579
488	0.390258	0.430734	0.474896	0.523034	0.575456	0.632493	0.694495
489	0.390137	0.430614	0.474779	0.522921	0.575351	0.632397	0.694411
490	0.390015	0.430495	0.474662	0.522810	0.575246	0.632301	0.694328

Unit	90	91	92	93	94	95	96
491	0.389895	0.430375	0.474546	0.522698	0.575141	0.632206	0.694244
492	0.389774	0.430256	0.474430	0.522587	0.575037	0.632111	0.694161
493	0.389654	0.430137	0.474314	0.522476	0.574932	0.632016	0.694078
494	0.389534	0.430019	0.474198	0.522365	0.574828	0.631921	0.693995
495	0.389414	0.429900	0.474083	0.522254	0.574725	0.631826	0.693913
496	0.389295	0.429782	0.473968	0.522144	0.574621	0.631732	0.693830
497	0.389175	0.429665	0.473853	0.522034	0.574518	0.631638	0.693748
498	0.389057	0.429547	0.473739	0.521924	0.574415	0.631544	0.693666
499	0.388938	0.429430	0.473624	0.521814	0.574312	0.631450	0.693584
500	0.388820	0.429313	0.473510	0.521705	0.574209	0.631357	0.693502
501	0.388702	0.429196	0.473397	0.521596	0.574107	0.631263	0.693421
502	0.388584	0.429080	0.473283	0.521487	0.574005	0.631170	0.693339
503	0.388466	0.428964	0.473170	0.521378	0.573903	0.631077	0.693258
504	0.388349	0.428848	0.473057	0.521270	0.573801	0.630984	0.693177
505	0.388232	0.428732	0.472944	0.521162	0.573699	0.630892	0.693096
506	0.388115	0.428617	0.472831	0.521054	0.573598	0.630799	0.693015
507	0.387999	0.428502	0.472719	0.520946	0.573497	0.630707	0.692935
508	0.387883	0.428387	0.472607	0.520839	0.573396	0.630615	0.692854
509	0.387767	0.428272	0.472495	0.520731	0.573296	0.630524	0.692774
510	0.387651	0.428158	0.472384	0.520624	0.573195	0.630432	0.692694
511	0.387536	0.428044	0.472272	0.520518	0.573095	0.630341	0.692614
512	0.387420	0.427930	0.472161	0.520411	0.572995	0.630249	0.692534
513	0.387306	0.427816	0.472051	0.520305	0.572895	0.630158	0.692455
514	0.387191	0.427703	0.471940	0.520199	0.572796	0.630068	0.692375
515	0.387077	0.427590	0.471830	0.520093	0.572696	0.629977	0.692296
516	0.386962	0.427477	0.471720	0.519987	0.572597	0.629887	0.692217
517	0.386849	0.427364	0.471610	0.519882	0.572498	0.629796	0.692138
518	0.386735	0.427252	0.471500	0.519777	0.572399	0.629706	0.692059
519	0.386622	0.427140	0.471391	0.519672	0.572301	0.629616	0.691981
520	0.386509	0.427028	0.471282	0.519567	0.572202	0.629527	0.691902
521	0.386396	0.426916	0.471173	0.519463	0.572104	0.629437	0.691824
522	0.386283	0.426805	0.471064	0.519358	0.572006	0.629348	0.691746
523	0.386171	0.426694	0.470956	0.519254	0.571909	0.629259	0.691668
524	0.386059	0.426583	0.470847	0.519150	0.571811	0.629170	0.691590
525	0.385947	0.426472	0.470739	0.519047	0.571714	0.629081	0.691512

Unit	90	91	92	93	94	95	96
526	0.385835	0.426362	0.470632	0.518943	0.571617	0.628993	0.691435
527	0.385724	0.426252	0.470524	0.518840	0.571520	0.628904	0.691357
528	0.385613	0.426142	0.470417	0.518737	0.571423	0.628816	0.691280
529	0.385502	0.426032	0.470310	0.518634	0.571327	0.628728	0.691203
530	0.385391	0.425923	0.470203	0.518532	0.571230	0.628640	0.691126
531	0.385281	0.425813	0.470096	0.518430	0.571134	0.628552	0.691050
532	0.385170	0.425704	0.469990	0.518328	0.571038	0.628465	0.690973
533	0.385061	0.425596	0.469884	0.518226	0.570943	0.628378	0.690897
534	0.384951	0.425487	0.469778	0.518124	0.570847	0.628290	0.690820
535	0.384841	0.425379	0.469672	0.518022	0.570752	0.628203	0.690744
536	0.384732	0.425271	0.469567	0.517921	0.570657	0.628117	0.690668
537	0.384623	0.425163	0.469461	0.517820	0.570562	0.628030	0.690593
538	0.384514	0.425055	0.469356	0.517719	0.570467	0.627944	0.690517
539	0.384406	0.424948	0.469251	0.517619	0.570372	0.627857	0.690441
540	0.384298	0.424841	0.469147	0.517518	0.570278	0.627771	0.690366
541	0.384190	0.424734	0.469042	0.517418	0.570184	0.627685	0.690291
542	0.384082	0.424627	0.468938	0.517318	0.570090	0.627599	0.690216
543	0.383974	0.424521	0.468834	0.517218	0.569996	0.627514	0.690141
544	0.383867	0.424414	0.468730	0.517118	0.569902	0.627428	0.690066
545	0.383760	0.424308	0.468627	0.517019	0.569809	0.627343	0.689991
546	0.383653	0.424203	0.468524	0.516920	0.569716	0.627258	0.689917
547	0.383546	0.424097	0.468420	0.516821	0.569623	0.627173	0.689843
548	0.383440	0.423992	0.468318	0.516722	0.569530	0.627088	0.689768
549	0.383333	0.423886	0.468215	0.516623	0.569437	0.627004	0.689694
550	0.383227	0.423782	0.468112	0.516525	0.569345	0.626919	0.689620
551	0.383121	0.423677	0.468010	0.516427	0.569252	0.626835	0.689547
552	0.383016	0.423572	0.467908	0.516329	0.569160	0.626751	0.689473
553	0.382911	0.423468	0.467806	0.516231	0.569068	0.626667	0.689399
554	0.382805	0.423364	0.467705	0.516133	0.568976	0.626583	0.689326
555	0.382700	0.423260	0.467603	0.516036	0.568885	0.626500	0.689253
556	0.382596	0.423156	0.467502	0.515939	0.568793	0.626416	0.689180
557	0.382491	0.423053	0.467401	0.515841	0.568702	0.626333	0.689107
558	0.382387	0.422950	0.467300	0.515745	0.568611	0.626250	0.689034
559	0.382283	0.422847	0.467199	0.515648	0.568520	0.626167	0.688961
560	0.382179	0.422744	0.467099	0.515551	0.568430	0.626084	0.688889

Unit	90	91	92	93	94	95	96
561	0.382075	0.422641	0.466999	0.515455	0.568339	0.626001	0.688817
562	0.381972	0.422539	0.466899	0.515359	0.568249	0.625919	0.688744
563	0.381869	0.422437	0.466799	0.515263	0.568159	0.625836	0.688672
564	0.381766	0.422335	0.466699	0.515167	0.568069	0.625754	0.688600
565	0.381663	0.422233	0.466600	0.515072	0.567979	0.625672	0.688528
566	0.381560	0.422131	0.466500	0.514977	0.567889	0.625590	0.688457
567	0.381458	0.422030	0.466401	0.514881	0.567800	0.625509	0.688385
568	0.381356	0.421929	0.466302	0.514786	0.567710	0.625427	0.688314
569	0.381254	0.421828	0.466204	0.514692	0.567621	0.625346	0.688242
570	0.381152	0.421727	0.466105	0.514597	0.567532	0.625264	0.688171
571	0.381051	0.421626	0.466007	0.514503	0.567443	0.625183	0.688100
572	0.380949	0.421526	0.465909	0.514408	0.567355	0.625102	0.688029
573	0.380848	0.421426	0.465811	0.514314	0.567266	0.625022	0.687958
574	0.380747	0.421326	0.465713	0.514220	0.567178	0.624941	0.687888
575	0.380647	0.421226	0.465616	0.514127	0.567090	0.624860	0.687817
576	0.380546	0.421127	0.465519	0.514033	0.567002	0.624780	0.687747
577	0.380446	0.421027	0.465421	0.513940	0.566914	0.624700	0.687677
578	0.380346	0.420928	0.465325	0.513847	0.566826	0.624620	0.687607
579	0.380246	0.420829	0.465228	0.513754	0.566739	0.624540	0.687537
580	0.380146	0.420730	0.465131	0.513661	0.566652	0.624460	0.687467
581	0.380046	0.420632	0.465035	0.513568	0.566565	0.624381	0.687397
582	0.379947	0.420533	0.464939	0.513476	0.566478	0.624301	0.687327
583	0.379848	0.420435	0.464843	0.513383	0.566391	0.624222	0.687258
584	0.379749	0.420337	0.464747	0.513291	0.566304	0.624143	0.687188
585	0.379650	0.420239	0.464651	0.513199	0.566218	0.624064	0.687119
586	0.379552	0.420141	0.464556	0.513108	0.566131	0.623985	0.687050
587	0.379453	0.420044	0.464460	0.513016	0.566045	0.623906	0.686981
588	0.379355	0.419947	0.464365	0.512925	0.565959	0.623827	0.686912
589	0.379257	0.419850	0.464270	0.512833	0.565873	0.623749	0.686844
590	0.379159	0.419753	0.464176	0.512742	0.565788	0.623671	0.686775
591	0.379062	0.419656	0.464081	0.512651	0.565702	0.623593	0.686706
592	0.378964	0.419560	0.463987	0.512561	0.565617	0.623515	0.686638
593	0.378867	0.419463	0.463893	0.512470	0.565532	0.623437	0.686570
594	0.378770	0.419367	0.463799	0.512380	0.565447	0.623359	0.686502
595	0.378673	0.419271	0.463705	0.512289	0.565362	0.623281	0.686434

Unit	90	91	92	93	94	95	96
596	0.378577	0.419175	0.463611	0.512199	0.565277	0.623204	0.686366
597	0.378480	0.419080	0.463518	0.512110	0.565192	0.623127	0.686298
598	0.378384	0.418984	0.463424	0.512020	0.565108	0.623049	0.686230
599	0.378288	0.418889	0.463331	0.511930	0.565024	0.622972	0.686163
600	0.378192	0.418794	0.463238	0.511841	0.564939	0.622896	0.686095
601	0.378096	0.418699	0.463145	0.511752	0.564856	0.622819	0.686028
602	0.378001	0.418604	0.463053	0.511663	0.564772	0.622742	0.685961
603	0.377905	0.418510	0.462960	0.511574	0.564688	0.622666	0.685894
604	0.377810	0.418416	0.462868	0.511485	0.564604	0.622589	0.685827
605	0.377715	0.418321	0.462776	0.511396	0.564521	0.622513	0.685760
606	0.377620	0.418227	0.462684	0.511308	0.564438	0.622437	0.685694
607	0.377526	0.418134	0.462592	0.511220	0.564355	0.622361	0.685627
608	0.377431	0.418040	0.462501	0.511132	0.564272	0.622285	0.685560
609	0.377337	0.417946	0.462409	0.511044	0.564189	0.622210	0.685494
610	0.377243	0.417853	0.462318	0.510956	0.564106	0.622134	0.685428
611	0.377149	0.417760	0.462227	0.510868	0.564024	0.622059	0.685362
612	0.377055	0.417667	0.462136	0.510781	0.563942	0.621983	0.685296
613	0.376962	0.417574	0.462045	0.510693	0.563860	0.621908	0.685230
614	0.376868	0.417482	0.461955	0.510606	0.563777	0.621833	0.685164
615	0.376775	0.417389	0.461864	0.510519	0.563696	0.621758	0.685098
616	0.376682	0.417297	0.461774	0.510432	0.563614	0.621684	0.685033
617	0.376589	0.417205	0.461684	0.510346	0.563532	0.621609	0.684967
618	0.376497	0.417113	0.461594	0.510259	0.563451	0.621535	0.684902
619	0.376404	0.417021	0.461504	0.510173	0.563369	0.621460	0.684837
620	0.376312	0.416930	0.461415	0.510087	0.563288	0.621386	0.684772
621	0.376220	0.416838	0.461325	0.510001	0.563207	0.621312	0.684707
622	0.376128	0.416747	0.461236	0.509915	0.563126	0.621238	0.684642
623	0.376036	0.416656	0.461147	0.509829	0.563046	0.621164	0.684577
624	0.375944	0.416565	0.461058	0.509743	0.562965	0.621090	0.684513
625	0.375853	0.416474	0.460969	0.509658	0.562885	0.621017	0.684448
626	0.375761	0.416384	0.460880	0.509573	0.562804	0.620943	0.684384
627	0.375670	0.416293	0.460792	0.509487	0.562724	0.620870	0.684319
628	0.375579	0.416203	0.460704	0.509402	0.562644	0.620797	0.684255
629	0.375488	0.416113	0.460615	0.509318	0.562564	0.620724	0.684191
630	0.375398	0.416023	0.460527	0.509233	0.562484	0.620651	0.684127

Unit	90	91	92	93	94	95	96
631	0.375307	0.415933	0.460439	0.509148	0.562405	0.620578	0.684063
632	0.375217	0.415844	0.460352	0.509064	0.562325	0.620505	0.683999
633	0.375127	0.415754	0.460264	0.508980	0.562246	0.620432	0.683935
634	0.375037	0.415665	0.460177	0.508896	0.562167	0.620360	0.683872
635	0.374947	0.415576	0.460090	0.508812	0.562088	0.620288	0.683808
636	0.374857	0.415487	0.460003	0.508728	0.562009	0.620215	0.683745
637	0.374768	0.415398	0.459916	0.508644	0.561930	0.620143	0.683682
638	0.374678	0.415309	0.459829	0.508561	0.561851	0.620071	0.683619
639	0.374589	0.415221	0.459742	0.508477	0.561773	0.620000	0.683556
640	0.374500	0.415133	0.459656	0.508394	0.561694	0.619928	0.683493
641	0.374411	0.415044	0.459569	0.508311	0.561616	0.619856	0.683430
642	0.374323	0.414956	0.459483	0.508228	0.561538	0.619785	0.683367
643	0.374234	0.414869	0.459397	0.508145	0.561460	0.619713	0.683304
644	0.374146	0.414781	0.459311	0.508062	0.561382	0.619642	0.683242
645	0.374057	0.414693	0.459226	0.507980	0.561304	0.619571	0.683179
646	0.373969	0.414606	0.459140	0.507898	0.561226	0.619500	0.683117
647	0.373881	0.414519	0.459055	0.507815	0.561149	0.619429	0.683055
648	0.373794	0.414431	0.458969	0.507733	0.561072	0.619358	0.682993
649	0.373706	0.414345	0.458884	0.507651	0.560994	0.619287	0.682931
650	0.373619	0.414258	0.458799	0.507569	0.560917	0.619217	0.682869
651	0.373531	0.414171	0.458714	0.507488	0.560840	0.619146	0.682807
652	0.373444	0.414085	0.458630	0.507406	0.560763	0.619076	0.682745
653	0.373357	0.413998	0.458545	0.507325	0.560687	0.619006	0.682684
654	0.373270	0.413912	0.458461	0.507243	0.560610	0.618936	0.682622
655	0.373184	0.413826	0.458377	0.507162	0.560534	0.618866	0.682561
656	0.373097	0.413740	0.458292	0.507081	0.560457	0.618796	0.682499
657	0.373011	0.413654	0.458208	0.507000	0.560381	0.618726	0.682438
658	0.372925	0.413569	0.458125	0.506920	0.560305	0.618657	0.682377
659	0.372838	0.413483	0.458041	0.506839	0.560229	0.618587	0.682316
660	0.372753	0.413398	0.457957	0.506759	0.560153	0.618518	0.682255
661	0.372667	0.413313	0.457874	0.506678	0.560078	0.618448	0.682194
662	0.372581	0.413228	0.457791	0.506598	0.560002	0.618379	0.682134
663	0.372496	0.413143	0.457708	0.506518	0.559927	0.618310	0.682073
664	0.372410	0.413058	0.457625	0.506438	0.559851	0.618241	0.682012
665	0.372325	0.412974	0.457542	0.506358	0.559776	0.618172	0.681952

Unit	90	91	92	93	94	95	96
666	0.372240	0.412889	0.457459	0.506279	0.559701	0.618104	0.681892
667	0.372155	0.412805	0.457377	0.506199	0.559626	0.618035	0.681831
668	0.372070	0.412721	0.457294	0.506120	0.559551	0.617967	0.681771
669	0.371986	0.412637	0.457212	0.506041	0.559476	0.617898	0.681711
670	0.371901	0.412553	0.457130	0.505961	0.559402	0.617830	0.681651
671	0.371817	0.412469	0.457048	0.505882	0.559327	0.617762	0.681591
672	0.371733	0.412386	0.456966	0.505804	0.559253	0.617694	0.681532
673	0.371649	0.412302	0.456884	0.505725	0.559179	0.617626	0.681472
674	0.371565	0.412219	0.456803	0.505646	0.559105	0.617558	0.681412
675	0.371481	0.412136	0.456721	0.505568	0.559031	0.617490	0.681353
676	0.371398	0.412053	0.456640	0.505489	0.558957	0.617422	0.681293
677	0.371314	0.411970	0.456559	0.505411	0.558883	0.617355	0.681234
678	0.371231	0.411887	0.456477	0.505333	0.558809	0.617287	0.681175
679	0.371148	0.411805	0.456397	0.505255	0.558736	0.617220	0.681116
680	0.371065	0.411722	0.456316	0.505177	0.558663	0.617153	0.681057
681	0.370982	0.411640	0.456235	0.505100	0.558589	0.617086	0.680998
682	0.370899	0.411558	0.456155	0.505022	0.558516	0.617019	0.680939
683	0.370817	0.411476	0.456074	0.504945	0.558443	0.616952	0.680880
684	0.370734	0.411394	0.455994	0.504867	0.558370	0.616885	0.680821
685	0.370652	0.411312	0.455914	0.504790	0.558297	0.616818	0.680763
686	0.370570	0.411231	0.455834	0.504713	0.558225	0.616752	0.680704
687	0.370488	0.411149	0.455754	0.504636	0.558152	0.616685	0.680646
688	0.370406	0.411068	0.455674	0.504559	0.558080	0.616619	0.680588
689	0.370324	0.410986	0.455595	0.504482	0.558007	0.616553	0.680529
690	0.370242	0.410905	0.455515	0.504406	0.557935	0.616486	0.680471
691	0.370161	0.410824	0.455436	0.504329	0.557863	0.616420	0.680413
692	0.370080	0.410744	0.455357	0.504253	0.557791	0.616354	0.680355
693	0.369998	0.410663	0.455277	0.504177	0.557719	0.616289	0.680298
694	0.369917	0.410582	0.455198	0.504101	0.557647	0.616223	0.680240
695	0.369836	0.410502	0.455120	0.504025	0.557575	0.616157	0.680182
696	0.369755	0.410422	0.455041	0.503949	0.557504	0.616092	0.680124
697	0.369675	0.410341	0.454962	0.503873	0.557432	0.616026	0.680067
698	0.369594	0.410261	0.454884	0.503797	0.557361	0.615961	0.680010
699	0.369514	0.410181	0.454806	0.503722	0.557290	0.615896	0.679952
700	0.369434	0.410102	0.454727	0.503646	0.557219	0.615830	0.679895

Unit	90	91	92	93	94	95	96
701	0.369353	0.410022	0.454649	0.503571	0.557148	0.615765	0.679838
702	0.369273	0.409943	0.454571	0.503496	0.557077	0.615700	0.679781
703	0.369193	0.409863	0.454493	0.503421	0.557006	0.615636	0.679724
704	0.369114	0.409784	0.454416	0.503346	0.556935	0.615571	0.679667
705	0.369034	0.409705	0.454338	0.503271	0.556865	0.615506	0.679610
706	0.368955	0.409626	0.454261	0.503197	0.556794	0.615442	0.679553
707	0.368875	0.409547	0.454183	0.503122	0.556724	0.615377	0.679497
708	0.368796	0.409468	0.454106	0.503048	0.556654	0.615313	0.679440
709	0.368717	0.409389	0.454029	0.502973	0.556584	0.615249	0.679384
710	0.368638	0.409311	0.453952	0.502899	0.556514	0.615184	0.679327
711	0.368559	0.409233	0.453875	0.502825	0.556444	0.615120	0.679271
712	0.368480	0.409154	0.453799	0.502751	0.556374	0.615056	0.679215
713	0.368402	0.409076	0.453722	0.502677	0.556304	0.614992	0.679159
714	0.368323	0.408998	0.453645	0.502603	0.556235	0.614929	0.679102
715	0.368245	0.408920	0.453569	0.502530	0.556165	0.614865	0.679047
716	0.368167	0.408843	0.453493	0.502456	0.556096	0.614801	0.678991
717	0.368088	0.408765	0.453417	0.502383	0.556027	0.614738	0.678935
718	0.368011	0.408687	0.453341	0.502309	0.555957	0.614674	0.678879
719	0.367933	0.408610	0.453265	0.502236	0.555888	0.614611	0.678823
720	0.367855	0.408533	0.453189	0.502163	0.555819	0.614548	0.678768
721	0.367777	0.408456	0.453113	0.502090	0.555750	0.614485	0.678712
722	0.367700	0.408379	0.453038	0.502017	0.555682	0.614422	0.678657
723	0.367623	0.408302	0.452962	0.501945	0.555613	0.614359	0.678602
724	0.367545	0.408225	0.452887	0.501872	0.555544	0.614296	0.678546
725	0.367468	0.408148	0.452812	0.501799	0.555476	0.614233	0.678491
726	0.367391	0.408072	0.452737	0.501727	0.555408	0.614171	0.678436
727	0.367314	0.407995	0.452662	0.501655	0.555339	0.614108	0.678381
728	0.367238	0.407919	0.452587	0.501583	0.555271	0.614046	0.678326
729	0.367161	0.407843	0.452512	0.501510	0.555203	0.613983	0.678271
730	0.367085	0.407767	0.452438	0.501439	0.555135	0.613921	0.678217
731	0.367008	0.407691	0.452363	0.501367	0.555068	0.613859	0.678162
732	0.366932	0.407615	0.452289	0.501295	0.555000	0.613797	0.678107
733	0.366856	0.407539	0.452214	0.501223	0.554932	0.613735	0.678053
734	0.366780	0.407464	0.452140	0.501152	0.554865	0.613673	0.677998
735	0.366704	0.407388	0.452066	0.501080	0.554797	0.613611	0.677944

Unit	90	91	92	93	94	95	96
736	0.366628	0.407313	0.451992	0.501009	0.554730	0.613549	0.677890
737	0.366552	0.407238	0.451919	0.500938	0.554663	0.613488	0.677836
738	0.366477	0.407163	0.451845	0.500867	0.554596	0.613426	0.677782
739	0.366401	0.407088	0.451771	0.500796	0.554528	0.613365	0.677727
740	0.366326	0.407013	0.451698	0.500725	0.554462	0.613303	0.677674
741	0.366251	0.406938	0.451624	0.500654	0.554395	0.613242	0.677620
742	0.366176	0.406863	0.451551	0.500583	0.554328	0.613181	0.677566
743	0.366101	0.406789	0.451478	0.500513	0.554261	0.613120	0.677512
744	0.366026	0.406714	0.451405	0.500442	0.554195	0.613059	0.677458
745	0.365951	0.406640	0.451332	0.500372	0.554128	0.612998	0.677405
746	0.365877	0.406566	0.451259	0.500302	0.554062	0.612937	0.677351
747	0.365802	0.406492	0.451186	0.500231	0.553996	0.612876	0.677298
748	0.365728	0.406418	0.451114	0.500161	0.553930	0.612815	0.677244
749	0.365654	0.406344	0.451041	0.500091	0.553864	0.612755	0.677191
750	0.365579	0.406270	0.450969	0.500022	0.553798	0.612694	0.677138
751	0.365505	0.406196	0.450897	0.499952	0.553732	0.612634	0.677085
752	0.365432	0.406123	0.450825	0.499882	0.553666	0.612574	0.677032
753	0.365358	0.406049	0.450752	0.499813	0.553600	0.612513	0.676979
754	0.365284	0.405976	0.450681	0.499743	0.553535	0.612453	0.676926
755	0.365210	0.405903	0.450609	0.499674	0.553469	0.612393	0.676873
756	0.365137	0.405830	0.450537	0.499605	0.553404	0.612333	0.676820
757	0.365064	0.405757	0.450465	0.499535	0.553338	0.612273	0.676768
758	0.364990	0.405684	0.450394	0.499466	0.553273	0.612213	0.676715
759	0.364917	0.405611	0.450322	0.499397	0.553208	0.612154	0.676662
760	0.364844	0.405538	0.450251	0.499329	0.553143	0.612094	0.676610
761	0.364771	0.405466	0.450180	0.499260	0.553078	0.612035	0.676558
762	0.364698	0.405393	0.450109	0.499191	0.553013	0.611975	0.676505
763	0.364626	0.405321	0.450038	0.499123	0.552949	0.611916	0.676453
764	0.364553	0.405249	0.449967	0.499054	0.552884	0.611856	0.676401
765	0.364481	0.405177	0.449896	0.498986	0.552819	0.611797	0.676349
766	0.364408	0.405105	0.449825	0.498918	0.552755	0.611738	0.676297
767	0.364336	0.405033	0.449755	0.498850	0.552691	0.611679	0.676245
768	0.364264	0.404961	0.449684	0.498781	0.552626	0.611620	0.676193
769	0.364192	0.404889	0.449614	0.498714	0.552562	0.611561	0.676141
770	0.364120	0.404818	0.449544	0.498646	0.552498	0.611502	0.676089

Unit	90	91	92	93	94	95	96
771	0.364048	0.404746	0.449473	0.498578	0.552434	0.611444	0.676038
772	0.363976	0.404675	0.449403	0.498510	0.552370	0.611385	0.675986
773	0.363905	0.404604	0.449333	0.498443	0.552306	0.611326	0.675934
774	0.363833	0.404533	0.449263	0.498375	0.552243	0.611268	0.675883
775	0.363762	0.404461	0.449194	0.498308	0.552179	0.611209	0.675832
776	0.363691	0.404390	0.449124	0.498241	0.552115	0.611151	0.675780
777	0.363619	0.404320	0.449054	0.498173	0.552052	0.611093	0.675729
778	0.363548	0.404249	0.448985	0.498106	0.551989	0.611035	0.675678
779	0.363477	0.404178	0.448916	0.498039	0.551925	0.610977	0.675627
780	0.363406	0.404108	0.448846	0.497972	0.551862	0.610919	0.675576
781	0.363336	0.404037	0.448777	0.497906	0.551799	0.610861	0.675525
782	0.363265	0.403967	0.448708	0.497839	0.551736	0.610803	0.675474
783	0.363194	0.403897	0.448639	0.497772	0.551673	0.610745	0.675423
784	0.363124	0.403827	0.448570	0.497706	0.551610	0.610687	0.675372
785	0.363054	0.403757	0.448501	0.497639	0.551547	0.610630	0.675322
786	0.362983	0.403687	0.448433	0.497573	0.551485	0.610572	0.675271
787	0.362913	0.403617	0.448364	0.497507	0.551422	0.610515	0.675220
788	0.362843	0.403547	0.448296	0.497441	0.551360	0.610457	0.675170
789	0.362773	0.403477	0.448227	0.497375	0.551297	0.610400	0.675119
790	0.362703	0.403408	0.448159	0.497309	0.551235	0.610343	0.675069
791	0.362634	0.403338	0.448091	0.497243	0.551173	0.610286	0.675019
792	0.362564	0.403269	0.448023	0.497177	0.551110	0.610229	0.674969
793	0.362495	0.403200	0.447955	0.497111	0.551048	0.610172	0.674918
794	0.362425	0.403131	0.447887	0.497046	0.550986	0.610115	0.674868
795	0.362356	0.403062	0.447819	0.496980	0.550924	0.610058	0.674818
796	0.362287	0.402993	0.447751	0.496915	0.550863	0.610001	0.674768
797	0.362217	0.402924	0.447684	0.496850	0.550801	0.609945	0.674718
798	0.362148	0.402855	0.447616	0.496784	0.550739	0.609888	0.674669
799	0.362079	0.402787	0.447549	0.496719	0.550678	0.609832	0.674619
800	0.362011	0.402718	0.447481	0.496654	0.550616	0.609775	0.674569
801	0.361942	0.402650	0.447414	0.496589	0.550555	0.609719	0.674520
802	0.361873	0.402581	0.447347	0.496524	0.550493	0.609662	0.674470
803	0.361805	0.402513	0.447280	0.496460	0.550432	0.609606	0.674420
804	0.361736	0.402445	0.447213	0.496395	0.550371	0.609550	0.674371
805	0.361668	0.402377	0.447146	0.496330	0.550310	0.609494	0.674322

Unit	90	91	92	93	94	95	96
806	0.361600	0.402309	0.447079	0.496266	0.550249	0.609438	0.674272
807	0.361532	0.402241	0.447013	0.496201	0.550188	0.609382	0.674223
808	0.361464	0.402173	0.446946	0.496137	0.550127	0.609326	0.674174
809	0.361396	0.402106	0.446880	0.496073	0.550067	0.609271	0.674125
810	0.361328	0.402038	0.446813	0.496009	0.550006	0.609215	0.674076
811	0.361260	0.401970	0.446747	0.495945	0.549945	0.609159	0.674027
812	0.361192	0.401903	0.446681	0.495881	0.549885	0.609104	0.673978
813	0.361125	0.401836	0.446615	0.495817	0.549824	0.609048	0.673929
814	0.361057	0.401769	0.446548	0.495753	0.549764	0.608993	0.673880
815	0.360990	0.401701	0.446483	0.495689	0.549704	0.608937	0.673832
816	0.360923	0.401634	0.446417	0.495626	0.549644	0.608882	0.673783
817	0.360855	0.401568	0.446351	0.495562	0.549584	0.608827	0.673734
818	0.360788	0.401501	0.446285	0.495499	0.549524	0.608772	0.673686
819	0.360721	0.401434	0.446220	0.495435	0.549464	0.608717	0.673637
820	0.360654	0.401367	0.446154	0.495372	0.549404	0.608662	0.673589
821	0.360588	0.401301	0.446089	0.495309	0.549344	0.608607	0.673541
822	0.360521	0.401234	0.446023	0.495246	0.549284	0.608552	0.673492
823	0.360454	0.401168	0.445958	0.495183	0.549225	0.608497	0.673444
824	0.360388	0.401102	0.445893	0.495120	0.549165	0.608443	0.673396
825	0.360321	0.401035	0.445828	0.495057	0.549106	0.608388	0.673348
826	0.360255	0.400969	0.445763	0.494994	0.549046	0.608334	0.673300
827	0.360189	0.400903	0.445698	0.494931	0.548987	0.608279	0.673252
828	0.360123	0.400837	0.445633	0.494869	0.548928	0.608225	0.673204
829	0.360057	0.400772	0.445569	0.494806	0.548869	0.608170	0.673156
830	0.359991	0.400706	0.445504	0.494744	0.548810	0.608116	0.673108
831	0.359925	0.400640	0.445440	0.494681	0.548751	0.608062	0.673060
832	0.359859	0.400575	0.445375	0.494619	0.548692	0.608008	0.673013
833	0.359793	0.400509	0.445311	0.494557	0.548633	0.607954	0.672965
834	0.359728	0.400444	0.445247	0.494495	0.548574	0.607900	0.672918
835	0.359662	0.400379	0.445182	0.494433	0.548516	0.607846	0.672870
836	0.359597	0.400313	0.445118	0.494371	0.548457	0.607792	0.672823
837	0.359531	0.400248	0.445054	0.494309	0.548398	0.607738	0.672775
838	0.359466	0.400183	0.444990	0.494247	0.548340	0.607685	0.672728
839	0.359401	0.400118	0.444926	0.494185	0.548282	0.607631	0.672681
840	0.359336	0.400053	0.444863	0.494124	0.548223	0.607578	0.672634

Unit	90	91	92	93	94	95	96
841	0.359271	0.399989	0.444799	0.494062	0.548165	0.607524	0.672586
842	0.359206	0.399924	0.444735	0.494001	0.548107	0.607471	0.672539
843	0.359141	0.399859	0.444672	0.493939	0.548049	0.607417	0.672492
844	0.359076	0.399795	0.444609	0.493878	0.547991	0.607364	0.672445
845	0.359012	0.399731	0.444545	0.493817	0.547933	0.607311	0.672399
846	0.358947	0.399666	0.444482	0.493756	0.547875	0.607258	0.672352
847	0.358883	0.399602	0.444419	0.493695	0.547817	0.607204	0.672305
848	0.358818	0.399538	0.444356	0.493634	0.547760	0.607151	0.672258
849	0.358754	0.399474	0.444293	0.493573	0.547702	0.607099	0.672212
850	0.358690	0.399410	0.444230	0.493512	0.547644	0.607046	0.672165
851	0.358626	0.399346	0.444167	0.493451	0.547587	0.606993	0.672118
852	0.358562	0.399282	0.444104	0.493390	0.547530	0.606940	0.672072
853	0.358498	0.399218	0.444042	0.493330	0.547472	0.606887	0.672025
854	0.358434	0.399155	0.443979	0.493269	0.547415	0.606835	0.671979
855	0.358370	0.399091	0.443917	0.493209	0.547358	0.606782	0.671933
856	0.358307	0.399028	0.443854	0.493149	0.547301	0.606730	0.671887
857	0.358243	0.398964	0.443792	0.493088	0.547244	0.606677	0.671840
858	0.358180	0.398901	0.443730	0.493028	0.547187	0.606625	0.671794
859	0.358116	0.398838	0.443667	0.492968	0.547130	0.606573	0.671748
860	0.358053	0.398775	0.443605	0.492908	0.547073	0.606520	0.670702
861	0.357990	0.398712	0.443543	0.492848	0.547016	0.606468	0.671656
862	0.357926	0.398649	0.443481	0.492788	0.546960	0.606416	0.671610
863	0.357863	0.398586	0.443420	0.492728	0.546903	0.606364	0.671564
864	0.357800	0.398523	0.443358	0.492668	0.546846	0.606312	0.671519
865	0.357737	0.398460	0.443296	0.492609	0.546790	0.606260	0.671473
866	0.357675	0.398398	0.443234	0.492549	0.546733	0.606208	0.671427
867	0.357612	0.398335	0.443173	0.492490	0.546677	0.606157	0.671382
868	0.357549	0.398273	0.443111	0.492430	0.546621	0.606105	0.671336
869	0.357487	0.398210	0.443050	0.492371	0.546565	0.606053	0.671290
870	0.357424	0.398148	0.442989	0.492311	0.546509	0.606002	0.671245
871	0.357362	0.398086	0.442928	0.492252	0.546453	0.605950	0.671200
872	0.357299	0.398024	0.442866	0.492193	0.546397	0.605899	0.671154
873	0.357237	0.397961	0.442805	0.492134	0.546341	0.605847	0.671109
874	0.357175	0.397900	0.442744	0.492075	0.546285	0.605796	0.671064
875	0.357113	0.397838	0.442684	0.492016	0.546229	0.605745	0.671018

Unit	90	91	92	93	94	95	96
876	0.357051	0.397776	0.442623	0.491958	0.546173	0.605694	0.670973
877	0.356989	0.397714	0.442562	0.491899	0.546118	0.605643	0.670928
878	0.356927	0.397652	0.442501	0.491840	0.546062	0.605591	0.670883
879	0.356866	0.397591	0.442441	0.491781	0.546007	0.605540	0.670838
880	0.356804	0.397529	0.442380	0.491723	0.545951	0.605490	0.670793
881	0.356742	0.397468	0.442320	0.491664	0.545896	0.605439	0.670748
882	0.356681	0.397407	0.442259	0.491606	0.545841	0.605388	0.670704
883	0.356619	0.397345	0.442199	0.491548	0.545786	0.605337	0.670659
884	0.356558	0.397284	0.442139	0.491490	0.545730	0.605286	0.670614
885	0.356497	0.397223	0.442079	0.491431	0.545675	0.605236	0.670569
886	0.356435	0.397162	0.442019	0.491373	0.545620	0.605185	0.670525
887	0.356374	0.397101	0.441959	0.491315	0.545565	0.605135	0.670480
888	0.356313	0.397040	0.441899	0.491257	0.545511	0.605084	0.670436
889	0.356252	0.396979	0.441839	0.491199	0.545456	0.605034	0.670391
890	0.356192	0.396919	0.441779	0.491142	0.545401	0.604983	0.670347
891	0.356131	0.396858	0.441720	0.491084	0.545346	0.604933	0.670303
892	0.356070	0.396797	0.441660	0.491026	0.545292	0.604883	0.670258
893	0.356009	0.396737	0.441600	0.490969	0.545237	0.604833	0.670214
894	0.355949	0.396676	0.441541	0.490911	0.545183	0.604783	0.670170
895	0.355888	0.396616	0.441482	0.490854	0.545128	0.604733	0.670126
896	0.355828	0.396556	0.441422	0.490796	0.545074	0.604683	0.670082
897	0.355768	0.396496	0.441363	0.490739	0.545020	0.604633	0.670038
898	0.355707	0.396436	0.441304	0.490682	0.544965	0.604583	0.669994
899	0.355647	0.396376	0.441245	0.490624	0.544911	0.604533	0.669950
900	0.355587	0.396316	0.441186	0.490567	0.544857	0.604483	0.669906
901	0.355527	0.396256	0.441127	0.490510	0.544803	0.604434	0.669862
902	0.355467	0.396196	0.441068	0.490453	0.544749	0.604384	0.669818
903	0.355407	0.396136	0.441009	0.490396	0.544695	0.604335	0.669775
904	0.355347	0.396077	0.440951	0.490340	0.544642	0.604285	0.669731
905	0.355288	0.396017	0.440892	0.490283	0.544588	0.604236	0.669688
906	0.355228	0.395957	0.440833	0.490226	0.544534	0.604186	0.669644
907	0.355169	0.395898	0.440775	0.490170	0.544481	0.604137	0.669600
908	0.355109	0.395839	0.440716	0.490113	0.544427	0.604088	0.669557
909	0.355050	0.395779	0.440658	0.490057	0.544373	0.604038	0.669514
910	0.354990	0.395720	0.440600	0.490000	0.544320	0.603989	0.669470

Unit	90	91	92	93	94	95	96
911	0.354931	0.395661	0.440542	0.489944	0.544267	0.603940	0.669427
912	0.354872	0.395602	0.440484	0.489888	0.544213	0.603891	0.669384
913	0.354813	0.395543	0.440425	0.489831	0.544160	0.603842	0.669341
914	0.354754	0.395484	0.440367	0.489775	0.544107	0.603793	0.669297
915	0.354695	0.395425	0.440310	0.489719	0.544054	0.603744	0.669254
916	0.354636	0.395367	0.440252	0.489663	0.544001	0.603696	0.669211
917	0.354577	0.395308	0.440194	0.489607	0.543948	0.603647	0.669168
918	0.354518	0.395249	0.440136	0.489551	0.543895	0.603598	0.669125
919	0.354460	0.395191	0.440079	0.489496	0.543842	0.603550	0.669082
920	0.354401	0.395132	0.440021	0.489440	0.543789	0.603501	0.669039
921	0.354343	0.395074	0.439963	0.489384	0.543737	0.603453	0.668997
922	0.354284	0.395015	0.439906	0.489329	0.543684	0.603404	0.668954
923	0.354226	0.394957	0.439849	0.489273	0.543631	0.603356	0.668911
924	0.354167	0.394899	0.439791	0.489218	0.543579	0.603307	0.668869
925	0.354109	0.394841	0.439734	0.489162	0.543526	0.603259	0.668826
926	0.354051	0.394783	0.439677	0.489107	0.543474	0.603211	0.668783
927	0.353993	0.394725	0.439620	0.489052	0.543421	0.603163	0.668741
928	0.353935	0.394667	0.439563	0.488996	0.543369	0.603115	0.668698
929	0.353877	0.394609	0.439506	0.488941	0.543317	0.603066	0.668656
930	0.353819	0.394551	0.439449	0.488886	0.543265	0.603018	0.668614
931	0.353761	0.394494	0.439392	0.488831	0.543213	0.602970	0.668571
932	0.353704	0.394436	0.439336	0.488776	0.543161	0.602923	0.668529
933	0.353646	0.394379	0.439279	0.488721	0.543109	0.602875	0.668487
934	0.353588	0.394321	0.439222	0.488666	0.543057	0.602827	0.668445
935	0.353531	0.394264	0.439166	0.488612	0.543005	0.602779	0.668403
936	0.353474	0.394206	0.439109	0.488557	0.542953	0.602732	0.668360
937	0.353416	0.394149	0.439053	0.488502	0.542901	0.602684	0.668318
938	0.353359	0.394092	0.438997	0.488448	0.542850	0.602636	0.668276
939	0.353302	0.394035	0.438940	0.488393	0.542798	0.602589	0.668235
940	0.353244	0.393978	0.438884	0.488339	0.542746	0.602541	0.668193
941	0.353187	0.393921	0.438828	0.488285	0.542695	0.602494	0.668151
942	0.353130	0.393864	0.438772	0.488230	0.542643	0.602447	0.668109
943	0.353073	0.393807	0.438716	0.488176	0.542592	0.602399	0.668067
944	0.353017	0.393750	0.438660	0.488122	0.542541	0.602352	0.668026
945	0.352960	0.393693	0.438604	0.488068	0.542489	0.602305	0.667984

Unit	90	91	92	93	94	95	96
946	0.352903	0.393637	0.438548	0.488014	0.542438	0.602258	0.667942
947	0.352846	0.393580	0.438493	0.487960	0.542387	0.602211	0.667901
948	0.352790	0.393524	0.438437	0.487906	0.542336	0.602164	0.667859
949	0.352733	0.393467	0.438381	0.487852	0.542285	0.602117	0.667818
950	0.352677	0.393411	0.438326	0.487798	0.542234	0.602070	0.667776
951	0.352620	0.393355	0.438270	0.487745	0.542183	0.602023	0.667735
952	0.352564	0.393298	0.438215	0.487691	0.542132	0.601976	0.667694
953	0.352508	0.393242	0.438160	0.487637	0.542081	0.601929	0.667652
954	0.352452	0.393186	0.438104	0.487584	0.542031	0.601883	0.667611
955	0.352395	0.393130	0.438049	0.487530	0.541980	0.601836	0.667570
956	0.352339	0.393074	0.437994	0.487477	0.541929	0.601789	0.667529
957	0.352283	0.393018	0.437939	0.487423	0.541879	0.601743	0.667488
958	0.352227	0.392962	0.437884	0.487370	0.541828	0.601696	0.667447
959	0.352172	0.392906	0.437829	0.487317	0.541778	0.601650	0.667406
960	0.352116	0.392851	0.437774	0.487264	0.541727	0.601603	0.667365
961	0.352060	0.392795	0.437719	0.487211	0.541677	0.601557	0.667324
962	0.352004	0.392739	0.437664	0.487158	0.541627	0.601511	0.667283
963	0.351949	0.392684	0.437610	0.487105	0.541576	0.601464	0.667242
964	0.351893	0.392629	0.437555	0.487052	0.541526	0.601418	0.667201
965	0.351838	0.392573	0.437500	0.486999	0.541476	0.601372	0.667160
966	0.351783	0.392518	0.437446	0.486946	0.541426	0.601326	0.667120
967	0.351727	0.392463	0.437392	0.486893	0.541376	0.601280	0.667079
968	0.351672	0.392407	0.437337	0.486841	0.541326	0.601234	0.667039
969	0.351617	0.392352	0.437283	0.486788	0.541276	0.601188	0.666998
970	0.351562	0.392297	0.437229	0.486735	0.541226	0.601142	0.666957
971	0.351507	0.392242	0.437174	0.486683	0.541177	0.601096	0.666917
972	0.351452	0.392187	0.437120	0.486630	0.541127	0.601051	0.666877
973	0.351397	0.392132	0.437066	0.486578	0.541077	0.601005	0.666836
974	0.351342	0.392078	0.437012	0.486526	0.541028	0.600959	0.666796
975	0.351287	0.392023	0.436958	0.486473	0.540978	0.600914	0.666756
976	0.351232	0.391968	0.436904	0.486421	0.540928	0.600868	0.666715
977	0.351178	0.391914	0.436851	0.486369	0.540879	0.600822	0.666675
978	0.351123	0.391859	0.436797	0.486317	0.540830	0.600777	0.666635
979	0.351068	0.391805	0.436743	0.486265	0.540780	0.600731	0.666595
980	0.351014	0.391750	0.436689	0.486213	0.540731	0.600686	0.666555

Unit	90	91	92	93	94	95	96
981	0.350960	0.391696	0.436636	0.486161	0.540682	0.600641	0.666515
982	0.350905	0.391641	0.436582	0.486109	0.540633	0.600595	0.666475
983	0.350851	0.391587	0.436529	0.486057	0.540584	0.600550	0.666435
984	0.350797	0.391533	0.436476	0.486006	0.540534	0.600505	0.666395
985	0.350743	0.391479	0.436422	0.485954	0.540485	0.600460	0.666355
986	0.350688	0.391425	0.436369	0.485902	0.540436	0.600415	0.666315
987	0.350634	0.391371	0.436316	0.485851	0.540388	0.600370	0.666275
988	0.350580	0.391317	0.436263	0.485799	0.540339	0.600325	0.666236
989	0.350527	0.391263	0.436209	0.485748	0.540290	0.600280	0.666196
990	0.350473	0.391209	0.436156	0.485696	0.540241	0.600235	0.666156
991	0.350419	0.391156	0.436104	0.485645	0.540193	0.600190	0.666117
992	0.350365	0.391102	0.436051	0.485594	0.540144	0.600145	0.666077
993	0.350312	0.391048	0.435998	0.485543	0.540095	0.600101	0.666038
994	0.350258	0.390995	0.435945	0.485491	0.540047	0.600056	0.665998
995	0.350204	0.390941	0.435892	0.485440	0.539998	0.600011	0.665959
996	0.350151	0.390888	0.435840	0.485389	0.539950	0.599967	0.665919
997	0.350098	0.390835	0.435787	0.485338	0.539902	0.599922	0.665880
998	0.350044	0.390781	0.435734	0.485287	0.539853	0.599878	0.665841
999	0.349991	0.390728	0.435682	0.485236	0.539805	0.599833	0.665801
1000	0.349938	0.390675	0.435629	0.485186	0.539757	0.599789	0.665762

Unit	90	91	92	93	94	95	96
1010	0.349409	0.390146	0.435108	0.484680	0.539278	0.599347	0.665372
1020	0.348886	0.389624	0.434593	0.484181	0.538803	0.598910	0.664986
1030	0.348369	0.389107	0.434083	0.483686	0.538334	0.598478	0.664604
1040	0.347858	0.388595	0.433579	0.483197	0.537870	0.598050	0.664226
1050	0.347352	0.388090	0.433080	0.482714	0.537411	0.597627	0.663852
1060	0.346852	0.387590	0.432587	0.482235	0.536956	0.597208	0.663481
1070	0.346357	0.387095	0.432098	0.481761	0.536507	0.596793	0.663115
1080	0.345868	0.386605	0.431615	0.481292	0.536061	0.596383	0.662751
1090	0.345384	0.386121	0.431137	0.480828	0.535620	0.595976	0.662392
1100	0.344905	0.385641	0.430663	0.480368	0.535184	0.595573	0.662036
1110	0.344430	0.385167	0.430195	0.479913	0.534752	0.595175	0.661683
1120	0.343961	0.384697	0.429731	0.479463	0.534324	0.594780	0.661333
1130	0.343497	0.384232	0.429272	0.479017	0.533900	0.594389	0.660987
1140	0.343037	0.383772	0.428817	0.478575	0.533480	0.594001	0.660644
1150	0.342582	0.383316	0.428367	0.478138	0.533064	0.593617	0.660305
1160	0.342131	0.382864	0.427921	0.477705	0.532653	0.593237	0.659968
1170	0.341685	0.382418	0.427479	0.477275	0.532245	0.592860	0.659635
1180	0.341244	0.381975	0.427042	0.476850	0.531840	0.592487	0.659304
1190	0.340806	0.381537	0.426608	0.476429	0.531440	0.592117	0.658976
1200	0.340373	0.381103	0.426179	0.476012	0.531043	0.591751	0.658652
1210	0.339944	0.380672	0.425754	0.475599	0.530650	0.591387	0.658330
1220	0.339519	0.380246	0.425333	0.475189	0.530260	0.591027	0.658011
1230	0.339098	0.379824	0.424915	0.474783	0.529874	0.590670	0.657695
1240	0.338681	0.379406	0.424501	0.474381	0.529491	0.590317	0.657381
1250	0.338267	0.378992	0.424091	0.473982	0.529111	0.589966	0.657070
1260	0.337858	0.378581	0.423685	0.473587	0.528735	0.589618	0.656762
1270	0.337452	0.378174	0.423282	0.473195	0.528362	0.589273	0.656456
1280	0.337050	0.377771	0.422883	0.472806	0.527992	0.588931	0.656153
1290	0.336652	0.377371	0.422488	0.472421	0.527626	0.588592	0.655852
1300	0.336257	0.376975	0.422095	0.472040	0.527262	0.588256	0.655554
1310	0.335865	0.376582	0.421706	0.471661	0.526902	0.587923	0.655258
1320	0.335477	0.376192	0.421321	0.471286	0.526544	0.587592	0.654965
1330	0.335093	0.375806	0.420938	0.470913	0.526189	0.587264	0.654674
1340	0.334711	0.375423	0.420559	0.470544	0.525838	0.586938	0.654385
1350	0.334333	0.375044	0.420183	0.470178	0.525489	0.586615	0.654099

Unit	90	91	92	93	94	95	96
1360	0.333958	0.374667	0.419810	0.469815	0.525143	0.586295	0.653814
1370	0.333587	0.374294	0.419441	0.469455	0.524799	0.585977	0.653532
1380	0.333218	0.373924	0.419074	0.469097	0.524459	0.585662	0.653253
1390	0.332853	0.373557	0.418710	0.468743	0.524121	0.585349	0.652975
1400	0.332490	0.373193	0.418349	0.468391	0.523786	0.585039	0.652699
1410	0.332131	0.372831	0.417991	0.468042	0.523453	0.584731	0.652426
1420	0.331774	0.372473	0.417636	0.467696	0.523123	0.584425	0.652154
1430	0.331420	0.372117	0.417284	0.467353	0.522795	0.584122	0.651885
1440	0.331069	0.371765	0.416934	0.467012	0.522470	0.583821	0.651617
1450	0.330721	0.371415	0.416587	0.466674	0.522147	0.583522	0.651352
1460	0.330376	0.371068	0.416243	0.466338	0.521827	0.583225	0.651088
1470	0.330033	0.370723	0.415901	0.466005	0.521509	0.582930	0.650826
1480	0.329694	0.370381	0.415562	0.465674	0.521194	0.582638	0.650567
1490	0.329356	0.370042	0.415225	0.465346	0.520881	0.582348	0.650309
1500	0.329022	0.369706	0.414891	0.465020	0.520570	0.582060	0.650052
1510	0.328689	0.369372	0.414560	0.464697	0.520261	0.581773	0.649798
1520	0.328360	0.369040	0.414231	0.464376	0.519955	0.581489	0.649546
1530	0.328033	0.368711	0.413904	0.464057	0.519650	0.581207	0.649295
1540	0.327708	0.368384	0.413580	0.463740	0.519348	0.580927	0.649046
1550	0.327386	0.368060	0.413258	0.463426	0.519048	0.580649	0.648798
1560	0.327066	0.367738	0.412939	0.463114	0.518750	0.580373	0.648553
1570	0.326748	0.367418	0.412621	0.462805	0.518454	0.580098	0.648309
1580	0.326433	0.367101	0.412306	0.462497	0.518161	0.579826	0.648066
1590	0.326120	0.366786	0.411993	0.462192	0.517869	0.579555	0.647826
1600	0.325810	0.366473	0.411683	0.461888	0.517579	0.579286	0.647586
1610	0.325501	0.366163	0.411374	0.461587	0.517291	0.579019	0.647349
1620	0.325195	0.365855	0.411068	0.461288	0.517006	0.578754	0.647113
1630	0.324891	0.365548	0.410764	0.460991	0.516722	0.578491	0.646878
1640	0.324589	0.365244	0.410462	0.460696	0.516440	0.578229	0.646645
1650	0.324289	0.364942	0.410162	0.460403	0.516159	0.577969	0.646414
1660	0.323991	0.364642	0.409864	0.460112	0.515881	0.577710	0.646184
1670	0.323696	0.364344	0.409568	0.459822	0.515605	0.577454	0.645955
1680	0.323402	0.364049	0.409274	0.459535	0.515330	0.577199	0.645728
1690	0.323111	0.363755	0.408982	0.459250	0.515057	0.576945	0.645503
1700	0.322821	0.363463	0.408691	0.458966	0.514786	0.576693	0.645278

Unit	90	91	92	93	94	95	96
1710	0.322533	0.363173	0.408403	0.458684	0.514516	0.576443	0.645056
1720	0.322248	0.362885	0.408117	0.458404	0.514249	0.576194	0.644834
1730	0.321964	0.362599	0.407832	0.458126	0.513983	0.575947	0.644614
1740	0.321682	0.362315	0.407550	0.457850	0.513718	0.575702	0.644395
1750	0.321402	0.362032	0.407269	0.457575	0.513455	0.575458	0.644178
1760	0.321123	0.361752	0.406990	0.457302	0.513194	0.575215	0.643962
1770	0.320847	0.361473	0.406712	0.457031	0.512935	0.574974	0.643747
1780	0.320572	0.361196	0.406437	0.456762	0.512677	0.574734	0.643533
1790	0.320300	0.360921	0.406163	0.456494	0.512421	0.574496	0.643321
1800	0.320028	0.360647	0.405891	0.456228	0.512166	0.574259	0.643110
1810	0.319759	0.360375	0.405621	0.455963	0.511913	0.574024	0.642900
1820	0.319491	0.360105	0.405352	0.455700	0.511661	0.573790	0.642691
1830	0.319225	0.359837	0.405085	0.455439	0.511411	0.573557	0.642484
1840	0.318961	0.359570	0.404819	0.455179	0.511162	0.573326	0.642278
1850	0.318698	0.359305	0.404555	0.454921	0.510915	0.573096	0.642073
1860	0.318437	0.359042	0.404293	0.454664	0.510669	0.572868	0.641869
1870	0.318178	0.358780	0.404032	0.454409	0.510424	0.572640	0.641666
1880	0.317920	0.358520	0.403773	0.454155	0.510182	0.572414	0.641465
1890	0.317664	0.358261	0.403516	0.453903	0.509940	0.572190	0.641265
1900	0.317409	0.358004	0.403260	0.453652	0.509700	0.571966	0.641065
1910	0.317156	0.357748	0.403005	0.453403	0.509461	0.571744	0.640867
1920	0.316904	0.357494	0.402752	0.453155	0.509224	0.571523	0.640670
1930	0.316654	0.357242	0.402500	0.452909	0.508988	0.571304	0.640474
1940	0.316405	0.356990	0.402250	0.452664	0.508753	0.571085	0.640279
1950	0.316158	0.356741	0.402002	0.452420	0.508519	0.570868	0.640085
1960	0.315913	0.356493	0.401754	0.452178	0.508287	0.570652	0.639893
1970	0.315668	0.356246	0.401508	0.451937	0.508056	0.570437	0.639701
1980	0.315425	0.356001	0.401264	0.451698	0.507827	0.570223	0.639510
1990	0.315184	0.355757	0.401021	0.451460	0.507598	0.570011	0.639320
2000	0.314944	0.355514	0.400779	0.451223	0.507371	0.569799	0.639132
2010	0.314705	0.355273	0.400539	0.450987	0.507146	0.569589	0.638944
2020	0.314468	0.355033	0.400300	0.450753	0.506921	0.569380	0.638757
2030	0.314232	0.354795	0.400062	0.450520	0.506697	0.569172	0.638571
2040	0.313997	0.354557	0.399826	0.450288	0.506475	0.568965	0.638387
2050	0.313764	0.354322	0.399590	0.450058	0.506254	0.568759	0.638203

Unit	90	91	92	93	94	95	96
2060	0.313532	0.354087	0.399357	0.449828	0.506034	0.568554	0.638020
2070	0.313301	0.353854	0.399124	0.449600	0.505816	0.568351	0.637838
2080	0.313072	0.353622	0.398893	0.449374	0.505598	0.568148	0.637657
2090	0.312844	0.353391	0.398663	0.449148	0.505382	0.567946	0.637477
2100	0.312617	0.353162	0.398434	0.448924	0.505166	0.567746	0.637298
2110	0.312391	0.352934	0.398206	0.448700	0.504952	0.567546	0.637120
2120	0.312167	0.352707	0.397980	0.448478	0.504739	0.567348	0.636942
2130	0.311944	0.352481	0.397754	0.448257	0.504527	0.567150	0.636766
2140	0.311722	0.352256	0.397530	0.448038	0.504316	0.566954	0.636590
2150	0.311501	0.352033	0.397308	0.447819	0.504106	0.566758	0.636415
2160	0.311281	0.351811	0.397086	0.447601	0.503898	0.566563	0.636241
2170	0.311063	0.351590	0.396865	0.447385	0.503690	0.566370	0.636068
2180	0.310845	0.351370	0.396646	0.447170	0.503483	0.566177	0.635896
2190	0.310629	0.351151	0.396428	0.446956	0.503278	0.565985	0.635725
2200	0.310414	0.350933	0.396210	0.446742	0.503073	0.565795	0.635554
2210	0.310200	0.350717	0.395994	0.446530	0.502869	0.565605	0.635384
2220	0.309987	0.350502	0.395779	0.446319	0.502667	0.565416	0.635216
2230	0.309776	0.350288	0.395565	0.446109	0.502465	0.565228	0.635047
2240	0.309565	0.350074	0.395352	0.445900	0.502264	0.565041	0.634880
2250	0.309356	0.349862	0.395141	0.445693	0.502065	0.564855	0.634714
2260	0.309147	0.349651	0.394930	0.445486	0.501866	0.564669	0.634548
2270	0.308940	0.349441	0.394720	0.445280	0.501668	0.564485	0.634383
2280	0.308733	0.349232	0.394512	0.445075	0.501471	0.564301	0.634219
2290	0.308528	0.349024	0.394304	0.444871	0.501276	0.564118	0.634055
2300	0.308324	0.348817	0.394097	0.444668	0.501081	0.563937	0.633893
2310	0.308120	0.348612	0.393892	0.444466	0.500887	0.563756	0.633731
2320	0.307918	0.348407	0.393687	0.444265	0.500693	0.563575	0.633569
2330	0.307717	0.348203	0.393483	0.444065	0.500501	0.563396	0.633409
2340	0.307517	0.348000	0.393281	0.443866	0.500310	0.563217	0.633249
2350	0.307317	0.347798	0.393079	0.443668	0.500120	0.563040	0.633090
2360	0.307119	0.347597	0.392878	0.443471	0.499930	0.562863	0.632932
2370	0.306922	0.347397	0.392679	0.443275	0.499741	0.562687	0.632774
2380	0.306725	0.347198	0.392480	0.443079	0.499554	0.562511	0.632617
2390	0.306530	0.347000	0.392282	0.442885	0.499367	0.562337	0.632461
2400	0.306336	0.346803	0.392085	0.442691	0.499181	0.562163	0.632306

Unit	90	91	92	93	94	95	96
2410	0.306142	0.346607	0.391889	0.442498	0.498995	0.561990	0.632151
2420	0.305949	0.346412	0.391694	0.442307	0.498811	0.561818	0.631997
2430	0.305758	0.346218	0.391499	0.442116	0.498627	0.561647	0.631843
2440	0.305567	0.346024	0.391306	0.441926	0.498445	0.561476	0.631690
2450	0.305377	0.345832	0.391114	0.441736	0.498263	0.561306	0.631538
2460	0.305188	0.345640	0.390922	0.441548	0.498081	0.561137	0.631387
2470	0.305000	0.345449	0.390731	0.441361	0.497901	0.560969	0.631236
2480	0.304813	0.345260	0.390541	0.441174	0.497722	0.560801	0.631086
2490	0.304626	0.345071	0.390352	0.440988	0.497543	0.560634	0.630936
2500	0.304441	0.344882	0.390164	0.440803	0.497365	0.560468	0.630787
2510	0.304256	0.344695	0.389977	0.440619	0.497188	0.560302	0.630639
2520	0.304072	0.344509	0.389790	0.440436	0.497011	0.560137	0.630491
2530	0.303889	0.344323	0.389605	0.440253	0.496835	0.559973	0.630344
2540	0.303707	0.344138	0.389420	0.440071	0.496661	0.559810	0.630198
2550	0.303526	0.343954	0.389236	0.439890	0.496486	0.559647	0.630052
2560	0.303345	0.343771	0.389053	0.439710	0.496313	0.559485	0.629907
2570	0.303165	0.343589	0.388870	0.439531	0.496140	0.559323	0.629762
2580	0.302986	0.343407	0.388689	0.439352	0.495968	0.559163	0.629618
2590	0.302808	0.343227	0.388508	0.439174	0.495797	0.559003	0.629475
2600	0.302631	0.343047	0.388328	0.438997	0.495626	0.558843	0.629332
2610	0.302455	0.342868	0.388148	0.438820	0.495457	0.558685	0.629190
2620	0.302279	0.342689	0.387970	0.438645	0.495288	0.558526	0.629048
2630	0.302104	0.342512	0.387792	0.438470	0.495119	0.558369	0.628907
2640	0.301930	0.342335	0.387615	0.438296	0.494951	0.558212	0.628766
2650	0.301756	0.342159	0.387439	0.438122	0.494784	0.558056	0.628626
2660	0.301583	0.341984	0.387263	0.437949	0.494618	0.557901	0.628487
2670	0.301411	0.341809	0.387089	0.437777	0.494452	0.557746	0.628348
2680	0.301240	0.341635	0.386915	0.437606	0.494288	0.557591	0.628210
2690	0.301070	0.341462	0.386741	0.437435	0.494123	0.557438	0.628072
2700	0.300900	0.341290	0.386569	0.437266	0.493960	0.557285	0.627935
2710	0.300731	0.341118	0.386397	0.437096	0.493797	0.557132	0.627798
2720	0.300563	0.340947	0.386226	0.436928	0.493634	0.556980	0.627662
2730	0.300395	0.340777	0.386055	0.436760	0.493473	0.556829	0.627526
2740	0.300228	0.340608	0.385885	0.436593	0.493312	0.556679	0.627391
2750	0.300062	0.340439	0.385716	0.436426	0.493151	0.556529	0.627257

Unit	90	91	92	93	94	95	96
2760	0.299896	0.340271	0.385548	0.436261	0.492991	0.556379	0.627122
2770	0.299732	0.340103	0.385380	0.436095	0.492832	0.556230	0.626989
2780	0.299567	0.339937	0.385213	0.435931	0.492674	0.556082	0.626856
2790	0.299404	0.339771	0.385047	0.435767	0.492516	0.555934	0.626723
2800	0.299241	0.339605	0.384881	0.435604	0.492359	0.555787	0.626591
2810	0.299079	0.339441	0.384716	0.435441	0.492202	0.555640	0.626460
2820	0.298918	0.339276	0.384552	0.435279	0.492046	0.555494	0.626329
2830	0.298757	0.339113	0.384388	0.435118	0.491890	0.555349	0.626198
2840	0.298597	0.338950	0.384225	0.434957	0.491736	0.555204	0.626068
2850	0.298437	0.338788	0.384063	0.434797	0.491581	0.555059	0.625938
2860	0.298278	0.338627	0.383901	0.434638	0.491428	0.554916	0.625809
2870	0.298120	0.338466	0.383740	0.434479	0.491274	0.554772	0.625681
2880	0.297963	0.338306	0.383579	0.434321	0.491122	0.554630	0.625553
2890	0.297806	0.338146	0.383419	0.434163	0.490970	0.554487	0.625425
2900	0.297649	0.337988	0.383260	0.434006	0.490819	0.554346	0.625298
2910	0.297494	0.337829	0.383101	0.433850	0.490668	0.554204	0.625171
2920	0.297338	0.337672	0.382943	0.433694	0.490518	0.554064	0.625045
2930	0.297184	0.337515	0.382786	0.433539	0.490368	0.553924	0.624919
2940	0.297030	0.337358	0.382629	0.433384	0.490219	0.553784	0.624793
2950	0.296877	0.337202	0.382473	0.433230	0.490070	0.553645	0.624668
2960	0.296724	0.337047	0.382317	0.433077	0.489922	0.553506	0.624544
2970	0.296572	0.336893	0.382162	0.432924	0.489776	0.553368	0.624420
2980	0.296421	0.336738	0.382007	0.432772	0.489628	0.553230	0.624296
2990	0.296270	0.336585	0.381853	0.432620	0.489481	0.553093	0.624173
3000	0.296119	0.336432	0.381700	0.432469	0.489336	0.552957	0.624050
3010	0.295970	0.336280	0.381547	0.432318	0.489190	0.552820	0.623928
3020	0.295820	0.336128	0.381395	0.432168	0.489045	0.552685	0.623806
3030	0.295672	0.335977	0.381244	0.432018	0.488901	0.552550	0.623685
3040	0.295524	0.335826	0.381092	0.431869	0.488757	0.552415	0.623564
3050	0.295376	0.335676	0.380942	0.431721	0.488614	0.552281	0.623443
3060	0.295229	0.335527	0.380792	0.431573	0.488471	0.552147	0.623323
3070	0.295083	0.335378	0.380643	0.431426	0.488329	0.552014	0.623203
3080	0.294937	0.335230	0.380494	0.431279	0.488187	0.551881	0.623084
3090	0.294792	0.335082	0.380345	0.431132	0.488046	0.551748	0.622965
3100	0.294647	0.334935	0.380198	0.430987	0.487905	0.551617	0.622846

Unit	90	91	92	93	94	95	96
3110	0.294503	0.334788	0.380050	0.430841	0.487765	0.551485	0.622728
3120	0.294359	0.334642	0.379904	0.430696	0.487625	0.551354	0.622611
3130	0.294216	0.334496	0.379757	0.430552	0.487486	0.551224	0.622493
3140	0.294073	0.334351	0.379612	0.430408	0.487347	0.551093	0.622376
3150	0.293931	0.334206	0.379466	0.430265	0.487209	0.550964	0.622260
3160	0.293790	0.334062	0.379322	0.430122	0.487071	0.550835	0.622144
3170	0.293649	0.333918	0.379178	0.429980	0.486934	0.550706	0.622028
3180	0.293508	0.333775	0.379034	0.429838	0.486797	0.550577	0.621913
3190	0.293368	0.333633	0.378891	0.429697	0.486660	0.550450	0.621798
3200	0.293229	0.333491	0.378748	0.429556	0.486524	0.550322	0.621683
3210	0.293090	0.333349	0.378606	0.429416	0.486389	0.550195	0.621569
3220	0.292951	0.333208	0.378464	0.429276	0.486254	0.550068	0.621455
3230	0.292813	0.333068	0.378323	0.429137	0.486119	0.549942	0.621341
3240	0.292675	0.332928	0.378183	0.428998	0.485985	0.549816	0.621228
3250	0.292538	0.332788	0.378043	0.428860	0.485852	0.549691	0.621116
3260	0.292402	0.332649	0.377903	0.428722	0.485718	0.549566	0.621003
3270	0.292266	0.332510	0.377764	0.428584	0.485586	0.549442	0.620891
3280	0.292130	0.332372	0.377625	0.428447	0.485453	0.549317	0.620780
3290	0.291995	0.332235	0.377487	0.428311	0.485321	0.549194	0.620668
3300	0.291860	0.332097	0.377349	0.428175	0.485190	0.549070	0.620557
3310	0.291726	0.331961	0.377212	0.428039	0.485059	0.548947	0.620447
3320	0.291592	0.331825	0.377075	0.427904	0.484928	0.548825	0.620337
3330	0.291459	0.331689	0.376938	0.427769	0.484798	0.548703	0.620227
3340	0.291326	0.331553	0.376802	0.427635	0.484668	0.548581	0.620117
3350	0.291194	0.331419	0.376667	0.427501	0.484539	0.548460	0.620008
3360	0.291062	0.331284	0.376532	0.427368	0.484410	0.548339	0.619899
3370	0.290931	0.331150	0.376397	0.427235	0.484282	0.548218	0.619791
3380	0.290800	0.331017	0.376263	0.427102	0.484154	0.548098	0.619683
3390	0.290669	0.330884	0.376129	0.426970	0.484026	0.547978	0.619575
3400	0.290539	0.330751	0.375996	0.426838	0.483899	0.547859	0.619467
3410	0.290409	0.330619	0.375863	0.426707	0.483772	0.547740	0.619360
3420	0.290280	0.330487	0.375731	0.426576	0.483645	0.547621	0.619253
3430	0.290151	0.330356	0.375599	0.426446	0.483519	0.547503	0.619147
3440	0.290023	0.330225	0.375468	0.426316	0.483394	0.547385	0.619041
3450	0.289895	0.330095	0.375336	0.426187	0.483268	0.547267	0.618935

Unit	90	91	92	93	94	95	96
3460	0.289767	0.329965	0.375206	0.426057	0.483144	0.547150	0.618829
3470	0.289640	0.329835	0.375076	0.425929	0.483019	0.547033	0.618724
3480	0.289514	0.329706	0.374946	0.425800	0.482895	0.546917	0.618619
3490	0.289387	0.329578	0.374816	0.425672	0.482771	0.546801	0.618515
3500	0.289262	0.329449	0.374687	0.425545	0.482648	0.546685	0.618411
3510	0.289136	0.329321	0.374559	0.425418	0.482525	0.546569	0.618307
3520	0.289011	0.329194	0.374431	0.425291	0.482403	0.546454	0.618203
3530	0.288887	0.329067	0.374303	0.425165	0.482281	0.546340	0.618100
3540	0.288762	0.328940	0.374175	0.425039	0.482159	0.546225	0.617997
3550	0.288639	0.328814	0.374049	0.424913	0.482037	0.546111	0.617894
3560	0.288515	0.328688	0.373922	0.424788	0.481916	0.545998	0.617792
3570	0.288392	0.328563	0.373796	0.424664	0.481796	0.545884	0.617690
3580	0.288270	0.328438	0.373670	0.424539	0.481675	0.545771	0.617588
3590	0.288147	0.328313	0.373545	0.424415	0.481555	0.545659	0.617487
3600	0.288026	0.328189	0.373420	0.424292	0.481436	0.545546	0.617385
3610	0.287904	0.328065	0.373295	0.424169	0.481317	0.545434	0.617285
3620	0.287783	0.327942	0.373171	0.424046	0.481198	0.545323	0.617184
3630	0.287662	0.327819	0.373047	0.423923	0.481079	0.545211	0.617084
3640	0.287542	0.327696	0.372924	0.423801	0.480961	0.545100	0.616984
3650	0.287422	0.327574	0.372801	0.423679	0.480843	0.544990	0.616884
3660	0.287303	0.327452	0.372678	0.423558	0.480726	0.544879	0.616785
3670	0.287184	0.327330	0.372556	0.423437	0.480609	0.544769	0.616686
3680	0.287065	0.327209	0.372434	0.423316	0.480492	0.544660	0.616587
3690	0.286947	0.327088	0.372312	0.423196	0.480376	0.544550	0.616488
3700	0.286828	0.326968	0.372191	0.423076	0.480260	0.544441	0.616390
3710	0.286711	0.326848	0.372070	0.422957	0.480144	0.544333	0.616292
3720	0.286594	0.326728	0.371950	0.422838	0.480029	0.544224	0.616194
3730	0.286477	0.326609	0.371830	0.422719	0.479914	0.544116	0.616097
3740	0.286360	0.326490	0.371710	0.422600	0.479799	0.544008	0.616000
3750	0.286244	0.326371	0.371591	0.422482	0.479685	0.543901	0.615903
3760	0.286128	0.326253	0.371471	0.422364	0.479571	0.543794	0.615806
3770	0.286013	0.326135	0.371353	0.422247	0.479457	0.543687	0.615710
3780	0.285897	0.326018	0.371234	0.422130	0.479344	0.543580	0.615614
3790	0.285783	0.325900	0.371117	0.422013	0.479231	0.543474	0.615518
3800	0.285668	0.325784	0.370999	0.421897	0.479118	0.543368	0.615423

Unit	90	91	92	93	94	95	96
3810	0.285554	0.325667	0.370882	0.421781	0.479005	0.543262	0.615327
3820	0.285440	0.325551	0.370765	0.421665	0.478893	0.543157	0.615232
3830	0.285327	0.325435	0.370648	0.421549	0.478782	0.543052	0.615138
3840	0.285214	0.325320	0.370532	0.421434	0.478670	0.542947	0.615043
3850	0.285101	0.325205	0.370416	0.421320	0.478559	0.542843	0.614949
3860	0.284989	0.325090	0.370300	0.421205	0.478448	0.542738	0.614855
3870	0.284877	0.324975	0.370185	0.421091	0.478338	0.542634	0.614761
3880	0.284765	0.324861	0.370070	0.420977	0.478228	0.542531	0.614668
3890	0.284654	0.324748	0.369956	0.420864	0.478118	0.542428	0.614575
3900	0.284542	0.324634	0.369841	0.420751	0.478008	0.542324	0.614482
3910	0.284432	0.324521	0.369728	0.420638	0.477899	0.542222	0.614389
3920	0.284321	0.324408	0.369614	0.420526	0.477790	0.542119	0.614297
3930	0.284211	0.324296	0.369501	0.420413	0.477681	0.542017	0.614205
3940	0.284101	0.324184	0.369388	0.420302	0.477573	0.541915	0.614113
3950	0.283992	0.324072	0.369275	0.420190	0.477465	0.541813	0.614021
3960	0.283883	0.323960	0.369163	0.420079	0.477357	0.541712	0.613930
3970	0.283774	0.323849	0.369051	0.419968	0.477250	0.541611	0.613839
3980	0.283666	0.323738	0.368939	0.419857	0.477143	0.541510	0.613748
3990	0.283557	0.323628	0.368828	0.419747	0.477036	0.541410	0.613657
4000	0.283450	0.323518	0.368717	0.419637	0.476929	0.541309	0.613566
4010	0.283342	0.323408	0.368606	0.419527	0.476823	0.541209	0.613476
4020	0.283235	0.323298	0.368496	0.419418	0.476717	0.541110	0.613386
4030	0.283128	0.323189	0.368386	0.419309	0.476611	0.541010	0.613296
4040	0.283021	0.323080	0.368276	0.419200	0.476506	0.540911	0.613207
4050	0.282915	0.322971	0.368166	0.419092	0.476400	0.540812	0.613118
4060	0.282809	0.322863	0.368057	0.418983	0.476296	0.540713	0.613029
4070	0.282703	0.322755	0.367948	0.418876	0.476191	0.540615	0.612940
4080	0.282598	0.322647	0.367839	0.418768	0.476087	0.540517	0.612851
4090	0.282492	0.322540	0.367731	0.418661	0.475983	0.540419	0.612763
4100	0.282388	0.322433	0.367623	0.418554	0.475879	0.540321	0.612675
4110	0.282283	0.322326	0.367515	0.418447	0.475775	0.540224	0.612587
4120	0.282179	0.322219	0.367408	0.418340	0.475672	0.540127	0.612499
4130	0.282075	0.322113	0.367301	0.418234	0.475569	0.540030	0.612412
4140	0.281971	0.322007	0.367194	0.418128	0.475467	0.539933	0.612325
4150	0.281868	0.321901	0.367088	0.418023	0.475364	0.539837	0.612238

Unit	90	91	92	93	94	95	96
4160	0.281765	0.321796	0.366981	0.417917	0.475262	0.539741	0.612151
4170	0.281662	0.321691	0.366875	0.417812	0.475160	0.539645	0.612064
4180	0.281559	0.321586	0.366770	0.417708	0.475059	0.539549	0.611978
4190	0.281457	0.321481	0.366664	0.417603	0.474957	0.539454	0.611892
4200	0.281355	0.321377	0.366559	0.417499	0.474856	0.539358	0.611806
4210	0.281253	0.321273	0.366454	0.417395	0.474756	0.539264	0.611720
4220	0.281152	0.321170	0.366350	0.417291	0.474655	0.539169	0.611635
4230	0.281051	0.321066	0.366245	0.417188	0.474555	0.539074	0.611549
4240	0.280950	0.320963	0.366141	0.417085	0.474455	0.538980	0.611464
4250	0.280849	0.320860	0.366038	0.416982	0.474355	0.538886	0.611380
4260	0.280749	0.320758	0.365934	0.416879	0.474255	0.538793	0.611295
4270	0.280649	0.320655	0.365831	0.416777	0.474156	0.538699	0.611211
4280	0.280549	0.320553	0.365728	0.416675	0.474057	0.538606	0.611126
4290	0.280451	0.320451	0.365625	0.416573	0.473958	0.538513	0.611042
4300	0.280351	0.320350	0.365523	0.416472	0.473860	0.538420	0.610959
4310	0.280252	0.320249	0.365421	0.416370	0.473762	0.538328	0.610875
4320	0.280153	0.320148	0.365319	0.416269	0.473664	0.538235	0.610792
4330	0.280055	0.320047	0.365217	0.416169	0.473566	0.538143	0.610709
4340	0.279956	0.319947	0.365116	0.416068	0.473468	0.538051	0.610626
4350	0.279858	0.319846	0.365015	0.415968	0.473371	0.537960	0.610543
4360	0.279761	0.319747	0.364914	0.415868	0.473274	0.537868	0.610460
4370	0.279663	0.319647	0.364814	0.415768	0.473177	0.537777	0.610378
4380	0.279566	0.319547	0.364713	0.415669	0.473081	0.537686	0.610296
4390	0.279469	0.319448	0.364613	0.415569	0.472985	0.537595	0.610214
4400	0.279373	0.319349	0.364513	0.415470	0.472889	0.537505	0.610132
4410	0.279276	0.319251	0.364414	0.415372	0.472793	0.537415	0.610050
4420	0.279180	0.319152	0.364315	0.415273	0.472697	0.537325	0.609969
4430	0.279084	0.319054	0.364216	0.415175	0.472602	0.537235	0.609888
4440	0.278989	0.318956	0.364117	0.415077	0.472507	0.537145	0.609807
4450	0.278893	0.318859	0.364018	0.414979	0.472412	0.537056	0.609726
4460	0.278798	0.318761	0.363920	0.414882	0.472317	0.536966	0.609646
4470	0.278703	0.318664	0.363822	0.414784	0.472223	0.536877	0.609565
4480	0.278609	0.318567	0.363724	0.414687	0.472129	0.536789	0.609485
4490	0.278514	0.318471	0.363627	0.414591	0.472035	0.536700	0.609405
4500	0.278420	0.318374	0.363529	0.414494	0.471941	0.536612	0.609325

Unit	90	91	92	93	94	95	96
4510	0.278326	0.318278	0.363432	0.414398	0.471847	0.536524	0.609245
4520	0.278232	0.318182	0.363336	0.414302	0.471754	0.536436	0.609166
4530	0.278139	0.318087	0.363239	0.414206	0.471661	0.536348	0.609087
4540	0.278046	0.317991	0.363143	0.414110	0.471568	0.536260	0.609008
4550	0.277953	0.317896	0.363047	0.414015	0.471476	0.536173	0.608929
4560	0.277860	0.317801	0.362951	0.413920	0.471383	0.536086	0.608850
4570	0.277767	0.317707	0.362855	0.413825	0.471291	0.535999	0.608771
4580	0.277675	0.317612	0.362760	0.413730	0.471199	0.535912	0.608693
4590	0.277583	0.317518	0.362664	0.413636	0.471107	0.535826	0.608615
4600	0.277491	0.317424	0.362570	0.413541	0.471016	0.535740	0.608537
4610	0.277400	0.317330	0.362475	0.413447	0.470924	0.535654	0.608459
4620	0.277308	0.317236	0.362380	0.413354	0.470833	0.535568	0.608381
4630	0.277217	0.317143	0.362286	0.413260	0.470743	0.535482	0.608304
4640	0.277126	0.317050	0.362192	0.413167	0.470652	0.535397	0.608227
4650	0.277036	0.316957	0.362098	0.413074	0.470561	0.535311	0.608149
4660	0.276945	0.316865	0.362005	0.412981	0.470471	0.535226	0.608073
4670	0.276855	0.316772	0.361911	0.412888	0.470381	0.535141	0.607996
4680	0.276765	0.316680	0.361818	0.412796	0.470291	0.535057	0.607919
4690	0.276675	0.316588	0.361725	0.412703	0.470202	0.534972	0.607843
4700	0.276586	0.316496	0.361633	0.412611	0.470112	0.534888	0.607767
4710	0.276496	0.316405	0.361540	0.412519	0.470023	0.534804	0.607690
4720	0.276407	0.316314	0.361448	0.412428	0.469934	0.534720	0.607615
4730	0.276318	0.316222	0.361356	0.412336	0.469845	0.534636	0.607539
4740	0.276230	0.316132	0.361264	0.412245	0.469757	0.534552	0.607463
4750	0.276141	0.316041	0.361173	0.412154	0.469669	0.534469	0.607388
4760	0.276053	0.315951	0.361081	0.412064	0.469580	0.534386	0.607313
4770	0.275965	0.315860	0.360990	0.411973	0.469492	0.534303	0.607238
4780	0.275877	0.315770	0.360899	0.411883	0.469405	0.534220	0.607163
4790	0.275789	0.315681	0.360809	0.411793	0.469317	0.534138	0.607088
4800	0.275702	0.315591	0.360718	0.411703	0.469230	0.534055	0.607013
4810	0.275615	0.315502	0.360628	0.411613	0.469143	0.533973	0.606939
4820	0.275528	0.315413	0.360538	0.411524	0.469056	0.533891	0.606865
4830	0.275441	0.315324	0.360448	0.411434	0.468969	0.533809	0.606791
4840	0.275354	0.315235	0.360358	0.411345	0.468882	0.533727	0.606717
4850	0.275268	0.315146	0.360269	0.411256	0.468796	0.533646	0.606643

Unit	90	91	92	93	94	95	96
4860	0.275182	0.315058	0.360179	0.411168	0.468710	0.533564	0.606570
4870	0.275096	0.314970	0.360090	0.411079	0.468624	0.533483	0.606496
4880	0.275010	0.314882	0.360001	0.410991	0.468538	0.533402	0.606423
4890	0.274925	0.314794	0.359913	0.410903	0.468452	0.533321	0.606350
4900	0.274839	0.314707	0.359824	0.410815	0.468367	0.533241	0.606277
4910	0.274754	0.314620	0.359736	0.410727	0.468282	0.533160	0.606204
4920	0.274669	0.314532	0.359648	0.410640	0.468197	0.533080	0.606131
4930	0.274584	0.314446	0.359560	0.410553	0.468112	0.533000	0.606059
4940	0.274500	0.314359	0.359473	0.410465	0.468027	0.532920	0.605987
4950	0.274415	0.314272	0.359385	0.410379	0.467943	0.532840	0.605914
4960	0.274331	0.314186	0.359298	0.410292	0.467858	0.532761	0.605842
4970	0.274247	0.314100	0.359211	0.410205	0.467774	0.532681	0.605770
4980	0.274164	0.314014	0.359124	0.410119	0.467690	0.532602	0.605699
4990	0.274080	0.313928	0.359037	0.410033	0.467606	0.532523	0.605627
5000	0.273997	0.313843	0.358951	0.409947	0.467523	0.532444	0.605556
5010	0.273913	0.313758	0.358865	0.409861	0.467440	0.532366	0.605485
5020	0.273830	0.313673	0.358779	0.409776	0.467356	0.532287	0.605413
5030	0.273748	0.313588	0.358693	0.409490	0.467273	0.532209	0.605343
5040	0.273665	0.313503	0.358607	0.409605	0.467190	0.532130	0.605272
5050	0.273582	0.313418	0.358522	0.409520	0.467108	0.532052	0.605201
5060	0.273500	0.313334	0.358436	0.409435	0.467025	0.531974	0.605131
5070	0.273418	0.313250	0.358351	0.409351	0.466943	0.531897	0.605060
5080	0.273336	0.313166	0.358266	0.409266	0.466861	0.531819	0.604990
5090	0.273255	0.313082	0.358182	0.409182	0.466779	0.531742	0.604920
5100	0.273173	0.312999	0.358097	0.409098	0.466697	0.531665	0.604850
5110	0.273092	0.312915	0.358013	0.409014	0.466616	0.531587	0.604780
5120	0.273011	0.312832	0.357928	0.408930	0.466534	0.531511	0.604711
5130	0.272930	0.312749	0.357844	0.408847	0.466453	0.531434	0.604641
5140	0.272849	0.312666	0.357761	0.408763	0.466372	0.531357	0.604572
5150	0.272768	0.312583	0.357677	0.408680	0.466291	0.531281	0.604503
5160	0.272688	0.312501	0.357593	0.408597	0.466210	0.531205	0.604434
5170	0.272608	0.312418	0.357510	0.408514	0.466130	0.531128	0.604365
5180	0.272528	0.312336	0.357427	0.408432	0.466049	0.531053	0.604296
5190	0.272448	0.312254	0.357344	0.408349	0.465969	0.530977	0.604227
5200	0.272368	0.312173	0.357261	0.408267	0.465889	0.530901	0.604159

Unit	90	91	92	93	94	95	96
5210	0.272288	0.312091	0.357179	0.408185	0.465809	0.530826	0.604090
5220	0.272209	0.312010	0.357097	0.408103	0.465729	0.530750	0.604022
5230	0.272130	0.311928	0.357014	0.408021	0.465650	0.530675	0.603954
5240	0.272051	0.311847	0.356932	0.407940	0.465570	0.530600	0.603886
5250	0.271972	0.311766	0.356850	0.407858	0.465491	0.530525	0.603818
5260	0.271893	0.311686	0.356769	0.407777	0.465412	0.530451	0.603751
5270	0.271815	0.311605	0.356687	0.407696	0.465333	0.530376	0.603683
5280	0.271737	0.311525	0.356606	0.407615	0.465254	0.530302	0.603616
5290	0.271658	0.311445	0.356525	0.407534	0.465176	0.530227	0.603548
5300	0.271580	0.311365	0.356444	0.407454	0.465097	0.530153	0.603481
5310	0.271503	0.311285	0.356363	0.407373	0.465019	0.530079	0.603414
5320	0.271425	0.311205	0.356282	0.407293	0.464941	0.530006	0.603347
5330	0.271348	0.311126	0.356202	0.407213	0.464863	0.529932	0.603281
5340	0.271270	0.311046	0.356122	0.407133	0.464785	0.529858	0.603214
5350	0.271193	0.310967	0.356041	0.407053	0.464708	0.529785	0.603148
5360	0.271116	0.310888	0.355961	0.406974	0.464630	0.529712	0.603081
5370	0.271039	0.310809	0.355882	0.406894	0.464553	0.529639	0.603015
5380	0.270963	0.310731	0.355802	0.406815	0.464476	0.529566	0.602949
5390	0.270886	0.310652	0.355723	0.406736	0.464399	0.529493	0.602883
5400	0.270810	0.310574	0.355643	0.406657	0.464322	0.529420	0.602817
5410	0.270734	0.310496	0.355564	0.406578	0.464245	0.529348	0.602752
5420	0.270658	0.310418	0.355485	0.406500	0.464169	0.529276	0.602686
5430	0.270582	0.310340	0.355406	0.406421	0.464092	0.529203	0.602621
5440	0.270506	0.310262	0.355328	0.406343	0.464016	0.529131	0.602555
5450	0.270431	0.310185	0.355249	0.406265	0.463940	0.529060	0.602490
5460	0.270355	0.310107	0.355171	0.406187	0.463864	0.528988	0.602425
5470	0.270280	0.310030	0.355093	0.406109	0.463788	0.528916	0.602360
5480	0.270205	0.309953	0.355015	0.406031	0.463713	0.528845	0.602295
5490	0.270130	0.309876	0.354937	0.405954	0.463637	0.528773	0.602231
5500	0.270056	0.309799	0.354859	0.405877	0.463562	0.528702	0.602166
5510	0.269981	0.309723	0.354782	0.405799	0.463487	0.528631	0.602102
5520	0.269907	0.309646	0.354704	0.405722	0.463412	0.528560	0.602038
5530	0.269832	0.309570	0.354627	0.405645	0.463337	0.528489	0.601973
5540	0.269758	0.309494	0.354550	0.405569	0.463262	0.528419	0.601909
5550	0.269684	0.309418	0.354473	0.405492	0.463188	0.528348	0.601845

Unit	90	91	92	93	94	95	96
5560	0.269611	0.309342	0.354396	0.405416	0.463113	0.528278	0.601782
5570	0.269537	0.309267	0.354320	0.405339	0.463039	0.528208	0.601718
5580	0.269464	0.309191	0.354243	0.405263	0.462965	0.528137	0.601654
5590	0.269390	0.309116	0.354167	0.405187	0.462891	0.528067	0.601591
5600	0.269317	0.309041	0.354091	0.405112	0.462817	0.527998	0.601528
5610	0.269244	0.308966	0.354015	0.405036	0.462743	0.527928	0.601464
5620	0.269171	0.308891	0.353939	0.404960	0.462670	0.527858	0.601401
5630	0.269098	0.308816	0.353863	0.404885	0.462596	0.527789	0.601338
5640	0.269026	0.308742	0.353788	0.404810	0.462523	0.527720	0.601276
5650	0.268953	0.308667	0.353712	0.404735	0.462450	0.527650	0.601213
5660	0.268881	0.308593	0.353637	0.404660	0.462377	0.527581	0.601150
5670	0.268809	0.308519	0.353562	0.404585	0.462304	0.527512	0.601088
5680	0.268737	0.308445	0.353487	0.404510	0.462231	0.527444	0.601025
5690	0.268665	0.308371	0.353412	0.404436	0.462159	0.527375	0.600963
5700	0.268593	0.308297	0.353338	0.404362	0.462086	0.527307	0.600901
5710	0.268522	0.308224	0.353263	0.404287	0.462014	0.527238	0.600839
5720	0.268450	0.308150	0.353189	0.404213	0.461942	0.527170	0.600777
5730	0.268379	0.308077	0.353115	0.404139	0.461870	0.527102	0.600715
5740	0.268308	0.308004	0.353040	0.404066	0.461798	0.527034	0.600653
5750	0.268237	0.307931	0.352967	0.403992	0.461726	0.526966	0.600592
5760	0.268166	0.307858	0.352893	0.403918	0.461655	0.526898	0.600530
5770	0.268096	0.307786	0.352819	0.403845	0.461583	0.526830	0.600469
5780	0.268025	0.307713	0.352746	0.403772	0.461512	0.526763	0.600408
5790	0.267955	0.307641	0.352672	0.403699	0.461441	0.526696	0.600347
5800	0.267884	0.307569	0.352599	0.403626	0.461370	0.526628	0.600286
5810	0.267814	0.307497	0.352526	0.403553	0.461299	0.526561	0.600225
5820	0.267744	0.307425	0.352453	0.403480	0.461228	0.526494	0.600164
5830	0.267674	0.307353	0.352380	0.403408	0.461157	0.526427	0.600103
5840	0.267605	0.307281	0.352308	0.403336	0.461087	0.526361	0.600043
5850	0.267535	0.307210	0.352235	0.403263	0.461016	0.526294	0.599982
5860	0.267466	0.307138	0.352163	0.403191	0.460946	0.526227	0.599922
5870	0.267396	0.307067	0.352091	0.403119	0.460876	0.526161	0.599862
5880	0.267327	0.306996	0.352019	0.403047	0.460806	0.526095	0.599802
5890	0.267258	0.306925	0.351947	0.402976	0.460736	0.526029	0.599742
5900	0.267189	0.306854	0.351875	0.402904	0.460666	0.525963	0.599682

Unit	90	91	92	93	94	95	96
5910	0.267120	0.306783	0.351803	0.402833	0.460596	0.525897	0.599622
5920	0.267052	0.306713	0.351732	0.402761	0.460527	0.525831	0.599562
5930	0.266983	0.306642	0.351660	0.402619	0.460458	0.525765	0.599503
5940	0.266915	0.306502	0.351589	0.402619	0.460388	0.525700	0.599443
5950	0.266847	0.306432	0.351518	0.402548	0.460319	0.525634	0.599384
5960	0.266779	0.306432	0.351447	0.402478	0.460250	0.525569	0.599324
5970	0.266711	0.306362	0.351376	0.402407	0.460181	0.525504	0.599265
5980	0.266643	0.306292	0.351305	0.402336	0.460113	0.525439	0.599206
5990	0.266575	0.306223	0.351235	0.402266	0.460044	0.525374	0.599147
6000	0.266507	0.306153	0.351164	0.402196	0.459975	0.525309	0.599088
6010	0.266440	0.306084	0.351094	0.402126	0.459907	0.525244	0.599030
6020	0.266373	0.306015	0.351024	0.402056	0.459839	0.525179	0.598971
6030	0.266305	0.305946	0.350954	0.401986	0.459771	0.525115	0.598912
6040	0.266238	0.305877	0.350884	0.401916	0.459703	0.525051	0.598854
6050	0.266171	0.305808	0.350814	0.401847	0.459635	0.524986	0.598796
6060	0.266105	0.305739	0.350744	0.401777	0.459567	0.524922	0.598737
6070	0.266038	0.305670	0.350674	0.401708	0.459499	0.524858	0.598679
6080	0.265971	0.305602	0.350605	0.401638	0.459432	0.524794	0.598621
6090	0.265905	0.305534	0.350536	0.401569	0.459364	0.524730	0.598563
6100	0.265839	0.305465	0.350467	0.401500	0.459297	0.524667	0.598506
6110	0.265772	0.305397	0.350398	0.401432	0.459230	0.524603	0.598448
6120	0.265706	0.305329	0.350329	0.401363	0.459163	0.524540	0.598390
6130	0.265640	0.305262	0.350260	0.401294	0.459096	0.524476	0.598333
6140	0.265575	0.305194	0.350191	0.401226	0.459029	0.524413	0.598275
6150	0.265509	0.305126	0.350123	0.401157	0.458963	0.524350	0.598218
6160	0.265443	0.305059	0.350054	0.401089	0.458896	0.524287	0.598161
6170	0.265378	0.304992	0.349986	0.401021	0.458830	0.524224	0.598103
6180	0.265313	0.304924	0.349918	0.400953	0.458763	0.524161	0.598046
6190	0.265247	0.304857	0.349850	0.400885	0.458697	0.524098	0.597989
6200	0.265182	0.304790	0.349782	0.400817	0.458631	0.524036	0.597933
6210	0.265117	0.304724	0.349714	0.400750	0.458565	0.523973	0.597876
6220	0.265053	0.304657	0.349646	0.400682	0.458499	0.523911	0.597819
6230	0.264988	0.304590	0.349579	0.400615	0.458433	0.523849	0.597763
6240	0.264923	0.304524	0.349511	0.400548	0.458368	0.523786	0.597706
6250	0.264859	0.304458	0.349444	0.400481	0.458302	0.523724	0.597650

Unit	90	91	92	93	94	95	96
6260	0.264794	0.304391	0.349377	0.400414	0.458237	0.523662	0.597594
6270	0.264730	0.304325	0.349310	0.400347	0.458172	0.523601	0.597537
6280	0.264666	0.304259	0.349243	0.400280	0.458106	0.523539	0.597481
6290	0.264602	0.304193	0.349176	0.400213	0.458041	0.523477	0.597425
6300	0.264538	0.304128	0.349109	0.400147	0.457976	0.523416	0.597369
6310	0.264474	0.304062	0.349043	0.400080	0.457912	0.523354	0.597314
6320	0.264411	0.303996	0.348976	0.400014	0.457847	0.523293	0.597258
6330	0.264347	0.303931	0.348910	0.399948	0.457782	0.523232	0.597202
6340	0.264284	0.303866	0.348843	0.399882	0.457718	0.523171	0.597147
6350	0.264221	0.303801	0.348777	0.399816	0.457653	0.523109	0.597091
6360	0.264157	0.303736	0.348711	0.399750	0.457589	0.523049	0.597036
6370	0.264094	0.303671	0.348645	0.399684	0.457525	0.522988	0.596981
6380	0.264031	0.303606	0.348580	0.399618	0.457461	0.522927	0.596926
6390	0.263968	0.303541	0.348514	0.399553	0.457397	0.522866	0.596871
6400	0.263906	0.303477	0.348448	0.399487	0.457333	0.522806	0.596816
6410	0.263843	0.303412	0.348383	0.399422	0.457269	0.522746	0.596761
6420	0.263781	0.303348	0.348318	0.399357	0.457206	0.522685	0.596706
6430	0.263718	0.303284	0.348252	0.399292	0.457142	0.522625	0.596651
6440	0.263656	0.303219	0.348187	0.399227	0.457079	0.522565	0.596597
6450	0.263594	0.303155	0.348122	0.399162	0.457015	0.522505	0.596542
6460	0.263532	0.303092	0.348057	0.399097	0.456952	0.522445	0.596488
6470	0.263470	0.303028	0.347993	0.399033	0.456889	0.522385	0.596433
6480	0.263408	0.302964	0.347928	0.398968	0.456826	0.522326	0.596379
6490	0.263346	0.302901	0.347864	0.398904	0.456763	0.522266	0.596325
6500	0.263285	0.302837	0.347799	0.398839	0.456701	0.522206	0.596271
6510	0.263223	0.302774	0.347735	0.398775	0.456638	0.522147	0.596217
6520	0.263162	0.302711	0.347671	0.398711	0.456575	0.522088	0.596163
6530	0.263100	0.302647	0.347607	0.398647	0.456513	0.522029	0.596109
6540	0.263039	0.302584	0.347543	0.398583	0.456450	0.521969	0.596056
6550	0.262978	0.302522	0.347479	0.398520	0.456388	0.521910	0.596002
6560	0.262917	0.302459	0.347415	0.398456	0.456326	0.521852	0.595948
6570	0.262856	0.302396	0.347351	0.398392	0.456264	0.521793	0.595895
6580	0.262795	0.302333	0.347288	0.398329	0.456202	0.521734	0.595842
6590	0.262735	0.302271	0.347224	0.398266	0.456140	0.521675	0.595788
6600	0.262674	0.302209	0.347161	0.398202	0.456078	0.521617	0.595735

Unit	90	91	92	93	94	95	96
6610	0.262614	0.302146	0.347098	0.398139	0.456017	0.521558	0.595682
6620	0.262553	0.302084	0.347035	0.398076	0.455955	0.521500	0.595629
6630	0.262493	0.302022	0.346972	0.398013	0.455894	0.521442	0.595576
6640	0.262433	0.301960	0.346909	0.397951	0.455833	0.521384	0.595523
6650	0.262373	0.301899	0.346846	0.397888	0.455771	0.521326	0.595470
6660	0.262313	0.301837	0.346783	0.397825	0.455710	0.521268	0.595418
6670	0.262253	0.301775	0.346721	0.397763	0.455649	0.521210	0.595365
6680	0.262194	0.301714	0.346658	0.397700	0.455588	0.521152	0.595312
6690	0.262134	0.301652	0.346596	0.397638	0.455527	0.521094	0.595260
6700	0.262075	0.301591	0.346533	0.397576	0.455467	0.521037	0.595208
6710	0.262015	0.301530	0.346471	0.397514	0.455406	0.520979	0.595155
6720	0.261956	0.301469	0.346409	0.397452	0.455346	0.520922	0.595103
6730	0.261897	0.301408	0.346347	0.397390	0.455285	0.520864	0.595051
6740	0.261838	0.301347	0.346285	0.397328	0.455225	0.520807	0.594999
6750	0.261778	0.301286	0.346224	0.397267	0.455164	0.520750	0.594947
6760	0.261720	0.301225	0.346162	0.397205	0.455104	0.520693	0.594895
6770	0.261661	0.301165	0.346100	0.397144	0.455044	0.520636	0.594843
6780	0.261602	0.301104	0.346039	0.397082	0.454984	0.520579	0.594792
6790	0.261543	0.301044	0.345978	0.397021	0.454924	0.520522	0.594740
6800	0.261485	0.300984	0.345916	0.396960	0.454865	0.520466	0.594689
6810	0.261427	0.300923	0.345855	0.396899	0.454805	0.520409	0.594637
6820	0.261368	0.300863	0.345794	0.396838	0.454745	0.520353	0.594586
6830	0.261310	0.300803	0.345733	0.396777	0.454686	0.520296	0.594534
6840	0.261252	0.300744	0.345672	0.396716	0.454627	0.520240	0.594483
6850	0.261194	0.300684	0.345612	0.396655	0.454567	0.520184	0.594432
6860	0.261136	0.300624	0.345551	0.396595	0.454508	0.520128	0.594381
6870	0.261078	0.300565	0.345491	0.396534	0.454449	0.520071	0.594330
6880	0.261021	0.300505	0.345430	0.396474	0.454390	0.520015	0.594279
6890	0.260963	0.300446	0.345370	0.396414	0.454331	0.519960	0.594228
6900	0.260905	0.300386	0.345310	0.396353	0.454272	0.519904	0.594178
6910	0.260848	0.300327	0.345249	0.396293	0.454214	0.519848	0.594127
6920	0.260791	0.300268	0.345189	0.396233	0.454155	0.519792	0.594076
6930	0.260733	0.300209	0.345129	0.396173	0.454096	0.519737	0.594026
6940	0.260676	0.300150	0.345069	0.396114	0.454038	0.519681	0.593975
6950	0.260619	0.300091	0.345010	0.396054	0.453980	0.519626	0.593925

Unit	90	91	92	93	94	95	96
6960	0.260562	0.300033	0.344950	0.395994	0.453921	0.519571	0.593875
6970	0.260505	0.299974	0.344890	0.395935	0.453863	0.519516	0.593824
6980	0.260449	0.299916	0.344831	0.395875	0.453805	0.519460	0.593774
6990	0.260392	0.299857	0.344772	0.395816	0.453747	0.519405	0.593724
7000	0.260335	0.299799	0.344712	0.395757	0.453689	0.519351	0.593674
7010	0.260279	0.299741	0.344653	0.395698	0.453631	0.519296	0.593624
7020	0.260223	0.299683	0.344594	0.395639	0.453574	0.519241	0.593574
7030	0.260166	0.299624	0.344535	0.395580	0.453516	0.519186	0.593525
7040	0.260110	0.299567	0.344476	0.395521	0.453458	0.519132	0.593475
7050	0.260054	0.299509	0.344417	0.395462	0.453401	0.519077	0.593425
7060	0.259998	0.299451	0.344359	0.395403	0.453344	0.519023	0.593376
7070	0.259942	0.299393	0.344300	0.395345	0.453286	0.518968	0.593326
7080	0.259886	0.299336	0.344241	0.395386	0.453229	0.518914	0.593277
7090	0.259830	0.299278	0.344183	0.395228	0.453172	0.518860	0.593228
7100	0.259775	0.299221	0.344125	0.395170	0.453115	0.518806	0.593178
7110	0.259719	0.299164	0.344066	0.395111	0.453058	0.518752	0.593129
7120	0.259664	0.299106	0.344008	0.395053	0.453001	0.518698	0.593080
7130	0.259608	0.299049	0.343950	0.394995	0.452945	0.518644	0.593031
7140	0.259553	0.298992	0.343892	0.394937	0.452888	0.518590	0.592982
7150	0.259498	0.298935	0.343834	0.394879	0.452831	0.518536	0.592933
7160	0.259443	0.298878	0.343776	0.394822	0.452775	0.518483	0.592885
7170	0.259388	0.298822	0.343719	0.394764	0.452718	0.518429	0.592836
7180	0.259333	0.298765	0.343661	0.394706	0.452662	0.518376	0.592787
7190	0.259278	0.298708	0.343604	0.394649	0.452606	0.518322	0.592739
7200	0.259223	0.298652	0.343546	0.394591	0.452550	0.518269	0.592690
7210	0.259168	0.298596	0.343489	0.394534	0.452494	0.518216	0.592642
7220	0.259114	0.298539	0.343432	0.394477	0.452438	0.518163	0.592593
7230	0.259059	0.298483	0.343374	0.394420	0.452382	0.518110	0.592545
7240	0.259005	0.298427	0.343317	0.394362	0.452326	0.518057	0.592497
7250	0.258950	0.298371	0.343260	0.394306	0.452270	0.518004	0.592449
7260	0.258896	0.298315	0.343203	0.394249	0.452215	0.517951	0.592400
7270	0.258842	0.298259	0.343147	0.394192	0.452159	0.517898	0.592352
7280	0.258788	0.298203	0.343090	0.394135	0.452104	0.517845	0.592304
7290	0.258734	0.298148	0.343033	0.394078	0.452048	0.517793	0.592257
7300	0.258680	0.298092	0.342977	0.394022	0.451993	0.517740	0.592209

Unit	90	91	92	93	94	95	96
7310	0.258626	0.298036	0.342920	0.393965	0.451938	0.517688	0.592161
7320	0.258573	0.297981	0.342864	0.393909	0.451882	0.517635	0.592113
7330	0.258519	0.297926	0.342807	0.393853	0.451827	0.517583	0.592066
7340	0.258465	0.297870	0.342751	0.393797	0.451772	0.517531	0.592018
7350	0.258412	0.297815	0.342695	0.393740	0.451718	0.517479	0.591971
7360	0.258358	0.297760	0.342639	0.393684	0.451663	0.517427	0.591923
7370	0.258305	0.297705	0.342583	0.393628	0.451608	0.517375	0.591876
7380	0.258252	0.297650	0.342527	0.393573	0.451553	0.517323	0.591829
7390	0.258199	0.297595	0.342471	0.393517	0.451499	0.517271	0.591782
7400	0.258146	0.297541	0.342416	0.393461	0.451444	0.517219	0.591734
7410	0.258093	0.297486	0.342360	0.393405	0.451390	0.517168	0.591687
7420	0.258040	0.297431	0.342305	0.393350	0.451335	0.517116	0.591640
7430	0.257987	0.297377	0.342249	0.393294	0.451281	0.517064	0.591593
7440	0.257934	0.297323	0.342194	0.393239	0.451227	0.517013	0.591547
7450	0.257882	0.297268	0.342138	0.393184	0.451173	0.516962	0.591500
7460	0.257829	0.297214	0.342083	0.393128	0.451119	0.516910	0.591453
7470	0.257776	0.297160	0.342028	0.393073	0.451065	0.516859	0.591406
7480	0.257724	0.297106	0.341973	0.393018	0.451011	0.516808	0.591360
7490	0.257672	0.297052	0.341918	0.392963	0.450957	0.516757	0.591313
7500	0.257619	0.296998	0.341863	0.392908	0.450904	0.516706	0.591267
7510	0.257567	0.296944	0.341808	0.392854	0.450850	0.516655	0.591220
7520	0.257515	0.296890	0.341754	0.392799	0.450796	0.516604	0.591174
7530	0.257463	0.296836	0.341699	0.392744	0.450743	0.516553	0.591128
7540	0.257411	0.296783	0.341645	0.392690	0.450690	0.516502	0.591082
7550	0.257359	0.296729	0.341590	0.392635	0.450636	0.516452	0.591036
7560	0.257308	0.296676	0.341536	0.392581	0.450583	0.516401	0.590989
7570	0.257256	0.296623	0.341481	0.392526	0.450530	0.516351	0.590943
7580	0.257204	0.296569	0.341427	0.392472	0.450477	0.516300	0.590898
7590	0.257153	0.296516	0.341373	0.392418	0.450424	0.516250	0.590852
7600	0.257101	0.296463	0.341319	0.392364	0.450371	0.516200	0.590806
7610	0.257050	0.296410	0.341265	0.392310	0.450318	0.516149	0.590760
7620	0.256999	0.296357	0.341211	0.392256	0.450265	0.516099	0.590714
7630	0.256947	0.296304	0.341157	0.392202	0.450212	0.516049	0.590669
7640	0.256896	0.296251	0.341104	0.392148	0.450160	0.515999	0.590623
7650	0.256845	0.296199	0.341050	0.392095	0.450107	0.515949	0.590578

Unit	90	91	92	93	94	95	96
7660	0.256794	0.296146	0.340996	0.392041	0.450055	0.515899	0.590532
7670	0.256743	0.296093	0.340943	0.391987	0.450002	0.515849	0.590487
7680	0.256692	0.296041	0.340889	0.391934	0.449950	0.515800	0.590442
7690	0.256642	0.295989	0.340836	0.391881	0.449898	0.515750	0.590396
7700	0.256591	0.295936	0.340783	0.391827	0.449846	0.515700	0.590351
7710	0.256540	0.295884	0.340729	0.391774	0.449793	0.515651	0.590306
7720	0.256490	0.295832	0.340676	0.391721	0.449741	0.515601	0.590261
7730	0.256439	0.295780	0.340623	0.391668	0.449689	0.515552	0.590216
7740	0.256389	0.295728	0.340570	0.391615	0.449638	0.515503	0.590171
7750	0.256339	0.295676	0.340517	0.391562	0.449586	0.515453	0.590126
7760	0.256288	0.295624	0.340465	0.391509	0.449534	0.515404	0.590081
7770	0.256238	0.295572	0.340412	0.391456	0.449482	0.515355	0.590037
7780	0.256188	0.295520	0.340359	0.391404	0.449431	0.515306	0.589992
7790	0.256138	0.295469	0.340307	0.391351	0.449379	0.515257	0.589947
7800	0.256088	0.295417	0.340254	0.391298	0.449328	0.515208	0.589903
7810	0.256038	0.295366	0.340202	0.391246	0.449276	0.515159	0.589858
7820	0.255989	0.295314	0.340149	0.391193	0.449225	0.515111	0.589814
7830	0.255939	0.295263	0.340097	0.391141	0.449174	0.515062	0.589769
7840	0.255889	0.295212	0.340045	0.391089	0.449123	0.515013	0.589725
7850	0.255840	0.295160	0.339993	0.391037	0.449071	0.514965	0.589681
7860	0.255790	0.295109	0.339941	0.390985	0.449020	0.514916	0.589637
7870	0.255741	0.295058	0.339889	0.390932	0.448969	0.514868	0.589592
7880	0.255691	0.295007	0.339837	0.390881	0.448919	0.514819	0.589548
7890	0.255642	0.294905	0.339785	0.390829	0.448868	0.514771	0.589504
7900	0.255593	0.294905	0.339733	0.390777	0.448817	0.514723	0.589460
7910	0.255544	0.294855	0.339681	0.390725	0.448766	0.514675	0.589416
7920	0.255495	0.294804	0.339630	0.390673	0.448716	0.514626	0.589373
7930	0.255446	0.294753	0.339578	0.390622	0.448665	0.514578	0.589329
7940	0.255397	0.294703	0.339527	0.390570	0.448615	0.514530	0.589285
7950	0.255348	0.294652	0.339475	0.390519	0.448564	0.514483	0.589241
7960	0.255299	0.294602	0.339424	0.390467	0.448514	0.514435	0.589198
7970	0.255250	0.294552	0.339373	0.390416	0.448464	0.514387	0.589154
7980	0.255202	0.294501	0.339322	0.390365	0.448414	0.514339	0.589111
7990	0.255153	0.294451	0.339270	0.390314	0.448363	0.514291	0.589067
8000	0.255105	0.294401	0.339219	0.390262	0.448313	0.514244	0.589024

BIBLIOGRAPHY

Books and Reports

Abernathy, W. J., *The Productivity Dilemma: Roadblock to Innovation in the Automobile Industry* (Baltimore: Johns Hopkins University Press, 1978).

Alchian, A. A., "Reliability of Progress Curves in Airframe Production," Report No. RM260-1, Rand Corporation, Santa Monica, Calif., April 14, 1958.

Anzanos, A., R. M. Field and R. E. Lorenz, *Progress Curves, Factors and Application* (St. Louis: McDonnell Aircraft Corp., 1958).

Arrow, K. S., "Methodological Problems in Airframe Cost-Performance Studies," Report No. RM-456, The Rand Corporation, Santa Monica, Calif., September 20, 1950.

Asher, H., "Cost-Quantity Relationships in the Airframe Industry," Report No. R-291, The Rand Corporation, Santa Monica, Calif., July 1, 1956, 191 pages.

Blume, E. J., and D. Peitzke, *Purchasing with the Learning Curve* (Inglewood, Calif.: North American Aviation, Inc., August 1953).

Burns, T., and G. M. Stalker, *The Management Innovation* (London: Tavistock, 1961).

Dahlhaus, F. J., "Learning Curve Methodology for Cost Analysis," AD-661052, Defense Documentation Center, Cameron Station, Alexandria, Va., October 1967.

Falk, S. A., *Improvement Curve Analysis Techniques* (Boston, Mass.: Harbridge House, Inc., 1959).

Guibert, P., *Le Plan de Fabrication Aeronautique* (Paris, France: Dunod, 1945).

Hancock, W. M., "The Learning Curve," *Industrial Engineering Handbook*, 3rd edition (New York: McGraw-Hill, 1971).

Hoffman, F. S., "Comments on the Modified Form of the Aircraft Progress Functions," Report No. RN-464, The Rand Corporation, Santa Monica, Calif., October 4, 1950.

Hollander, S., *The Sources of Increased Efficiency: A Study of DuPont Rayon Plants* (Cambridge, Mass.: M.I.T. Press, 1965).

Hughes, R. C., and H. G. Golem, *Production Efficiency Curve and Its Application* (San Diego: Arts and Crafts Press, 1944).

Karlin, S., "A Mathematical Treatment of Learning Models," Report No. RM-291, The Rand Corporation, Santa Monica, Calif., September 2, 1962.

Lippencott, C. E., "Learning Curve Tables—Planning and Estimating Tool," IBM Report, TN 20-0214, Data Systems Division, Poughkeepsie, N.Y., August 1963.

McDonald, P. M., "Improvement Curves," Procurement Association, Inc., Covina, Calif., 1966.

Morgan, A. W., "Experience Curves Applicable to the Aircraft Industry," Glen L. Martin Company, Baltimore, 1959.

Orisini, J. A., "An Analysis of Theoretical and Empirical Advances in Learning Curve Concepts Since 1966," AD 875892, Wright Patterson A.F.B., Ohio, Air Force Institute of Technology, 1970.

Pardee, F. W., "Weapons System Cost Sensitivity Analysis," The Rand Corporation, Santa Monica, Calif., June 15, 1960.

Rand Corporation, "Reliability of Cost Estimates," Report No. RM-481, Santa Monica, Calif., October 30, 1950.

Richmond, S. B., *Operations Research for Management Decisions* (New York: The Ronald Press Company, 1968).

Securities and Exchange Commission, Accounting Series Release No. 33-5492 (S.E.C., Washington, D.C., 1974).

Shepard, A. H., and D. Lewis, "Prior Learning as a Factor in Performance Curves," Library of Congress Publication, No. 101487, U.S. Navy Technical Report, SOC 938-1-4 (Washington, D.C.: Government Printing Office).

Stanford Research Institute, SRI (1), "Development of Production Acceleration Curves for Airframes" (for USAF-AMCF, 1949).

Stanford Research Institute SRI (2), "An Improved Rational and Mathematical Explanation of the Progress Curve in Airframe Production" (for USAF-AMCF, August 1949).

Stanford Research Institute SRI (3), "Relationships for Determining the Optimum Expansibility of the Elements of a Peacetime Aircraft Procurement Program" (for USAF-AMCF, December 1949).

Stanford Research Institute SRI (4), "Acceleration of Airframe Production as a Function of Direct Labor Application and Productivity" (for USAF-AMCF, February 1949).

Stanley, P. J., "The Time to Achieve Peak Output with Special Reference to Aircraft Production," College of Aeronautics, Report No. 30, Cranfield, England, 1949.

Subcommittee on Armed Services, House of Representatives, 84th Congress, Second Session, "Report on Aircraft Production Costs and Profits" (Washington, D.C.: Government Printing Office, July 13, 1956).

United States Air Force, "Air Force Procurement Instructions," Department of the Air Force (Washington, D.C.: Government Printing Office, September 1960).

United States Army Missile Command, "Alpha and Omega and the Experience Curve," April 12, 1965.

Wertman, L., "Construction and Use of MTF Curves," *Manufacturing Planning and Estimating Handbook* (New York: McGraw-Hill, 1963).

Articles

Abernathy, W. J., and N. Baloff, "A Methodology for Planning New Product Start-Ups," *Decision Sciences* (Vol. 4, No. 1, January 1973), pp. 1–20.

Abernathy, W. J., and P. L. Townsend, "Technology, Productivity and Process Change," *Technological Forecasting and Social Change* (Vol. 7, No. 4, August 1975), pp. 379–396.

Abernathy, W. J., and K. Wayne, "Limits of the Learning Curve," *Harvard Business Review* (Vol. 52, No. 5, September–October 1974), pp. 109–119.

Alchian, A. A., "Reliability of Progress Curves in Airframe Production," *Econometrica* (Vol. 31, No. 4, October 1963), pp. 679–693.

Alden, R. J., "Learning Curves: An Example," *Industrial Engineering* (Vol. 6, No. 12, 1974), pp. 34–37.

Anderlohr, G., "Determining tbe Cost of Production Breaks," *Management Review* (Vol. 58, No. 12, 1969), pp. 16–19.

———, "What Production Breaks Cost," *Industrial Engineering* (Vol. 1, No. 9, September 1969), p. 346.

Andress, F., "The Learning Curve as a Production Tool," *Harvard Business Review* (Vol. 32, No. 1, January–February 1954), pp. 87–97.

Ansoff, H., and J. M. Stewart, "Strategies for a Technology-Based Business," *Harvard Business Review* (Vol. 45, No. 6, 1967), pp. 71–83.

Arrow, K. J., "The Economic Implications of Learning by Doing," *Review of Economic Studies* (Vol. 29, 1962), pp. 154–174.

Arrow, K. J., H. B. Chenery, B. Minbas and R. M. Solow, "Capital Labor Substitution and Economic Efficiency," *Review of Economics and Statistics* (Vol. 43, 1961), pp. 225–250.

Baird, B. F., "A Note on the Confusion Surrounding Learning Curves," *Production and Inventory Management* (April 1966), pp. 71–78.

Baloff, N., "Startups in Machine Intensive Production Systems," *Journal of Industrial Engineering* (Vol. 17, No. 1, January 1966), pp. 25–32.

———, "The Learning Curve—Some Controversial Issues," *Journal of Industrial Economics* (July 1966), pp. 275–282.

———, "Estimating the Parameters of the Startup Model—An Empirical Approach," *Journal of Industrial Engineering* (Vol. 18, No. 4, April 1967), pp. 248–253.

———, "Startup Management," *IEEE Transactions Engineering Management* (Vol. EM-17, No. 4, November 1970), pp. 132–141.

———, "Extension of the Learning Curve—Some Empirical Results," *Operational Research Quarterly* (Vol. 22, No. 4, 1971), pp. 329–340.

Baloff, N., and S. Becker, "A Model of Group Adaptation to Problem Solving

Tasks," *Human Performance and Organizational Behavior* (August 1968), pp. 217–238.

Baloff, N., and J. Kennelly, "Accounting Implications of Product and Process Startups," *Journal of Accounting Research* (Vol. 5, No. 2, Autumn 1967), pp. 131–143.

Baloff, N., and R. B. McKersie, "Motivating Startups," *Journal of Business* (Vol. 39, No. 4, October 1966), pp. 473–484.

Barron, L. A., "Learner Curves Boost Team Output," *American Machinist* (Vol. 102, No. 25, December 1, 1958), pp. 100–101.

Belkaoui, A., "Costing Through Learning," *Cost and Management* (May–June 1976), pp. 36–40.

Bevis, F. W., C. Finniear and D. R. Towill, "Prediction of Operator Performance During Learning of Repetitive Tasks," *International Journal of Production Research* (Vol. 8, No. 4, 1970), pp. 293–305.

Billion, S. A., "Industrial Learning Curves and Forecasting," *Management International Review* (Vol. 6, No. 6, 1966), pp. 65–96.

Bodde, L., "Riding the Experience Curve," *Technology Review* (Vol. 78, No. 5, 1976), pp. 53–59.

Boren, W. H., "Some Applications of the Learning Curve to Government Contracts," *NAA Bulletin* (Vol. 46, No. 2, October 1964), pp. 21–22.

Bowers, W. H., "Who's Afraid of the Learning Curve," *Purchasing* (March 24, 1966), p. 9.

Brenneck, R., "Breakeven Charts Reflecting Learning," *NAA Bulletin* (Vol. 40, No. 10, January 1959, pp. 34–38.

———, "The Learning Curve for Labor Hours—for Pricing," *NAA Bulletin* (Sec. 1, June 1959), pp. 77–78.

———, "Learning Curve Techniques for More Profitable Contracts," *NAA Bulletin* (Sec. 2, Vol. 40, No. 11, July 1959), pp. 59–69.

Broadston, J. A., "Learning Curve Wage Incentives," *Management Accounting* (Vol. 49, No. 12, 1968), pp. 15–23.

Bruns, J. H., "Forecasting the Cost of Redesign," *Machine Design* (Vol. 42, No. 6, 1970), pp. 113–115.

Bump, E. A., "Effects of Learning on Cost Projections," *Management Accounting* (Vol. 55, No. 11, May 1974), pp. 19–24.

Carlson, J. G., "How Management Can Use the Improvement Phenomenon," *California Management Review* (Vol. 3, No. 2, 1961), pp. 83–94.

———, "Cubic Learning Curves: Precision Tool for Labor Estimating," *Manufacturing Engineering and Management* (Vol. 71, No. 5, 1973), pp. 22–25.

Carlson, J. G., and R. J. Rowe, "How Much Does Forgetting Cost?" *Industrial Engineering* (Vol. 8, No. 9, 1976), pp. 40–47.

Clark, S., "Applying Learning Curves to the Maintenance Force," *Plant Engineering* (Vol. 21, No. 8, 1967), pp. 126–127.

Cochran, E. B., "New Concepts of the Learning Curve," *Journal of Industrial Engineering* (Vol. 11, No. 4, 1960), pp. 317–327.

———, "Learning: New Dimension in Labor Standards," *Industrial Engineering* (Vol. 1, No. 1, 1969), pp. 38–47.

_____, "Dynamics of Work Standards," *Manufacturing Engineering and Management* (Vol. 70, No. 4, 1973), pp. 28–31.

Cole, R., "Increasing Utilization of the Cost Quantity Relationship in Manufacturing," *Journal of Industrial Engineering* (Vol. 9, No. 3, 1958), pp. 173–177.

Conley, P., "Experience Curves as a Planning Tool," *IEEE Spectrum* (Vol. 7, No. 6, 1970), pp. 63–68.

Conway, R. W. "Some Tactical Problems in Digital Simulation," *Management Science* (October 1963), p. 49.

Conway, R. W., and A. Schultz, Jr., "The Manufacturing Progress Function," *Journal of Industrial Engineering* (Vol. 13, No. 1, January–February 1959), pp. 39–54.

Corlett, E. N., and V. J. Morcombe, "Straightening Out Learning Curves," *Personnel Management* (June 1970), pp. 14–19.

DeJong, J. R., "The Effects of Increasing Skill on Cycle Time and Its Consequences for Time Standards," *Ergonomics* (November 1957), pp. 51–60.

Demski, J. S., "An Accounting System Structured on a Linear Programming Model," *The Accounting Review* (October 1967), pp. 701–712.

Ebert, R. J., "Aggregate Planning with Learning Curve Productivity," *Management Science* (Vol. 23, No. 2, 1976), pp. 171–182.

Ferrara, W. L., and J. C. Hayya, "Toward Probabilistic Budgeting," *Management Accounting* (October 1970), pp. 23–28.

Garg, A., and P. Milliman, "The Aircraft Progress Curve—Modified for Design Changes," *Journal of Industrial Engineering* (Vol. 12, No. 1, 1961), pp. 23–28.

Givens, H. R., "An Application of Curvilinear Breakeven Analysis," *The Accounting Review* (January 1966), pp. 141–143.

Glover, J. H., "Manufacturing Progress Functions: I. An Alternative Model and Its Comparison with Existing Functions," *International Journal of Production Research* (Vol. 4, No. 4, 1966), pp. 279–300.

_____, "Manufacturing Progress Functions: II. Selection of Trainees and Control of Their Progress," *International Journal of Production Research* (Vol. 5, No. 1, 1966).

Goel, S. N., and R. H. Becknell, "Learning Curves That Work," *Industrial Engineering* (Vol. 4, No. 5, 1972), pp. 28–31.

Goggans, T. P., "Breakeven Analysis with Curvilinear Functions," *The Accounting Review* (October 1965), pp. 867–871.

Greenberg, L., "The Measurement of the Work-Accident Experience in the American Petroleum Industry," *American Society of Safety Engineers* (Vol. 15, No. 2, 1970), pp. 11–13.

_____, "Why the Mine Injury Is Out of Focus," *Mining Engineering* (Vol. 23, No. 3, 1971), pp. 51–53.

Hall, L. H., "Experience with Experience Curves for Aircraft Design Changes," *NAA Bulletin* (Vol. 39, No. 4, 1957), pp. 59–66.

Hancock, W. M., "Prediction of Learning Rates for Manual Operations," *Journal of Industrial Engineering* (Vol. 18, No. 1, 1967), pp. 42–47.

Hartley, K., "The Learning Curve and Its Application to the Aircraft Industry," *Journal of Industrial Economics* (Vol. 13, No. 2, 1965), pp. 122–128.

Harvey, D. W., "Financial Planning Information for Production Start-Ups," *Accounting Review* (Vol. 51, No. 4, 1976), pp. 838–845.

Hilliard, J. E., and R. A. Leitch, "Cost-Volume-Profit Analysis under Uncertainty: A Log Normal Approach," *The Accounting Review* (January 1975), pp. 69–80.

Hirsch, W. Z., "Manufacturing Progress Functions," *Review of Economics and Statistics* (Vol. 34, No. 2, 1952), pp. 143–155.

———, "Firm Progress Ratios," *Econometrica* (Vol. 24, No. 2, 1956), pp. 136–143.

Hirschmann, W. B., "Learning Curve," *Chemical Engineering* (Vol. 71, No. 7, 1964), pp. 95–100.

———, "Profit from the Learning Curve," *Harvard Business Review* (Vol. 42, No. 1, 1964), pp. 125–139.

Hirshleiffer, J., "The Firm's Cost Function: A Successful Reconstruction?" *Journal of Business* (Chicago), (Vol. 35, No. 3, 1962), pp. 235–255.

Hoffmann, J. R., "Effects of Prior Experience on Learning Curve Parameters," *Journal of Industrial Engineering* (Vol. 19, No. 8, 1968), pp. 412–413.

Jaedick, R. K., and A. A. Robichek, "Cost-Volume-Profit Analysis under Conditions of Uncertainty," *The Accounting Review* (October 1964), pp. 917–926.

Janzen, J., "The Manufacturing Progress Function Applied to a Wage Incentive Plan," *Journal of Industrial Engineering* (Vol. 17, No. 4, 1966), pp. 197–200.

Jordan, R., "Learning How to Use the Learning Curve," *NAA Bulletin* (Sec. 2, January 1958), pp. 27–39.

Katz, R., "Understanding and Applying Learning Curves," *Automation* (Vol. 16, No. 11, 1969), pp. 50–53.

Keachie, E. C., and R. J. Fontana, "Effects of Learning on Optimal Lot Size," *Management Science* (Vol. 13, No. 2, 1966), pp. 102–108.

Kilbridge, M. D., "Predetermined Learning Curves for Clerical Operations," *Journal of Industrial Engineering* (Vol. 10, No. 3, 1959), pp. 203–209.

———, "A Model for Industrial Learning Costs," *Management Science* (Vol. 8, No. 4, 1962), pp. 516–527.

Knecht, G. R., "Costing Technological Growth and Generalized Learning Curves," *Operations Research Quarterly* (Vol. 25, No. 3, 1974), pp. 487–491.

Kneip, J. G., "The Maintenance Progress Function," *Journal of Industrial Engineering* (Vol. 16, No. 6, 1965), pp. 398–400.

Levy, F. K., "Adaptation in the Production Process," *Management Science* (Vol. 11, No. 6, April 1965), pp. B136–B154.

Liao, M., "Model Sampling: A Stochastic Cost-Volume-Profit Analysis," *The Accounting Review* (October 1964), pp. 780–790.

Lundberg, R. H., "Learning Curve Theory as Applied to Production Costs," *S.A.E. Journal* (Vol. 64, No. 6, 1956), pp. 48–49.

McIntyre, E. V., "Cost-Volume-Profit Analysis Adjusted for Learning," *Management Science* (Vol. 24, No. 2, 1977), pp. 149–160.

Montgomery, F., "Increased Productivity in the Construction of Liberty Vessels," *Monthly Labor Review* (Vol. 57, No. 5, 1943), pp. 861–864.

Morse, W. J., "Reporting Production Costs That Follow the Learning Curve Phenomenon," *The Accounting Review* (Vol. 47, No. 4, 1972), pp. 761–773.

_____, "Learning Curve Cost Projections with Constant Unit Costs," *Managerial Planning* (March–April 1974), pp. 15–21.

_____, "Use of Learning Curves in Financial Accounting," *CPA Journal* (Vol. 44, No. 1, 1974), pp. 51–55.

Nagely, R., "Learning Curve Short-Cut to Cost Reduction," *Purchasing* (September 29, 1958), pp. 80–83.

Nathanson, D. M., "Forecasting Petrochemical Prices," *Chemical Engineering Progress* (Vol. 68, No. 11, 1972), pp. 89–96.

Parsons, G. W. S., "The 80% Learning Curve," *Modern Machine Shop* (March 1960).

Pegels, C. C., "On Startup or Learning Curves: An Expanded View," *AIIE Transactions* (Vol. 1, No. 3, 1969), pp. 216–222.

_____, "Start Up or Learning Curves—Some New Approaches," *Decision Sciences* (Vol. 7, No. 4, 1976), pp. 705–713.

Pooler, V. H., "How to Use the Learning Curve," *Purchasing* (July 17, 1961).

Preston, L. E., and E. C. Keachie, "Cost Functions and Progress Functions: An Integration," *American Economic Review* (Vol. 54, No. 2, 1964), pp. 100–107.

Rice, J. W., "Throw Prices a Curve," *Purchasing* (Vol. 69, No. 1, 1970), pp. 47–49.

Russell, J. H., "Progress Function Models and Their Deviations," *Journal of Industrial Engineering* (Vol. 19, No. 1, January 1968), pp. 5–10.

Sanders, B. T., and E. E. Blystone, "Progress Curve: An Aid to Decision Making," *NAA Bulletin* (Vol. 48, June 1961), pp. 81–86.

Searle, A. D., "Productivity of Labor and Industry," *Monthly Labor Review* (Vol. 61, No. 6, 1945), pp. 1132–1147.

Sheshinski, E., "Tests of the Learning by Doing Hypothesis," *Review of Economics and Statistics* (Vol. 49, No. 4, 1967), pp. 568–578.

Shroad, V. J., "Control of Labor Costs Through the Use of Learning Curves," *NAA Bulletin* (Vol. 46, No. 2, 1964), pp. 15–20.

Solomons, D., "Break-even Analysis under Absorption Costing," *The Accounting Review* (July 1968), pp. 447–452.

Summers, E. L., and G. A. Welsch, "How Learning Curve Models Can Be Applied to Profit Planning," *Management Sciences* (Vol. 7, No. 2, 1970), pp. 45–50.

Thomopoulos, N. T., and M. Lehman, "The Mixed Model Learning Curve," *AIIE Transactions* (Vol. 1, No. 2, 1969), pp. 127–132.

Towill, D. R., "An Industrial Dynamics Model for Start-Up Management," *IEEE Transactions on Engineering Management* (Vol. EM-20, No. 2, 1973), pp. 44–51.

Turban, E., "Incentives During Learning—An Application of the Learning Curve Theory and a Survey of Other Methods," *Journal of Industrial Engineering* (Vol. 19, No. 12, 1968), pp. 600–607.

Utterback, J. M., and W. J. Abernathy, "A Dynamic Model of Process and Product Innovation," *Omega* (Vol. 3, No. 6, 1975), pp. 639–656.

Wertmann, L., "Putting Learning Curves to Work," *Tool Engineer* (Vol. 43, No. 3, 1959), pp. 99–102.

White, J., "The Use of Learning Curve Theory in Setting Management Goals," *Journal of Industrial Engineering* (Vol. 12, No. 6, 1961), pp. 409–411.

Wright, T. P., "Factors Affecting the Cost of Airplanes," *Journal of Aeronautical Sciences* (Vol. 3, No. 2, 1936), pp. 122–128.

Wyer, R., "Learning Curve Helps Figure Profits, Control Costs," *National Association of Cost Accountants Bulletin* (Vol. 35, No. 4, 1953), pp. 490–502.

———, "Industrial Accounting with the Learning Curve," *California CPA* (February 24, 1956), p. 23.

———, "Learning Curve Techniques for Direct Labor Management," *NAA Bulletin* (Sec. 2, July 1958), pp. 19–25.

Yelle, L. E., "Technological Forecasting: A Learning Curve Approach," *Industrial Management* (Vol. 16, No. 1, 1974), pp. 6–11.

———, "Estimating Learning Curves for Potential Products," *Industrial Marketing Management* (Vol. 5, No. 2/3, 1976), pp. 147–154.

———, "The Learning Curve: Historical Review and Comprehensive Review," *Decision Sciences* (Vol. 10, 1979), pp. 302–328.

Young, S. L., "Misapplications of the Learning Curve Concept," *Journal of Industrial Engineering* (Vol. 17, No. 8, 1966), pp. 410–415.

INDEX

About the Author

AHMED BELKAOUI is Professor of Accounting at the Chicago campus of the University of Illinois. He is the author of *Industrial Bonds and the Rating Process, Socio-Economic Accounting, International Accounting* (Quorum Books, 1983, 1984, 1985), *Accounting Theory, Conceptual Foundations of Management Accounting, Cost Accounting, Theorie Comptable*, and numerous articles.